Lecture Notes in Computer Science 5435

Commenced Publication in 1973
Founding and Former Series Editors:
Gerhard Goos, Juris Hartmanis, and Jan van Leeuwen

Volkmar Pipek   Mary Beth Rosson
Boris de Ruyter   Volker Wulf (Eds.)

End-User Development

2nd International Symposium, IS-EUD 2009
Siegen, Germany, March 2-4, 2009
Proceedings

 Springer

Volume Editors

Volkmar Pipek
University of Siegen
57068 Siegen, Germany
E-mail: volkmar.pipek@uni-siegen.de

Mary Beth Rosson
The Pennsylvania State University
University Park, PA 16802, USA
E-mail: mrosson@psu.edu

Boris de Ruyter
Philips Research Europe
5656 AE Eindhoven, The Netherlands
E-mail: Boris.de.Ruyter@philips.com

Volker Wulf
University of Siegen
57068 Siegen, Germany
E-mail: volker.wulf@fit.fraunhofer.de

Library of Congress Control Number: 2009921810

CR Subject Classification (1998): D.2, D.1, I.7, K.6

LNCS Sublibrary: SL 3 – Information Systems and Applications,
incl Internet/Web, and HCI

ISSN   0302-9743
ISBN-10   3-642-00425-3 Springer Berlin Heidelberg New York
ISBN-13   978-3-642-00425-4 Springer Berlin Heidelberg New York

springer.com

© Springer-Verlag Berlin Heidelberg 2009
Printed in Germany

Typesetting: Camera-ready by author, data conversion by Scientific Publishing Services, Chennai, India
Printed on acid-free paper   SPIN: 12624331   06/3180   5 4 3 2 1 0

Preface

Work practices and organizational processes vary widely and evolve constantly. The technological infrastructure has to follow, allowing or even supporting these changes. Traditional approaches to software engineering reach their limits whenever the full spectrum of user requirements cannot be anticipated or the frequency of changes makes software reengineering cycles too clumsy to address all the needs of a specific field of application. Moreover, the increasing importance of 'infrastructural' aspects, particularly the mutual dependencies between technologies, usages, and domain competencies, calls for a differentiation of roles beyond the classical user–designer dichotomy.

End user development (EUD) addresses these issues by offering lightweight, use-time support which allows users to configure, adapt, and evolve their software by themselves. EUD is understood as a set of methods, techniques, and tools that allow users of software systems who are acting as non-professional software developers to create, modify, or extend a software artifact[1]. While programming activities by non-professional actors are an essential focus, EUD also investigates related activities such as collective understanding and sense-making of use problems and solutions, the interaction among end users with regard to the introduction and diffusion of new configurations, or delegation patterns that may also partly involve professional designers.

EUD concepts have found widespread use in commercial software with some success: recording macros in word processors, setting up spreadsheets for calculations, defining e-mail-filters, configurating desktop widgets, or composing mesh-ups. Although these applications only realize a fraction of EUD potential and still suffer from many flaws, they illustrate why empowering end-users to develop their applications is such an important issue. It contributes to the economic performance of organizations that depend increasingly on their IT infrastructure and enables citizens to become active members of the information society.

EUD integrates different threads of discussions from human–computer interaction (HCI), software engineering (SE), computer–supported cooperative work (CSCW), and artificial intelligence (AI). Concepts such as tailorability, configurability, end-user programming, visual programming, natural programming, and programming by example already form a fruitful base, but they need to be better integrated and the synergy between them more fully exploited.

Driven by developments in the context of Web 2.0, the number of end-user developers compared to the number of software professionals will grow strongly. This underlines the importance of systematic research into EUD. The potential to provide EUD-based adaptation over the Internet may create a shift from the conventional few-to-many distribution model of software adaptations to a many-to-many model.

EUD can lead to considerable competitive advantage in adapting to dynamically changing (economic) environments. The increasing amount of software embedded

---

[1] Lieberman, H.; Paternó, F.; Wulf, V. (eds): End User Development, Springer, London 2006.

within consumer and professional products also points to a need in promoting EUD to enable effective use of these products. This momentum may also be picked up to improve software (re-)design based on user-driven innovation tools and strategies.

On the political level, EUD is important for full participation of citizens in the emerging information society. While techniques of Web 2.0 already contribute to a democratization of the creation of content, the modification of the software infrastructure is difficult for non-professional programmers. This often leads to a division of labor between those who produce and those who consume. EUD has the potential to counterbalance these effects.

The Second International Symposium on End User Development focused on an emergent discussion which so far has taken place in many different forums. In these proceedings, we document 12 full papers and two notes that report on the latest advances in the field. Full papers and notes were chosen in a quality-oriented selection process in which each contribution was reviewed by at least three members of the Program Committee.

We are grateful to the distinguished members of our Program Committee.

Six invited speakers shared their insights with us during the symposium. Their work has largely contributed to shaping EUD as a research field. We would like to thank Jörg Beringer (SAP), Margaret Burnett (Oregon State University), Pele Ehn (University of Malmo), Gerhard Fischer (University of Colorado), Yasmin Kafai (University of Pennsylvania), and Frank Piller (RWTH Aachen). Burnett's and Fischer's contributions are additionally documented in these proceedings.

Organizing an international symposium requires team effort over a considerable period of time. We would like to thank Gunnar Stevens (Fraunhofer FIT) and Christopher Scaffidi (Carnegie Mellon University), who put together the work-in-progress section. Andrea Bernards, Matthias Korn, Karin Ofterdinger, Marion Schulte, Martin Stein, Marcel Tweer, and Timm Wunderlich supported us in many different ways, such as maintaining the website, formatting the proceedings, or running the registration process. We are deeply indebted to their high engagement.

Finally, we are grateful to the sponsors of the symposium: the President of the University of Siegen, Philips Research, Sparkasse Siegen, the German Science Foundation's Research Centre on 'Media Upheavals' (DFG-FK 615), and the International Institute for Socio-Informatics (IISI).

January 2009

Organization

Program Committee

Sasche Alda	Accenture, Germany
Jörg Beringer	SAP, Palo Alto, USA
Alan Blackwell	Cambridge University, UK
Margaret Burnett	Oregon State University, USA
Maria Francesca Costabile	University of Bari, Italy
Clarisse Sieckenius De Souza	Catholic University, Rio de Janeiro, Brazil
Anid Dey	Carnegie Mellon University, USA
Yvonne Dittrich	IT University Copenhagen, Denmark
John Daughtry	Penn State University, USA
Christian Dörner	University of Siegen, Germany
Gregor Engels	University of Paderborn, Germany
Roman Englert	T-Labs, Ben Gurion University, Israel
Umer Farooq	Microsoft, USA
Gerhard Fischer	University of Colorado, Boulder, USA
Jörg Haake	Fernuniversität Hagen, Germany
Austin Henderson	Pitney Bull, USA
Jan Hess	University of Siegen, Germany
Thomas Herrmann	University of Bochum, Germany
Yasmin Kafai	Penn State University, USA
John Karat	IBM T.J. Watson Research center, USA
Roger Kilian-Kehr	SAP Research, Karlsruhe, Germany
Markus Klann	Fraunhofer FIT, Germany
Kari Kuutti	University of Oulu, Finland
Catherine Letondal	Institute Pasteur, Paris, France
Henry Lieberman	MIT Media Lab, USA
Wendy Mackay	INRIA, France
Nikolay Mehandjiev	UMIST, UK
Rob Miller	MIT, USA
Anders Morch	University of Oslo, Norway
Piero Mussio	University of Milan, Italy
Brad Myers	Carnegie Mellon University, USA
Horst Oberquelle	University of Hamburg, Germany
Reinhard Oppermann	Fraunhofer FIT, Germany
Philippe Palanque	Univerity of Toulouse, France
Fabio Paternó	CNR-ISTI, Pisa, Italy
Alexander Repenning	University of Colorado, Boulder, USA
Markus Rohde	University of Siegen, Germany
Stefan Scheidl	SAP Research, Germany
Albrecht Schmidt	University of Duisburg-Essen, Germany

Carla Simone	University of Milano-Bicocca, Italy
Brian Smith	Penn State University, USA
Gunnar Stevens	University of Siegen and Fraunhofer FIT, Germany
Giuseppe Strina	RWTH Aachen, Germany
Alistair Sutcliffe	UMIST, UK
Bettina Törpel	Technical University of Denmark, Copenhagen, Denmark
Michael Veith	University of Siegen, Germany
Markus Won	Deutsche Post, Bonn, Germany
Fahri Yetim	University of Siegen, Germany
Jürgen Ziegler	University of Duisburg-Essen, Germany
Heinz Züllighoven	University of Hamburg, Germany

Table of Contents

Part I: Invited Talks

End-User Development and Meta-design: Foundations for Cultures of
Participation 3
  Gerhard Fischer

What Is End-User Software Engineering and Why Does It Matter? 15
  Margaret Burnett

Part II: Refereed Papers

Mutual Development: A Case Study in Customer-Initiated Software
Product Development 31
  Renate Andersen and Anders I. Mørch

Appropriation Infrastructure: Supporting the Design of Usages 50
  Gunnar Stevens, Volkmar Pipek, and Volker Wulf

Supporting End Users to Be Co-designers of Their Tools 70
  Maria Francesca Costabile, Piero Mussio,
  Loredana Parasiliti Provenza, and Antonio Piccinno

Improving Documentation for eSOA APIs through User Studies 86
  Sae Young Jeong, Yingyu Xie, Jack Beaton, Brad A. Myers,
  Jeff Stylos, Ralf Ehret, Jan Karstens, Arkin Efeoglu, and
  Daniela K. Busse

End-User Development of Enterprise Widgets 106
  Michael Spahn and Volker Wulf

End-User Development for E-Government Website Content Creation ... 126
  Daniela Fogli

LWOAD: A Specification Language to Enable the End-User Develoment
of Coordinative Functionalities 146
  Federico Cabitza and Carla Simone

Shaping Collaborative Work with Proto-patterns.................... 166
  Till Schümmer and Jörg M. Haake

Web Design Patterns: Investigating User Goals and Browsing
Strategies 186
  Paloma Díaz, Mary Beth Rosson, Ignacio Aedo, and John. M. Carroll

Males' and Females' Script Debugging Strategies   205
    Valentina Grigoreanu, James Brundage, Eric Bahna,
    Margaret Burnett, Paul ElRif, and Jeffrey Snover

Hypertextual Programming for Domain-Specific End-User
Development   225
    Sebastian Ortiz-Chamorro, Gustavo Rossi, and Daniel Schwabe

Fast, Accurate Creation of Data Validation Formats by End-User
Developers   242
    Chris Scaffidi, Brad Myers, and Mary Shaw

Part III: Refereed Notes

Cicero Designer: An Environment for End-User Development of
Multi-Device Museum Guides   265
    Giuseppe Ghiani, Fabio Paternò, and Lucio Davide Spano

Observing End-User Customisation of Electronic Patient Records   275
    Cecily Morrison and Alan F. Blackwell

Author Index   285

Part I
Invited Talks

End-User Development and Meta-design: Foundations for Cultures of Participation

Gerhard Fischer

Center for LifeLong Learning and Design (L3D)
University of Colorado
Boulder, CO 80309-0430 USA
gerhard@colorado.edu

Abstract. The first decade of the World Wide Web predominantly enforced a clear separation between designers and consumers. New technological developments, such as the cyberinfrastructure and Web 2.0 architectures, have emerged to support a participatory Web. These developments are the foundations for a fundamental shift from a consumer culture (specialized in producing finished goods to be consumed passively) to a culture of participation (in which all people are provided with the means to participate actively in personally meaningful activities). End-user development and meta-design provide foundations for this fundamental transformation. They explore and support new approaches for the design, adoption, appropriation, adaptation, evolution, and sharing of artifacts by all participating stakeholders. They take into account that cultures of participation are not dictated by technology alone: they are the result of incremental shifts in human behavior and social organizations.

1 Introduction

Cultures are defined in part by their media and their tools for thinking, working, learning, and collaborating [McLuhan, 1964]. In the past, the design of most media emphasized a clear distinction between producers and consumers [Benkler, 2006]. Television is the medium that most obviously exhibits this orientation [Postman, 1985] and in the worst case contributes to the degeneration of humans into *"couch potatoes"* [Fischer, 2002] for whom remote controls are the most important instruments of their cognitive activities. In a similar manner, our current educational institutions often treat learners as consumers, fostering a mindset in students of "consumerism" [Illich, 1971] rather than "ownership of problems" for the rest of their lives [Bruner, 1996]. As a result, learners, workers, and citizens often feel left out of decisions by teachers, managers, and policymakers, denying them opportunities to take active roles in personally meaningful and important problems.

The personal computer can produce, in principle, an incredible increase in the creative autonomy of the individual. But historically these possibilities were often of interest and accessible only to a small number of "high-tech scribes." End-user development (EUD) is focused on the challenge of allowing users of software systems who

V. Pipek et al. (Eds.): IS-EUD 2009, LNCS 5435, pp. 3–14, 2009.
© Springer-Verlag Berlin Heidelberg 2009

are not primarily interested in software per se to modify, extend, evolve, and create systems that fit their needs.

What the personal computer has done for the individual, the Internet has done for groups and communities. The first decade of Internet use was dominated by broadcast models and thereby extended the existing strong separation of "designers" and "users" imposed by existing media. Meta-design is an evolving conceptual framework to exploit computational media in support of collaboration and communication (such as table-top computing and wikis) to foster cultures of participation.

2 End-User Development

Familiarity with software applications has become an essential requirement for professionals in a variety of complex domains: architects, doctors, electrical engineers, biochemists, statisticians, and film directors (among many others) all depend for their livelihood on the mastery of various collections of applications [Eisenberg & Fischer, 1994]. These applications, to be at all useful, must provide domain professionals with complex, powerful functionality. In doing so, however, these systems likewise increase the cognitive cost of mastering the new capabilities and resources that they offer. Moreover, the users of these applications will notice that *"software is not soft"*—that is, that the behavior of a given application cannot be changed or meaningfully extended without substantial reprogramming.

The need for end-user development is not a luxury but a necessity: computational systems modeling some particular "world" are never complete; they must evolve over time because (1) the world changes and new requirements emerge; and (2) skilled domain professionals change their work practices over time—their understanding and use of a system will be very different after a month and certainly after several years. If systems cannot be modified to support new practices, users will be locked into existing patterns of use.

These problems were recognized early in the context of expert systems and domain-oriented environments (here we present just two examples for illustration):

- *Expert systems:* The TEIRESIAS system [Davis, 1984] was a module to support domain professionals to augment the existing knowledge base of a medical expert system; the objective of this component was to establish and support interaction at a discourse level that would allow domain professionals to articulate their knowledge without having to program in Lisp.
- *Domain-oriented environments*: The JANUS-MODIFIER system [Fischer & Girgensohn, 1990; Girgensohn, 1992] supported not just human-computer interaction but *human problem-domain interaction* to allow kitchen designers to introduce new components and new critiquing rules into design environments in support of kitchen design.

From a more theoretical perspective, end-user developments can cope with ill-defined (or wicked) problems and breakdowns:

- *Ill-defined or wicked problems* [Rittel & Webber, 1984] cannot be delegated from domain professionals to software professionals, but require the creation of externalizations that talk back to the owner of the problem [Schön, 1983].

- *Breakdowns* [Fischer, 1994] are experienced by domain professionals and not by the system developers; if domain professionals can respond to these breakdowns without relying on a "high-tech scribe," systems will evolve in response to real needs.

Professional programmers and domain professionals define the endpoints of a continuum of computer users. The former like computers because they can program, and the latter because they get their work done. The goal of supporting domain professionals to develop and modify systems does not imply transferring the responsibility of good system design to the end-user [Burnett et al., 2004]. Normal users will in general not build tools of the quality a professional designer would (which was recognized as one of the basic limitations of second-generation design methods [Rittel, 1984]). However, if the tool does not satisfy the needs or the tastes of the end-users (who know best what these requirements are), then end-users should be able to adapt the system without requiring the assistance of developers.

3   A "New World" Based on Cultures of Participation

As the research community interested EUD gathers in 2009 for the *Second International Symposium on End-user Development*, an interesting question is: What has changed since the first symposium that took place in 2003 (as documented in the book *End-User Development* [Lieberman et al., 2006], which includes a chapter about the future of EUD [Klann et al., 2006])? The major innovation and transformation that emerged is the participatory web (or Web 2.0 [O'Reilly, 2006]), complementing and transcending the broadcast web (or Web 1.0), which dominated the first decade of the web.

The Web 1.0 model primarily supports web page publishing and e-commerce, whereas the Web 2.0 model is focused on collaborative design environments, social media, and social networks creating feasibility spaces for new cultures that allow people to participate rather than being confined to passive consumer roles.

This transformation represents a fundamental shift from *consumer cultures* (focused on passive consumption of finished goods produced by others) [Postman, 1985] to *cultures of participation* (in which all people are provided with the means to participate actively in personally meaningful activities) [Fischer, 2002; von Hippel, 2005]. End-user development is obviously an essential component of this transformation, but its impact is much broader: this transformation represents a change and new opportunity for social production, for mass collaboration, for civic and political life, and for education.

The EUD research community has struggled to make its objectives and techniques known to the world, whereas the Web 2.0 world is being defined by breaking down the boundaries between producers and consumers. New broad-based developments (including open source software, Wikipedia, Second Life, YouTube, and 3D Warehouse, to name just a few) attracted a very large number of contributors. The research community interested in EUD now has an opportunity to apply its research findings to create an analytical framework to deeply understand these new developments and evolve them further.

This "new world" has established new levels of discourse, including the following:

- From the dichotomy between consumers and producers, new, middle-ground models have emerged such as
  - *prosumers* [Tapscott & Williams, 2006], who are techno-sophisticated and comfortable with the technologies with which they grew up; they have little fear of hacking, modifying, and evolving their artifacts to their own requirements. They do not wait for someone else to anticipate their needs, and they can decide what is important for them. They participate in learning and discovery and engage in experimenting, exploring, building, tinkering, framing, solving, and reflecting.
  - *professional amateurs* [Brown, 2005; Leadbeater & Miller, 2008], who are innovative, committed, and networked amateurs working to professional standards; they are a new social hybrid, and their activities are not adequately captured by the traditional dichotomous definitions of work and leisure, professional and amateur, consumption and production.
  - *social production* and *mass collaboration* [Benkler, 2006], which are based on the following facts: (a) a tiny percentage of a very large base is still a substantial number of people; (b) beyond quantitative numbers exists a great diversity of interests and passions in the Long Tail [Anderson, 2006]; and (c) while human beings often act for material rewards, they can also be motivated by social capital, reputation, connectedness, and the enjoyment derived from giving things of value away (contributing).
- An emphasis on *open systems*, which are systems focused on the "unfinished" and take into account that design problems have no stopping rule, need to remain open and fluid to accommodate ongoing change, and for which "continuous beta" becomes a desirable rather than a to-be-avoided attribute.
- The importance of *user-generated content*, in which "content" is broadly defined: creating artifacts with existing tools (e.g., writing a document with a word processor) or changing the tools (e.g., writing macros to extend the word processor as a tool). In specific environments (such as open source software), the content is subject to the additional requirement of being computationally interpretable).
- Moving from guidelines, rules, and procedures to *exceptions, negotiations, and work-arounds* to complement and integrate accredited and expert knowledge with informal, practice-based, and situated knowledge [Suchman, 1987; Orr, 1996; Winograd & Flores, 1986].
- Exploiting the Long Tail [Anderson, 2006] of knowledge distribution, allowing people from around the world to engage in topics and activities about which they feel passionate.
- Fostering and supporting richer *ecologies of participation* (see Section 4.2).
- Creating a new understanding of motivation, creativity, control, ownership, and quality (see Section 4.3).

4 Meta-design

Meta-design [Fischer & Giaccardi, 2006] is focused on "design for designers." It creates open systems at design time that can be modified by their users acting as co-designers, requiring and supporting more complex interactions at use time. Meta-design is grounded in the basic assumption that future uses and problems cannot be completely anticipated at design time, when a system is developed. At use time, users will invariably discover mismatches between their needs and the support that an existing system can provide for them.

Open systems allow significant modifications when the need arises. The successes of open source software systems and open content environments have demonstrated that, given the right conditions, design through the collaboration of many can create new kinds of systems.

Meta-design tries to reduce the gap in the world of computing between a population of elite high-tech scribes who can act as designers and a much larger population of intellectually disenfranchised knowledge workers who are *forced* into consumer roles. The *seeding, evolutionary growth, and reseeding (SER) model* [Fischer & Ostwald, 2002] is an emerging descriptive and prescriptive model in support of meta-design. In the past, large and complex software systems were built as complete artifacts through the large efforts of a small number of people. Instead of attempting to build complete systems, the SER model advocates building *seeds* (in participatory design activities with meta-designers and end-users) that can evolve over time through small contributions of a large number of people (being the defining characteristics of a culture of participation). It postulates that systems that evolve over a sustained time span must continually alternate between periods of planned activity and unplanned evolution and periods of deliberate (re)structuring and enhancement. A seed is something that has the potential to change and grow. In socio-technical environments, seeds need to be designed and created for the *technical* as well as the *social* component of the environment.

4.1 The Ubiquity of Meta-design

Meta-design transcends end-user development by studying and supporting cultures of participation not only in the area of software artifacts, but also in every domain of information and cultural production. Meta-design explores different purposes associated with the artifacts under development, ranging from reliability and efficiency to reaching a deeper understanding of problems and developing more creative and innovative solutions.

In our research, we have explored meta-design [Fischer & Giaccardi, 2006] in the following areas:

- *design of computational artifacts* [Lieberman et al., 2006], with an emphasis on customization, personalization, tailorability, end-user modifiability, design for diversity, and design for a "universe of one" [Carmien & Fischer, 2008];
- *architectural design* [Brand, 1995], with an emphasis on underdesign and support for an "unself-conscious culture of design" [Alexander, 1964];
- *new models of teaching and learning* [Brown, 2005; Rogoff et al., 1998], with an emphasis on challenging the assumption that information must move from teachers and other credentialed producers to passive learners and consumers [Illich, 1971], such as learning communities, teachers as meta-designers, and courses-as-seeds [dePaula et al., 2001];

- *open source* [Raymond & Young, 2001], with an emphasis on open source as a success model of decentralized, collaborative, evolutionary development [Scharff, 2002]; and
- *interactive art* [Giaccardi, 2004], with an emphasis on collaboration and co-creation facilitated by putting the tools rather than the object of design in the hands of users.

In our currently active research, we are further deepening our understanding of meta-design and cultures of participation with the following projects:

- *3D WAREHOUSE*, an environment in which people from around the world can share 3D models created with SketchUp, and how these models can be referenced and displayed in Google Earth;
- *SAP DEVELOPER NETWORK*, an example of a successful socio-technical environment consisting of more than one million registered users forming a highly active online community; and
- *CREATIVEIT*, a wiki-based environment fostering and supporting the evolving scientific community participating in the NSF Program on "Creativity and IT."

4.2 Richer Ecologies of Participation

The traditional notions of developer and user are unable to reflect the fact that many socio-technical environments nowadays are developed with the participation of many people with varied interests and capabilities. Cultures of participation require contributors with diverse background knowledge who need to provide support and value different ways of participating. Many collaborative design environments serve *only as content management* systems: participants contribute and share their *own* interests and abilities, and additional activities such as critiquing, rating, tagging, deliberating, extending, improving, and negotiating do not take place and are not adequately supported; their value is therefore not sufficiently recognized.

Early studies [Gantt & Nardi, 1992] already identified that EUD is more successful if supported by collaborative work practices rather than focusing on individuals. Gantt and Nardi observed the emergence of "gardeners" (also known as "power users" and "local developers"), who are technically interested and sophisticated enough to perform system modifications that are needed by a community of users but that other end-users are not able or inclined to perform.

A detailed analysis of open-source software systems [Ye & Fischer, 2007] revealed a variety of different roles: (1) *passive users* (using the system); (2) *readers* (trying to understand how the system works by reading the source code); (3) *bug reporters* (discovering and reporting bugs); (4) *bug fixers* (fixing bugs); (5) *peripheral developers* (occasionally contributing new functionality or features); (6) *active developers* (regularly contributing new features and fixing bugs); and (7) *project leader(s)* (initiating the project and being responsible for its vision and overall direction).

In the SketchUp/3D Warehouse/Google Earth environments, a similar role distribution can be observed: contributors create new models with SketchUp, raters and taggers evaluate and describe these models, and curators organize models in collections and create narratives.

To be more specific about the role of *meta-designers*: what do they do? They use their own creativity to create socio-technical environments in which other people can be creative. The main activity of meta-designers shifts from determining the meaning, functionality, and content of a system to encouraging and supporting users to engage in these activities. Meta-designers must be willing to share control of how systems will be used, which content will be contained, and which functionality will be supported. They do so with a focus on *underdesign* (1) by creating contexts and content creation tools rather than content; (2) by creating technical and social conditions for broad participation in design activities; and (3) by supporting "hackability" and "remixability."

4.3 Motivation, Control, Ownership, Creativity, and Quality

As argued before, understanding and fostering cultures of participation with meta-design requires paying attention to factors from political, economical, and social domains. This section takes a brief look at a few of those factors.

Motivation. Human beings are diversely motivated beings. We act not only for material gain, but for psychological well-being, for social integration and connectedness, for social capital, for recognition, and for improving our standing in a reputation economy. The motivation for going the extra step to engage in EUD was articulated by Rittel [Rittel, 1984]: *"The experience of having participated in a problem makes a difference to those who are affected by the solution. People are more likely to like a solution if they have been involved in its generation; even though it might not make sense otherwise."* Meta-design relies on intrinsic motivation for participation and it has the potential to influence this by providing contributors with the sense and experience of joint creativity, by giving them a sense of common purpose and mutual support in achieving it, and in many situations by replacing common background or geographic proximity with a sense of well-defined purpose, shared concerns, and the successful common pursuit of these [Anderson, 2006; Fischer, 2001].

Control. Meta-design supports users as active contributors who can transcend the functionality and content of existing systems. By facilitating these possibilities, *control* is distributed among all stakeholders in the design process. The importance of this distribution of control has been emphasized as important for architecture [Alexander, 1984]: *"I believe passionately in the idea that people should design buildings for themselves. In other words, not only that they should be involved in the buildings that are for them but that they should actually help design them."* Other arguments indicate that shared control will lead to more innovation [von Hippel, 2005]: *"Users that innovate can develop exactly what they want, rather than relying on manufacturers to act as their (often very imperfect) agents."*

Ownership. Our experiences gathered in the context of the design, development, and assessment of our systems indicate that meta-design methodologies are less successful when users are brought into the process late (thereby denying them ownership) than when users are "misused" to fix problems and to address weaknesses of systems that the developers did not fix themselves. Meta-design does work when users are part of the participatory design effort in establishing a meta-design framework, including support for intrinsic and extrinsic motivation, user toolkits for reducing the effort to make contributions, and the seeding of use communities in which individuals can share their contributions [Dawe, 2007].

Social Creativity. Where do new ideas come from in meta-design environments and cultures of participation? The creativity potential is grounded in (1) user-driven innovations, (2) taking advantage of breakdowns as sources for creativity, and (3) exploiting the symmetry of ignorance and conceptual collisions. To increase social creativity requires: (1) *diversity* (each participants should have some unique information or perspective); (2) *independence* (participants' opinions are not determined by the opinions of those around them) [Surowiecki, 2005]; (3) decentralization (participants are able to specialize and draw on local knowledge) [Anderson, 2006]; and (4) *aggregation* (mechanisms exist for turning individual contributions into collections, and private judgments into collective decisions). In addition, participants must be able to express themselves (requiring EUD competencies), must be willing to contribute (motivation), and must be allowed to have their voices heard (control).

Quality. Many teachers will tell their students that they will not accept research findings and argumentation based on articles from Wikipedia. This exclusion is usually based on considerations such as: *"How are we to know that the content produced by widely dispersed and qualified individuals is not of substandard quality?"*

The online journal *Nature* (http://www.nature.com/) has compared the quality of articles found in the *Encyclopedia Britannica* with Wikipedia and has come to the conclusion that *"Wikipedia comes close to Britannica in terms of the accuracy of its science entries."* This study and the interpretation of its findings has generated a controversy, and Tapscott and Williams [Tapscott & Williams, 2006] have challenged the basic assumption that a direct comparison between the two encyclopedias is a relevant issue: *"Wikipedia isn't great because it's like the Britannica. The Britannica is great at being authoritative, edited, expensive, and monolithic. Wikipedia is great at being free, brawling, universal, and instantaneous."*

There are many more open issues to be investigated about quality and trust [Kittur et al., 2008] in cultures of participation, including: (1) errors will always exist, resulting in learners acquiring the important skill of always being critical of information rather than blindly believing in what others (specifically experts or teachers) are saying; and (2) ownership may be a critical dimension: the community at large has a greater sense of ownership and thereby is more willing to put an effort into fixing errors. This last issue has been explored in open source communities and has led to the observation that *"if there are enough eyeballs, all bugs are shallow"* [Raymond & Young, 2001].

5 Drawbacks of Cultures of Participation

Cultures of participation open up unique new opportunities for mass collaboration and social production, but they are not without drawbacks. One such drawback is that humans may be forced to cope with the burden of being active contributors in *personally irrelevant activities*.

This drawback can be illustrated with "do-it-yourself" societies. Through modern tools, humans are empowered to perform many tasks themselves that were done previously by skilled domain workers serving as agents and intermediaries. Although this shift provides power, freedom, and control to customers, it also has forced people to act as contributors in contexts for which they lack the experience that professionals have acquired and maintained through the daily use of systems, as well as the broad background knowledge to do these tasks efficiently and effectively (e.g., companies offloading work to customers).

Substantially more experience and assessment is required to determine whether the *advantages* of cultures of participation (such as extensive coverage of information, creation of large numbers of artifacts, creative chaos by making all voices heard, reduced authority of expert opinions, and shared experience of social creativity) will outweigh the *disadvantages* (accumulation of irrelevant information, wasting human resources in large information spaces, and lack of coherent voices). Such a determination will depend on creating a deeper understanding of these trade-offs [Carr, 2008; Lanier, 2006].

6 Implications and Conclusions

For a couple of decades the rise of digital media has been providing new powers for the *individual*. The world's networks are now providing enormous unexplored opportunities for *groups and communities*. Providing all citizens with the means to become co-creators of new ideas, knowledge, and products in personally meaningful activities presents one of the most exciting innovations and transformations, with profound implications in the years to come.

This paper has described numerous reasons why EUD environments (for customizing, tailoring, and evolving systems) are highly desirable. Despite the fact that some EUD environments and their supporting research have been around for years and some success models exist [Lieberman et al., 2006], there is evidence that the impact of academic research efforts in this area has been limited.

We do know, however, that digital media are powerful catalysts of cultural change. The challenge for the EUD research community is not only understanding, supporting, and participating in existing cultures, but also shaping, transforming, and fostering new cultures. Humans all over the world have the opportunity today not only to be exposed to cultures of consumerism [Postman, 1985], but to become active contributors in cultures of participation. Without an analytic model and a demystification of media to deeply understand and explain new emerging phenomena and environments, however, we will only be able to treat them as curiosities or transient fads [Benkler, 2006]. The potential impact of cultures of participation supported by meta-design is substantial: they erode monopolistic positions held by professions, educational institutions, and experts, and they increase the diversity of perspectives on the way the world is and the way it could be. They require new metaphors, new levels of discourse, and new environments to think, reflect, and support working, learning, and collaboration for alternative and more democratic futures.

Acknowledgments

I thank the members of the Center for LifeLong Learning & Design at the University of Colorado, who have made major contributions to the ideas described in this paper.

I have learned much over the years by interacting with my professional colleagues and collaborators in the EUD and EUSE communities.

The research was supported in part by (1) grants from the National Science Foundation, including: (a) IIS-0613638 *"A Meta-Design Framework for Participative Software Systems"*, (b) IIS-0709304 *"A New Generation Wiki for Supporting a Research Community in 'Creativity and IT'"* and (c) IIS-0843720 *"Increasing Participation and Sustaining a Research Community in 'Creativity and IT'"*; (2) a Google research award, *"Motivating and Empowering Users to Become Active Contributors: Supporting the Learning of High-Functionality Environments"*; and (3) a SAP research project, *"Giving All Stakeholders a Voice: Understanding and Supporting the Creativity and Innovation of Communities Using and Evolving Software Products."*

References

1. Alexander, C.: The Synthesis of Form, Part I. Harvard University Press, Cambridge (1964)
2. Alexander, C.: The State of the Art in Design Methods. In: Cross, N. (ed.) Developments in Design Methodology, pp. 309–316. John Wiley & Sons, New York (1984)
3. Anderson, C.: The Long Tail: Why the Future of Business Is Selling Less of More. Hyperion, New York (2006)
4. Benkler, Y.: The Wealth of Networks: How Social Production Transforms Markets and Freedom. Yale University Press, New Haven (2006)
5. Brand, S.: How Buildings Learn: What Happens after They're Built. Penguin Books, New York (1995)
6. Brown, J.S.: New Learning Environments for the 21st Century (2005),
   `http://www.johnseelybrown.com/newlearning.pdf`
7. Bruner, J.: The Culture of Education. Harvard University Press, Cambridge (1996)
8. Burnett, M., Cook, C., Rothermel, G.: End-User Software Engineering. Communications of the ACM 47(9), 53–58 (2004)
9. Carmien, S.P., Fischer, G.: Design, Adoption, and Assessment of a Socio-Technical Environment Supporting Independence for Persons with Cognitive Disabilities. In: Proceedings of Chi 2008, pp. 597–607. ACM, Florence (2008)
10. Carr, N.: Is Google Making Us Stupid? (2008),
    `http://www.theatlantic.com/doc/200807/google`
11. Davis, R.: Interactive Transfer of Expertise. In: Buchanan, B.G., Shortliffe, E.H. (eds.) Rule-Based Expert Systems: The Mycin Experiments of the Stanford Heuristic Programming Project, pp. 171–205. Addison-Wesley Publishing Company, Reading (1984)
12. Dawe, M.: Reflective Design-in-Use: Co-Designing an Assistive Remote Communication System with Individuals with Cognitive Disabilities and Their Families, Ph.D. Dissertation, University of Colorado at Boulder (2007),
    `http://l3d.cs.colorado.edu/~meliss/diss/`
13. dePaula, R., Fischer, G., Ostwald, J.: Courses as Seeds: Expectations and Realities. In: Dillenbourg, P., Eurelings, A., Hakkarainen, K. (eds.) Proceedings of the European Conference on Computer-Supported Collaborative Learning, Maastricht, The Netherlands, pp. 494–501 (2001)
14. Eisenberg, M., Fischer, G.: Programmable Design Environments: Integrating End-User Programming with Domain-Oriented Assistance. In: Human Factors in Computing Systems, Chi 1994, Boston, MA, pp. 431–437. ACM, New York (1994)

15. Fischer, G.: Turning Breakdowns into Opportunities for Creativity. Knowledge-Based Systems, Special Issue on Creativity and Cognition 7(4), 221–232 (1994)
16. Fischer, G.: Communities of Interest: Learning through the Interaction of Multiple Knowledge Systems. In: 24th Annual Information Systems Research Seminar In Scandinavia (IRIS 1924), Ulvik, Norway, pp. 1–14 (2001)
17. Fischer, G.: Beyond 'Couch Potatoes': From Consumers to Designers and Active Contributors," Firstmonday (Peer-Reviewed Journal on the Internet) (2002), http://firstmonday.org/issues/issue7_12/fischer/
18. Fischer, G., Giaccardi, E.: Meta-Design: A Framework for the Future of End User Development. In: Lieberman, H., Paternò, F., Wulf, V. (eds.) End User Development, pp. 427–457. Kluwer Academic Publishers, Dordrecht (2006)
19. Fischer, G., Girgensohn, A.: End-User Modifiability in Design Environments. In: Human Factors in Computing Systems (Chi 1990), Seattle, WA, pp. 183–191. ACM, New York (1990)
20. Fischer, G., Ostwald, J.: Seeding, Evolutionary Growth, and Reseeding: Enriching Participatory Design with Informed Participation, Malmö University, Sweden, pp. 135–143 (2002)
21. Gantt, M., Nardi, B.A.: Gardeners and Gurus: Patterns of Cooperation among CAD Users. In: Bauersfeld, P., Bennett, J., Lynch, G. (eds.) Proceedings of ACM CHI 1992 Conference on Human Factors in Computing Systems, pp. 107–117. ACM, New York (1992), http://www.acm.org/pubs/articles/proceedings/chi/142750/p107-gantt/p107-gantt.pdf
22. Giaccardi, E.: Principles of Metadesign: Processes and Levels of Co-Creation in the New Design Space, Ph.D. Dissertation, CAiiA-STAR, School of Computing, Plymouth, UK (2004)
23. Girgensohn, A.: End-User Modifiability in Knowledge-Based Design Environments, Ph.D. Dissertation, University of Colorado at Boulder (1992)
24. Illich, I.: Deschooling Society. Harper and Row, New York (1971)
25. Kittur, A., Suh, B., Chi, E.H.: Can You Ever Trust a Wiki? Impacting Perceived Trustworthiness in Wikipedia. In: Proceedings of CSCW 2008 (2008)
26. Klann, M., Paterno, F., Wulf, V.: Future Perspectives in End-User Development. In: Lieberman, H., Paternò, F., Wulf, V. (eds.) End User Development, pp. 475–486. Kluwer Academic Publishers, Dordrecht (2006)
27. Lanier, J.: Digital Maoism: The Hazards of the New Online Collectivism (2006), http://www.edge.org/3rd_culture/lanier06/lanier06_index.html
28. Leadbeater, C., Miller, P.: The Pro-Am Revolution—How Enthusiasts Are Changing Our Economy and Society (2008), http://www.demos.co.uk/files/proamrevolutionfinal.pdf
29. Lieberman, H., Paterno, F., Wulf, V. (eds.): End User Development. Kluwer Publishers, Dordrecht (2006)
30. McLuhan, M.: Understanding Media: The Extensions of Man. MIT Press, Cambridge (1964)
31. O'Reilly, T.: What Is Web 2.0—Design Patterns and Business Models for the Next Generation of Software (2006), http://www.oreillynet.com/pub/a/oreilly/tim/news/2005/09/30/what-is-web-20.html
32. Orr, J.: Talking About Machines—an Ethnography of a Modern Job. ILR Press/Cornell University Press, Ithaca, NY (1996)

33. Postman, N.: Amusing Ourselves to Death—Public Discourse in the Age of Show Business. Penguin Books, New York (1985)
34. Raymond, E.S., Young, B.: The Cathedral and the Bazaar: Musings on Linux and Open Source by an Accidental Revolutionary. O'Reilly & Associates, Sebastopol (2001)
35. Rittel, H.: Second-Generation Design Methods. In: Cross, N. (ed.) Developments in Design Methodology, pp. 317–327. John Wiley & Sons, New York (1984)
36. Rittel, H., Webber, M.M.: Planning Problems Are Wicked Problems. In: Cross, N. (ed.) Developments in Design Methodology, pp. 135–144. John Wiley & Sons, New York (1984)
37. Rogoff, B., Matsuov, E., White, C.: Models of Teaching and Learning: Participation in a Community of Learners. In: Olsen, D.R., Torrance, N. (eds.) The Handbook of Education and Human Development—New Models of Learning, Teaching and Schooling, pp. 388–414. Blackwell, Oxford (1998)
38. Scharff, E.: Open Source Software, a Conceptual Framework for Collaborative Artifact and Knowledge Construction, Ph.D. Dissertation, University of Colorado at Boulder (2002)
39. Schön, D.A.: The Reflective Practitioner: How Professionals Think in Action. Basic Books, New York (1983)
40. Suchman, L.A.: Plans and Situated Actions. Cambridge University Press, Cambridge (1987)
41. Surowiecki, J.: The Wisdom of Crowds. Anchor Books, New York (2005)
42. Tapscott, D., Williams, A.D.: Wikinomics: How Mass Collaboration Changes Everything, Portofolio. Penguin Group, New York (2006)
43. von Hippel, E.: Democratizing Innovation. MIT Press, Cambridge (2005)
44. Winograd, T., Flores, F.: Understanding Computers and Cognition: A New Foundation for Design. Ablex Publishing Corporation, Norwood (1986)
45. Ye, Y., Fischer, G.: Designing for Participation in Socio-Technical Software Systems. In: Stephanidis, C. (ed.) Proceedings of 4th International Conference on Universal Access in Human-Computer Interaction, Beijing, China, pp. 312–321. Springer, Heidelberg (2007)

What Is End-User Software Engineering and Why Does It Matter?

Margaret Burnett

Oregon State University, School of Electrical Engineering and Computer Science,
Corvallis, Oregon, 97331 USA
burnett@eecs.oregonstate.edu

Abstract. End-user programming has become ubiquitous, so much so that there are more end-user programmers today than there are professional programmers. End-user programming empowers—but to do what? Make really bad decisions based on really bad programs? Enter software engineering's focus on quality. Considering software quality is necessary, because there is ample evidence that the programs end users create are filled with expensive errors. In this paper, I consider what happens when we add to end-user programming environments considerations of software quality, going beyond the "create a program" aspect of end-user programming. I describe a philosophy to software engineering for end users, and then survey several projects in this area. A basic premise is that end-user software engineering can only succeed to the extent that it respects the fact that the user probably has little expertise or even interest in software engineering.

Keywords: End-user software engineering, End-user programming, End-user development.

1 Introduction

It all started with end-user programming.

End-user programming enables end users to create their own programs. Researchers and developers have been working on empowering end users to do this for a number of years, and they have succeeded: today, end users create numerous programs.

The "programming environments" used by end users include spreadsheet systems, web authoring tools, and graphical languages for creating educational simulations (e.g., [6, 16, 18, 22, 23]). Using these systems, end users create programs in forms such as spreadsheets, dynamic web applications, and educational simulations. Some ways in which end users create these programs include writing and editing formulas, dragging and dropping objects onto a logical workspace, connecting objects in a diagram, or demonstrating intended logic to the system.

In fact, research based on U.S. Bureau of Census and Bureau of Labor data shows that there are about 3 million professional programmers in the United States—but over 12 million more people who say they do programming at work, and over 50 million who use spreadsheets and databases [28]. Fig. 1 shows the breakouts. Thus,

V. Pipek et al. (Eds.): IS-EUD 2009, LNCS 5435, pp. 15–28, 2009.

the number of end-user programmers in the U.S. alone probably falls somewhere between 12 million and 50 million people—several times the number of professional programmers.

Clearly then, end-user programming empowers—it has already empowered millions of end users to create their own software.

Unfortunately, there is a down side: the software they are creating with this new power is riddled with errors. In fact, evidence abounds of the pervasiveness of errors in software end users create. (See, for example, the EUSPRIG web site's 89 news stories recounting spreadsheet errors [9].) These errors can have significant impact. For example, one school faced a £30,000 shortfall because values in a budget spreadsheet had not been added up correctly [9 story # 67]. TransAlta Corporation took a $24 million charge to earnings after a bidding error caused it to buy more U.S. power transmission hedging contracts than it bargained for, at higher prices than it wanted to pay, due to a spreadsheet error [10].

Even when the errors in end-user-created software are non-catastrophic, however, their effects can matter. Web applications created by small-business owners to promote their businesses do just the opposite if they contain bad links or pages that display incorrectly, resulting in loss of revenue and credibility. Software resources linked by end users to monitor non-safety-critical medical conditions can cause unnecessary pain or discomfort for users who rely on them. Such problems are ubiquitous in two particularly rapidly growing types of software end users develop: open resource coalitions and dynamic web applications.

Thus, the problem with end-user programming is that end users' programs are all too often turning out to be of too low quality for the purposes for which they were created.

1.1 A New Area: End-User Software Engineering

A new research area is emerging to address this problem. The area is known as *end-user software engineering* [7], and it aims to address the problem of end users' software quality by looking beyond the "create" part of software development, which is already well supported, to the rest of the software lifecycle. Thus, *end-user programming* is the "create" part of end-user software development, and end-user software engineering adds consideration of software quality issues to both the "create" and the "beyond create" parts of software development.

More formally, Ko et al. define *end-user software engineering* as "end-user programming involving systematic and disciplined activities that address software quality issues (such as reliability, efficiency, usability, etc.). In essence, end-user programming focuses mainly on how to allow end users to create their own programs, and end-user software engineering considers how to support the entire software lifecycle and its attendant issues" [14].

End-user software engineering is similar to the notion of *end-user development* [17], but not quite the same. According to Wikipedia, "end-user development (EUD) is a research topic within the field of computer science, describing activities or techniques that allow people who are not professional developers to create or modify a software artifact. A typical example of EUD is programming to extend and adapt an

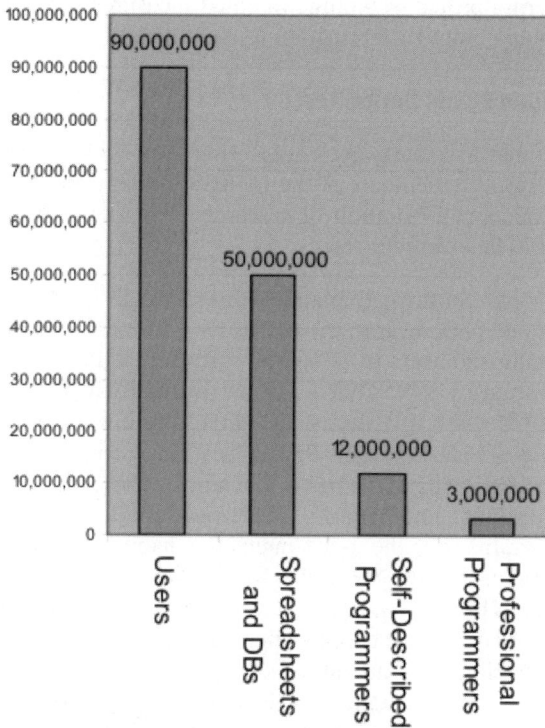

Fig. 1. U.S. users in 2006 and those who do forms of programming [28]

existing package (e.g. an office suite)" [30]. Thus, end-user software engineering is end-user development with the additional notion of the software's quality.

In my view, end-user software engineering (done well) is inherently different from traditional software engineering, because simply mimicking traditional approaches would not be likely to produce successful results. One reason is that end users often have very different training and background than professional programmers. Even more important, end users also face different motivations and work constraints than professional programmers. They are not likely to know about quality control mechanisms, formal development processes, modeling diagrams, or test adequacy criteria, and are not likely to invest time learning about such things. This is because in most cases, end users are not striving to create the best software they can; rather, they have their "real goals" to achieve: such as accounting, teaching, managing safety, understanding financial data, or authoring new media-based experiences.

The strategy my collaborators and I have used in our end-user software engineering research to support these users in pursuing their real goals has been to gently alert them to dependability problems, to assist them with their explorations into those problems to whatever extent they choose to pursue such explorations, and to work within the contexts with which they are familiar. This strategy represents a paradigm shift from traditional software engineering and end-user programming research, because it marries dependability with end-user software development. Thus, our end-user software engineering projects combine in equal measures software engineering foundations with human-computer interaction foundations.

1.2 Organization of This Paper

I'll illustrate the end-user software engineering area with examples of projects that have been conducted by members of the EUSES Consortium (http://eusesconsortium. org), an NSF-funded collaboration of researchers working in the end-user software engineering area. The examples are:

- WYSIWYT and Surprise-Explain-Reward: WYSIWYT is a methodology for supporting systematic testing by end users. Surprise-Explain-Reward is a strategy for enticing end users to engage in software engineering practices such as the testing supported by WYSIWYT. Since WYSIWYT's success depends on Surprise-Explain-Reward, I'll discuss the two of these works together.
- Debugging Machine-Learned Programs: In recent times, a new kind of "programmer" has entered the mix—machines. These machines, through machine-learning algorithms, automatically create programs on the user's computer, deriving these programs from the user's interaction habits and data history. I'll discuss a debugging approach and early results for one type of program in this class.
- Gender in End-User Software Engineering: If end-user software engineering is to properly blend HCI-based people-oriented foundations with software engineering foundations, then it must attend to both 50%s of the people who are end users—both the males and the females. I'll discuss emerging information about gender differences' implications for the design of end-user software engineering tools.

2 WYSIWYT Testing and Surprise-Explain-Reward

WYSIWYT (What You See Is What You Test) [26] supports *systematic testing* by end-user programmers. It has mostly been implemented in the spreadsheet paradigm, so I'll present it here from that perspective. Its motivation is the following: empirical studies have shown that users often assume their spreadsheets are correct, but even if they try to consider whether there are errors, they do so by looking at the immediate value recalculations they see when they enter or change formulas. Empirical work has shown that this "one test only" feedback is tied to overconfidence about the correctness of their spreadsheets.

WYSIWYT helps to address this problem. With WYSIWYT, as a user incrementally develops a spreadsheet, he or she can also test that spreadsheet. As the user changes cell formulas and values, the underlying evaluation engine automatically evaluates cells, and the user (validates) checks off resulting values that are correct. Behind the scenes, these validations are used to measure the quality of testing in terms of a dataflow adequacy criterion, which tracks coverage of interactions between cells caused by cell references.

For example, in Fig. 2, the user has noticed that Smith's letter grade (row 4) is correct, so the user checked it off. The Average row's values under HWAVG, MIDTERM, and FINAL are also correct, so the user checks them off too. As a results, the cell borders turn closer to blue on a red-blue continuum, in which red means untested, blue means tested, and colors between red and blue (shades of purple) mean partially tested.

But, pause to reflect: Why *should* a user whose interests are simply to get their spreadsheet results as efficiently as possible choose to spend extra time learning about these unusual new checkmarks, let alone think carefully about values and whether they should be checked off? Let's further assume that these users have never seen software engineering devices before. To succeed at enticing the user to use these devices, we require a strategy that will both motivate these users to make use of software engineering devices and provide the just-in-time support they need to effectively follow up on this interest.

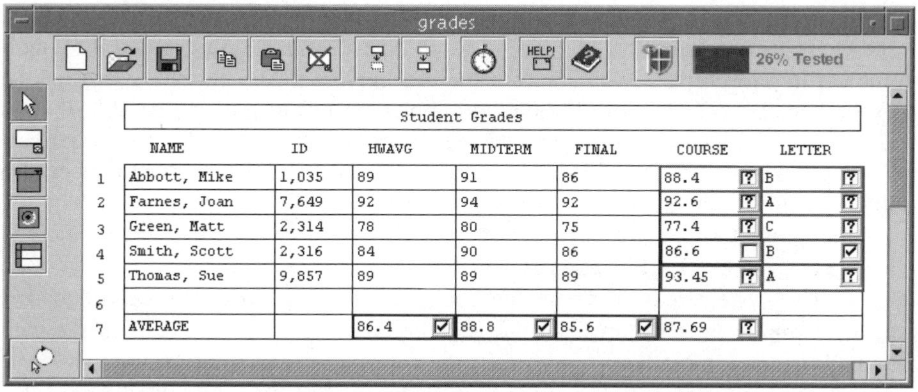

Fig. 2. At any time, the user can test by checking off a value that turned out to be correct, and this test causes borders of the cells involved to become more blue, reflecting coverage of the tests so far

We call our strategy for enticing the user down this path Surprise-Explain-Reward [31]. The strategy attempts to first arouse users' curiosity about the software engineering devices through surprise, and to then encourage them, through explanations and rewards, to follow through with appropriate actions. This strategy has its roots in three areas of research: (1) research about curiosity (psychology) [20], (2) Blackwell's model of attention investment [4] (psychology/HCI), and (3) minimalist learning (educational theory, HCI) [8].

Research into curiosity indicates that surprising by violating a user's assumptions can trigger a search for an explanation. The violation of assumptions indicates to the user the presence of something they do not understand. According to the information-gap perspective [20], a revealed gap in the user's knowledge focuses the user's attention on the gap and leads to curiosity, which motivates the user to close the gap by searching for an explanation.

This is why the first component of our surprise-explain-reward strategy is needed: to arouse users' curiosity enough, through surprise, to cause them to search for explanations. Blackwell's model of attention investment [4] considers the costs, benefits, and risks users weigh in deciding how to complete a task. For example, if a user's goal is to forecast a budget using a spreadsheet, then exploring an unknown feature has perceived costs, perceived benefits, and a perceived risk — such as that using the new feature will waste time or, worse, leave the spreadsheet in a state from which it is difficult (and thus incurs more costs) to recover. The model of attention investment implies that the second (explanation) component of the surprise-explain-reward strategy must provide motivation by promising specific rewards (benefits). The third component must then follow through with at least the rewards that were promised.

For example, we instantiate the surprise-explain-reward strategy with the red borders and the checkboxes in each cell, both of which are unusual for spreadsheets. These surprises (information gaps) are non-intrusive: the user is not forced to attend to them if they view other matters to be more worthy of their time. However, if they become curious about these features, they can ask them to explain themselves at a very low cost, simply by hovering over them with their mouse. Thus, the surprise component delivers to the explain component.

The explain component is also very low in cost. In its simplest form, it explains the object in a tool tip. For example, if the user hovers over a checkbox that has not yet been checked off, the tool tip says (in one variant of our prototype): "*If this value is right,* √ *it; if it's wrong, X it. This testing helps you find errors.*" Thus, it explains the semantics very briefly, gives just enough information for the user to succeed at going down this path, and gives a hint at the reward.

As the above tool tip has pointed out, it is also possible for the user to "X out" a value that is incorrect. For example, in Fig. 3, the user has noticed two incorrect values. The system reasons about the backward slice (contributing cells and their values), taking correct values also into account, and highlights the cells in the dataflow path deemed most likely to contain the formula error. In the figure, two cells were X'd out, and those same two are highlighted, but one is highlighted darker than the other, because it was both identified as having a wrong value and also contributed to the other one that had the wrong value.

The main reward is finding errors through checking values off and X'ing them out to narrow down the most likely locations of formula errors, but a secondary reward is

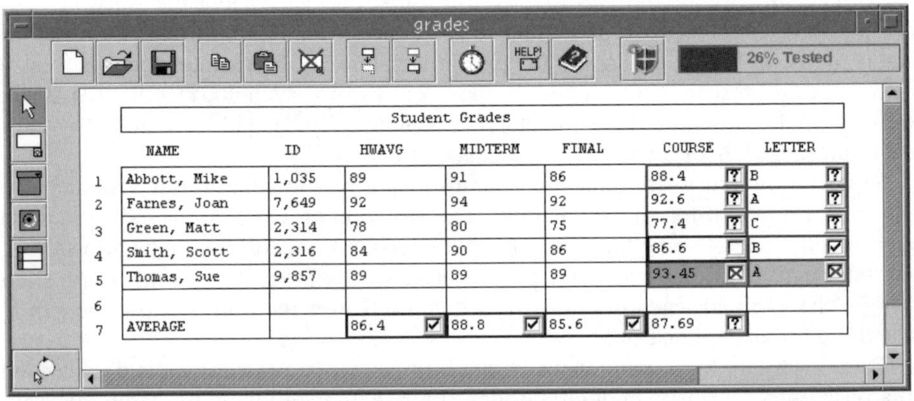

Fig. 3. If the user also notices that a value is incorrect, the user can X it out, and this causes the fault localization algorithm to suggest which cell formulas are most likely to contain the error

a "well tested" (high coverage) spreadsheet, which at least shows evidence of having fairly thoroughly looked for errors. To help achieve testing coverage, question marks point out where more decisions about values will make progress (cause more coverage under the hood, cause more color changes on the surface), and the progress bar at the top shows overall coverage/testedness so far. Our empirical work has shown that these devices are quite motivating, and further more lead to more effectiveness [27].

3 Debugging Machine-Learned Programs

But what if the program that has gone wrong was not written by a human at all? How do you debug a program that was written by a machine instead of a person?

This is the problem faced by users of a new sort of program, namely, one generated by a machine learning system that customizes itself to the user. For example, intelligent user interfaces, recommender systems, and categorizers of email use machine learning to adapt their behavior to users' preferences. This learned set of behaviors is a *program*. These learned programs do not come into existence until the learning environment has left the hands of the machine-learning specialist: they are learned on the user's computer. Thus, if these programs make a mistake, the only one present to fix them is the end user. These attempts to "fix" the system can be viewed as debugging—the user is aware of faulty system behavior, and wants to change the system's logic so as to fix the flawed behavior.

Sometimes correctness is not critical; "good enough" will suffice. For example, a spam filter that successfully collects 90% of dangerous, virus-infested spam leaves the user in a far better situation than having no spam filter at all. However, as the applications of machine learning expand, these programs are becoming more critical. For example, recommender systems that recommend substandard suppliers or incorrect parts, language translators that translate incorrectly, decision support systems that lead the user to overlook important factors, and even email classifiers that misfile important messages could cause significant losses to their users and raise significant liability issues for businesses.

My collaborators and I have begun to investigate how to support end-user debugging of machine-learned programs [15]. Inspired by the success of the Whyline's support of end-user debugging [13, 21], we designed a method to allow end users to ask Why questions of machine-learned software. Our approach is novel in the following ways: (1) it supports *end users* asking questions of machine-learned programs, and (2) the answers aim at providing suggestions for these end users to *debug* the learned programs.

We have built a prototype of our approach, so that we could investigate both barriers faced by end users when debugging machine-learned programs, and challenges to machine learning algorithms themselves. Our prototype was an e-mail application with several predefined folders. The system utilized a machine-learned program to predict which folder each message in the inbox should be filed to, thus allowing the user to easily archive messages. Our prototype answers the Why questions shown in Table 1.

Table 1. The Why questions [15]

Why will this message be filed to <Personal>?
Why won't this message be filed to <Bankruptcy>?
Why did this message turn red?
Why wasn't this message affected by my recent changes?
Why did so many messages turn red?
Why is this email undecided?
Why does <banking> matter to the <Bankruptcy> folder?
Why aren't all important words shown?
Why can't I make this message go to <Systems>?

For example, the answer to Table 1's second question (with dynamically-replaced text in <brackets>) is:

The message will be filed to <Personal> instead of <Bankruptcy> because <Personal> rates more words in this message near Required than <Bankruptcy> does, and it rates more words that aren't present in this message near Forbidden. (Usage instructions followed this text.)

In addition to the textual answers, three questions are also answered visually. These are shown in Table 2. The bars indicate the weight of each word for predictions to a given folder; the closer to Required/Forbidden, the more/less likely messages containing this word will be classified to this folder.

Fig. 4 shows a thumbnail of the entire prototype. The top half is not readable at this size, but it is simply a traditional email program. The bottom middle panel provides visual answers, shown at a readable size in Table 2.

Using this prototype, we conducted a formative empirical study to unearth barriers faced by the end user in debugging in this fashion, as well as challenges faced by machine-learning systems that generate the programs that ultimately will be debugged

Table 2. Visual explanations for three Why questions [15]

Why does <word> matter to <folder>?	Why will this message be filed to <folder>?	Why won't this message be filed to <folder>?

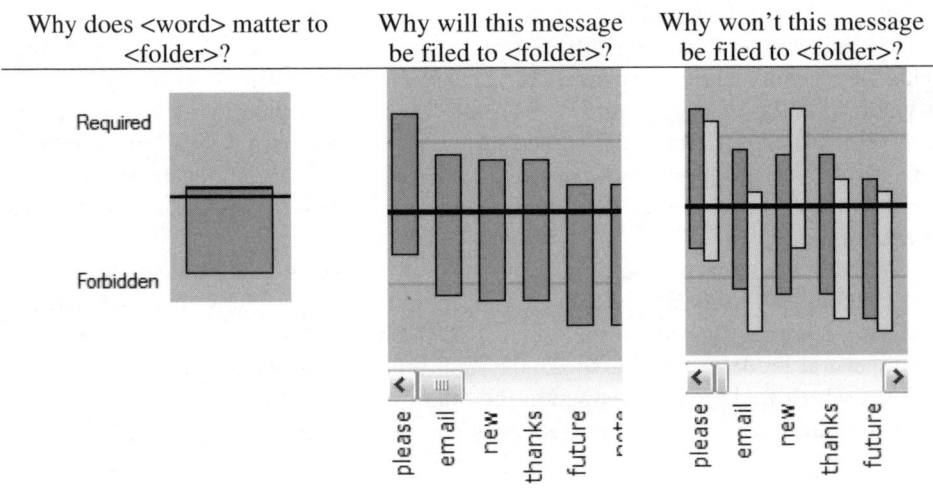

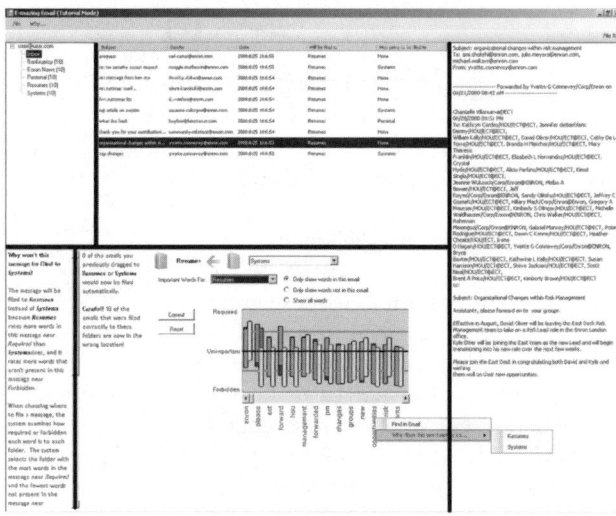

Fig. 4. A thumbnail view of the prototype [15]

by end users [15]. One of our primary results was that end users faced great difficulty in determining *where* would be the effective places to correct errors—much more so than in than in *how* to do so. The sheer number of these instances strongly suggests the value of providing end users with information about where to give feedback to the machine-learned program in order to debug effectively.

4   Gender in End-User Software Engineering

Another important result in the Kulesza et al. study was that gender differences were present in the *number* of barriers encountered, the *sequence* of barriers, and *usage* of debugging features. This is one of many studies conducted by EUSES Consortium collaborators in recent years that show gender differences in how male and female end-user programmers can best be supported in developing software effectively.

For example, evidence has emerged indicating gender differences in programming environment appeal, playful tinkering with end-user software engineering features, attitudes toward and usage of end-user software engineering features, and end-user debugging strategies [1, 2, 5, 12, 19, 24, 25, 29]. In essence, in these studies females have been shown to both use different features and to use features differently than males. Even more critically, the features most conducive to females' success are different from the features most conducive to males' success—and are the features least supported in end-user programming environments. This is the opposite of the situation for features conducive to males' success [29].

To begin to address this problem, we proposed two theory-based features that aimed to improve female performance without harming male performance [3]. We evolved these features over three years through the use of formative investigations, drawing from education theory, self-efficacy theory, information processing theory, metacognition, and curiosity theory.

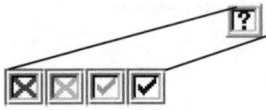

Fig. 5. Clicking on the checkbox turns it into four choices whose tool tips say "it's wrong," "seems wrong maybe," "seems right maybe," "it's right." [3]

The first feature was to add "maybe" nuances to the checkmarks and X-marks of the WYSIWYT approach (Fig. 5) [3]. The empirical work leading to this change suggested that the original "it's right" and "it's wrong" checkmark and X-mark might seem too assertive a decision to make for low self-efficacy users, and we therefore added "seems right maybe" and "seems wrong maybe" checkmark and X-mark options. The change was intended to communicate the idea that the user did not need to be confident about a testing decision in order to be "qualified" to make judgments.

The second change was a more extensive set of explanations, to explain not only concepts but also to help close Norman's "gulf of evaluation" by enabling users to better self-judge their problem-solving approaches. We proposed it in [3] and then evolved that proposal, ultimately providing the strategy explanations of Fig. 6. Note that these are explanations of testing and debugging strategy, not explanations of software features per se.

The strategy explanations are provided as both video snippets and hypertext (Fig. 6). In each video snippet, the female debugger works on a debugging problem and a male debugger, referring to the spreadsheet, helps by giving strategy ideas. Each snippet ends with a successful outcome. The video medium was used because theory and research suggest that an individual with low self-efficacy can increase self-efficacy by observing a

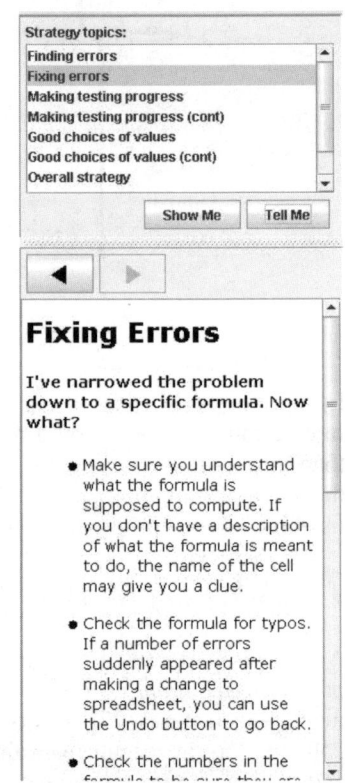

Fig. 6. (Top): 1-minute video snippets. (Bottom): Hypertext version [11].

person similar to oneself struggle and ultimately succeed at the task. The hypertext version had exactly the same strategy information, with the obvious exception of the animation of the spreadsheet being fixed and the talking heads. We decided on hypertext because it might seem less time-consuming and therefore more attractive to users from an attention investment perspective [4], and because some people prefer to learn from text rather than pictorial content. Recent improvements to the video explanations include shortening the explanations, revising the wording to sound more like a natural conversation, and adding an explicit lead-in question to immediately establish the purpose of each explanation.

We evaluated the approach in a controlled laboratory study, in which a Control group used the original WYSIWYT system as described in Section 2 and a Treatment group used the system with the two changes just described in this system [11]. The Treatment females did not fix more bugs than Control females, but we would not expect them to: Treatment females had both lower self-efficacy than Control females and more things to take their time than Control females did. However, taking the self-efficacy and time factors into account reveals that the new features helped to close the gender gap in numerous ways.

First we found that our feature changes reduced the debugging feature *usage* gap between males and females. When we compared the males and females in the Treatment group to their counterparts in the Control group, the feature changes were tied to greater interest among the Treatment group. Compared to females in the Control group, Treatment females made more use of debugging features such as checkmarks and X-marks, and had stronger ties between debugging feature usage and strategic testing behaviors.

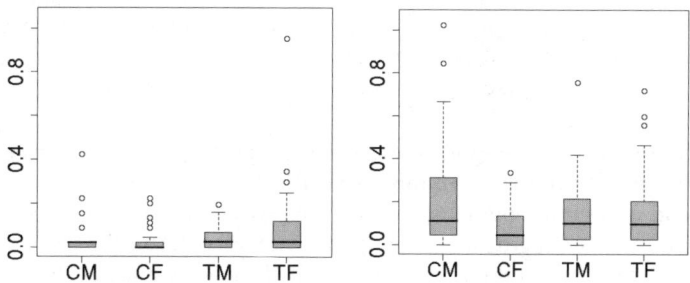

Fig. 7. Tinkering with X-marks (left) and √-marks (right), in marks per debugging minute. Note the gender gaps between the Control females' and males' medians. These gaps disappear in the Treatment group [11].

Second, we considered playful experimentation with the checkmarks and X-marks (trying them out and then removing them) as a sign of interest. Past studies reported that females were unwilling to approach these features, but that if they did choose to tinker, their effectiveness improved [1, 2]. Treatment females tinkered with the features significantly more than Control females, and this pattern held for both checkmarks and X-marks. Fig. 7 illustrates these differences.

Even more important than debugging feature usage per se was the fact that the feature usage was helpful. The total (playful plus lasting) number of checkmarks used per debugging minute, when accounting for pre-self-efficacy, predicted the maximum percent testedness per debugging minute achieved by females in both the Control group and in the Treatment group. Further, for all participants, maximum percent testedness, accounting for pre-self-efficacy, was a significant factor in the number of bugs fixed.

Finally, Treatment females' post-session verbalizations showed that their attitudes toward the software environment were more positive than Control females', and

Treatment females' confidence levels were roughly appropriate indicators of their actual ability levels, whereas Control females' confidence levels were not.

Taken together, the feature usage results show marked differences between Treatment females versus Control females, all of which were beneficial to the Treatment females. In contrast, there were very few significant differences between the male groups. Most important, none of the changes benefiting the females showed adverse effects on the males.

These results serve to reconfirm previous studies' reports of the existence of a gender gap related to the software environments themselves in the realm of end-user programming. However, the primary contribution is that they show, for the first time, that it is possible to design features in these environments that lower barriers to female effectiveness and help to close the gender gap.

5 Conclusion

End-user software engineering matters when software quality matters. End-user software engineering takes end-user programming beyond the "create" stage, expanding to consider other elements of the software lifecycle. It matters because sometimes end users' software creations have flaws, and it empowers the end users to do something about these flaws.

End-user software engineering's success rests on respecting end users' real goals and work habits. As the work in this paper illustrates, we do not advocate trying to transform end users into engineers, nor do we propose to mimic the traditional engineering approaches of segregated support for each element of the software life cycle, or even to ask the user to think in such terms. Instead, we advocate promoting systematic ways an end-user programmer can guard against and solve software quality problems through mechanisms meant especially for end-user programmers.

References

1. Beckwith, L., Burnett, M., Grigoreanu, V., Wiedenbeck, S.: Gender HCI: What About the Software? Computer, 83–87 (2006)
2. Beckwith, L., Inman, D., Rector, K., Burnett, M.: On to the Real World: Gender and Self-Efficacy in Excel. In: IEEE Symposium on Visual Languages and Human-Centric Computing, pp. 119–126. IEEE, Los Alamitos (2007)
3. Beckwith, L., Sorte, S., Burnett, M., Wiedenbeck, S., Chintakovid, T., Cook, C.: Designing Features for Both Genders in End-User Programming Environments. In: IEEE Symposium on Visual Languages and Human-Centric Computing, pp. 153–160. IEEE, Los Alamitos (2005)
4. Blackwell, A.: First Steps in Programming: A Rationale for Attention Investment Models. In: IEEE Symposium on Visual Languages and Human-Centric Computing, pp. 2–10. IEEE, Los Alamitos (2002)
5. Brewer, J., Bassoli, A.: Reflections of Gender, Reflections on Gender: Designing Ubiquitous Computing Technologies. In: Gender & Interaction: Real and Virtual Women in a Male World, Workshop at AVI, pp. 9–12 (2006)

6. Burnett, M., Chekka, S., Pandey, R.: FAR: An End-User Language to Support Cottage E-Services. In: Human-Centric Computing Languages and Environments, pp. 195–202. IEEE, Los Alamitos (2001)
7. Burnett, M., Cook, C., Rothermel, G.: End-User Software Engineering. Communications of the ACM 47(9), 53–58 (2004)
8. Carroll, J., Rosson, M.: Paradox of the Active User. In: Carroll, J. (ed.) Interfacing Thought: Cognitive Aspects of Human-Computer Interaction, pp. 80–111. MIT Press, Cambridge (1987)
9. EUSPRIG Spreadsheet Mistakes News Stories, http://www.eusprig.org/stories.htm
10. French, C.: TransAlta Says Clerical Snafu Costs It $24 Million. Globe and Mail (June 3, 2003)
11. Grigoreanu, V., Cao, J., Kulesza, T., Bogart, C., Rector, K., Burnett, M., Wiedenbeck, S.: Can Feature Design Reduce the Gender Gap in End-User Software Development Environments? In: IEEE Symposium on Visual Languages and Human-Centric Computing, pp. 149–156. IEEE, Los Alamitos (2008)
12. Kelleher, C., Pausch, R., Kiesler, S.: Storytelling Alice Motivates Middle School Girls to Learn Computer Programming. In: ACM Conference on Human Factors in Computing Systems, pp. 1455–1464. ACM, New York (2007)
13. Ko, A., Myers, B.: Designing the Whyline: A Debugging Interface for Asking Questions about Program Behavior. In: ACM Conference on Human Factors in Computing Systems, pp. 151–158. ACM, New York (2004)
14. Ko, A.J., Abraham, R., Beckwith, L., Blackwell, A., Burnett, M., Erwig, M., Lawrance, J., Lieberman, H., Myers, B., Rosson, M.B., Rothermel, G., Scaffidi, C., Shaw, M., Wiedenbeck, S.: The State of the Art in End-User Software Engineering (submitted, 2008)
15. Kulesza, T., Wong, W., Stumpf, S., Perona, S., White, R., Burnett, M., Oberst, I., Ko, A.: Fixing the Program My Computer Learned: Barriers for End Users, Challenges for the Machine. In: ACM Conference on Intelligent User Interfaces. ACM, New York (to appear, 2009)
16. Lieberman, H. (ed.): Your Wish Is My Command: Programming By Example. Morgan Kaufmann Publishers, San Francisco (2001)
17. Lieberman, H., Paterno, F., Wulf, V. (eds.): End-User Development. Springer, Heidelberg (2006)
18. Little, G., Lau, T., Cypher, A., Lin, J., Haber, E., Kandogan, E.: Koala: Capture, Share, Automate, Personalize Business Processes on the Web. In: ACM Conference on Human Factors in Computing Systems, pp. 943–946. ACM, New York (2007)
19. Lorigo, L., Pan, B., Hembrooke, H., Joachims, T., Granka, L., Gay, G.: The Influence of Task and Gender on Search and Evaluation Behavior Using Google. Information Processing and Management, 1123–1131 (2006)
20. Lowenstein, G.: The psychology of curiosity. J. Psychological Bulletin 116(1), 75–98 (1994)
21. Myers, B., Weitzman, D., Ko, A., Chau, D.H.: Answering Why and Why Not Questions in User Interfaces. In: ACM Conference on Human Factors in Computing Systems, pp. 397–406. ACM, New York (2006)
22. Pane, J., Myers, B., Miller, L.: Using HCI Techniques to Design a More Usable Programming System. In: Proc. IEEE Human-Centric Computing Languages and Environments, pp. 198–206. IEEE, Los Alamitos (2002)

23. Repenning, A., Ioannidou, A.: AgentCubes: Raising the Ceiling of End-User Development in Education through Incremental 3D. In: IEEE Symposium on Visual Languages and Human-Centric Computing, pp. 27–31. IEEE, Los Alamitos (2006)
24. Rode, J.A., Toye, E.F., Blackwell, A.F.: The Fuzzy Felt Ethnography - Understanding the Programming Patterns of Domestic Appliances. Personal and Ubiquitous Computing 8, 161–176 (2004)
25. Rosson, M., Sinha, H., Bhattacharya, M., Zhao, D.: Design Planning in End-User Web Development. In: IEEE Symposium on Visual Languages and Human-Centric Computing, pp. 189–196. IEEE, Los Alamitos (2007)
26. Rothermel, G., Burnett, M., Li, L., DuPuis, C., Sheretov, A.: A Methodology for Testing Spreadsheets. ACM Transactions on Software Engineering 10(1) (January 2001)
27. Ruthruff, J., Phalgune, A., Beckwith, L., Burnett, M., Cook, C.: Rewarding Good Behavior: End-User Debugging and Rewards. In: IEEE Symposium on Visual Languages and Human-Centric Computing, pp. 115–122. IEEE, Los Alamitos (2004)
28. Scaffidi, C., Shaw, M., Myers, B.: Estimating the Numbers of End Users and End User Programmers. In: IEEE Symp. Visual Lang. Human-Centric Computing, pp. 207–214. IEEE, Los Alamitos (2005)
29. Subrahmaniyan, N., Beckwith, L., Grigoreanu, V., Burnett, M., Wiedenbeck, S., Narayanan, V., Bucht, K., Drummond, R., Fern, X.: Testing vs. Code Inspection vs.. What Else? Male and Female End Users' Debugging Strategies. In: ACM Conference on Human Factors in Computing Systems, pp. 617–626. ACM, New York (2008)
30. Wikipedia, End-User Development,
    http://en.wikipedia.org/wiki/End_user_development
31. Wilson, A., Burnett, M., Beckwith, L., Granatir, O., Casburn, L., Cook, C., Durham, M., Rothermel, G.: Harnessing Curiosity to Increase Correctness in End-User Programming. In: ACM Conference on Human Factors in Computing Systems. ACM, New York (2003)

Part II
Refereed Papers

Mutual Development: A Case Study in Customer-Initiated Software Product Development

Renate Andersen and Anders I. Mørch

InterMedia, University of Oslo,
P.O. Box 1161 Blindern, N-0318 Oslo, Norway
renate.andersen@ementor.no, anders.morch@intermedia.uio.no

Abstract. The paper is a case study of customer-initiated software product development. We have observed and participated in system development activities in a commercial software house (company) over a period of two years. The company produces project-planning tools for the oil and gas industry, and relies on interaction with customers for further development of its products. Our main research question is how customers and professional developers engage in mutual development mediated by shared software tools (products and support systems). We have used interviews with developers and customers as our main source of data, and identified the activities (from use to development) where customers have contributed to development. We analyze our findings in terms of co-configuration, meta-design and modding in order to name and compare the various stages of development (adaptation, generalization, improvement request, specialization, and tailoring).

Keywords: customer-initiated product development, software development, case study, empirical analysis, theoretical perspectives, mutual development.

1 Introduction

The goal of the research reported here is to identify areas where end-user development (EUD) and professional software development interact. We have observed and participated in development activities in a commercial software house (referred to as company in the remainder of the paper) over a period of two years. We propose a model of the activities, which we refer to as mutual development. The model consists of the 5 sub-processes, which connects EUD and professional development.

1.1 The Case

The company is engaged in commercial software development in the area of project planning and management and provides consultancy services in using its tools. At present, the company employs 25-30 people, but they intend to grow and is concurrently expanding their staff and searching for new markets. The main market has been the Nordic oil and gas industry. To expand into new markets, particularly building and construction, the company has started to modify and improve its knowledge management practices regarding customer relations. As researchers, we were invited by

V. Pipek et al. (Eds.): IS-EUD 2009, LNCS 5435, pp. 31–49, 2009.

the company to give advice for how to improve knowledge management practices with customers.

The company is known for their customer initiated product development approach, i.e. close interaction with customers to develop tailor-made products [1][31]. Customers are encouraged to report problems, innovative use, and local development to the company. This has been stimulated through long-term relationships (maintenance contracts) and user forums. Each year the company hosts a large showcase where customers are invited, and developers provide communication and information sharing tools for customer interaction. This started with the telephone, then supplemented by mail, later extending to a Helpdesk interface, then a Customer Relationship Management (CRM) system, and most recently a Web 2.0 prototype created by the research team [29].

Despite their small size, the company is recognized as a major player in the business of project planning tools. They have several hundred customers and they have long-term commitments with many of them. One of their recent products is an add-on to Microsoft Project.

Our main research question and objective is how there is mutual development between customers, professional developers mediated by software products and ICT support systems in the company we studied. By *mutual development* we mean that both professional developers and end users contribute to development as active participants in both design and use. We identify the range of end-user development activities (from use to design) taking place in the interaction between the company's developers and some of their customers.

We have identified five sub-processes (adaptation, generalization, improvement requests, specialization, and tailoring) by pinpointing what developers and customers are doing and where their activities meet and overlap. We base our analysis on interviews with developers, consultants, and customers, and on data from a video-recorded workshop. The findings are compared with previous research in EUD and analyzed in terms of co-configuration [7][8], meta-design [10][12] and modding [15][16]. The goal is to identify the interdependencies of EUD and professional development and to construct a model for their mutual development.

The rest of the paper is organized as follows. It starts with an overview of EUD. Next, we present a survey of research in the intersection of EUD and software development. Then we present three theoretical perspectives on EUD. We analyze our findings by comparing with the three perspectives. At the end open issues for further research is suggested.

2   End-User Development

End-user development is an umbrella term for research and development in end-user tools for application development. This originated with research that dealt with technological and organizational issues of an emerging field, such as end-user programming in spreadsheets and tailorable systems [22]. Most recently, web application development has introduced a new line of R&D that shares many similarities with EUD (e.g., mashups, Yahoo pipes). However, EUD was perhaps first established as a research field with its own agenda in the European EUD-Net project (2002-3), which defines EUD as "a set of methods, activities, techniques, and tools that allow people who are non-professional software developers, at some point to create or modify a software artifact" [21]. The different approaches to EUD vary with respect to how they emphasize methods, activities, techniques, and tools, and whether they focus on creation or modification of software artifacts. Furthermore, what a software artifact means also varies among researchers. Software tools, source code, design diagrams, application units, and application development environments have been mentioned. As an example, end-user tailoring is about methods, activities, techniques, and tools for adaptation and further development of existing software applications based on direct activation of tailoring tools from the applications' user interface [25] [39].

EUD is multidisciplinary and its rationale (the *"why"* of EUD) has multiple dimensions: human-computer interaction (HCI), software engineering, and organizational use. From a *human-computer interaction* perspective, EUD is about leveraging the deployment of easy-to-use ICT and turning them into easy-to-further-develop systems [21][28][40]. From a *software engineering* perspective, EUD is supportive of the trend of producing *generic applications* [2][24]. By "generic" is meant multifunctional, domain independent, or application generators, i.e. "over designed" functionality that can be configured to different user needs [26], or domain independent tools like groupware and basic drawing functionality, or "under designed" environments that support users in creating new applications [12]. For example, a groupware system can provide different users with different access rights to shared objects [33]. From the perspective of *organizational use*, the rationale for EUD is associated with the user diversity found in organizations employing advanced ICT. Users have different cultural, educational, training, and employment backgrounds. They are novice and experienced computer users (e.g. super user), ranging from the young to the mature, and they have many different abilities and disabilities [3][23][26].

2.1 Integrated EUD

EUD interrelates with software development in multiple ways, but (to the best of our knowledge) there are few studies that have examined EUD in terms of boundary crossing of two types of organizations (developer and customers). We survey the related work below EUD. We also include work that is not commonly associated with EUD in the survey.

Stevens and Wulf [33] presented a case study of inter-organizational cooperation from the steel industry in Germany. They analyzed the relationship between two engineering offices and a steel mill to identify patterns of cooperation that can serve as requirements for new designs. They found that there was tight coupling across organizational boundaries, but also competition between the units. EUD was proposed in terms of a component-based framework for tailoring a groupware application at runtime. The focus was on flexible access control for sharing material stored in electronic repositories among the interacting units. The new access mechanisms could be decomposed and integrated and the users were able to realize new access mechanisms that did not already exist in the groupware. By decomposing application components into simpler ones and assembling the parts into new compounds (intermediate building blocks) and applications, users can modify existing applications and create new ones, without accessing the underlying program code [40].

Eriksson and Dittrich [9] identified the reasons why tailoring should be integrated with software development. In a case study of a Swedish telecom provider, they found it was possible to provide end-user developers with the means to tailor not only individual applications, but also the infrastructure in which applications are integrated. According to the authors, this is an area that might change faster than applications, especially in rapidly changing business contexts. To support this form of tailoring in the organization, they studied tailoring needs to coordinate better with software development activities. In another study, Dittrich and Vaucouleur [4] found that customization practices of an ERP system they studied at several sites were at odds with software engineering practices, resulting in a discrepancy in terms of integrated environments for end-user development.

In a case study in an accounting company in Norway, the activities of end user developers were followed and analyzed using Activity Theory [26]. The authors show how the organization successfully initiated a program to train super users [17] in conjunction with introducing a new software application, Visma Business (VB). The research was formulated to address how super users engage in EUD activities in order to achieve an efficient use of VB, and how EUD activities were organized. In terms of organization, there was a certain division of labor within the community: 1) between the regular users and the super users, 2) between the super users and the application coordinator (acting as local developer), and 3) between the application coordinator and the professional developers. It was also interesting to find a new role for a local developer. This person's responsibility was primarily to perform EUD activities at a general level, to work closely with some of the more experienced super users in the offices, and to communicate with the professional developers. This person generalized the results of useful EUD activities and made local solutions available throughout the company.

Explicit and implicit channels for communication between developers and users for the purpose of end user development have been proposed in a variety of contexts, especially in the area of CSCW. For example Mørch and Mehandjiev [27] demonstrated that design rationale integrated with a tailor-enabled application could support indirect communication between developers and users and thus help end user developers to further develop their applications. Along the same lines, Stevens and Wiedenhöfer [34] developed a wiki-based help system for communication and information sharing to be integrated with standalone applications. It provides online help to a community of users and thus enhances communication between developers and users with the affordances of Web 2.0. The authors claim this form of integration creates a more seamless transition between the use context and the resolution of a problem due to the familiarity users have with Wiki-based systems [34].

3   Concepts for Analysis

We analyze our findings in terms of three theoretical perspectives on end-user development in order to account for a broad array of relevant concerns, ranging from computer science to application domains to organization of work: meta-design, modding, and co-configuration.

3.1   SER Model and Meta-design

SER (Seeding, Evolutionary growth, Reseeding) is a process model for integrating end-user development with software engineering [11]. It is different from user-centered design in HCI (e.g., prototyping) and from software engineering (e.g., specification driven methods). It has more in common with aspects of participatory design in that the SER model describes a sociotechnical environment for tailorable applications to be used over an extended period of time. It postulates that systems that evolve over a sustained time span must continually alternate between periods of unplanned evolutions by end users (evolutionary growth), and periods of deliberate restructuring and enhancement (reseeding), involving users in collaboration with designers [11].

The SER model makes a distinction between design time and use time, which distinguishes developers' activity from users' activity. Integrating these two types of software development activities is the aim of *meta-design*: a framework to provide end users with tools that allow them to tailor and further develop professional tools in their own context [10][12]. Meta-designers use their creativity to develop sociotechnical environments in which other (less technical oriented) users can be creative in their own areas of expertise. Meta-design as viewed from a software engineering viewpoint defines flexible design spaces for end-user developers. Examples are tailoring languages, application frameworks and EUD tools integrated with applications. This means the users interested in being active contributors should be supported in exploring an application's potential for being incorporated in new activities, and evolving its functionally to support new needs [10]. To the extent this can be accomplished without end users having detailed knowledge of programming, meta-design becomes a powerful framework and perspective for EUD.

The SER model has influenced the mutual development model we present below. In particular, we elaborate on evolutionary growth and reseeding and the dynamic interaction between them in the company we studied.

3.2   Modding

Modding is when users modify products by themselves, without the direct intervention of professional developers. The term is a slang expression derived from the word modify that refers to the act of modifying a piece of software or hardware, originally conceived in the gaming industry. Modding is an alternative way of including customers in product development processes. Modding can be seen to combine EUD and participatory design, in that it combines the inclusion of customers in both early and later stages of product development, depending on the customer's needs. By adopting this activity, modding can be seen as extending the design environment approach to EUD [12][28][40] by making it possible for customers to promote an array of ideas and needs in the early stages of product development, even before a given framework exists.

The outcomes of modding, called mods, range from minor alterations to very extensive variations of the original product [15][16]. An example of modding from the gaming industry is when hardcore players create hacks and figure out how to develop software add-ons to twist games' parameters, such as the creation of a "No Jealousy" patch, which lets characters have more than one lover without either one getting jealous [20]. What is even more interesting is how the original product serves as a platform for further modding for customers.

Modding as an alternative approach to including customers in product development processes is a noteworthy concept since it engages the customer in different stages of the product development process. Modding is based on further development of an already existing platform. However, this must not be misunderstood. It does not mean the narrowing down of product development to simply be further development of already existing products, as is often the case with tailorable applications and evolutionary application development [24]. On the contrary, it appears that already existing products may be "opened up" by end-user contributions in terms of generating new ideas for functionality, new features, and even new products. In many ways, it is the concrete (executable) applications rather than the more abstract application frameworks and tailoring languages that best serve as a platform for end-user development [24].

3.3 Co-configuration

Engeström [7] [8] adopted the term co-configuration from Victor & Boynton [35] to enhance the theory of expansive learning in order to address a new form of work that involves user participation from customers and employees in the development of products. Co-configuration implies both a new form of work and a new way of learning. Engeström draws on the empirical findings of a broadband telecommunications firm in Finland, focusing on learning as joint creation of new knowledge and new practices by multiple stakeholders [7]. Engeström, following Victor and Boynton [35], defines co-configuration as an emerging historical type of work with the following general characteristics [7]:

- Adaptive and adaptable customer products or services, or more typically integrated product-service combinations
- A continuous relationship of mutual exchange between customers, producers, and the product-service combinations
- Continuous co-configuration and customization of the product-service-customer relationship over lengthy time periods
- Active customer involvement and input in the co-configuration work
- Multiple collaborating producers that need to operate together in networks within or between organizations
- Mutual learning from interactions between the parties involved in configuration actions.

From this description, we can understand the term co-configuration as a type of work that includes active participation from customers in developing their products. One of the characteristics of co-configuration work is the great degree of customer participation required in order for it to work. For example, when developing project planning software to fit a user organization and its work tasks, it is important to include users as participants in the process since they are the ones who know what kind of work tasks the project planning tools are supposed to support. However, not all companies will benefit by such a strategy. For example, to what degree is the company dependent on involvement from customers? What happens if some customers do not see the value of being part of such co-configuration work? To what degrees do the customers actually participate? To what degree is it reasonable to expect that customers will continue to participate over lengthy time periods? It is probably realistic to assume that in today's world of mass consumption the majority of end users will not want to design or contribute to further development of the products they use. We chose to focus on those customers who took an active part in the case we report.

4   Method

Our objective is to construct a model of mutual development between customers and professional developers as seen from a EUD perspective. The case study is designed to extend our own previous efforts by treating the interaction of two organizations (developer and customer) as the unit of analysis [26][31]. We identify the sub-processes of the product development process studied. EUD is one component in this picture, but not the only one. By presenting the whole picture we wish to provide a comprehensive view of mutual development, which we present as different stages of activity, using examples and theoretical analyses to justify our claims. We used a qualitative approach as part of a case study. In addition, we used video and audio recorders to gather data. Moreover, we used open-ended interviews, focus groups and participant observations.

4.1   Categorizing Data

This section will elaborate on how the intermediate terms used to describe mutual development emerged as a result of analysis done while screening and analyzing data. The form of analysis used is 'template analysis,' which is the process whereby "the researcher produces a list of codes (a template) representing themes identified in their textual data [19]." This is both a top-down and bottom up process. Below, we have named some terms, more precisely the different stages of mutual development, representing different themes identified in the empirical findings. After identifying these themes, the data was analyzed with this in mind, using these themes as a template. King distinguishes three features in template analysis: *defining codes*, *hierarchical coding* and *parallel coding* [19].

Defining codes is to label a section of text with a code in order to index it as relating to a theme or issue in the data that the researcher has identified as important to his or her interpretation [19]. We had the research questions in mind the first time we went through the data, but in the second round of selecting data we categorized it accordingly. The categorization of "outer loop" and "inner loop" were used as "high-level codes," and may be connected with what King defines as *hierarchical coding*.

Hierarchical coding "is codes that are arranged hierarchically with groups of similar codes clustered together to produce more general higher order codes" [19]. The high-level codes of "inner loop" and "outer loop" roughly clustered the data into two different terrains, one about customer-initiated development activity (outer) and the other about software engineering (inner). This was done deliberately to create an overview of the data. Knowing that our area of interest was mostly on the "outer loop" product development process, the data was analyzed again for topics within this domain. It was found that within the interviews there existed some sub-processes of outer loop product development. They were identified as *Adaptation, Generalization,*

Tailoring, Improvement Request and *Specialization*. Using these terms or codes as a template, the data was searched again in order to support these sub-processes with empirical evidence.

Parallel coding is when the same segment of data is classified within two (or more) different codes at the same level [19]. In one instance, the same set of data excerpts was classified within the intermediate code "outer loop" and the lower order code Specialization, which is a stage within the inner loop product development. Therefore, parallel coding was used in this context.

5 Data and Analysis

At the end of the coding we ended up with the following five sub-processes (stages) of customer-initiated product development:

- *Adaptation*: Adaptation is when a customer requests an improvement to an existing product and the company chooses to fulfill the request. It becomes an Adaptation just for this customer. Sometimes, the customer has to pay for this, sometimes not.
- *Generalization*: Generalization occurs when a new version of an existing product is released and is available to more than one customer.
- *Improvement Requests*: This is when customers request the company for extra functionality, report bugs and usability problems, and is viewed from the customers' perspectives.
- *Specialization*: Specialization is when the professional developers at the company create in-house builds. This is common in inner loop development processes where professional developers improve the products for their own internal work. This could potentially result in new features, but most often it entails refining the product, reorganizing program code, and removing bugs.
- *Tailoring* is about active end users who make adaptations on their own.

We justify these stages using the data extracts and analysis below. The two first extracts define basic issues (types of process) that resurface in the other extracts and in the analyses. The last three extracts represent four of the five stages.

5.1 Excerpt 1: Types of Improvement Request

In the first excerpt, the focus is on how a developer (informant) judges the Improvement Requests of the customer. This includes making a power decision as to what kinds of Improvement Requests to consider. The power to judge whether or not a customer Improvement Request should be accepted lies in the hands of the company's professional developers. This excerpt does not go into detail about how exactly these Improvement Requests enter the company, but it does elaborate in what way the customers ask for Improvement Requests.

Informant: *Often when they (the customers) want Improvement Requests they ask me if I can make a change (to the existing product), according to some needs they have. In addition they put it (the Improvement Request) into a list we have on the Internet. We receive a lot of Improvement Requests and some of them are actually such good ideas that we want to integrate them into our products. And there are other ideas that are really bad. There are also some ideas that are not so good (but they are doable), therefore we incorporate them if they pay for it. When doing this we make special libraries for that particular customer. Then this does not become a part of the system (the product).*

Improvement Requests turned out to be an important activity for communication with the company, requiring less technical expertise than Tailoring. Excerpt 1 is an example of how customers propose changes to the company's products without doing any local development. Excerpt 1 shows that an Improvement Request is one of the prerequisite sub-processes of Adaptation. It is when a professional developer creates a new feature for an already existing product in accordance with the customer's demands. At the end of this excerpt, the informant introduces the theme of how they get good, possible (doable) and bad ideas for further development. If an idea is labeled *good* it is accepted as is. When an idea is categorized as *possible* it means that the idea is plausible, but will not become a part of the general product. It might be accepted under contract (with payment), and turns into a local Adaptation. Finally, an idea labeled *bad* is rejected outright. Implicit in this example is the assumption that the company's employees are the ones who judge whether the Improvement Requests are *good*, *possible* or *bad* and have the freedom to make those distinctions.

As seen from a meta-design and SER perspective [11][12], Excerpt 1 may be interpreted as an example of boundary crossing, namely that submitting, receiving and handling of improvement request cross the boundary of two organizations (customer and developer). It also indicates some of the decisions that have to be made before the "evolutionary growth" of an application at a specific site can be accepted into the "reseeding" phase by company developers. In this way, Improvement Requests can help to bridge the gap between EUD and professional development.

The data in Excerpt 1 may have some commonalities with Engeström's notion of co-configuration. Item number two in the definition of co-configuration (see Integrated EUD) is about the *mutual exchange between customers, producers and the product-service combinations* [8]. Mutual exchange can be seen in this excerpt as well, between the customers issuing requests to the company and the professional developers handling these requests. The exchange for customers is getting the development they want, while the company receives money for performing the development (or more satisfied customers).

If a request is categorized as good or possible, the next stage of Adaptation takes place. During the second stage of Adaptation terms like patch, build and version become relevant, which we discuss below.

5.2   Excerpt 2: Types of Generalization

This is part of an interview one of the researchers had with one of the developers. The informant explains the software deployment (packaging) terms *patch*, *build* and *version* as part of an elaborated answer to a question about improvement requests:

Informant: *There are three levels: we have a so-called patch, which is a quick fix to some sort of a problem. This is being sent out to the customer, which*

> *is a (solution) right there and then. After the customer installs the patch, he tests if it works and then the problem is fixed. After a while, when we have made enough patches like this, we find new errors and the customers find errors and then we make a new complete program. That is what we call a build. On top of this, we have something we call versions; they could be (called) 3.4, 3.5, 3.5.1. They have more content and much more functionality.*

Patch, build and version are the developers' responses to customers forwarding Improvement Requests in the Adaptation stage, which again can lead to Specialization and Generalization. *Patch* is understood as a quick fix to a problem. Patches are packaged extensions that fit specific versions. For example, if Word is being used to write some text and one's references in EndNote are lost each time text is converted into PDF, the company could be contacted. They will fix it and send back a so-called *patch,* which is small program (a software component) that may be installed on the computer and linked with the main program, and the problem is fixed. *Builds* result if the company has had many quick fixes, similar to the example with Word, and 2nd order problems emerge (i.e., problems connected to the compatibility of patches). Then they create a *build,* which is a compiled program. Builds are associated with Specialization. Finally, a new *version* is both an extension and a generalization. It is an extension (improvement) of a build, and a generalization when a new *version* is made available to new customers and to the existing customers when they are due for an upgrade according to their contract. Generalization is a borderline activity between inner loop and outer loop product development.

In Excerpt 2 it is evident that to a large extent, software development at the company proceeds with the SER model, as Fischer describes [11]. Excerpt 2 has a lot in common with the example Fischer uses to explain the reseeding phase, where open source software systems take some time to evolve, aided by using local (user created) extensions and the integration of patches (*evolutionary growth*), but eventually require major reorganizing in order to incorporate the patches and extensions in a coherent fashion (*reseeding*) [11]. In the company it happened like this: First the product evolves locally as a result of *patches* created in response to customer requests, and when this becomes unwieldy the company's professional developers create a *build.* Lastly, when the modifications become too numerous or are judged to be useful (good) for other (potential) customers, the developers create a new *version* of the product. However, Fischer does not distinguish between build and version. He uses the term *reseeding* for all developer activity associated with reorganizing multiple adaptations (patched systems) into unified (seamless) versions. Due to the complexity of this activity, it is useful to distinguish the multiple sub processes (types) of reseeding and the interaction between evolutionary growth and reseeding.

5.3 Excerpt 3: Improvement Request and Adaptation

Excerpt 3 below illustrates how the Improvement Requests, as elaborated in the excerpt above, are differentiated. It also shows what is meant by Adaptation.

Question: So, the rationale for a given upgrade lies with a specific customer, which means that a customer can be a part of setting the standards for what other customers receive.

Answer: Mm, but if what one customer suggests is far off, then we just make a local adaptation for that specific customer.

Question: So, this becomes a new version for you then?

Answer: What we have in addition to every menu choice is a so-called user option, it is placed in an "own" library, which can be linked, and allows us to do further product development.

What triggered the statement above is that one of the interviewers asked how the company develops their products. In sentence number two, the informant answers that if the customer's request is "far off" they just make an Adaptation for this particular customer, as long as the customer pays for it. As mentioned above, this corresponds with an Improvement Request labeled *possible*. Excerpt 3 shows how an Improvement Request labeled *good* may become available to all customers. The informant acknowledges after some hesitation and with elaboration that the customers are to some extent "defining" what other customers receive of product upgrades. They do this by suggesting Improvement Requests and other customer-initiated activities such as Tailoring. However in most cases Improvement request that are responded to by an Adaptation, providing a custom-made product for this customer by using patches or user options with the current released version of the product. In the last sentence in Excerpt 3, the informant explains what is meant by (local) Adaptation. It is associated with a patched system installation that can be continually adapted (further developed) by user options that are deployed in a separate package (own library). When installed in the system, it appears as a separate menu with items for the various user options.

5.4   Excerpt 4: Generalization

The above excerpt introduced the term "user option," which is a special kind of patch. The related terms user option, patch and new version will be clarified in Excerpt 4 below. The excerpt illustrates the generalization process.

Question: Do you have other examples of customers initiating new functionality to the product?

Answer: Yes, we have done it for BuildingCompany and ABB... (two large European engineering and consultancy companies)

Question: What sort of new functionality did they want?

Answer: Yes, well, it is. I don't remember - it was years ago. I know that when they bought the product they had specific requirements that were originally not part of the product. But we wrote it into the contract as the functionality they wanted.

Question: Ok, so it was a part of the contract?

Answer: Yes, they wanted it within a specific time period. Their requirements were rather demanding regarding what they wanted us to make.

Question: Was it an add-on specifically made for BuildingCompany or..

Answer: No, it became a part of the product. Yes, it started as a patch, what we call a user option.

The informant underlines that a request for new functionality eventually became part of the company's general product portfolio and was made available to all their customers. It is an example of *Generalization*. It becomes clear that in this situation the request for new functionality that BuildingCompany asked for was something specific they needed. The company wrote their demands into the contract. This excerpt reiterates a point made above, that *good* Improvement Requests would be incorporated into the next version of one of their products.

The transition from Adaptation to Generalization is evident in Excerpt 4 since it describes an activity that involves one specific product (Planner) based on interaction with specific customers (Building Company in particular). The product has developed from small local extensions (patches and user options) to a basic core (in-house) version to a new (released) version where generally useful local adaptations are incorporated into the new release. We interpret the last sentence of the excerpt to mean a step-wise integration into the product (from specific to general) along three steps. It is associated with the combination of the utterance of *"No"* and *"Yes"* that signify a contradiction and disruptive (non incremental) transition (from Adaptation to Generalization). 1-2) Yes, it started as a special type of patch (user option), which is Adaptation, 3) no, it was only later incorporated into the product, which is Generalization. Adaptation represents the two first steps. First, the extra functionality BuildingCompany asked for is a *user option*, which means it is only available for this specific customer. Second, they want to make this available for later use, so they make a *patch* that the other customers can access upon demand, for example via the company's web pages. Third, when there is a *new version* of the product, the extra functionality (patches and user options) have been incorporated in the product and therefore made available to potentially all customers. In other words, we may say that there is a gradual development of the company's products over the years, many of which are based on local development initiatives and Improvement Requests to generalized versions and back to new initiatives for further development, as new user contexts appear.

Fischer and Ostwald's SER model [11] suggests mutual dependency of evolutionary growth and reseeding, and this is supported by the findings reported here, namely that use time activity (Improvement Requests) can trigger design-time (Generalization) activity. It is also related to SER in a more indirect way, in that Adaptation as a user-oriented design-time activity can lead to Generalization.

Jeppesen underlines how a defining characteristic of modding is how *"final mods often are freely revealed,"* meaning that no users are excluded from using the new modified version" [15]. In the same way as final mods are freely available, the Adaptations made to products based on some customers' ideas become available for all customers in the Generalization stage, when the suggestions from customers are accepted and integrated into a new version of the product, as shown in the excerpt above.

5.5 Excerpt 5: Tailoring

Excerpt 5 shows how customers locally adjust a software product by end-user programming to create their own extensions. Excerpt 5, from an interview with a customer in the building industry, shows a customer stating that he has adjusted the product himself by writing code in the domain-specific language SQL.

Question: *Have you requested any wishes or needs for local adaptations?*
Answer: *No, we have not got any special adaptations of the products (from the company). The reason for this is because I knew a great deal about SQL from earlier experience; therefore I managed to find a shortcut (of how to do it myself). I do not know the whole structure of the system, but it is available through ordinary documentation. There you get the whole (database) table structure and that has made it possible for me to find a shortcut through Access (a proprietary database management system) and allowed me to make some special (local) adaptations.*
Question: *So, in reality you have made your own adaptations to the products?*
Answer: *Yes, you may say that.*

This excerpt illustrates Tailoring, which is the sub-process that most closely resembles EUD as a standalone activity. Microsoft Office Access is used in conjunction with one of the company's project planning tools for data storage.

In the first sentence of this excerpt the customer states that the company has not adjusted the products for them. It is discovered that the reason for this is because the customer has made some adaptations to the product himself. He has *tailored* the product. This was possible for the customer because the products are well documented. In addition, because this customer was familiar with SQL, a high-level database query language, it was natural for him to fix the problem himself to suit his needs. This excerpt is an example of what we refer to as *Tailoring*. In Tailoring, the customer actually locally adapts the product without any company involvement. This might mean creating a small program to work around an inefficient solution as shown in this excerpt.

The reason the customer is able to tailor the product himself is because he is an expert project manager and is interested in learning how to work around a problem or inefficient solution when it appears. In other words, he is a super user. As an example, he describes how he can access and reorganize database tables as he sees fit and in a way that meets his organization's needs. The cost of this is his time and the skills required for programming, albeit simplified with a database query language like SQL compared to programming languages like Java. The advantage is that he will be able to see results of his ideas implemented relatively quickly as compared to the turn-around time when ideas for change are submitted to the company via improvement requests. The interviewer asks if this is a way of doing local adaptation, and he confirms that his SQL programming can be perceived as such. If Tailoring is followed with an Improvement request, tailoring might contribute to further development at the general levels, as was illustrated in the previous excerpt.

In previous work, tailoring has been viewed as evolutionary application development [24]. This view ignored the role of professional development and reseeding, and explored the design space of evolutionary growth for end-user developers. According to the mutual development perspective, this view must be updated. Based on the data reported here, tailoring is better conceived of as *evolutionary design*, in the sense that the local (customer) solution serves as a design for the general (company) solution, assuming it is accepted.

The findings reported in this section have been condensed and depicted in the mutual development model shown in Figure 1. Excerpt 1 can be seen as clarifying the informants' perception of the terms *good, possible* and *bad.* Excerpt 2 has a similar role for the terms *patch, build* and *version (user options* are further distinguished in Excerpts 3 and 4). Excerpt 3 also underlines the processes of *Improvement Request* and *Adaptation,* which are related in that one feeds into the other. Excerpt 4 exemplifies the stage of *Generalization.* It illustrates how a product becomes available to all customers. Finally, Excerpt 5 illustrates *Tailoring* by showing how a customer with some programming knowledge modified the product himself. It should be stressed that we have focused on the activities that involve end users (company customers) and multiple perspectives on developer-user interaction. We do not yet have sufficient data to illustrate the *Specialization* stage.

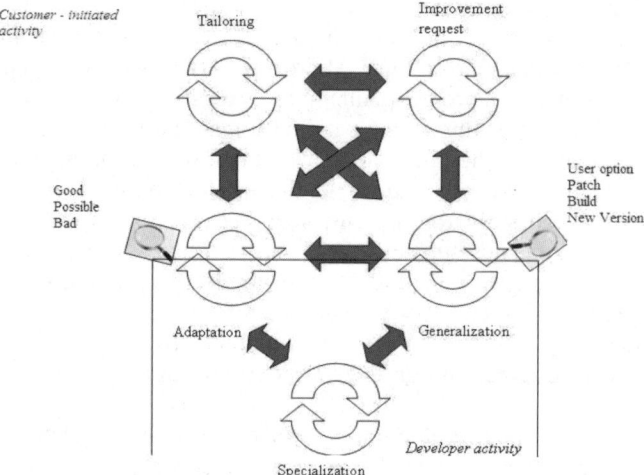

Fig. 1. Different stages of mutual development: developer activity and customer-initiated activity co-evolve; the arrows indicate dependencies. Specialization is not addressed in this paper because it does not interrelate directly with end-user activities.

6   Conclusions and Directions for Further Work

Our main research question and objective is how there is mutual development between customers, professional developers mediated by software products and ICT support systems in the company we studied. Our findings points to the components of the product development process studied. It was found that within the interviews there existed some sub-processes of mutual development (initially formulated during the preliminary analysis as customer-initiated product development) [1]. They were identified as *Adaptation, Generalization, Improvement Request, Specialization,* and *Tailoring.*

Mutual development is depicted in Figure 1. It is our first attempt to construct a model to integrate professional and end-user development [1]. Looking back, we see there are additional questions we would have liked to ask our informants, for example about the details of the customer-developer interactions. This was not possible in the current study. We cannot rule out that there may be sub-processes that have not been identified, some that may have to be modified, and yet others that need to be elaborated. This is part of future work.

In spite of this, it is clear that EUD and professional development are interdependent, and represent two different activity systems, one (customer-initiated activity) feeds into the other (developer activity) and they co-evolve. This relationship is maintained because the developer organization (company) relies on input from active customers for continuation of its products as part of maintenance and consultation contracts, and to get innovative ideas for new products that can attract new customers. This is to some extent a result of the company's small size and its operation in a niche market. On the other hand, customers rely on the company for project planning tools, training and constancy services, the ability to interact with the company's developers, and in general the pleasure they get from seeing their suggestions for modification being incorporated in a later version of the product.

The five excerpts we have shown to justify our claims illustrate how the products in the company have evolved from specialized and locally adapted instances to more general and stable ones in interaction with customers. It goes through an elaborated process of specialization (refinement), adaptation (domain orientation) and generalization (one to many instances), starting with a stable (but non optimal) product version that is gradually extended with locally developed extensions, user options, and patches. At some point this configuration becomes unwieldy and the system is rebuilt. The new build may lead into a new version of the product if it will benefit the company and its other customers. Interaction between the stages is not unidirectional because new versions may lead to new local development and improvement requests, which repeat the process.

We have used theories and concepts developed by other researchers in EUD and adjoining disciplines, in particular meta-design [10][12], co-configuration [7][8], and modding [15][16] to discuss our findings at a more theoretical level. These findings are summarized as follows.

Findings According to the Meta-design and SER Perspective

- Customers being active either as designers of aspects of solutions or as producers of new ideas
- Interaction between customers and professional developers is the driving force of evolutionary development
- Professional developers adapting the products in accordance with customers' needs as main method to further develop the products
- Project planning tools evolving as a result of being used in specific contexts

Findings According to the Co-configuration Perspective

- Both customers and professional developers gain from customer-initiated product development
- Customers forwarding Improvement Requests and the company handling these form a sort of network
- Customers are active in the product development process
- Customer-initiated product development is a continuous process lasting for a long time

- When customers and professional developers interact in intimate ways to develop products, they can be considered collaborators

Findings According to the Modding Perspective

- Changes made to the company's products by users vary in complexity
- There are changes made solely by users
- Some modifications become available to all customers.
- Customer-initiated product development motivates technical-minded users
- Customers suggesting or designing new features of a product in a way "open it up" for further development
- When customers develop new features, it can be seen as a decentralized development activity

6.1 Directions for Further Work

Our results can furthermore be extended along directions advocated by researchers in user-driven innovation, participatory design, and evolution of technology.

Users can be creative and contribute to development without designing, and end-user development is often triggered by innovative use of a tool as a first step to address a breakdown in use. Norman [30] suggests workarounds and hacks as two techniques people draw on in everyday situations when coping with difficult-to-use tools. Many companies are starting to realize that innovation can arise not only from the IT department, but also from the interaction with partners, suppliers, and customers. Eric von Hippel, a pioneer and long-time champion of studying users as innovators in product development coined the term user-driven innovation. He has introduced a method for identifying sources of innovation, following "lead users" [38]. Many of the innovations he has studied originated with lead users' novel use of an existing product or an adaptation of a product based on knowledge of a related product. For example the motocross series of bikes manufactured for teenagers during the 1960s and 1970s originated as result of teenagers' desire for their bikes to resemble adult motocross bikes.

Researchers in information systems have used terms like super users [17], gurus [14], and boundary spanners [36] for a similar role as lead user. They share the view that these users help to democratize the design process, and study them by drawing on insights derived from empirical data gathered from user organizations, like we have done in this paper.

In the area of software development, participatory design [6][18], directed observation [30], and strategic ethnography [32] are methods for addressing similar issues. Directed observation means to seek out and analyze the workarounds, hacks, and clever improvisations lead users and ordinary people create at work and at home [30]. Strategic ethnography is longitudinal studies following artifacts (packaged software) as they evolve over time, which has been referred to as capturing the biography of these artifacts [32].

Based on a study of user driven innovation in an open source community von Hippel [37] observed "the ability of user communities to develop and sustain exceedingly complex products without any manufacturer involvement is remarkable." He identifies the conditions that favor user innovation and explores how circumstances evolve, sometimes to include commercial manufacturers and sometimes not [37]. When commercial manufactures are included in the loop, the resulting inter-organization activity structure can be compared with "mutual development." When commercial manufactures are not included in the loop, the resulting organization can be compared with the emerging "user manufacturing" model. Aided by the Internet and Web 2.0 applications to support communication and information sharing and most recently "mashing" (combining existing web 2.0 applications to create new ones), this model has the potential to attract new interest in end-user development due to the enormous success of this platform to attract self-motivated contributors [13]. To leverage this potential for end-user tailoring and evolutionary design is an area for further research in EUD.

In their study, Douthwaite and colleagues [5] state the following "as technology and system complexity increase so does the need for interaction between the originating R&D team and the key stakeholders (those who will directly benefit and be penalized from the innovation)." This is a hypothesis that requires further testing. It implies when software products increase in complexity, the interaction between developers and customers must proportionally increase in order to successfully manage further development and sustain the product. Otherwise, users will seek out other products that are simpler to use. The reason for increasing customer interaction as complexity unfolds is that a successful technology represents a synthesis of the developers and key stakeholder knowledge sets, and creating this synthesis requires more iteration and negotiation as complexity increases [5]. This is a hypothesis that ought to be explored in software evolution as well, in particular when end-users are enabled by EUD environments and rich feedback channels to more experienced developers.

Acknowledgements

The authors thank Annett Hillestad who was the co-supervisor to the first author. The members of the KIKK project at InterMedia, University of Oslo: Shazia Mushtaq, Damir Nedic, Kathrine Nygård, and Espen Olsen contributed to the ideas presented here. Sten Ludvigsen and Anne Moen gave us constructive comments throughout the project. The project is part of the KP-Lab (Knowledge Practices Laboratory) and supported financially by the European Commission's contract FP6-2004-IST-4 027490.

References

1. Andersen, R.: Customer-initiated product development: A case study of adaptation and co-configuration, Master's thesis, Dept. of Informatics, University of Oslo, Norway (2008)
2. Bansler, J.P., Havn, E.: Information systems development with generic systems. In: Walter, W.R.J. (ed.) Proceedings from Second European Conference on Information Systems, pp. 30–31. Nijenrode University Press, Breukelen (1994)
3. Costabile, M.F., Foglia, D., Fresta, G., Mussio, P., Piccinno, A.: Software environments for end-user development and tailoring. PsychNology Journal 2(1), 99–122 (2004)
4. Dittrich, Y., Vaucouleur, S.: Practices around customization of standard systems. In: Proceedings of the 2008 international Workshop on Cooperative and Human Aspects of Software Engineering (CHASE 2008), pp. 37–40. ACM Press, New York (2008)

5. Douthwaite, B., Keatinge, J.D.H., Park, J.R.: Why promising technologies fail: The neglected role of user innovation during adoption. Research Policy 30(5), 819–836 (2001)
6. Ehn, P., Kyng, M.: Cardboard computers: Mocking-it-up or hands-on the future. In: Greenbaum, J., Kyng, M. (eds.) Design at Work: Cooperative Design of Computer Systems, pp. 169–195. Lawrence Erlbaum, Hillsdale (1991)
7. Engeström, Y.: New forms of learning in co-configuration work. The Journal of Workplace Learning 16, 11–21 (2004)
8. Engeström, Y.: Enriching the Theory of Expansive Learning: Lessons From Journeys Toward Coconfiguration. Mind, culture and activity 14(1-2), 23–29 (2007)
9. Eriksson, J., Dittrich, Y.: Combining tailoring and evolutionary software development for rapidly changing business systems. Journal of Organizational and End-User Computing 19(2), 47–64 (2007)
10. Fischer, G., Giaccardi, E., Ye, Y., Sutcliffe, A.G., Mehandjiev, N.: Meta-design: A manifesto for end-user development. Comm. ACM 47(9), 33–37 (2004)
11. Fischer, G., Ostwald, J.: Seeding, evolutionary growth, and reseeding: Enriching participatory design with informed participation. In: Proceedings of the Participatory Design Conference (PDC 2002), pp. 135–143. ACM Press, New York (2002)
12. Fischer, G., Scharff, E.: Meta-design: Design for designers. In: Proceedings 3rd International Conference on Designing Interactive Systems (DIS 2000), New York, pp. 396–405 (2000)
13. Floyd, I.R., Jones, M.C., Rathi, D., Twidale, M.B.: Web mash-ups and patchwork prototyping: User-driven technological innovation with Web 2.0 and open source software. In: Proceedings of the 40th annual Hawaii international Conference on System Sciences, pp. 86–96 (2007) .
14. Gantt, M., Nardi, B.: Gardeners and gurus: Patterns of cooperation among CAD. users. In: Proceedings of the Conference on Computer-Human Interaction (CHI 1992), pp. 107–117. ACM Press, New York (1992)
15. Jeppesen, L.B.: Profiting from innovative user communities: How firms organize the production of user modifications in the computer industry. Working Papers 2003-2004, Dept. of Industrial Economics and Strategy, Copenhagen Business School, Denmark (2004)
16. Jeppesen, L.B., Molin, M.J.: Consumers as co-developers: Learning and innovation outside the firm. Working Papers, 2003-01, Dept. of Industrial Economics and Strategy, Copenhagen Business School, Denmark (2003)
17. Kaasbøll, J., Øgrim, L.: Super-users: Hackers, management hostages or working class heroes? A Study of user influence on redesign in distributed organizations. In: Proceedings of the 17th Information Systems Research Seminar in Scandinavia (IRIS-17), pp. 784–798. Dept. of Information Processing Science, University of Oulu, Finland (1994)
18. Kanstrup, A.M., Christiansen, E.: Selecting and evoking innovators: Combining democracy and creativity. In: Proceedings of the 4th Nordic Conference on HCI (NordiCHI 2006), pp. 321–330. ACM Press, New York (2006)
19. King, N.: Template analysis. In: Symon, G., Cassell, C. (eds.) Qualitative methods and analysis in organizational research: A practical guide, pp. 118–134. Sage, London (1994)
20. Knight, W.: Supernatural powers become contagious in PC game (April 28, 2008), http://www.newscientist.com/article.ns?id=dn6857
21. Lieberman, H., Paterno, F., Wulf, V. (eds.): End-user development: Empowering people to flexibly employ advanced information and communication technology. Kluwer, Dordrecht (2006)
22. Mehandjiev, N., Bottaci, L. (eds.): End-user development: Special issue of the Journal of End User Computing 10(2) (1998)

23. Mehandjiev, N., Sutcliffe, A.G., Lee, D.: Organisational views of end-user development. In: Lieberman, H., Paterno, F., Wulf, V. (eds.) End user development: Empowering people to flexibly employ advanced information and communication technology. Kluwer Academic Publishers, Dordrecht (2005)

24. Mørch, A.: Evolving a generic application into a domain-oriented design environment. Scandinavian Journal of Information Systems 8(2), 63–90 (1996)

25. Mørch, A.: Three levels of end-user tailoring: Customization, integration, and extension. In: Kyng, M., Mathiassen, L. (eds.) Computers and Design in Context, pp. 51–76. MIT Press, Cambridge (1997)

26. Mørch, A.I., Hansen Åsand, H.R., Ludvigsen, S.R.: The Organization of End User Development in an Accounting Company. In: Clarke, S. (ed.) End User Computing Challenges and Technologies: Emerging Tools and Applications, pp. 102–123. Information Science Reference, Hershey (2007)

27. Mørch, A.I., Mehandjiev, N.D.: Tailoring as collaboration: The mediating role of multiple representations and application units. Computer Supported Cooperative Work 9(1), 75–100 (2000)

28. Mørch, A.I., Stevens, G., Won, M., Klann, M., Dittrich, Y., Wulf, V.: Component-based technologies for end-user development. Comm. ACM 47(9), 59–62 (2004)

29. Nedic, D., Olsen, E.A.: Customizing an open source web portal framework in a business context: Integrating participatory design with an agile approach. Master's thesis, Dept. of Informatics, University of Oslo, Norway (2007)

30. Norman, D.A.: Workarounds and hacks: The leading edge of innovation. Interactions 15(4), 47–48 (2008)

31. Nygård, K.A., Mørch, A.I.: The Role of Boundary Crossing for Knowledge Advancement in Product Development. In: Proceedings Int'l Conf. Computers in Education (ICCE 2007), pp. 183–186. IOS Press, Amsterdam (2007)

32. Pollock, N., Williams, R.: The biography of the enterprise-wide system or how SAP conquered the World. Routledge, London (2008)

33. Stevens, G., Wulf, V.: A new dimension in access control: Studying maintenance engineering across organizational boundaries. In: Proceedings of CSCW 1992, pp. 196–205. ACM Press, New York (2002)

34. Stevens, G., Wiedenhofer, T.: CHIC - A pluggable solution for community help in context. In: Proceedings of the 4th Nordic Conference on HCI (NordiCHI 2006), pp. 212–221. ACM Press, New York (2006)

35. Victor, B., Boynton, A.C.: Invented here: Maximizing your organization's internal growth and profitability. Harvard Business School Press, Boston (1998)

36. Volkoff, O., Strong, D.M., Elmes, M.B.: Between a Rock and a Hard Place: Boundary Spanners in an ERP Implementation. In: Proceedings of the 8th Americas Conference on Information Systems, pp. 958–962 (2002)

37. von Hippel, E.: Innovation by User Communities: Learning From Open-Source Software. MIT Sloan Management review 42(4), 82–86 (2001)

38. von Hippel, E.: Democratizing Innovation. MIT Press, Cambridge (2005)

39. Wulf, V., Golombek, B.: Direct activation: A concept to encourage tailoring activities. Behaviour & Information Tech. 20(4), 249–263 (2001)

40. Wulf, V., Pipek, V., Won, M.: Component-based tailorability: Enabling highly flexible software applications. Int. J. Hum.-Comput. Stud. 66(1), 1–22 (2008)

Appropriation Infrastructure: Supporting the Design of Usages

Gunnar Stevens, Volkmar Pipek, and Volker Wulf

University of Siegen and Fraunhofer FIT

Abstract. End User Development offers technical flexibility to encourage the appropriation of software applications within specific contexts of use. Appropriation needs to be understood as a phenomenon of many collaborative and creative activities. To support appropriation, we propose integrating communication channels into software applications. Such an appropriation infrastructure provides communication and collaboration support to stimulate knowledge sharing among users and between users and developers. It exploits the technological flexibility of software applications to enable these actors to change usages and configurations. Taking the case of the BSCWeasel groupware, we demonstrate how an appropriation infrastructure can be realized. Empirical results from the BSCWeasel project demonstrate the impact of such an infrastructure on the appropriation and design process. Based on these results, we argue that appropriation infrastructures should be tightly integrated in the application using the IT artifact itself as a boundary object as well as a bridge between design and use.

1 Introduction

We interpret the appropriation of information technology not as a phenomenon that somehow happens once a software application is in its 'application field', but as a network of activities that users continuously perform in order to make a software 'work' in a new work environment, shaping the artifact as a material as well as a meaningful object. Existing practices evolve and result in new practices. Technical flexibility to redesign the application according to specific local needs play a major role in enabling appropriation work. Appropriation work may lead to software usages that go beyond what has been envisioned by the designers of the software application [cf. 29]. It is a specific part of an IT artifact's usage, but it remains also linked (through the artifact's materiality) with its design process and the designer's work environments. Appropriation work needs to be understood as a core concept in the field of End User Development (EUD).

To deal appropriately with the combined efforts of users and designers to successfully establish a software tool usage that satisfies the needs of practice requires a fundamental shift in perspectives on the concepts of 'design' and 'use'. If the target of a design process is not a technology/software/tool, but a certain *usage* (that is stimulated by a certain new technology/software/tool), traditional notions of design processes and product structures become problematic. When does usage design start, when

V. Pipek et al. (Eds.): IS-EUD 2009, LNCS 5435, pp. 50–69, 2009.

does it stop? Is it a continuous or a discrete process? Who initiates 'design' phases – the developer side or the user side? For which parts of designing a usage are professional designers responsible, and for which parts the 'users' (they may be considered as professional usage designers just with a different expertise profile)? Which competencies and experiences are necessary to perform certain activities of appropriation work?

We see the cracks in the idea of a strict separation of design and use spheres everywhere in practice: In the necessity for software development in cycles, in the frequent software updating procedures, in continuous helpline support provided by software manufacturers, in the differentiation of user roles (scale between end users and power/lead users), in software development contract structures that include 'maintenance', in the practice of user forums in the Internet (that may have been provided by software manufacturers, but also third parties), and also in scientific conceptualizations e.g. with regard to 'tailoring' functions that support design-in-use ([15] and many others), with regard to integrating users into software design (e.g. [12]), with regard to professionalization structures in design and the problems they may cause (e.g. [38]) or with regard to the integration of user-driven innovation in (re-)design processes (e.g. [42]). In fact, the blurring notions of design and use spheres point towards collaboration necessities and opportunities which, we claim should become a central research area in the field of End User Development.

We will first connect our perspective to the scientific discourse in HCI and SE. Based on the perspective of usage design, we will describe a framework for an appropriation infrastructure that allows to bridge between design and use by supporting user-user- and user-designer-collaboration in usage design. We have implemented a first example of an appropriation infrastructure when designing the BSCWeasel groupware. To evaluate the utility of appropriation infrastructures, empirical results from the BSCWeasel project are presented.

2 Appropriation Work and Technical Flexibility

We now describe in more detail what we see as relevant aspects of appropriation work. We then discuss how the HCI and SE research communities tackle the issue of technical flexibility. Both disciplines understood the need for flexibility on different levels, a product-oriented perspective can be typically found in HCI discussions, and a process-oriented perspective is typical for SE. We will argue that a linkage between these approaches is essential.

2.1 Appropriation Work

Several case studies have investigated appropriation processes of IT artefacts in a long term perspective [17, 25, 27, 31, 40, 43]. They offer empirical insights into the appropriation activities and the resulting changes in work practices, and they also showed that a significant part of the work being done to make software applications work is collaborative. Based on these studies, in [29] we lined out opportunities for collaboration support: (1) articulation support (support for technology-related articulations - real and online), (2) historicity support (visualize appropriation as a process

of emerging technologies and usages, e.g. by documenting earlier configuration decisions, providing retrievable storage of configuration and usage descriptions), (3) decision support (in a collaborative appropriation activity, providing voting, polling, etc.),
(4) demonstration support (provide communication channels to demonstrate usages
from one user or a group to another user or a group), (5) observation support (support
the visualization of – accumulated, anonymized - information on the use of tools and
functions in an organizational context), (6) simulation/exploration support (show effects of possible usages in a exemplified or actual organizational setting, maybe allow
configuration manipulations in a sandbox), (7) explanation support (explain reasons
for application behavior, automated vs. communication with experts), (8) delegation
support (support delegation patterns within configuration activities), and (9) (re-) design support (feedback to designers on the appropriation processes). This list focuses
on user-user-collaboration, and most support ideas still remain challenges that have to
be met with appropriate technological support.

But *when* is appropriation work? Orlikowski and Hofman [28] focused on the types
of work that are not closely related to the new technology, but that rather result in organizational changes. In their conceptual model to classify organizational changes resulting from the appropriation of collaborative infrastructures, they distinguish three
cases: *anticipated*, *opportunity-based*, and *emergent* changes. Anticipated changes are
organizational transformations, which can be planned and implemented purposefully
when the technology is introduced into the organization. The corresponding appropriation work activities can be most likely anticipated, support may be easily provided.
Opportunity-based changes occur spontaneously, but can be planed once the opportunity is clear. It may be hard to estimate occurrence, duration and intensity of appropriation work activities here, but once the opportunity becomes clear, the necessary
support may also be obvious (see [31] for an example of a group of users that integrated a technological functionality into their practice in an innovative, unforeseen
manner). Emergent changes happen spontaneously, and when they happen, they also
can't be planned or anticipated, they show that there is a necessity to continuously
provide easy access to a broad variety of means for appropriation work (see [41] for an
example of creating spontaneous learning opportunities between end users).

There are several approaches that address spontaneous change activities, such as
help systems, exploration environments, user hotlines, or the general technical in-use
flexibility of tools [cf. 43]. However, these approaches are fragmented and do not
refer to each other conceptually and technically.

2.2 Product-Oriented Flexibility

The HCI community, and the EUD community in its mainstream, regards technical
flexibility mainly as a product feature which allows tailoring computer applications
within their contexts of use [15]. Tailoring takes place after the original design and
implementation phase of an application; it typically starts during or right after the
installation in its field of application. Tailoring is usually carried out by ordinary
users, local experts, system's support or helpdesk staff in a collaborative manner.
The users may find themselves confronted with technical flexibility on three
levels of complexity: (1) choosing between alternatives of anticipated behavior,
(2) constructing new behavior from existing pieces and (3) altering the artifact
(i.e. reprogramming).

Highly tailorable software artifacts have been developed, commercial products (e.g. spreadsheets and CAD systems) as well as research prototypes ([22], [23]). With the emergence of collaborative tool infrastructures that support communication, cooperation, and knowledge exchange, the need for tailorable software artifacts even increased [3, 46]. The distributed nature of these systems and the potential interrelation of individual tailoring activities posed new challenges to the design of tailorable applications [26]. OVAL [21], Prospero [7], and FreEvolve [37, 47] answered this challenge by providing highly tailorable groupware application frameworks grounded in different paradigms of software engineering.

However, offering technical flexibility is not enough, we also need methods to find the right kind of flexibility to address the requirements of particular contexts of use, considering that things may change over time. It is a short coming of the EUD discussion around tailorable systems that the approaches address the issue of flexibility on the product level only, and do not study how their products are related to the appropriation dynamics and process-oriented flexibility.

2.3 Process-Oriented Flexibility

With the idea of designing usages, the traditional design work extends into the use phase. Requirements for tailoring functions can hardly be foreseen completely; inevitably breakdown situations will appear which cannot be fixed using the given tailoring possibilities. Therefore, the development of tailorable software should remain connected to a flexible software development process. The development process needs to be organized to cover rather spontaneous requests for software revisions, as well.

The STEPS software development process model by Floyd [12] extends earlier models of iterative software development with a stronger focus on user-designer collaboration and the gathering of actual use experience (not only laboratory evaluations) in the process of refining software. However, it remained pretty abstract and rather unspecific with regard to the types of work that would be required in addition to 'programming' and 'using'. As a pre-WWW approach, it did also not address issues of collaboration support. An extension of STEPS towards remote participation was suggested in the CommSy project [8]. CommSy uses its own groupware functionality to allow dedicated end users to participate remotely in the design process. Wulf and Rohde [46] proposed, as a part of their OTD approach, to enhance the STEPS model by integrating tailoring as a use activity with design relevance. An implementation architecture for component-based tailorability has been developed within the FreEvolve project [37, 47]. However, the approach did not address the underlying software development process or any necessities to support appropriation processes. Some of these issues were addressed in the concept of a use discourse infrastructure [29].

Coming from a different angle, Fischer discussed end-user modifiability for general design environments [9]. In his early work, he chose approaches similar to other product-oriented concepts dealing with flexibility. Later he developed a design process model called SER (Seeding, Evolutionary Growth and Reseeding; [10]). Similar to STEPS, the concept does neither describe the collaborative work tasks necessary to perform the process, nor does it specifically address the issue of supporting these tasks. The different work on end-user modifiability and participatory oriented design are currently integrated on a conceptual level by the Meta-design framework [11].

Agile software processes, like SCRUM or eXtreme Programming (XP), provide extreme short release cycles and allow customers to change requirements at any time during the design process. In particular XP suggests several methods to make such changes economical and technological feasible. Major software engineering approaches to ensure this type of flexibility are test driven development, continuous integration and continuous refactoring [2].

eXtreme Programming suggests that there should not be any extra effort to fulfill requirements that may appear in the future. This is the counterpart to the concept of radical tailoring. Radical tailorability wants to solve the problem of non-anticipated requirements by building highly flexible products, XP wants to solve this problem by providing flexible processes.

Since XP does not care about the appropriation processes in the use context, the model does not make any suggestion about a shared infrastructure to foster mutual learning processes. Instead, the programmers just get indirect feedback mediated by the "costumer on site"-principle [2], although in practice it is difficult to find these customers [32].

A pragmatic application of agile methods is offered by the development process of the Eclipse platform, called the Eclipse way [13, 20]. The Eclipse way is a mediating position between the dogma of radical tailorability and eXtreme Programming. It follows the position of radical tailorability since all development is based on components to keep the software adaptable and extendable in order to deal with the heterogeneities and dynamics in the fields of application. However, the Eclipse way does not assume that product-oriented flexibility will fully solve the problem of future requirements. It has developed some techniques to foster feedback from users. However, Eclipse does not provide a technical infrastructure to bridge the gap between designers and users. Moreover, the Eclipse way has never been applied to domains in which users are non professional designers.

3 An Infrastructure for Appropriation Support

The state of the art does not provide technical support for appropriation work from a 'design for usages' perspective. To fill the gap, a technical infrastructure for user-user and user-designer collaboration is proposed here. The design of the infrastructure is based on two basic assumptions:

(1) Appropriation processes require knowledge sharing among users. Therefore, communication channels should support communities of users to reflect upon the usage of their software.

(2) Support for appropriation processes needs to bridge between product- and process-oriented flexibility. Therefore it is necessary to provide communication channels between users and developers.

Figure 1 illustrates our model of an appropriation infrastructure. We assume that different users, power users, or system administrators work with a software application that is assumed to be flexible in a product-oriented sense. In an EUD sense it could consist of software modules which are represented at the user interface, are meaningful to the users, and can be tailored by them. The communication channels

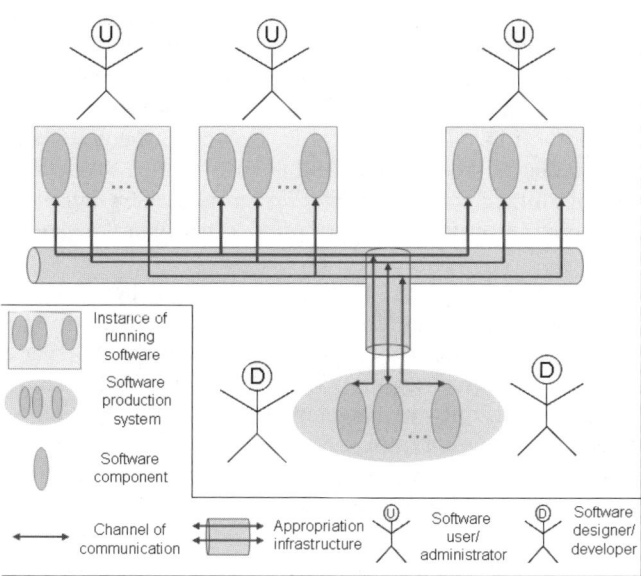

Fig. 1. Infrastructure for Appropriation Support

among users should hence be integrated into the user's interface and refer to the modularized structure of the functionality (see section 5).

Moreover, our approach is based on the assumption that a team of designers and engineers deal with the modularized code for maintenance and redesign purposes. Communication channels should allow users to express design requirements towards the software team referring to the modularized structure of the user's interface (see section 6). The content of the functionality-related communication among users should become visible for designers as well.

To act as a boundary object among users, the functions of the application and their tailoring options need to be understandable from different backgrounds of practice and levels of expertise. Developers should be equipped with support that enables them to perceive the usage of the application and to recognize break-down situations. Moreover, they need tools to efficiently provide additional flexibility, implement changes or refactor an application. We believe that access to a repository of components could contribute to more efficient work processes.

4 BSCWeasel

To explore the idea of an infrastructure for appropriation support, we have developed a groupware application, BSCWeasel, which contains communication channels for appropriation support.

BSCWeasel is a rich client based on the BSCW platform. BSCW (Basic Support for Cooperative Work) was one of the first web-based groupware applications. It was developed at the German National Center for Research in Information Technology (GMD) during the mid 90s [4]. It offers a 'shared workspace' which supports a group of users to up- and download documents. Additionally, awareness services, differentiated access rights, a group management tool, email distribution lists, a discussion forum, and a shared calendar complement the functionality of the groupware.

The fully web-based solution of BSCW has specific advantages. Obviously, there is not any installation effort on the client side. However, there are also considerable technical limitations due to the fact that BSCW just offers a thin client. There is not any redundant local storage for important files, a permanent internet connection is required, and streaming information (e.g. to provide peripheral awareness) is difficult to implement.

Therefore, we have developed a rich client extension, called BSCWeasel which is based on Eclipse. BSCWeasel started as an open source project in spring 2004 (cf.: http://www.bscweasel.de). So far we still follow the basic client server architecture of BSCW where the clients interact with a BSCW server. To implement rich clients, we used the component-based software development environment Eclipse Rich Client Platform (RCP) as the application framework [34, 35].

Eclipse is a development environment for component-based applications. Eclipse RCP is a core component of Eclipse, which allows running component-based applications on a variety of different operating systems. Moreover, the Eclipse Foundation promotes the growth of the Eclipse Ecosystem which allows benefiting from the results of a large community of developers. Eclipse provides a well supported and stable environment to build component-based applications. Another reason to choose Eclipse was the fact that the framework is open source. So the source code is available and enabled us to change the framework where necessary.

In a first version of BSCWeasel, we basically implemented the main features of the web-based BSCW client [cf.: 1]. Later on, we added components, called plugins in the Eclipse terminology, to realize new functionality. A set of new plugins offer tools for synchronous cooperation based on the XMPP/Jabber instant message protocol. We also developed a plugin which allows the fat client to deal with more than one BSCW server. Additionally, we extended the awareness functionality of BSCW and implemented a caching mechanism.

5 Collaboration among Users

To support collaborative appropriation activities among users, we suggest making help functions highly context sensitive and to augment help functions by functionalities of a community system. In our work, we draw on Wikis to augment help functions. Wikis are widely spread and allow editing texts in a collaborative manner.

We decided to represent the traditional help text of each function within a Wiki. Users can extend, change or annotate these texts. They can create different local descriptions of purpose, usage, or outcome of a function and exchange knowledge concerning the appropriation of this function within their local practices. Access to the Wiki needs to be highly contextualized at the user interface to select those Wiki entries which are associated with the current usage. In our approach, we took the state of the application as a proxy for the actual context of use. By means of the Meta Object Protocol and runtime reflection [18], we linked Wiki/help pages technically to specific states of the application.

From a user's perspective, a Wiki page refers to a function perceived by the users at the interface of the application, and therefore, supports appropriation discourses among communities of users (also addressing diversifying sub-communities). The user first selects the object in question and then presses F1 to open the corresponding help/wiki page. So, the software application offers a built-in communication channel among users and therefore acts as a boundary object for contextualizing the discussion among users (see section 3).

The Wiki discourse infrastructure was realized using standardized software interfaces, but the realization of context sensitivity is more challenging. We used context identifiers in the applications source code to anchor wiki widgets in a certain functionality area. However, this implementation strategy turned out to be hard to maintain since designers may either forget to write help texts for an identifier or place the context identifier at the wrong position in the source code.

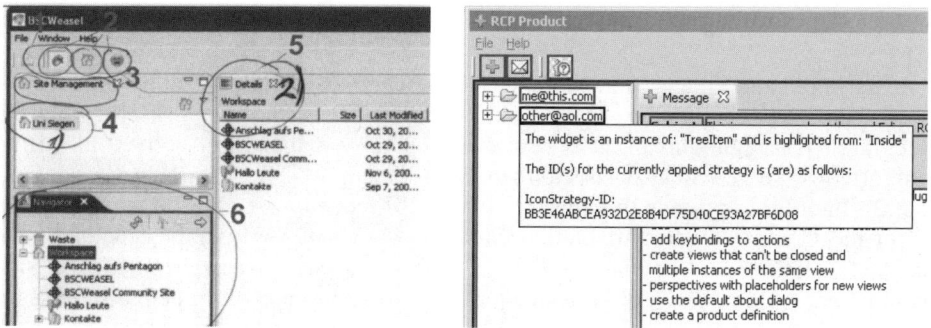

Fig. 2. Highlighting the point of interest: (left) from a user perception (right) from a computational perceptive (the tool tip refers to information that can be gathered by algorithmic reflection on current state of the application)

However, the situatedness of work activities ([37]) is a tough challenge for the underlying assumption that the execution position in the code is an appropriate measure for the current work context. Still manual maintenance of context identifiers would be quite error prone, as well. Therefore, we studied in which way users make sense of the "set of pixels generated and managed by a computational process that is the result of the computer interpretation of a program P." [5]. In our empirical studies of users' perception we present the users several screenshots of known and unknown programmes and ask them to highlight their point of interest (cf. Figure 2 left). In these studies, we observe that the way users give the pixel a meaning is related to the widget hierarchy of the interface. Based on this observation we created an algorithm which identifies function compounds as they are perceived by the users and maps them with stable context identifies. The calculation of the stable context identifier use the runtime reflection feature [18] to gather information that allows a computational identification of the point of interest (the tool tip in Figure 2 shows some of the information that was available for that widget via runtime reflection) [cf. 14].

The identified widget was highlighted as a potential point of interest at the interface (cf. Figure 2) and using the calculated context identifier as a shared reference point it offers access to the corresponding public Wiki page (cf. Figure 4) .

To implement the communication channels among users as described above, we have developed the CHIC-architecture (Community Help in Context) [36]. CHIC consists of three generic software modules: Application Integration Module (AIM), Context-Aware Adaptation Module (CAM), and Community-based Help System (CBHS) (see Figure 3).

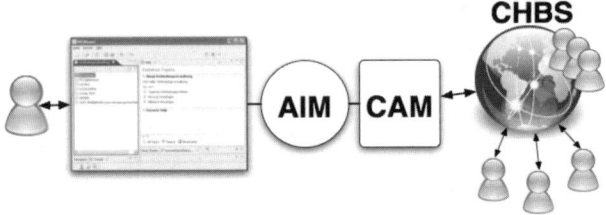

Fig. 3. Architecture of Community Help in Context (ChiC)

The Application Integration Module (AIM) integrates CHiC into an existing application and the user interacts with CHiC using it. When the user asks for help by pressing F1, it highlights the user perceived functions mapped to a context identifier and offers a "single-click" access to the CBHS-System [45] (for the interface see Figure 2). In order to provide this functionality, AIM requests the necessary information from the Context-Aware Adaptation Module (CAM). CAM mainly calculates the context identifier and mediates between AIM and CBHS. The CBHS can be any community system, like a Wiki, which provides an infrastructure for help discourses.

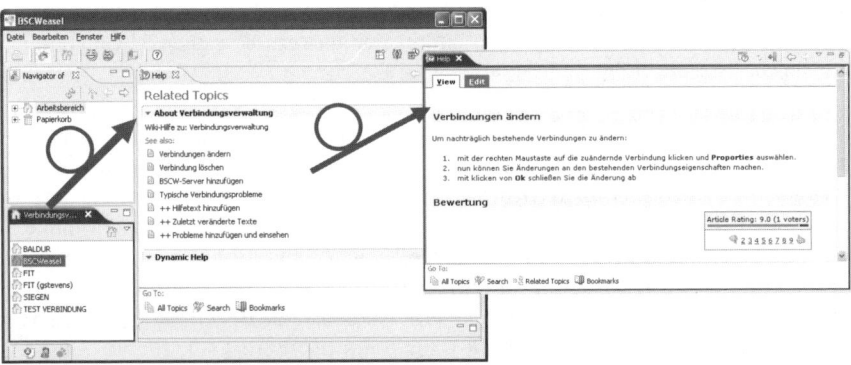

Fig. 4. Changing the selected interface element triggers a recalculation of the help entries (1). A click on one of the help entries opens the Wiki page via the internal web browser (2).

In the BSCWeasel case, we use the Eclipse framework to integrate the Wiki help into the application context. We benefit from the Eclipse architecture which allows adding new help items dynamically. A help item implements the interface IHelpResource which delivers the subject labels of help texts and the URLs of the corresponding Wiki pages. The subject labels of help items are displayed as links in the help window of Eclipse. When a user clicks on the label, Eclipse opens the internal web browser and loads the associated web page (cf. Figure 4). To realize CAM under Eclipse, we extended the IContextProvider. IContextProvider is invoked whenever the state of the application has changed. CAM uses this trigger to inspect the actual system state and requests CBHS to return a set of help entries.

The CBHS module was realized by integrating the Atlassian Confluence Wiki[1] because it provides a commenting function, several notification mechanisms like mail, RSS, and the recently changed pages. Moreover, it provides a well defined Web Service API.

6 Collaboration between Users and Developers

To offer collaboration support for users and designers, we have integrated a professional requirements tracking system into the BSCWeasel application and have equipped it with a specific interface for the users.

With regard to designers' needs, our goal was to minimize the overhead from the administration of direct user feedback together with other sources of requirements. To encourage contributions from a wide variety of different users, we wanted to provide a gentle slope of increasingly more complex levels of participation [22] in the requirements specification process. Legitimate peripheral participation in the requirements specification process is supported by allowing end users to just mark shortcomings in their current interface. However, lead users can use the system to discuss and test newly designed features in interaction with the professional designers who can use the system also for their work (e.g. design planning and scheduling).

To realize this part of the appropriation infrastructure, we came up with a hybrid approach which combines an external requirements tracking system with an Eclipse plugin which is integrated into the BSCWeasel user interface. The plugin provides specific views on the requirements tracking system. Technologically we drew on the Web Service API/remote method invocation interface of the requirements tracking system to integrate its user interface into the BSCWeasel application.

We decide to use a professional requirements tracking system, called JIRA. JIRA is a web based application supporting the interaction among developers. JIRA allows saving requirements in textual form, which can be annotated with attachments, e.g. log files or screenshots. Users of JIRA can discuss these requirements, prioritize and vote for them. A configurable workflow allows processing these requirements within the team of developers. The functionality of JIRA can be used via a web-based interface or it can be integrated into 3rd party products via the Web Service API.

The integration into BSCWeasel was realized implementing an Eclipse plugin called PaDU (Participatory Design in Use). PaDU packages JIRA's Web Service API and makes it available for Eclipse RCP applications. If a requirement is submitted to JIRA or information is retrieved from JIRA, PaDU will carry it out via the XML RPC. To lower the barriers for users, PaDU uses the integrated web browser of Eclipse. When the user wants to see detailed information about his contribution, PaDU will open the corresponding web page.

---

[1] http://www.atlassian.com/software/confluence/

PaDU allows contributing to the design process directly from the BSCWeasel user interface. PaDU integrates two buttons into the user interface of the BSCWeasel application (see Figure 5). The buttons help distinguishing between critical incidents (a subjective breakdown of tool usage) and use innovations (a new way of using existing functionality or a new idea for interesting functionality). These buttons are always visible and they are used as access points to document problems or suggest new design ideas.

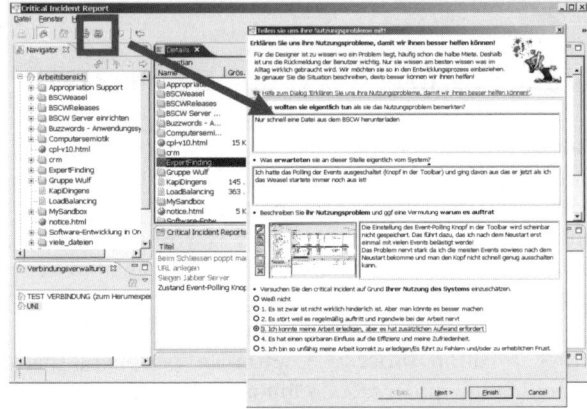

Fig. 5. PaDU's access point is in the button bar which activates the requirements tracking system

When a user presses one of these buttons, a multi-page dialog window appears. The dialog is adapted from the critical incident dialog [4] by Hartson et al [8]. Beyond purely textual descriptions of the requirements, we integrated features which allow for ostensive and deictic references to the software artefact in order to clarify design ideas. We have, for instance, extended the dialog window to enable users to add screenshots, annotate them textually or graphically, and attach own sketches. PaDU automatically takes a snapshot of the current state of the BSCWeasel interface at the moment it is activated. A drawing tool is available to edit the screenshots.

Designers can deal with the contributions of the users in the same way they do with any other requirements documented in the system. They can discuss these requirements, prioritize them and vote for them. To offer accountability with regard to their inputs, users can see all activities that happen in the requirements tracking system. Via their interface, users can track the state of their contributions. They are informed via email in case someone comments on their input. They can also set up links to other entries in order to be informed about the state of their procedure. Additionally, designers can send a direct email to a user to clarify open issues.

However, the discourse culture which emerged in the BSCWeasel project was slightly different. Instead of writing an email, questions to a contributor were attached as a comment. The contributor received an email containing this comment and had the option to answer to the email by adding a new comment. As a result, a public discourse around certain requirement emerged.

We understand design to be a communicative process which needs to be transparent to those who want to participate.[2] In order to satisfy this requirement users and designers should have similar rights with regard to inspecting the requirements database and adding comments. To support users in becoming familiar with the web interface and to increase their awareness of the design process, PaDU's start page contains all the contributions made by this particular user.

Additionally, we save a user's contributions locally. So, writing a design suggestion can happen before it is published within the requirement tracking system. Users can see all of their ideas in a list. A double click on published design ideas opens the web browser and shows the corresponding web page in the requirement tracking system. The web page shows the contribution in detail, the state of the contribution in the overall design process, and discussions and comments added in reaction to the contribution.

7 Bridging between Product-Oriented and Process-Oriented Flexibility

With regard to product-oriented flexibility, the current BSCWeasel implementation is grounded in the features which Eclipse RCP provides. A plugin is in a technical sense *the smallest application unit of the Eclipse Platform function that can be developed and delivered separately [16].* Such a component must be designed according to the Eclipse plugin mode which is an extension of the common OSGi standard. Roughly spoken a component is a bundle of java code, additional resources, and a description of the component's properties.

Product-oriented flexibility is basically limited to extensibility. The Eclipse Update Manager allows high-level components to be integrated at runtime into a composition to provide additional functionality. Plugins for an application are stored in specific web sites and have to follow the update site's specification. From this site they can be downloaded to the local plugin directory.

Compositions of plugins cannot be reassembled during runtime by end users since Eclipse RCP does not provide any specific user interface for that. Contrary to FreEvolve [37], Eclipse does not connect the component structure with the corresponding elements at the user interface.

Beyond extensibility, Eclipse RCP implements an interface-related aspect of product-oriented flexibility which is part of the Eclipse workbench concept. The user interface of an application is subdivided into different areas in which different interface elements (called views) can be placed. These areas can be recursively split when needed. Users can reposition these interface elements to compose a new integrated user interface and enhance the functionality by adding new views.

---

[2] This aspect distinguish our approach, e.g. from the concept of remote evaluation promoted by Hartson et al. (1996). In their work end users should only deliver information of shortcomings in the design. However, their participation in the design-related discussions of these shortcomings is not technically supported.

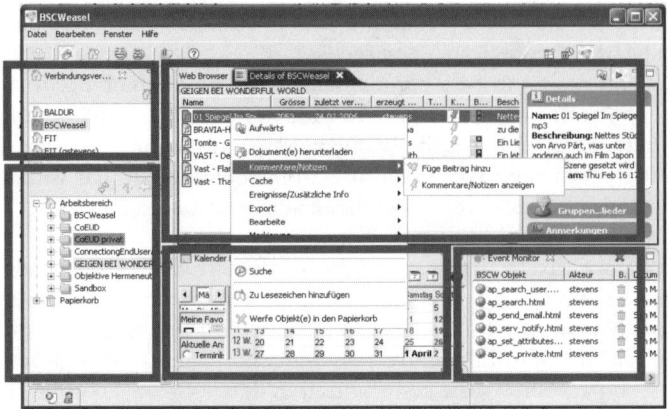

Fig. 6. Screen shot of an Eclipse workbench with a set of BSCWeasel related views (outlined with a rectangle)

Figure 6 provides a screenshot of the interface of the BSCWeasel, which illustrates the Eclipse workbench concept. Typically at the beginning the BSCWeasel user interface displays only some views and with the time the user interfaces become more complex, presenting more sophisticated features (like the Event Monitor in Figure 6, which presents awareness information).

We have set up an agile software development process to be able to react immediately to user requirements expressed within PaDU. To bridge between product- and process oriented flexibility, the developers can build new plugins or modify existing ones by means of short release cycles. We practice refactoring, as a method for architectural evolution. Eclipse as a software development environment offers tool suites to support these approaches to process-oriented flexibility, like refactoring feature, Release Engineering support, etc.

8   Case Study

Both prototypes which we described here were implemented based on the Eclipse plugin framework. Together with further applications that are being used at the periphery of other implementations (e.g. email clients), they form an infrastructure to support appropriation work in the late phase of usage design. Any application which operates on the same infrastructural background (Eclipse) would be able to use our concepts.

To evaluate our concepts, we implemented them into the BSCWeasel client. BSCWeasel was developed by a research group of a German university. The core group consisted of two developers which were complemented temporarily by different student teams. Contrary to most work in the area of product-oriented flexibility, we applied an agile development process which was directed towards short release cycles and an immediate evaluation in practice.

In May 2005 an initial version of BSCWeasel was used by the developers and their student team. Later versions were announced towards the research group at the university (about 15 members) and towards two groups at a research institute in applied computer science (about 15 researchers) 100 km away from the university. All researchers were basically familiar with BSCW, though the system was applied to rather different degrees. The appropriation process of BSCWeasel was analyzed via the discussion threads provided by PaDU and CHIC. Moreover, observations and informal interviews were carried out to explore the appropriation of BSCWeasel further on. Additionally, two studies were conducted based on the ISO 9241-10/12 standards to improve the usability of the application. The first study was carried out in April 2005 with nine users. It focused on the basic functionality of BSCWeasel. In January 2006, a second study with six users looked particularly into the usability of the CHiC and PaDU functionality.

With regard to the appropriation of BSCWeasel at the university and the research institute, we know about 10 regular users. They were intense users of BSCW before and identified specific BSCWeasel functions to be incorporated into their practice. The individual "killer" functions were not part of the BSCW thin client and covered a wide range of functionality. Some of them were requested via PaDU – like the option to download more than one file or complete folder structures, or a synchronized view on local and remote directory structures. Other functions were communicated directly towards the team of developers.

About half of the BSCWeasel users have made use of PaDU. From September 2005 to July 2007 130 design requirements were expressed via PaDU. Due to the relatively small number of active users the design team was rather reactive towards their suggestions. About 50% of these proposals got implemented.

In evaluating our experiences, we will focus on two main issues. First, we will investigate into the impact the appropriation infrastructure had on the design process. Secondly, we will look into the relations and interferences among the different functions of the appropriation infrastructure.

8.1 Grounding Design in Practice

After the roll-out of PaDU, the designers got more feedback from users. Since PaDU items were stored in the Bug Tracking System, the feedback was more systematic and easier to handle and became an integral part of the coordination work carried out by the designers.

PaDU is mainly used by users to make designers aware of a usability problem and/or feature request, however discussions among designers and users happened rarely. This may be due to the fact that PaDU does not disclose the users' identity. However, we found frequent instances in which contributions made in PaDU triggered a reflection process within the design team, e.g. discussing design alternatives related to a concrete user experience. Sometimes designers react to a user comment, when requirements expressed by the users were not clear (e.g. a designer wrote: "Well, technically this is a little thing [to implement the feature request]. However, for the moment is not yet clear to me how you would like to use it") or different solutions were possible, (e.g. asking which of different options to implement an "open file with …" feature would be needed).

Most of the contributions made by the users referred to cases in which they were able to accomplish their task, often by means of a workaround, but wanted a better support from BSCWeasel. The snapshot annotation tool was typically used to point to the referred area in the user interface. The suggested redesign would render more control or efficiency to their work. For example, with regard to the upload function a user made the following proposal: "It would be a nice thing to know the data volume ahead of an upload. In this case one would know how long it takes and whether there is sufficient space available".

Analyzing the contributions made via PaDU, we found little design requirements which went far beyond the given functionality. Most of the suggestions were rooted in practical experiences using BSCWeasel in the users' daily work. Accessing PaDU directly from their context of use seems to stimulate users to focus on present-at-hand technology when contributing. It seems to result in incremental rather than highly innovative suggestions for redesign.

However, these contributions, based on practical experience, had a considerable impact on the design process. One of the developers came up with the following bon mot: "If programming is understood as theory building [24], PaDU helps making it a 'grounded theory'".

Nevertheless, PaDU should be perceived as an additional instrument to improve distributed, continuous Participatory Design and not as a replacement for traditional, creativity oriented Participatory Design instruments like Future workshops.

8.2 Integrating Different Functions in an Appropriation Infrastructure

When integrating the different parts of the appropriation infrastructure and studying them simultaneously, we became aware of the phenomena of interference. The lacking integration of users' communication channels with those channels between users and designers created problems. The segregation of the different appropriation support functionalities – such as help, adaptation, or requirements articulation – seems to be dysfunctional.

We observe that CHiC was mainly used as a traditional help system with only little discussions among users going on. It seems that CHiC and PaDU cannibalized each other since both could be applied when BSCWeasel was not present-at-hand. This fact became obvious in the second usability study. An interviewee stated that he is occasionally uncertain whether to address other users or better the developers. He had a problem in connecting the BSCWeasel client with the BSCW server. Reflecting on his problem, he was not sure whether it was caused by bad design or inappropriate use. So he could not decide easily whether to discuss his problem in PaDU or CHiC. In another case a user explained that she put a question into PaDU but later cancelled it. She was not sure whether this issue was just her personal problem, ("just not knowing enough about the system"), or if the issue was more generally relevant for the design of BSCWeasel. These findings seem to indicate a need for a deeper integration of PaDU and CHiC.

Another example for lacking integration is the gap between flexibilization at the level of the user interface compared to the level of the component structure of the application and its missing integration into a communication infrastructure. Eclipse's "viewer" concept offers an elegant solution for the composition of interface elements compared to user interfaces of web-based clients augmented by applets. All interface elements can be integrated into a combined view, called perspective. We observed that this feature was applied by the users to individualize their user interface. However, Eclipse still suffers from the fact that this interface layer of a user centric composition is not connected to the underlying component structure. So, the underlying structure is not visible and cannot directly explore from the user interface taking the actual use context into account. Obviously, lacking references between software structure and user interface leads to confusion and does not support users in understanding the linkage between the user interface and the software architecture [6].

As a result, users may develop a mental model which diverges strongly from the software architecture. It leads specifically to problem in cases where applications, such as Eclipse IDE or BSCWeasel, are composed by hundreds of components provided by different vendors. During our usability study we found an example for these phenomena.. It turned out that users assumed that our chat tool (a 3rd party component) and the BSCW system where tightly coupled because the interface elements were integrated. In another case we observed an Eclipse IDE user who had problems in finding out which vendor was responsible for a specific view which he had added to his user interface. He was looking for more information about the object in question.

Moreover, Eclipse suffers from lacking integration of the component management features into a community-oriented communication infrastructure. The Eclipse community starts to become aware of this problem. In particular, some commercial companies like Innoopract have started to extend Eclipse with a component repository service with thousand of plug-ins. They support end users to assemble their personal Eclipse configuration out of the repository in an easy way. Furthermore one can observe that traditional centralized provisioning strategies will be enhanced by concepts that support a grassroots diffusion of composition and tailored artifacts.

9 Conclusion

Support for appropriation work has to be understood as a core challenge in the field of End User Development. From the perspective of appropriation work, the concept of design needs to be re-interpreted. It should be understood as designing usages, not tools. In such a perspective, activities of end users such as configuring, tailoring, sense making, or negotiating conventions of usage have to be linked to the work performed by software developers. Appropriation and realization are dialectic moments in usage design, while in the late phase it is mainly driven by actors and stakeholders from the use sphere, not from the design sphere. These activities can be considered as inherently collaborative and should be explicitly supported by appropriate infrastructures build into the applications. Extending earlier research, we aimed for an infrastructure that does not only support user-user-collaboration, but also integrates the professional designers' work sphere. When supporting appropriation work, it seems to be necessary to go beyond traditional EUD techniques such as configurating or tailoring and connect professional designers with end users.

As a first case of an appropriation infrastructure, we developed collaborative functionalities based on the Eclipse plugin architecture. We integrated this infrastructure into BSCWeasel, a rich client for the web-based groupware system BSCW. The first functionality we provided – supporting user-user collaboration - was a context-aware extensible help system based on a wiki metaphor. Help texts could be complemented or specialized for certain situations of usage. The second functionality we provided – supporting user-designer collaboration – was a requirements tracking system that allowed for rich technology-related articulations and collaborative requirements management and was integrated into the application, as well. Together with additional tools which were integrated, they form an infrastructure for appropriation work.

We collected first evaluation data by means of an empirical case study covering the infrastructure's appropriation in three research groups. Some of the assumptions guiding our design have been confirmed by the study. First of all, there is an interest, if not even a need, for collaboration in the appropriation of technology. It makes sense to understand the application to be appropriated not only as a boundary object between design and use, but also as a communication anchor and medium for appropriation activities. Figure 1 illustrates the fact that both the appropriation infrastructure and the component-repositories mediate between the developers and user communities if such a modularized design is meaningful for the different actors.

From a user perspective, the following activities seem to be expressions of appropriation work which are grounded in the reflective use of an application:

- consulting help systems,
- making requirement inquiry and (re-)design contributions,
- tailoring and updating an application.

Therefore, appropriation activities should be conceptualized from a holistic perspective. Appropriation infrastructure should integrate the different support features to a wider extend than BSCWeasel has done so far. The infrastructure needs to be tightly integrated into the software artifact for an optimal support of usage design:

- the communication channels should be activated directly from the access point of the functions they refer to [cf.: 44],
- the communication channels should be structured according to the way the users perceive the functionality,
- the communication channels should offer opportunities to create deictic references towards specific aspects of the functionality.

In order to better support appropriation work, the linkage between product- and process-oriented aspects of flexibility implies further fundamental design challenges. Users and designers need to build common ground with regard to the component structure of an application. Users build their mental models of technology based on the *perceived* functionality. Designers work is typically grounded in a long professional tradition of software modularization which has led to a separation of application logic and user interface. However, when supporting appropriation work, this tradition needs to be challenged since it is the source of misunderstandings between designers and users.

Our research needs to be extended to a theoretical level (e.g. connecting it to the discourse around 'infrastructuring', [33]) as well as on a technological level (e.g. fine grained component based tailorability beyond plug-in integration, additional support functions, different infrastructural background technologies, e.g. service-oriented architectures). Ultimately we hope to be able to establish a methodological perspective on end user development understood as software (usage!) design which is not dominated by the traditions of programmers but respects the work of all stakeholders involved.

We conclude this paper with a refinement of the definition of EUD, picking up the consideration that EUD should support a continuous co-evolution of both, the system and the user [5, 10]. In times where software development methodology conceptions like 'perpetual beta' [48] becomes general accepted designers, co-workers and other stakeholders of the software artifacts are essential participants in the continuous co-evolution. This also means that personal and shared design activities as highly interwoven. A definition of EUD should be reflected this issue, thus we suggest a refinement as follows: *EUD denotes a set of methods, tools and techniques to support end users to enforce their interests in the continuous co-evolutionary process by modifying individual artifacts or participating in the modification of shared artifacts.*

Acknowledgements

We would like to thank IBM for supporting our research by means of an Eclipse Innovation Award. We are also grateful to the German Science Foundation and the German Ministry of Research and Education (BMBF) for funding in the field of End User Development (EUD).

References

1. Appelt, W.: What Groupware Functionality do Users Really Use? In: Proceedings of the 9th Euromicro Workshop on PDP 2001. IEEE Computer Society, Los Alamitos (2001)
2. Beck, K.: Extreme Programming Explained: Embrace Change. Addison-Wesley, Pearson Education (2000)
3. Bentley, R., Dourish, P.: Medium versus mechanism: Supporting collaboration through customisation. In: Proceedings of ECSCW 1995. Kluwer Academic Publishers, Stockholm (1995)
4. Bentley, R., et al.: Supporting Collaborative Information Sharing with the World Wide Web: The BSCW Shared Workspace System. In: The World Wide Web Journal: Proceedings of the 4th International WWW Conference, vol. 1, pp. 63–74 (1995)
5. Costabile, M.F., Fogli, D., Mussio, P., Piccinno, A.: Visual Interactive Systems for End-User Development: a Model-based Design Methodology. IEEE Trans. on SMC - Part A: Systems and Humans 37(6), 1029–1046 (2007)
6. de Souza, C.S., Barbosa, S.D.J., Silva, S.R.P.: Semiotic engineering principles for evaluating end-user programming environments. Interacting with Computers 13 (2001)
7. Dourish, P.: Developing a Reflective Model of Collaborative Systems. ACM Transactions on Computer-Human Interaction 2(1), 40–63 (1995)
8. Finck, M., Gumm, D., Pape, B.: Using Groupware for Mediated Feedback. In: Proceedings of the Participation Design Conference 2004 (2004)
9. Fischer, G., Girgensohn, A.: End-user modifiability in design environments. In: Proceedings of the SIGCHI conference on Human factors in computing systems. ACM Press, Washington (1990)
10. Fischer, G., Ostwald, J.: Seeding, Evolutionary Growth, and Reseeding: Enriching Participatory Design with Informed Participation. In: Proceedings of the Participatory Design Conference (PDC 2002). 2002. CPSR, Malmö (2002)

11. Fischer, G., Giaccardi, E.: Meta-Design: A Framework for the Future of End User Development. In: Lieberman, H., Paternò, F., Wulf, V. (eds.) End User Development, pp. 427–458. Springer, Heidelberg (2006)
12. Floyd, C., Reisin, F.-M., Schmidt, G.: STEPS to Software Development with Users Source. In: Proceedings of the 2nd European Software Engineering Conference. LNCS. Springer, London (1989)
13. Gamma, E., Wiegand, J.: The eclipse way processes that adapt (2005)
14. Grüttner, M.: Entwicklung eines generischen Visualisierungs- und Interaktionskonzepts für kontextsensitive Hilfesysteme und prototypische Implementierung für das Eclipse RCP-Framework. In: Wirtschaftsinformatik. University of Siegen: Siegen (2007)
15. Henderson, A., Kyng, M.: There's No Place Like Home: Continuing Design in Use. In: Greenbaum, J.K. (ed.) Design at Work - Cooperative Design of Computer Artifacts, Hillsdale, pp. 219–240 (1991)
16. IBM, Draft: Eclipse Platform Technical Overview, IBM Corporation and The Eclipse Foundation (2005)
17. Karsten, H., Jones, M.: The long and winding road: Collaorative IT and organisational change. In: Int. Conference on Computer Supported Work (CSCW 1998). ACM Press, New York (1998)
18. Kiczales, G., des Rivières, J., Bobrow, D.: The Art of the Meta-Object Protocol. MIT Press, Cambridge (1991)
19. Lieberman, H., Paternó, F., Wulf, V. (eds.): End User Development. Springer, Berlin (2006)
20. Lippert, M.: Eclipse Core - Unter der Haube, Teil 2: Ein Blick auf den Entwicklungsprozess des Eclipse-Plattform-Projekts. Eclipse Magazin (2006)
21. Malone, T.W., Lai, K.-Y., Fry, C.: Experiments with Oval: a radically tailorable tool for cooperative work. ACM TOIS 13(2), 177–205 (1995)
22. McLean, A., et al.: User tailorable systems: Pressing the issues with buttons. In: Proceedings of CHI 1990, Seattle, Washington (1990)
23. Mørch, A.: Three Levels of End-user Tailoring: Customization, Integration and Extension. In: Kyng, M., Henderson, H. (eds.) Computers and Design in context, pp. 51–76. MIT Press, Cambridge (1997)
24. Naur, P.: Programming as Theory Building. Microprocessing and Microprogramming 15, 253–261 (1985)
25. Ngwenyama, O.K.: Groupware, social action and organizational emergence: on the process dynamics of computer mediated distributed work. Accounting, Management and Information Technologies 8(4), 123–143 (1998)
26. Oberquelle, H.: Situationsbedingte und benutzerorientierte Anpassbarkeit von Groupware. In: Hartmann, A., et al. (eds.) Menschengerechte Groupware - Software-ergonomische Gestaltung und partizipative Umsetzung, pp. 31–50. Stuttgart, Teubner (1994)
27. Orlikowski, W.J.: Evolving with Notes: Organizational change around groupware technology. In: Ciborra, C. (ed.) Groupware & Teamwork, pp. 23–60. J. Wiley, Chichester (1996)
28. Orlikowski, W.J., Hofman, J.D.: An Improvisational Model for Change Management: The Case of Groupware Technologies. Sloan Management Review, pp. 11–21 (Winter 1997)
29. Pipek, V.: From Tailoring to Appropriation Support: Negotiating Groupware Usage. In: Faculty of Science, Department of Information Processing Science 2005. University of Oulu, Oulu (2005)
30. Pipek, V., Kahler, H.: Supporting Collaborative Tailoring. In: Lieberman, H., Paterno, F., Wulf, V. (eds.) End-User Development. Springer, Berlin (2006)

31. Pipek, V.W.: A Groupware's Life. In: Proceedings of the Sixth European Conference on Computer Supported Cooperative Work (ECSCW 1999). Kluwer, Dordrecht (1999)
32. Rumpe, B., Schröder, A.: Quantitative Untersuchung des Extreme Programming Prozesses (2001)
33. Star, S.L., Bowker, G.C.: How to infrastructure. In: Lievrouw, L.A., Livingstone, S. (eds.) Handbook of New Media - Social Shaping and Consequences of ICTs, pp. 151–162. SAGE Pub., London (2002)
34. Stevens, G.: BSCWeasel – How to make an existing Groupware System more flexible. In: Demo presentation on the 9th European Conference on Computer-Supported Cooperative Work (2005)
35. Stevens, G., Budweg, S., Pipek, V.: The BSCWeasel and Eclipse-powered Cooperative End User Development. In: Proc. Workshop Eclipse as a Vehicle for CSCW Research at the Int. Conf. on CSCW 2004, Chicago, IL, USA (2004)
36. Stevens, G., Wiedenhöfer, T.: CHIC - A pluggable solution for community help in context. In: Proc of the 4th NordiCHi (2006)
37. Stiemerling, O.: Component-Based Tailorability. In: Institut für Informatik III, Rheinische Friedrich-Wilhelms-Universität, Bonn (2000)
38. Suchman, L.: Located accountabilities in technology production. Scandinavian Journal of Information Systems 14(2), 91–105 (2002)
39. Suchman, L.A.: Plans and situated actions: the problem of human-machine communication. Cambridge University Press, Cambridge (1990)
40. Törpel, B., Pipek, V., Rittenbruch, M.: Creating Heterogeneity - Evolving Use of Groupware in a Network of Freelancers. Special Issue on Evolving Use of Groupware, Computer Supported Cooperative Work: The Journal of Collaborative Computing (JCSCW) 12(1-2) (2003)
41. Twidale, M.B.: Over the Shoulder Learning: Supporting Brief Informal Learning. Computer Supported Cooperative Work 14(6), 505–547 (2005)
42. von Hippel, E., Katz, R.: Shifting Innovation to Users via Toolkits. Management Science 48(7), 821–833 (2002)
43. Wulf, V.: Evolving Cooperation when Introducing Groupware – A Self-Organization Perspective. Cybernetics and Human Knowing 6(2), 55–75 (1999)
44. Wulf, V., Golombek, B.: Exploration environments: concept and empirical evaluation. In: Proc. of the GROUP (2001)
45. Wulf, V., Golombek, B.: Direct Activation: A Concept to Encourage Tailoring Activities. Behaviour & Information Technology 20(4), 249–263 (2001)
46. Wulf, V., Rohde, M.: Towards an Integrated Organization and Technology Development. In: ACM Proceedings of the Symposium on Designing Interactive Systems (1995)
47. Wulf, V., Pipek, V., Won, M.: Component-based tailorability: Enabling highly flexible software applications. Int. J. Hum.-Comput. Stud. 66(1), 1–22 (2008)
48. Wikipedia: Perpetual beta. Online resource (November 28, 2008), http://en.wikipedia.org/wiki/Perpetual_beta

Supporting End Users to Be Co-designers of Their Tools

Maria Francesca Costabile[1], Piero Mussio[2],
Loredana Parasiliti Provenza[2], and Antonio Piccinno[1]

[1] Dipartimento di Informatica, Università di Bari, Bari, Italy
[2] Dipartimento di Informatica e Comunicazione, Università di Milano, Milano, Italy
{costabile,piccinno}@di.uniba.it,
{mussio,parasiliti}@dico.unimi.it

Abstract. Nowadays very different people use computer systems for their daily
working activities, but also for fun and entertainment or only to satisfy their
information needs. Designers are doing their best to create computer systems
that work as end users expect, but it must be honestly admitted that they often
fail and end users have all rights to complain. In order to improve this situation
and create better systems, participatory approaches have been proposed, which
involve end users in the design and development process. However, this
solution is not without flaws, mainly because timing and ways of users'
participation are very critical. In this paper we discuss our approach to create
working systems, which is based on a star model of the software life cycle that
drives system design, development and evolution, since software design and
development is seen as an evolutive process, driven by end-users activities in
the real life. System development does not end with its first release; it is
experimented by its end users and further evolved on the basis of their
feedbacks. End users are truly engaged in the software life cycle as co-designers
and experimenters of the software tools they will use in various application
domains.

Keywords: Design Methodology, Star Life Cycle, Co-Evolution of Users and
Systems, End-User Development.

1 Introduction

Current development of Information and Communication Technology (ICT) leads to a
continuous growth of both computer systems and end-user population. Designers are
doing their best to create computer systems that work as end users expect, but it must
be admitted that they often fail [1]. Consequently, people are not satisfied with the
system they use and companies investing in ICT are unhappy because a lot of money
and resources are wasted.

In order to design successful interactive systems that meet users' expectations and
improve their daily life, a designers' major issue is: "How to define an interaction
language that allows end users to easily perform their activities". This language must
be expressive enough to allow end users to formulate the solutions to their problems,
and yet not so rich to generate user disorientation. Thus, on one side there is a

V. Pipek et al. (Eds.): IS-EUD 2009, LNCS 5435, pp. 70–85, 2009.
© Springer-Verlag Berlin Heidelberg 2009

notation problem, while, on the other side there is a problem of system complexity. As to notation, each element of the end user-system dialog must be expressed with symbols the user can correctly interpret in her/his context and application domain. As to complexity, the language should offer to its users all and only the tools they need to perform their activities in a certain time and context.

Many questions arise. Who can define and evaluate notations understandable by users? Who can identify the set of tools required in a certain context during a certain activity? The answer is: the end users themselves. User involvement in the design team is the key point of participatory design approaches [2]. However, this solution is not without flaws, as clearly stated in [1]. Indeed, it is well known that end users are unreliable when requested to explicitly explain their needs and envision system functionalities, while they are very capable of detecting problems and difficulties when using a software system [1], [3].

We consider end users as domain experts and have worked with them in the design and development of systems in various application domains [4], [5]. Based on this experience, over the past few years we have been developing the Software Shaping Workshop (SSW) design methodology. We show in this paper that the SSW methodology is able to truly engage users at times they can provide valuable indications, as recommended in [1]. This goal is achieved by localizing the interface to user culture and allowing users to interact directly with the system under development. In this way, users are better engaged since they experiment the system in their 'sphere of work' [1]. In other words, the SSW methodology adopts a star model of the software life cycle, which anticipates the time when users test the system in their work practice [6]. This methodology acknowledges software design as an evolutive process, driven by user activities in the field. System development does not end with its first release; it is experimented by its end users and further evolved on the basis of their feedback. The system keeps evolving during time, since its use changes users' working practices, so that they require new functionalities and new tools [7].

End users are willing to be more involved in designing and developing their tools. The boom of the Web 2.0 is pushing people not only to use software, but also to create it. The Web already supports some kind of End-User Development activities, ranging from simple parameter customization to modification and assembly of components, creating simulations, games and web contents [8]. We will show in this paper how the SSW methodology supports the creation of computer systems that evolve in time and allow end users to be co-designers of their tools. In this way, it provides a contribution towards computer systems that work successfully in the real life.

The paper is organized as follows. Section 2 discusses motivations of this work. Sections 3 and 4 describe our approach to system design, development and evolution. Section 5 reports a case study that illustrates the practical application of the described concepts. Section 6 concludes the paper.

2 Background and Motivation

The diffusion of the World Wide Web as the platform for a wide variety of applications raises many expectations about the possibilities offered by web-based interactive systems. The interaction dimension creates new challenges for system specification, design and implementation. First of all, the use of an interactive system cause the working environment and organization to evolve, and force the system to adapt to the evolved user, organization and environment (called *co-evolution* of users and systems, see [5], [9]). Moreover, current techniques for software specification and design, such as UML, are very useful for software engineers, but they are often unfamiliar to users' experience, language, and background so that they fail to provide a good communication between application designers and users. This communication gap is a reason why software systems are often poorly usable [10]. To overcome these problems, software development methodologies aiming at participatory design [2] and open-ended design [11] are invoked. However, designers must make sure that end users are engaged at opportune moments, when they can provide useful suggestions.

A further reason that makes very difficult the creation of successful systems is the diversity of end users: they have very different physical, cognitive and cultural abilities, needs, interests and activities they want to perform with computer systems. This diversity calls for general, adaptive systems [10]. The temptation is to develop very general systems, which may easily become Turing Tar Pits in which "everything is possible but nothing of interest is easy" [12]. The opposite temptation is to create specialized systems, focused on the activity of a well-specified user – or a well specified and restricted community of users linked by similar practices or similar interests – working in a restricted context. In such systems Fischer warns about the perils of this tendency: beware of the Turing Tar Pit inverse, i.e., overspecialized systems that permit only a limited number of activities, which cannot be generalized nor adapted and evolved [13]; they become a strict cage for end users by limiting their strategies for achieving their goals. Indeed, domain-specific systems support certain problem contexts but the ability to extend them is very limited; even minor incremental changes are often impossible.

The design methodology we have developed in the last few years is suitable for developing interactive systems that are not Turing Tar Pits or the inverse. The methodology stems from our experience in participatory design of several applications. However, our participatory approach is very different from the traditional one [2] that recommends to involve end users in the design team just to provide advice on their needs and expectations. They are more engaged in the overall design and development process, being not only co-designers but also experimenters of the evolving system.

Involving users in software project initiatives has been frequently indicated as a critical factor in the creation of successful software [14]. It is well acknowledged that it is good practice to involve users in designing the software applications with which they will be working. This principle of participatory design is reflected in a wide spectrum of methodologies in use today, such as agile programming.

Recent researches show that, because end users are busy with their work, they will generally not be fully engaged in analyzing and evaluating new systems [1]. They become committed only when the system impacts on their daily life, i.e. when the system is released in the field. In the design and development phases, attempts to increase user participation are helpful, but only partially effective. Our experience is in line with this view: only when a new system impacts their daily practices, end users are able to evaluate it and raise significant issues about its functionalities and usability. This does not mean that involving end users in early phases of the design process is of no value, because they certainly provide useful feedback; it suggests that we have to revise the different stages of system development. Wagner and Piccoli recommend that post-implementation activities that try to solve the many problems raised by end users when they start working with the final system must be legitimized: they are not signs of system failure, but they are the only useful way of facing with actual users' needs and expectations [1].

One of the novelties of the SSW methodology is the proposal of modifying the traditional software life cycle by considering software design as an evolutive process, during which end users have the possibility of working in real settings with prototypes that will be evolved on the basis of the results of this work. Thus, end users are not required to *envision* since they *experience* what the end product will be and how it will impact on their work practice, being able to provide very valuable feedback.

In today information and communication society, end users are no longer passive consumers of computer tools, but they are shifting toward a more active role of information and software artifacts producers [15]. This is also highlighted by Shneiderman's claim: "the old computing was about what computers could do; the new computing is about what users can do" [16].

Our approach aims at developing software environments that support end users in performing their activities of interest, but also allow them to tailor these environments to better adapt them to their needs, and even to create or modify software artifacts. The latter are defined activities of End-User Development (EUD), to which a lot of attention is currently devoted by various researchers in Europe and all over the world [17], [18], [19], [20].

EUD implies the active participation of end users in the software development process. In this perspective, tasks that are traditionally performed by professional software developers are transferred to the users, who need to be specifically supported in performing these tasks. User participation in the software development process can range from providing information about requirements, use cases and tasks, as required in traditional participatory design, to creating/modifying software artefacts. Some EUD-oriented techniques have already been adopted by software for the mass market such as the adaptive menus in MS Word™ or some Programming by Example techniques in MS Excel™. However, we are still quite far from their systematic adoption.

To permit EUD activities, we consider a two-phase process, the first phase being designing the design environment (meta-design phase), the second one being designing the applications by using the design environment. The two phases are not clearly distinct, and are executed several times in an interleaved way, because the design environments evolve both as a consequence of the progressive insights the different stakeholders gain into the design process and as a consequence of the feedbacks provided by end users working with the system in the field. This two-phase process requires a shift in the design paradigm, which must move from user-centered and participatory design to meta-design [4], [21].

3   A Strategy for Supporting Users' Co-design

Meta-design refers to the design of environments that allow end users to be actively involved in the continuous development, use and evolution of systems. In this perspective, meta-design underlines a novel vision of system design, which is the basis of our approach and considers end users as co-designers of the tools they will use. All stakeholders of an interactive system, including end users, are 'owners' of a part of the problem: software engineers know the technology, end users know the application domain, Human-Computer Interaction (HCI) experts know human factors, etc.; they must all contribute to system design by bringing their own expertise. Stakeholders need different software environments, specific to their culture, knowledge and abilities, through which they can contribute to shape software artifacts. They should also exchange among themselves the results of these activities, to converge toward a common design. Moreover, co-evolution of users and systems forces all stakeholders to take part in a continuous evolution of the system [6], [20]. This can be carried out, on one hand, by end users, who can perform tailoring activities to adapt the software environments they use to their evolved needs and habits. On the other hand, end users should collaborate with all the other stakeholders in the evolution of the interactive system rather than just in the original design.

Because of the diversity of end users, the challenge is to ensure the universal access and universal usability of interactive systems. The slogan "one size fits all" cannot be applied to the user interface; it is well known that people experience many difficulties when they interact with an interface presenting a huge number of functionalities, being overwhelmed with unnecessary interaction possibilities and often disoriented by them. Our approach aims at providing different communities of users with software environments that they may access and manipulate by exploiting their own system of signs (notation) [22]. We recognize, with Iverson, that a notation developed by users during years of experiences is a tool of thought [23]. However, we do not seek for a universal notation, but acknowledge that each user community has developed a notation that properly expresses the concepts and activities of that community.

The interaction language exploited in each software environment is derived from the notation used by the community the environment is devoted to. This strategy has a drawback: it makes difficult for the user to understand the improvements on the system proposed by other stakeholders. To overcome this drawback and make fruitful this clash among laguages (and cultures), the proposed approach exploits system prototypes as boundary objects, supporting the communication among the different stakeholders. Each stakeholder describes the improvement s/he wants to add to the prototype by creating an updated executable prototype and possibly annotating it. The others stakeholders receive the annotated prototype and evaluate the proposal by reading annotations and concretely experimenting the prototype in their own environment while performing their work activity, thus living concretely the experience designed by the proposer.

The *Software Shaping Workshop* (SSW) methodology we have described in [4] adopts a meta-design participatory approach that does not end with the release of the software, but continues throughout the whole software life cycle. A team of experts, including software engineers, HCI experts and domain experts, designs, implements and evolves an application throughout its life cycle. The aim of this methodology is to design interactive systems that are easily understood by their users because they "speak" users' languages. An interactive system is designed as a network of software environments, called Software Shaping Workshops (SSW or briefly workshops), each of them being either an environment through which end users perform their activities or an environment through which stakeholders participate in the design of the whole system, even at use time. An SSW is designed in analogy with an artisan or engineer workshop, the workroom where an expert finds all and only those tools necessary to carry out her/his activities. The tools reflect the experts' needs. For example, the blacksmith's hammer is suitable for heavy work and has different features than the shoemaker's hammer, suitable for more precise work. Following the analogy, each SSW adopts a domain-oriented interaction language tailored to end-user culture, in that it is shaped and defined by evolving the traditional end-user notations and system of signs. In this sense, we refer to it as end-user language. Moreover, each SSW provides all and only those tools that are required to perform the specific activities to which the workshop is devoted. The data on which end users operate are thus represented as elements of the language. Note that using the word 'workshop' to denote the workroom we adopt the point of view of our users rather than the one of computer scientists who denotes, by this word, a brief intensive meeting.

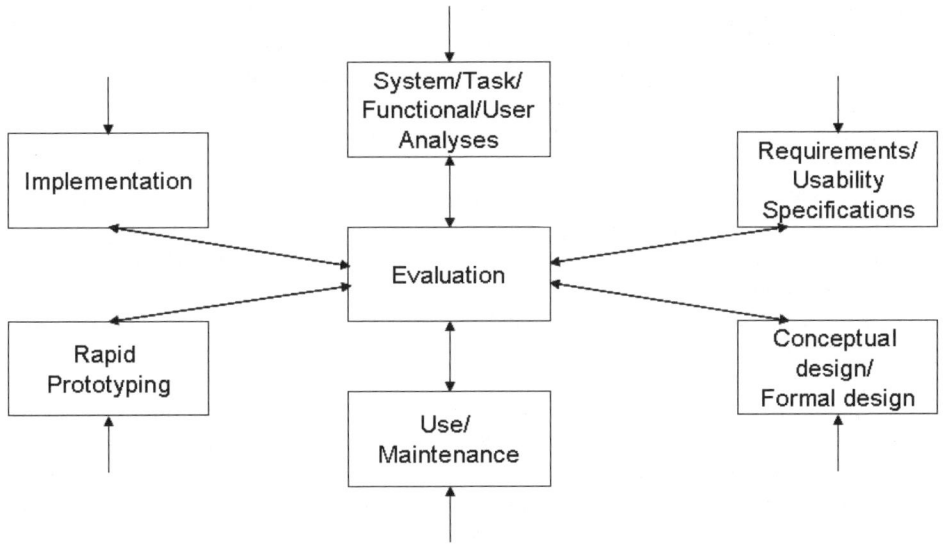

Fig. 1. The star life cycle model [1]

The SSWs are continually updated both because experience shows that the first release of a system does not generally work properly [1] and because the use of a system changes the work practice and determines user evolution (for more details on user and system co-evolution see [5]). In other words, system design and development do not end with its first release, since it evolves by following a star life cycle represented in Fig. 1 [6]. This model includes the use and maintenance activities performed during the working life of the system. The novelty of the SSW approach is that the activities in the life cycle are performed by a team including users representatives. System development can start from any point in the star (as shown by the entry arrows in the model in Fig. 1), followed by any other stage (as shown by the double arrows), always performing evaluation, which is at the center of the star. In this way, the requirements, the design and the product gradually evolve, becoming step by step well defined. The *Use/Maintenance* box refers to activities in which end users are truly engaged; they practice in the field with the current version of the system. They can enrich the system by creating new tools and, possibly, find out new ways to use it; they also discover flaws in its use [1], [24]. All this is possible when people use the system in real life, it cannot be imagined before. New iterations of design and development are then necessary.

Results reached at each stage of the system life must be evaluated before passing to the next stage. This is why evaluation is the star center. In the SSW methodology, end users are always required to experiment the current version of the system under development: they express their observations and suggestions, resulting from such experiments. To this aim, they are allowed to annotate their own environment and to make these annotations available to the design team [25]. More details about the communications among workshops in the network, in order to evolve the system, are in [4], [5], [26]. Analogously, Software Engineering (SE) experts and HCI experts operate on prototypes and update them. The negotiation among the members of the design team is based on the use of prototypes. A modification of the system is either accepted and executed, or rejected by the team after each member has experienced it and the different findings have been discussed [25].

The SSW architecture supports the methodology: a) each stakeholder operates according to her/his mental model by using a SSW customized to her/his notations; b) prototypes (as executable specifications) and annotations, by which each stakeholder describes why and how a prototype must be updated, are exchanged among SSWs.

On the whole, the SSW methodology brings to a process of software design, development and evolution that fosters the active participation of end users, involving them when they can be more useful and productive. The process always starts with defining a prototype, which is the seed of the whole process. This prototype can be an existing system that must be improved, or a mock up that embodies the client specification, if the process starts from scratch. Each stakeholder in the design team experiments the prototype using it in her/his SSW, and finds out usability problems, or unnecessary elements, or inadequacies of the system with respect to the work organization. Each stakeholder can modify and/or annotate the prototype at hand to make explicit her/his observations. From these experiments, several proposals emerge as different improvements of the original prototype. Such different proposals are concurrently developed, subjected to a continuous experimentation and negotiation among the stakeholders, until an agreed proposal emerges. The interaction language, i.e., the set of user actions, their notation and interaction style, is progressively defined in the process, under the critical influence of the domain experts and all involved end users. As to the notation, the lexicon (textual and graphical) and the syntax are computerized versions of those used by the end users in their domain, properly enriched and formalized to be executable by a computer. The formalization process implies the careful design of the presentation elements of the user interface.

4   SSW Architecture as a Network of Customized Environments

Fig. 2 shows the SSW architecture, organized as a network of SSWs, that supports a community of end users in performing their activities as well as the design team in designing the seed of the workshops and in evolving them. The case study refers to the development of a web application to support the activities of a consortium of small and medium-sized Italian companies operating in the confectionery field, called CIDD ("Consorzio Italiano Distribuzione Dolciaria"). More details on the case study are given in the next subsection.

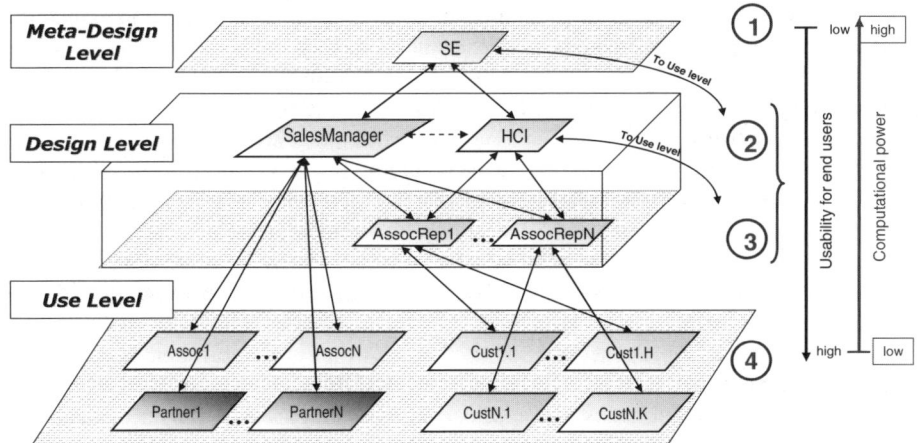

Fig. 2. The SSW network for the case study

The SSW network of an interactive system is organized in three different levels based on the different types of activities the workshops are devoted to: the *use level* includes workshops that are used by end users to perform their tasks (called application workshop); the *design level* includes workshops for designing and adapting the application workshops in accordance with the evolving knowledge and user needs (called system workshops); and the *meta-design level* includes the system workshop for software engineers, which allows them to generate and maintain all the workshops in the network.

The workshops in the architecture are of three types:

- *SE workshop* ("1" in Fig. 2): this workshop supports the software engineers in designing and evolving all the other workshops in the architecture, according to the requests of the different stakeholders. Interacting with SE workshop, software engineers perform their activities using programming languages and other development tools; they have high professional competence on software, low competence on domain activities. Even if software engineers may be considered end users when they interact with software environments, case tools, etc. created by others, in this paper end users are the domain experts for whom the system is developed and they do not have generally any expertise in computer science. The interaction languages in the SE workshop are characterized by high computational power (Turing Machine equivalent) but cannot in general be understood and managed by end users, i.e., they have low usability with respect to end users. Hence, the SE workshop would be a Turing Tar Pit for end users. In order to avoid this, more usable environments are designed for end users even if with lower computational power.

- *Design workshops* ("2" and "3" in Fig. 2): these workshops support the members of the design team other than software engineers in designing and evolving the application workshops. Such stakeholders have no (or little) competence in computer science; some of them have competence on HCI design, so that they can bring human factors in system design; other stakeholders have competence on domain activities. These team members use specialized interaction languages that have less computational power than the ones used by software engineers, in that they permit a limited set of operations. However, they are more usable for end users in that they can be correctly interpreted by end users.
- *Application workshops* ("4" in Fig. 2): these workshops are devoted to end users to perform their activities in the real world. Interacting with application workshops, end users perform their well-defined set of activities using domain-oriented languages that reflect and empower their traditional notations. Such languages permit the definition and execution of a limited set of computations, those of interest for the end-user community and are characterized by a low computational power. The characteristic structures of the alphabet elements used by an application workshop are words, icons, symbols that are significant for end users and can be correctly interpreted. Hence, the usability with respect to end users is high. Due to these languages, the application workshops are in danger of becoming the inverse of the Turing Tar Pit, where *everything is easy and very little of interest is possible*. Anyhow, this danger is avoided thanks to the support to co-evolution offered by our approach. Indeed, new functionalities can be provided to end users when they need them.

5 A Case Study

To provide a concrete example of these concepts, let us describe how the SSW methodology is being applied to the development of a web application supporting the activities of CIDD consortium. The application provides the consortium companies with several services such as price lists, discounts, order management, etc. and permits some of the consortium stakeholders to exchange information and cooperate through the Web.

After a field study, we identified the following stakeholders:

- the chairman, who is the official responsible for the consortium (e.g. he organizes and chairs meetings of associated companies, signs the balance sheet, etc.);
- the sales manager, who manages all the consortium activities;
- the consortium secretary, who works closely with the sales manager;
- the partner companies, which hold agreements with the consortium to provide goods to associated companies at special prices;
- the associated companies, which purchase products from the partner companies;
- the customers of associated companies.

A special role in the consortium is played by the sales manager, who needs to tailor the software environments to be used by the associated companies and by the partner companies, since he wants to decide about the services to provide to them. In turn, each associated company needs to define the environments to be used by their customers.

This is a typical case where various users want to co-design software environments and tools, thus the meta-design approach of the SSW methodology can be successful.

In the studies carried out for requirement analysis, four types of end users have been identified:

- *power users*: they are able to visualize, insert, modify and delete workshop contents, define access rules and even design application workshops; the role of the power user is played by the sales manager and his secretary, who works on his behalf;
- *associated companies*: their representatives can access contracts, catalogues, promotions, competitions, make orders and design/tailor the application workshops for their customers;
- *registered guests*: they are the customers of the associated companies and, through their workshops, they can visualize specific contents;
- *unregistered guests*: any user who visualizes the portal home page when browsing on the web.

The chairman is a political stakeholder, not interested in the portal use. Company customers and partners are different communities of registered guests.

A system used by different user communities is often overgeneralized for some and overspecialized for others. The SSW methodology avoids this: a system is generated as network of workshops, each one specific for tasks and needs of a user community.

The seed of the current version of the CIDD portal was a first release of the application developed as a static web site made of HTML pages that the CIDD manager had commissioned to a company. The first user of that release was the manager himself, who was not satisfied at all. The application lacked some functionalities he considered necessary and presented various usability problems; more importantly, his main complain was that he did not have the possibility of shaping the web pages for the other end users (associated companies, partner companies, etc.). In fact, one of the primary concerns of the manager is that he wants to decide the services and the functionalities of the other end users. He is a demanding user that wants to design software environments and tools used by himself and by the other users of the consortium portal.

Taking into account all manager's complains and requests, the new version of the CIDD portal was developed with the SSW methodology. By considering the different types of end users, the network architecture shown in Fig. 2 was defined. At the design level there is a workshop for HCI experts, a workshop for the sales manager and a number of workshops for representatives of associated companies ("AssocRep1", ..., "AssocRepN" in Fig. 2). The latter are used by representatives of associate companies to create and modify the application workshops devoted to their customers ("Cust1.1",..., "Cust1.H",.., "CustN.1",..., "CustN.K"). At use level there are application workshops used by associated companies ("Assoc1",..., "AssocN") and application workshop used by partner companies ("Partner1",..., "PartnerN") for their consortium activities.

Through their system workshop at the top level of the network, software engineers design and develop a first release of the system workshops for different experts (in the case study, sales manager and representatives of associated companies). By interacting with their own system workshops, such experts, who know end

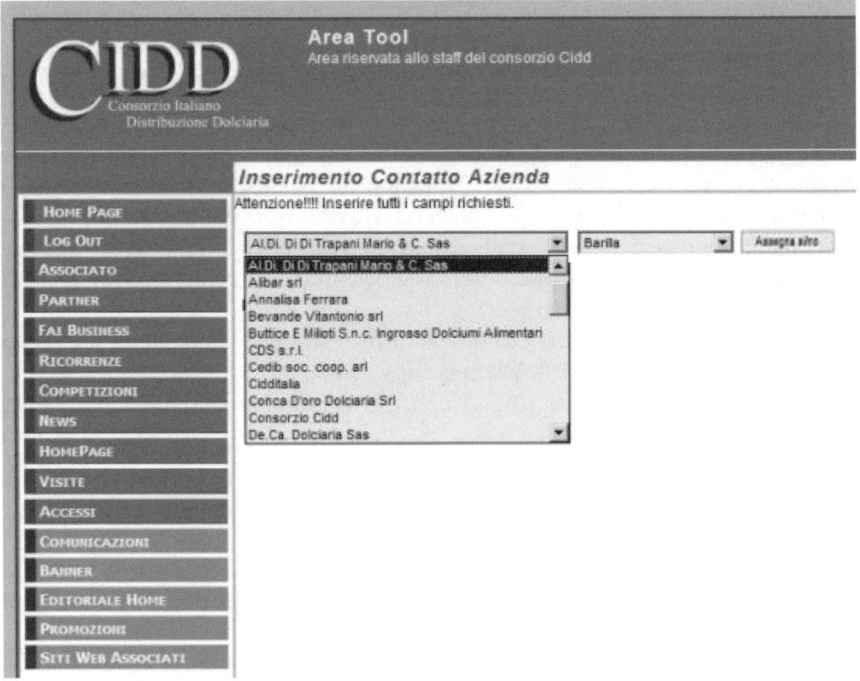

Fig. 3. The SalesManager workshop. The sales manager is generating services for associated companies.

usersworking context and habits, design and develop the application workshops tailored/specialized for different end-user communities (CIDD customers, associated companies, partners). CIDD customers, associated companies and partners use their workshops to carry out their tasks. When a user requires to perform new tasks not supported by her/his specialized workshop, s/he annotates the problems and sends it to corresponding domain expert, who evolves the workshop according to the new user requirements, by collaborating, if necessary, with HCI experts to fix usability problems. Whenever the domain expert system workshop is not so powerful to evolve another workshop, s/he asks software engineers for the missing tools by sending them an annotation. Software engineers thus evolve the workshop of the domain expert who is then able to evolve the application workshop as required.

Some examples on how end users act as co-designers are provided in the following. In the *SalesManager* workshop, the sales manager finds tools that allow him to design the application workshops for each associated company and each partner company, and the system workshops for associate company representatives ("AssocRep1",..., "AssocRepN" in Fig. 2). This workshop is shown in Fig. 3. Let us suppose that the sales manager wants to design the system workshop to be used by the representatives of an associated company, also providing it with some services. He designs this workshop by direct manipulation. Specifically, he selects the company from a drop-down list available in the central area of his workshop (the list is shown in Fig. 3); he also selects a service he wants to provide from another drop-down list

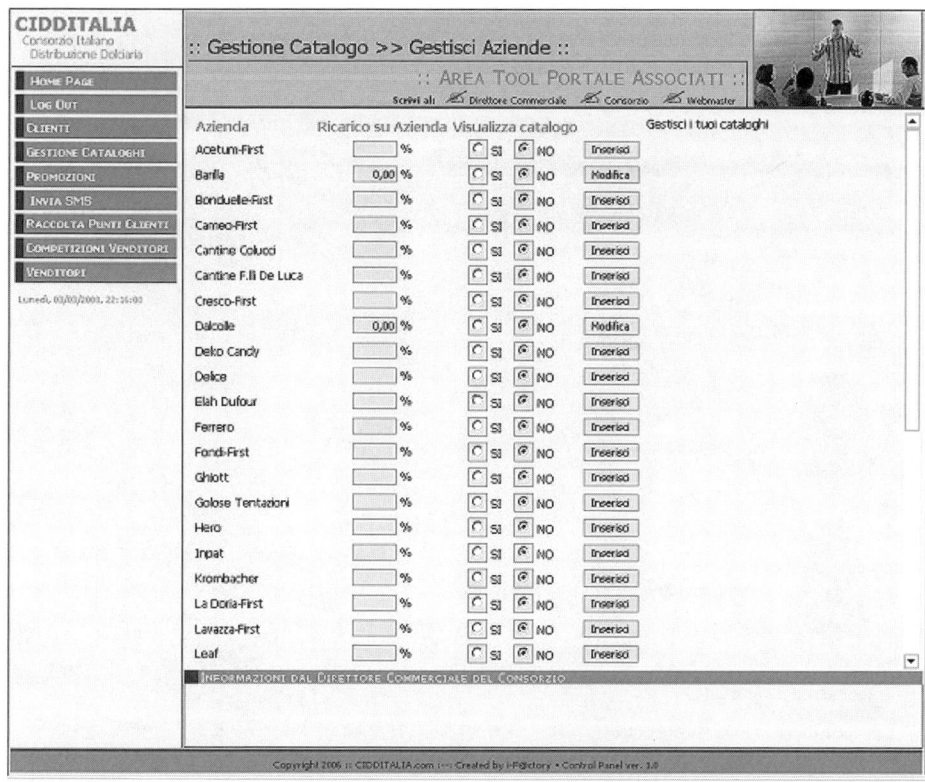

Fig. 4. A screen shot of the workshop for associated company representatives.

(available on the right of the previous one, not open in Fig. 3) and clicks on the association button (the latter on the right in Fig. 3) to actually associate the service to that company workshop. He does this for all services he wants to provide. As a result, the workshop for the representatives of the selected company is created, shown in Fig. 4. Nine services are available and they are listed in the left panel of the workshop. Fig. 4 actually shows a situation in which the user has selected a service from the left panel and the central area shows the tools available to the user for using that service. Such tools are provided through an interaction language that is suited to the culture and skills of the users, who understand the meaning of all language elements and easily work with them.

Similarly, the associated company's representatives use their workshop to design the workshops to be used by their customers (registered users). Referring again to Fig. 4, here the user defines the product catalogues for a customer, with prices and percentage of revenues, and how it can be visualized. The central area shows all companies that provide products to the customer. For each company, the user specifies in the appropriate field the percentage of revenues, and also decides whether to show prices in the catalogue or not, by clicking on a radio button. Fig. 5 shows how the catalogue is visualized in the customer workshop. Again, the user activity is specified through direct manipulation of the elements of the interaction language

Fig. 5. A screenshot of the workshop for a customer

implemented in that workshop. It is worth noting that the workshop in Fig. 4 provides its users with a communication area (the rectangular area at the bottom of Fig. 4) through which representative of associated companies can exchange messages in the network to foster the co-evolution process [5].

Through the developed system, each CCID user has available a workshop tailored to her/his needs, which allows users to interact through a domain-oriented language familiar to their culture and skills, thus avoiding the system to be a Turing Tar Pit. On the other side, users do not perceive their workshops as the inverse of Turing Tar Pits, which limit their activities, since the co-evolution process is supported throughout the software life cycle, making possible to add new functionalities, as required by end users.

We agree that the design of such complex systems requires "more knowledge than any one single person can possess, and the knowledge relevant to a problem is often distributed and controversial" [27]. The SSW methodology allows a community of stakeholders to create a system through their collaborative negotiations. This negotiation is based on the exchange of messages which are of two types: executable specifications of workshops; and annotations about these workshops. These specifications are XML-based documents [28]. A stakeholder designing or updating a workshop (the example of sales manager designing the workshop for an associated company, depicted in Fig. 3) modifies the executable specification that, when interpreted by the browser, generates the new workshop. The user interface of this new workshop is created by:

1. the browser interpreting the document resulting from the design process;
2. the user, who can set configuration parameters (the associated company representative configures her/his workshop).

Therefore, the stakeholder designing another workshop performs a programming activity that goes beyond configuration. By configuration we intend to set parameters in order to select among functionalities available in that workshop.

In this case study, there is a variety of end users that are experts in a specific domain, but not in computer science. They need to use the web application to perform their work tasks, but they are not and do not want to become computer scientists. They are permitted to shape and modify software artefacts through interaction languages, whose elements (technical words, icon, etc.) are familiar to them. When they modify and update the CIDD application, they actually program, but they are not aware of this, also because they do not use conventional programs that would be too unfamiliar to their culture and skills. They use a language through which they compose new software artefacts by construction, similarly to children's program construction [29]. Working with these languages, CIDD users perceive that they are simply carrying out their work activities and they are highly motivated. The simplicity of the user interface is a strength of the SSW approach: "let user do simple things to generate powerful results". In other words, they are *unwitting* software developers, as analysed in [15].

6   Conclusions

This paper has discussed an approach aimed at creating interactive systems that address the needs of different communities of users, in which operations are easy to perform and many interesting activities, including end-user development activities, can be carried out. In this way, it is possible to avoid that the systems are perceived by their users as Turing Tar Pit in which "everything is possible but nothing of interest is easy". The opposite temptation is also avoided, namely the creation of overspecialized systems, in which operations are easy to perform but only specific activities, which cannot be generalized nor adapted and evolved, are possible; these systems are perceived as the inverse of Turing Tar Pits, i.e. a strict cage that limits the activities of their users.

The approach requires that an interactive system is designed as a network of software environments, called Software Shaping Workshops, through which the different stakeholders involved in system design, including end-users' representatives, are able to collaborate in the design and the evolution of the network of workshops and to carry out activities of interest in their application domain.

The SSW methodology goes beyond the traditional participatory design that has been in practice for the last two decades [2]. End users are not only involved in the design phase to provide advice on their needs and expectations, they are truly engaged in the whole process having the possibility of working in real settings with prototypes that will be evolved on the basis of their feedback. The overall software life cycle is revised. System development does not end with its first release; it is used by people in their work practice and continuously evolved to comply with further users' needs, organization requirements and/or novel technology.

The concepts are explained through examples taken from a case study relative to the development of a web application to support the activities of a consortium of small and medium-sized Italian companies, which operate in the confectionery field.

Acknowledgments

This work was supported by the Italian MIUR and by EU and Regione Puglia under grant DIPIS. We thank the CIDD consortium and Nicola Claudio Cellamare for their collaboration in the development of the CIDD application.

References

1. Wagner, E.L., Piccoli, G.: Moving Beyond User Participation to Achieve Successful Is Design. Commun. ACM 50, 51–55 (2007)
2. Schuler, D., Namioka, A.: Participatory Design: Principles and Practices. Lawrence Erlbaum Associates, Inc., Mahwah (1993)
3. Mayhew, D.J.: The Usability Engineering Lifecycle: A Practitioner's Handbook for User Interface Design. Morgan Kaufmann Publishers Inc., San Francisco (1999)
4. Costabile, M.F., Fogli, D., Mussio, P., Piccinno, A.: Visual Interactive Systems for End-User Development: A Model-Based Design Methodology. IEEE Transactions on System Man and Cybernetics Part A-Systems and Humans 37, 1029–1046 (2007)
5. Costabile, M.F., Fogli, D., Marcante, A., Piccinno, A.: Supporting Interaction and Co-Evolution of Users and Systems. In: International Conference on Advanced Visual Interface, pp. 143–150. ACM Press, Venice (2006)
6. Bianchi, A., Bottoni, P., Mussio, P.: Issues in Design and Implementation of Multimedia Software Systems. In: IEEE International Conference on Multimedia Computing and Systems (ICMCS 1999), pp. 91–96. IEEE Computer Society, Los Alamitos (1999)
7. Nielsen, J.: Usability Engineering. Academic Press, San Diego (1993)
8. Fogli, D., Colosio, S., Sacco, M.: Managing Accessibility in Local E-Government Websites through End-User Development: A Case Study. Int. J. Universal Access in the Information Society (to appear)
9. Bourguin, G., Derycke, A., Tarby, J.C.: Beyond the Interface: Co-Evolution inside Interactive Systems - a Proposal Founded on Activity Theory. In: IHM-HCI, pp. 297–310. Springer, Heidelberg (2001)
10. Folmer, E., van Welie, M., Bosch, J.: Bridging Patterns: An Approach to Bridge Gaps between SE and HCI. Information and Software Technology 48, 69–89 (2006)
11. Hix, D., Hartson, H.R.: Developing User Interfaces: Ensuring Usability through Product & Process. John Wiley & Sons, Inc., Chichester (1993)
12. Perlis, A.J.: Special Feature: Epigrams on Programming. SIGPLAN Not. 17, 7–13 (1982)
13. Fischer, G.: Beyond Binary Choices: Understanding and Exploiting Trade-Offs to Enhance Creativity. First Monday 11 (2006)
14. Buono, P., Simeone, A.L.: An Experience About User Involvement for Successful Design. In: D'Atri, A., De Marco, M., Casalino, N. (eds.) Interdisciplinary Aspects of Information Systems Studies. Springer, Heidelberg (to appear)

15. Costabile, M.F., Mussio, P., Parasiliti Provenza, L., Piccinno, A.: End Users as Unwitting Software Developers. In: Proceedings of the 4th international workshop on End-user software engineering (WEUSE 2008), pp. 6–10. ACM, Leipzig (2008)
16. Shneiderman, B.: Leonardo's Laptop: Human Needs and the New Computing Technologies. MIT Press, Cambridge (2002)
17. Burnett, M., Cook, C., Rothermel, G.: End-User Software Engineering. Commun. ACM 47, 53–58 (2004)
18. Fischer, G., Giaccardi, E.: Meta-Design: A Framework for the Future of End User Development. In: Lieberman, H., Paternò, F., Wulf, V. (eds.) End User Development, vol. 9, pp. 427–457. Springer, Dordrecht (2006)
19. Myers, B., Hudson, S.E., Pausch, R.: Past, Present, and Future of User Interface Software Tools. ACM Trans. Comput.-Hum. Interact. 7, 3–28 (2000)
20. Sutcliffe, A., Mehandjiev, N.: Introduction. Communications of the ACM 47, 31–32 (2004)
21. Fischer, G., Giaccardi, E., Ye, Y., Sutcliffe, A., Mehandjiev, N.: Meta-Design: A Manifesto for End-User Development. Communications of the ACM 47, 33–37 (2004)
22. De Souza, C.S., Barbosa, S.D.J.: A Semiotic Framing for End-User Development. End User Development. In: Lieberman, H., Paternò, F., Wulf, V. (eds.) End User Development, vol. 9, pp. 401–426. Springer, Dordrecht (2006)
23. Iverson, K.E.: Notation as a Tool of Thought. Communications of the ACM 23, 444–465 (1980)
24. Costabile, M.F., Fogli, D., Mussio, P., Piccinno, A.: A Meta-Design Approach to End-User Development. In: IEEE Symposium on Visual Languages and Human-Centric Computing, pp. 308–310. IEEE Computer Society, Dallas (2005)
25. Fogli, D., Fresta, G., Mussio, P.: On Electronic Annotation and Its Implementation. In: Proceedings of the working conference on Advanced visual interfaces, pp. 98–102. ACM, Gallipoli (2004)
26. Carrara, P., Fogli, D., Fresta, G., Mussio, P.: Toward Overcoming Culture, Skill and Situation Hurdles in Human-Computer Interaction. Universal Access in the Information Society 1, 288–304 (2002)
27. Fischer, G.: Symmetry of Ignorance, Social Creativity, and Meta-Design. In: Proceedings of Creativity & Cognition 1999, pp. 116–123. ACM Press, New York (1999)
28. Costabile, M.F., Fogli, D., Marcante, A., Mussio, P., Piccinno, A.: A Design Methodology for Tailorable Visual Interactive Systems. In: Int. Conference on Software Engineering and Knowledge Engineering, San Francisco Bay, CA, USA, pp. 450–455 (2006)
29. Petre, M., Blackwell, A.F.: Children as Unwitting End-User Programmers. In: IEEE Symposium on Visual Languages and Human-Centric Computing, VL/HCC 2007, pp. 239–242 (2007)

Improving Documentation for eSOA APIs
through User Studies

Sae Young Jeong[1], Yingyu Xie[1], Jack Beaton[1], Brad A. Myers[1], Jeff Stylos[1],
Ralf Ehret[2], Jan Karstens[2], Arkin Efeoglu[2], and Daniela K. Busse[3]

[1] School of Computer Science
Carnegie Mellon University
Pittsburgh, PA, USA 15213
[2] SAP, AG
Walldorf, Germany
[3] SAP Labs, LLC Palo Alto, CA 94304
tooth2@gmail.com, clare.xie@gmail.com, jackbeaton@cmu.edu,
bam@cs.cmu.edu, jsstylos@cs.cmu.edu,
{ralf.ehret,jan.karstens,arkin.efeoglu,daniela.busse}@sap.com

Abstract. All software today is written using libraries, toolkits, frameworks and
other application programming interfaces (APIs). We performed a user study of
the online documentation a large and complex API for Enterprise Service-
Oriented Architecture (eSOA), which identified many issues and recommendations for making API documentation easier to use. eSOA is an appropriate
testbed because the target user groups range from high-level business experts
who do not have significant programming expertise (and thus are end-
participant developers), to professional programmers. Our study showed that
the participants' background influenced how they navigated the documentation.
Lack of familiarity with business terminology was a barrier we observed for
developers without business application experience. Participants with business
software experience had difficulty differentiating similarly named services.
Both groups avoided areas of the documentation that had an inconsistent visual
design. A new design for the documentation that supports flexible navigation
strategies seem to be required to support the wide range of users for eSOA. This
paper summarizes our study and provides recommendations for future documentation for developers.

Keywords: Usability, API Design, Service-Oriented Architecture, Web Services, Documentation, Business Solution Architects.

1 Introduction

"Service-Oriented Architecture" (SOA) is a way to structure large and distributed
software systems, where services communicate over a network with the client and
with other services, and can be combined into composite applications. Enterprise
SOA (eSOA) is focused specifically on supporting business processes across an
enterprise by reusing existing services. When an eSOA application is being planned
and developed, many kinds of people are involved, some of whom are end-user

V. Pipek et al. (Eds.): IS-EUD 2009, LNCS 5435, pp. 86–105, 2009.

developers (EUD). For example, business process experts, who might be titled "Solution Architects," are knowledgeable about the business context but may not necessarily be professional programmers, and are often responsible for identifying and selecting which services will be used. Specifications they write will then be passed to professional programmers, who are responsible for writing code that uses the actual services. Therefore, the documentation and some of the tools must be accessible to both EUDs and professional programmers.

In a service-oriented architecture, code on the user's machine communicates with a remote service using messages across the internet. The communication is usually encoded in XML, and the format of the messages is usually described using a WSDL (Web Services Description Language) file, which has been formalized by the World Wide Web Consortium (see, for example, http://www.w3.org/TR/wsdl).

As part of the "Natural Programming Project" [11], we are interested in a whole range of usability issues around programming. Recently, we have begun to focus on the usability of libraries, frameworks, toolkits, and other application programming interfaces (APIs) [6, 14, 17]. APIs are crucial to professionals and EUDs alike, since most of modern development of all kinds involves finding, understanding, and connecting pre-built items, from small library calls to large-scale components. SOA APIs are particularly interesting to study, because they are often large and complex, and therefore expose interesting issues of scale, and because they often target a wide range of developers. As one typical example, we studied a sales order scenario from SAP's SOA services. SAP provides a large number of SOA services (over 2000) with interdependencies between services, and each service has many parameters, with interdependencies about which parameters are optional and required and what values are allowed based on values of other parameters.

Our previous research has shown that programming using eSOA APIs is not simple if APIs are providing access to powerful business functionality [1, 2]. Some barriers we identified included long names for services, different behaviors of services due to different business behavior, parameters of the services as hierarchies of objects with complex dependencies driven by internal, not exposed, business logic, and lack of example code [1, 2]. The current paper presents the results of a new user study of the usability of the online documentation provided by SAP for their SOA product.

In summary, our results are that when navigating eSOA API documentation, users with business backgrounds did better, and they experienced the most benefit from process component documentation. The process component documentation provides diagrams showing the architecture of an eSOA API in terms of service interfaces, the service operations they contain, and the business objects to which they are connected. All users avoided sites with visual designs that were inconsistent with their starting pages. Developers without business application experience were unfamiliar with business terminology and so they focused on searching and scanning for individual terms with limited success. Based on these results, we recommend that documentation provide flexible ways to navigate for different users with different backgrounds.

2 Related Work

Some of the first work on applying usability principles to APIs comes out of Microsoft, focused on specific APIs [4]. Inspired by this, we began working on the usability of

API design patterns [6, 15, 17], and the barriers to programming faced by EUDs, which includes the difficulties of identifying and understanding the appropriate resources in the documentation, which we called "Selection Barriers" [10].

We also reported on our previous studies of the usability of eSOA APIs for programming. We identified many barriers for installing and using the eSOA development environments, including issues with generating the stubs that will interface between the user's code and the XML messages that are required to communicate over the web, and issues with the long and confusing names of the services [2]. In a second study, we asked experienced programmers to use four services which had already been identified for them [1]. The current study complements these other works by focusing on the task of finding the services in the first place.

Many other people have provided recommendations and guidelines for APIs, but most of these are just based on the writer's intuitions or personal experience, rather than usability studies with users. For example, API designers with experience building the Java [3] and Microsoft .NET [5] APIs have published API design guidelines. For SOA, Jones lists anecdotal common mistakes made when developing SOA architectures, such as problems caused by service hierarchies that are either too fine-grained or too coarse-grained [9].

Focusing on documentation in general, Purho adapted Nielsen's 10 heuristics to apply to documentation [13]. Friendly [8] applied an informal methodology of user testing to JavaDoc, which is automatically generated from a Java project, and derived clear and succinct recommendations for future API documentation designers. Unlike JavaDoc, the eSOA documentation we studied contains a large amount of hand-created content and addresses a larger, more complex framework.

Others have focused on the internal documentation for projects, focusing on the software developers themselves (e.g., [7]), but this is not relevant for understanding how documentation for external users should be designed.

3 Methodology

3.1 Participants

Based on the success of our earlier studies [15], we decided to use an informal lab study with users who were representative of the target populations for the eSOA API. Since we were told by SAP that the target API was designed for developers with a wide range of expertise and background, we selected some experienced programmers with little business background, and some experienced business EUDs with little programming background, and some in between. We had 8 participants, all of whom were male Masters students at our university, although all but one of them had work experience before returning to school (see Table 1). The age ranged from about 25 to 35. None of the participants had ever seen the specific documentation web site we were testing, and none had used the API that the documentation was for. Of the 8 participants, 4 had significant experience with business application development using business software such as SAP, PeopleSoft and Oracle. All four of these participants had experience with Enterprise Resource Planning (ERP), which is one of the major areas of business software. Participant p2 had the most business application experience, having used the SAP development environment and SAP's programming language called ABAP. The other 4 participants had no experience with business applications. Three of the participants had moderate to extensive programming experience with Java (4 years or more), and the others had some experience. All of the participants except p2 were enrolled in a Web Services course, but our study was performed before they had gotten very far along. This means that the participants all had an interest in SOA and had been introduced to some of the terms. Thus, we feel that subject p5 could be representative of new hires who might be assigned to do SOA work, p6-p8 might be representative of system integrators, p2 represents an all-around expert, and p1, p3 and p4 be representative of Solution Architects who have moderate knowledge of both business and programming. The experiment lasted about two hours, and the participants were each paid $20.

Table 1. Characteristics of the participants in the user study, and whether the search feature was available when they performed the study

	p1	p2	p3	p4	p5	p6	p7	p8
Years of Work Experience	3	3	3	1	0	2	1	2.5
Business Application Experience	yes	YES	yes	yes	no	no	no	no
Years Programming Experience	2	3	3	4	2	5	4	2.5
Were able to use Search				yes				yes

3.2 Tasks

The tasks for this study were to find the specific services necessary to perform a "Create Sales Order" using the documentation. The participants did not use any programming tools such as an Interactive Development Environment (IDE) and did not have to produce any code. They were shown the introductory page of the documentation web site and were given a brief tutorial (about 10 minutes) describing the document layout including the various ways to navigate away from the front page. We told participants that they should consider themselves to be high-level architects in a company that was planning to implement a new sales order system using an existing ERP system. They should find the services needed to create a sales order, starting from the string names of a buying company, a selling company, and a product. They did not need to actually implement an application; they only needed to identify the correct services so that another developer could later implement the system. They were given about 2 hours to finish all tasks.

One challenging part of this task was that when participants read the "Create Sales Order" service documentation, they would discover that this service does not take string names for the seller, product and buyer, but instead takes IDs, which the participants had to find other service calls to look up. Therefore, successful task completion required finding four services we refer to here as "Create Sales Order", "Find Customer", "Find Supplier", and "Find Product" (although the actual names were much longer and less clear). Participants were not told in advance about the need for multiple inter-related services. Discovering that inter-related services were necessary from the documentation was an essential part of the task.

During the study, we used the "think-aloud" protocol, in which participants are encouraged to talk to themselves and the moderator, because we were interested in gaining insights as to what participants were thinking while performing the task. In order to be able to gain as much useful information from each participant as possible, after seeing enough confusion to confirm that the participant was experiencing a usability breakdown, we would offer help so the participant would not remain stuck on one problem for the entire session. We wanted to know why problems occurred, not the length of delays. However, explicit help was relatively rare because it was difficult to give advice without giving away the whole solution.

3.3   Context – SOA Documentation

The participants used the actual then-released (February, 2008) online documentation of SAP's eSOA product. Based in part on the results of our study, SAP has since improved the site significantly, and many parts now no longer match what the participants saw, which is described below.

There are several different paths that participants could use to navigate from the starting page down to the pages of individual service operations (see Fig. 1). One path grouped services into Enterprise Service (ES) "Bundles" that collected together a set of services that are often used together. The ES Bundles navigation path was implemented using a user-editable Wiki, so that users of the documentation could add and update the bundles to show what services were actually used together in practice. Since this navigation path led to a Wiki, the visual formatting of these pages was quite different from other parts of the documentation web site. The bundles contained a list of service operations, and from there, users could eventually navigate down to the individual services, at which point they would leave the Wiki and return to the previous "normal" format.

A second path used the Enterprise Service Index, which listed business "process components" in alphabetical order. The Process Component pages each contained a

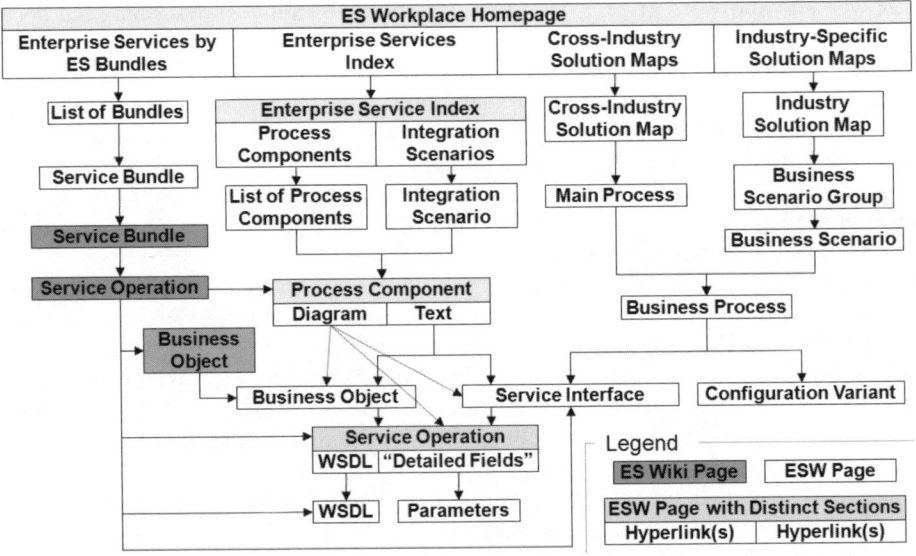

Fig. 1. Different possible navigation paths

Table 2. Descriptions of webpage content for pages shown in Figure 1

Documentation	Content
Solution Map	Business value chains displayed as colorful diagrams. Colored bars hyperlink to processes and scenarios. May apply across industries (ERP, CRM, etc.) or for one industry. (Oil, Retail, etc.) (Fig. 2)
Scenario Group	Similar to a Solution Map, but specific to a part of one industry.
Main or Business Process, Scenario	Text description of a business process or scenario. Hyperlinks lead further down, but often do not link to Service Interfaces.
Configuration Variant	Text description of business use cases that may not be intended for developers, but rather business analysts. Hyperlinks go only to other Configuration Variants, and upwards.
Process Component	This page contained both a diagram and text. The diagram linked to a group of Business Objects, and all Service Interfaces and Service Operations using those Business Objects. Text links below the diagram went to the Objects and Interfaces only. (Fig. 3a)
Service Interface	Text hyperlinks to some Service Operations sharing a Business Object, which may have one or more Service Interfaces.
Service Operation	Description of a service operation. Hyperlinks to the service WSDL and parameters. (Fig. 3b)
Business Object	Description of a distinct business "entity" (such as a sales order, supplier, etc.) with links to Service Operations acting upon it.
WSDL	XML file that describes the service in machine-readable form.

process component diagram and a textual description of the process component (see Fig. 3a). From the process component diagram, participants could then navigate to the relevant business objects and service interfaces. Participants could navigate using hyperlinks located in the process component diagram or in a table below the diagram listing the contents of the process component as text.

The third and fourth paths used two different kinds of graphical tables called "Solution Maps." The cross industry solution maps (see Fig. 2) provided categories such as ERP (Enterprise Resource Planning), CRM (Customer Relation Management), SCM (Supply Chain Management), and then at the next level, groups of services such as "analytics," "financials," and "sales and service.". The industry solution maps provided categories like "Retail," "Airlines," or "Oil & Gas", and then groups of services such as "Sales & Marketing" and "Vehicle Maintenance". As shown in Fig. 1, all of the links in the Solution Maps lead to "Business Process" pages. Unfortunately, some of these Business Process pages linked only to Configuration Variants, and not to the Service Interfaces that link to Service Operations pages and the technical information necessary for implementation. The Configuration Variant pages were dead ends and apparently not intended for use by developers. Instead they linked to other variants or back to Business Processes, so this path proved useless to our participants.

Once participants had navigated down to the "service operation" page (Fig. 3b), they could find out information about the specific service, including the WSDL files to download. On each of the service operation pages, there was a hyperlink to a separate "Detailed Field" page with collapsible tree hierarchies of the input and output parameters for calling the service. Since the web services can be accessed from a variety of programming languages, coding examples were not provided in the API

documentation. Instead, a browser-based service "testing jig" was available. By showing all available fields of the complex input and output parameter structures of the
web services in a tree view, this testing jig allowed users to test service consumption
with real values. However, at the time, the only link to the testing jig was provided
inside a "Handbook" PDF guide hyperlinked from the main starting page of the
documentation. This guide provided an end-to-end walkthrough of the documentation
site and screenshots of pages along the navigational paths.

When we began this study, the web site had a search box, but it appeared to be in-
operable, in that all searches returned no results. By the time we ran the last two subjects (p5, p8 – see Table 1), the search seemed to be fixed and began working.[1]

In summary, the documentation provided several architectural description pages to
help understanding of the overall architecture. Table 2 shows some of the different
architectural description pages, and their content.

4 Results

Table 3 shows a summary of the overall results – only two of the 8 participants (25%)
were able to find all of the services during the two-hour session. Three of the four
participants with business backgrounds (75%) were able to find the correct first service ("create sales order"), however one was not sure that he had found the right one.
Similarly, two of the participants without business backgrounds found the right sales
order service, but were not sure, and none found any of the other services. Since there
are such a small number of participants, we are not able to establish statistical signifi-
cance between the two groups, although the trend is striking. From our observations
and the think-aloud comments of the participants, we were able to understand the
participants' strategies and barriers at a much more detailed level.

4.1 Paths through the Documentation

Given the four starting entry points for navigating from a home page (Fig. 1), participants were confused with which one to use, and spent significant time reading text on
the home page to try to figure it out. The main page did not explain the motivations
and goals of the four different paths, leaving participants confused about why there
were multiple choices and which might be the most useful. This confusion made participants feel frustrated right at the beginning. Table 3 summarizes where the participants started.

An interesting observation was the use of what we call *rally points* by participants
while navigating through unfamiliar areas (see Table 3). Participants would choose a
path, go down that path until they decided whether or not it was worth continuing, and
then return to an earlier page multiple times. Participant's selection of a rally point
indicated a level of certainty that the navigation up to that point, at least, was correct.

Fig. 4 summarizes the paths of all of participants when trying to find the Create
Sales Order Service. Each row represents a type of web page, as described in Table 2.
Each circle represents web pages that the participant visited, with the size of the circle

---

[1] A hazard of using a commercial on-line system for a study – one cannot guarantee all participants will have the identical system!

representing how long the participant stayed at that page. In Table 3 and Fig. 4, we can see that the page at which the participant started was a natural rallying point at first, but participants would move the rally point around as they gained and lost confidence in the usefulness of various paths through the documentation.

Most participants showed a tendency to choose the Solution Maps as a starting point (as shown in Table 3), but five of the participants changed to the Enterprise Service Index after failing to use the solution maps. The Enterprise Service Index page only provided process component lists and integration scenario lists in alphabetical order. In the process component lists, there were prominent business software categories such as CRM, ERP, SCM and SRM. Participants with business application backgrounds used the "Enterprise Service Index" pages as a rally point, and when they found the "Sales Order Processing" component in the ERP and SRM category, they felt they were on the right track. Most participants were frustrated by new and unfamiliar terms and acronyms, but participants without business application backgrounds were particularly confused by the large number of prominent acronyms such as ERP, CRM, SCM, SRM and other business-specific terms that they did not understand.

When participants navigated to the Enterprise Service Bundles page (which was a Wiki), they were surprised by the different look and feel of this part of the web site, and felt they must have gone astray, so they quickly back-tracked. None of the participants made use of the Bundles pages, so they do not appear in Fig. 4.

Participants spent a lot of time trying to use the solution maps (Fig. 2). Some participants selected cross industry solution map, possibly because they were not told about any specific industry in the task instructions, but others guessed an industry they thought might be appropriate, and used an industry-specific map. However, the

Fig. 2. Cross industry solution map for ERP

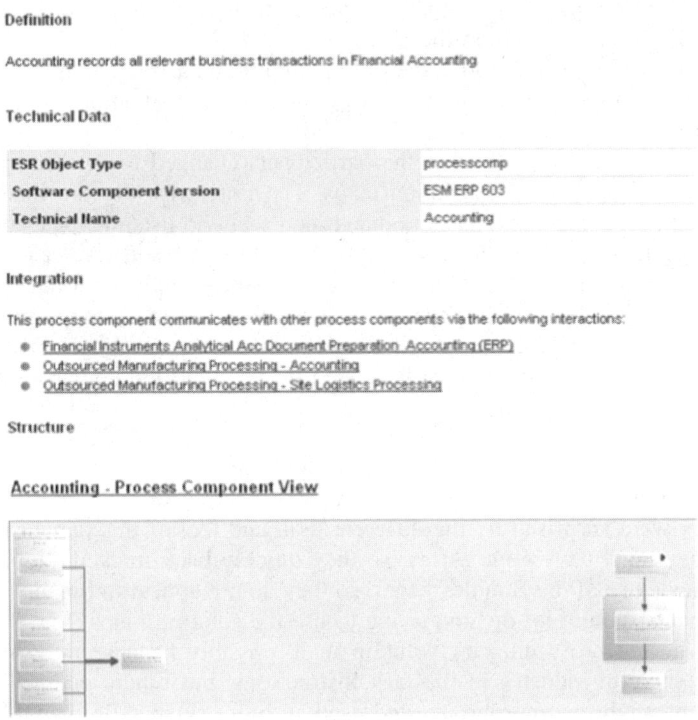
Definition
Accounting records all relevant business transactions in Financial Accounting
Technical Data
ESR Object Type
processcomp
Software Component Version
ESM ERP 603
Technical Name
Accounting
Integration
This process component communicates with other process components via the following interactions:
Financial Instruments Analytical Acc Document Preparation_Accounting (ERP)
Outsourced Manufacturing Processing - Accounting
Outsourced Manufacturing Processing - Site Logistics Processing
Structure
Accounting - Process Component View

(a)

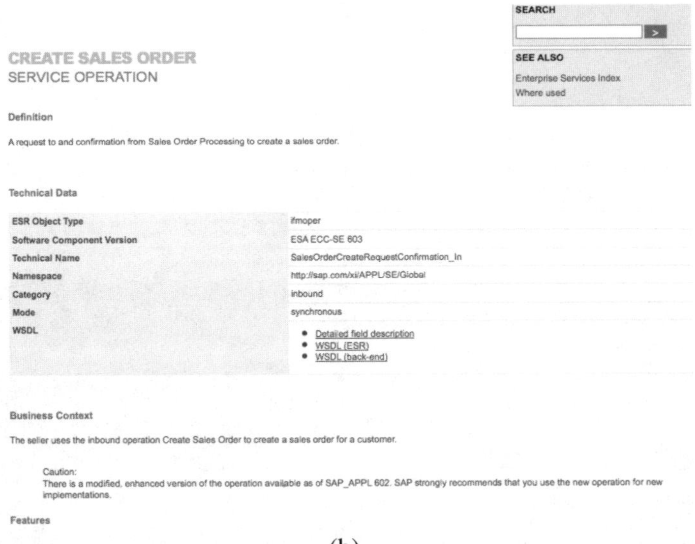
SEARCH
SEE ALSO
Enterprise Services Index
Where used
CREATE SALES ORDER
SERVICE OPERATION
Definition
A request to and confirmation from Sales Order Processing to create a sales order.
Technical Data
ESR Object Type
ifmoper
Software Component Version
ESA ECC-SE 603
Technical Name
SalesOrderCreateRequestConfirmation_In
Namespace
http://sap.com/xi/APPL/SE/Global
Category
inbound
Mode
synchronous
WSDL
Detailed field description
WSDL (ESR)
WSDL (back-end)
Business Context
The seller uses the inbound operation Create Sales Order to create a sales order for a customer.
Caution:
There is a modified, enhanced version of the operation available as of SAP_APPL 602. SAP strongly recommends that you use the new operation for new implementations.
Features

(b)

Fig. 3. (a) Process Component View Page for the Accounting process component which includes a diagram and text below the diagram (not shown). (b) Service Operation page for Create Sales Order.

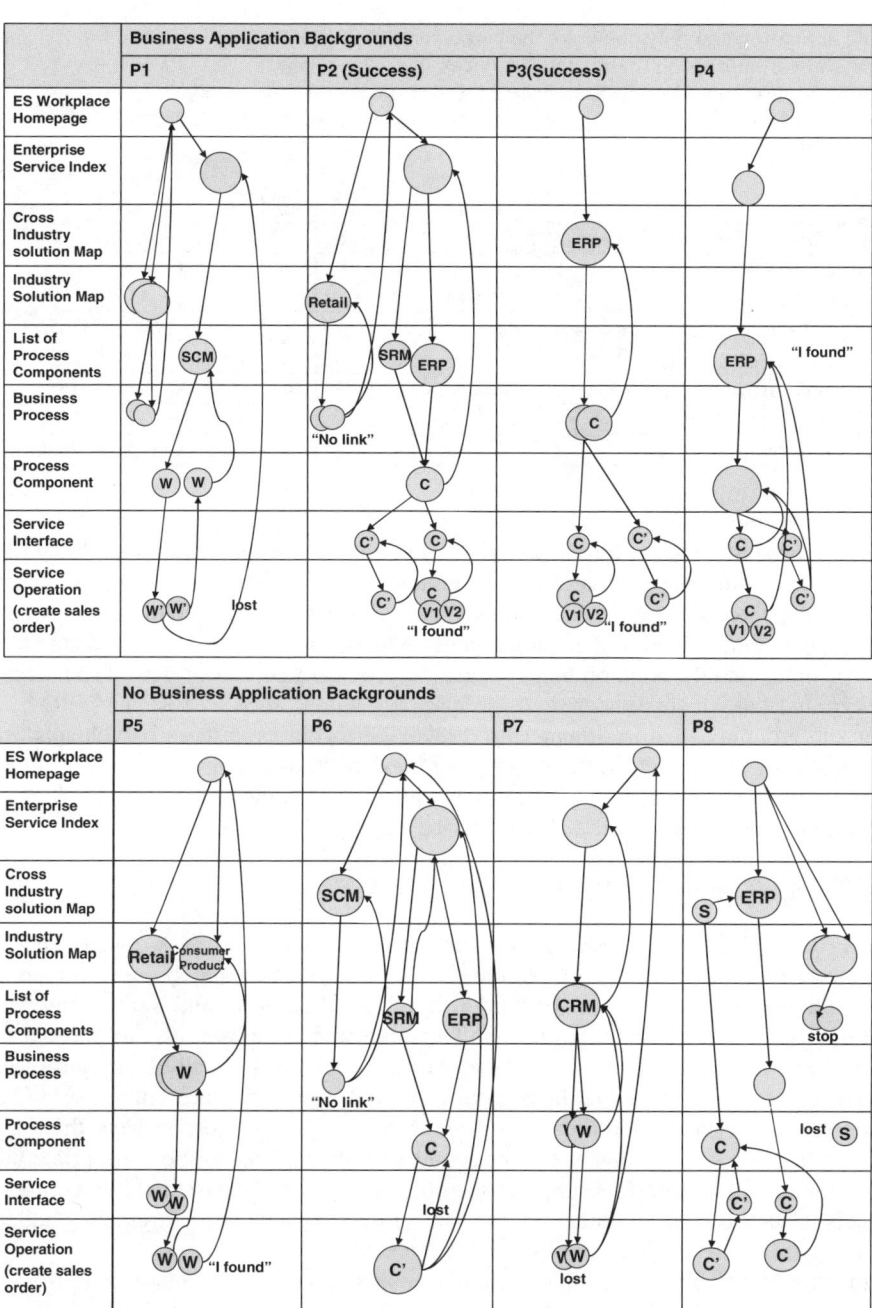

Fig. 4. Summaries of the navigational paths of all of the participants when trying to find the Create Sales Order service. The sizes of the circles represent the amount of time spent at web pages of the type in the first column.

Table 3. Starting and rally points for the participants (using page categories from Fig. 1), and success of participants on finding the 4 services.

Key: **M**=Solution **M**ap; **S**=**S**earch; **I**= **E**S **I**ndex, **P**=**P**rocess Component,
        L=**L**ist of Process Components, **B**=**B**usiness Process
        √=Success; √- =Success but not sure; **X**=Failure

	p1	p2	p3	p4	p5	p6	p7	p8	Total
Was able to use Search				yes				yes	
First Entry Point	M	M	M	I	M	M	I	S	
Other Rally Points	I,P	I,P	B	L,P	M,B	I,P	L,P	M,P	
Found Correct Service Operation:									
Create Sales Order	X	√	√	√-	X	√-	X	√-	62.5%
Find Customer Service	X	√	√	X	X	X	X	X	25%
Find Supplier Service	X	√	√	X	X	X	X	X	25%
Find Product Service	X	√	√	X	X	X	X	X	25%

participants without business backgrounds had difficulties in using the any of these solution maps to navigate further due to the unfamiliar terminology and the large number of choices making a brute-force systematic search difficult. However, half of the participants without business backgrounds used a map page as a rallying point (see Fig. 4). In the think-alouds, the participants expressed a desire to understand the "big picture," and the solution maps seemed to provide a good overview. The business-background participants understood the category names such as ERP and SRM, and their sub-grouping such as "financials," "retail," etc., but even these participants often only had experience with some of the categories and sub-groupings. However, all participants were confused by classifications with similar names such as: "sales", "sales execution", "sales order" and "sales & service" in the solution maps.

4.2 Process Component View

The Process Component view shows one or more related business objects and services (see Fig. 3a). For example, in the "Sales Order Processing" process component view, the user can navigate to the "ordering in" and "ordering out" service interfaces and the "sales order" business objects. The page was composed of two parts: a diagram, and a table. The diagram displayed business objects as small blocks and service interfaces as large blocks that held groups of smaller blocks representing service operations. The service operations were connected to the business objects they acted upon with arrows. The titles of the blocks acted as hyperlinks to the appropriate business object, service interface, and service operation pages. Due to the large number of objects to be shown in the diagram, the font of the elements was extremely small and yet horizontal and vertical scrolling was still needed.

In spite of these barriers, some participants spent an extensive amount of effort trying to understand the diagrams. Many of the participants found this view to be a good rallying point, since it provides a well-organized collection of related items to explore. However, some of the participants who were familiar with UML (Unified Modeling Language) notation mentioned that they would have preferred UML class diagrams, which have a standard notation for classes and their relationships.

Another cause for confusion was that the system provided many similar-sounding services in the process component view, and even multiple versions of the same service with similar names such as "create sales order v1", "create sales order v2", and "check sales order creation". Participants could not find any relevant information to differentiate those three different versions of services from the process component view. The participants had to drill down to the service operation level for each, to try to determine which should be used. If the user could recognize the differences among these different services at the process component view, this would have saved significant time and confusion.

Beneath the diagram, a table contained text descriptions and hyperlinks to many of the same locations as the diagram, with the exception of the service operations.

4.3 Service Descriptions

In the tasks we gave the participants, it was important to investigate the input and outputs of the various services. However, this was difficult to verify from the detailed service pages. Only three participants were able to find the "buyerID", "sellerID" and "materialID" parameters for the "Create Sales Order" service operation, which was crucial to determining what other services were needed.

Other problems with understanding the services included unfamiliar technical terms such as synchronous and asynchronous mode and inbound and outbound messages. The participants did not find any explanations of these terms in the documentation, although they are pervasive throughout all services. Some of the details of the operation, such as which fields were required versus optional, were actually not documented anywhere except in the generated WSDL XML files themselves, which was too long and difficult to read to be effective documentation.

The detailed page for each service listed three classes of messages: input message, output message and fault message, which participants did not understand. In fact, only input messages are relevant (messages that go "in" to the server), but this was not explained anywhere.

In general, many participants found the correct target service, but then were unsure whether it was correct or not, and continued searching. For example, Table 3 and Fig. 4 show that participants p4, p6 and p8 found the right service operation for Sales Order, but then navigated away and kept looking. Participant p4 eventually decided that a *different* service was actually right, and p6 and p8 were never confident of which service should be used.

4.4 Using Search

As mentioned above, the search box was present for all participants, but only began working for the last two (Table 1). All of the participants expressed a desire to use search to try to find the services. In general, if the participants knew the name of what they wanted, they preferred to use search, and the participants for whom search worked often returned to try searching when they were lost. Participants often tried to search for phrases we used in the instructions, such as "create sales order", "selling company", "buying company" and "product", but these were not helpful, and then participants tried related terminology such as "agency", "supplier", "customer," etc.

In general, participants were not successful at using search because there were always either no results or too many matching results. Even the most experienced participants had difficulty mapping the product in the instructions with the actual parameter name of "material".

When search began working, the results were presented grouped by the various API documentation types shown in Table 2, such as solution map pages, process component view pages, and service operation pages. This grouping proved helpful to participants, and made it easy to find the appropriate process components and business objects when they recognized them in the results. However, since there were often too many search results, and the listing was in alphabetical order, often participants missed the answer even when it was included.

4.5 Individual Strategies

By performing a detailed time analysis of each participant, we were able to break down their activities into various categories. We identified four categories of activities, with two opposing strategies in each:

- Focusing on scanning textual descriptions ("scan text") vs. focusing on scanning process diagrams ("scan diagrams").
- Trying to understand how to use the web site by reading the provided PDF documentation ("PDF overview"), or just by looking through the web site itself, relying on the documentation to be self-explanatory ("Self-explanatory"). Five participants found the PDF document but three of them did not use it, because it was a separate document.
- Browsing the documentation with a single specific key word in mind from the task instructions, such as "buyer" ("Single word"), or else using a set of interrelated synonyms ("Synonyms").
- Skimming the documentation focusing on only the prominent text, such as the headers ("Skim"), or systematically reading the pages line-by-line ("Line-by-line").

We then analyzed each of the participants, looking for whether they tried to use each of these strategies, and whether it worked for them. Note that each participant might have used different strategies at different times. Fig. 5 provides a radar chart averaged over all participants for the strategies. The opposing strategies are shown at opposite ends of each line. The outer black line (connecting the circles) shows the average of whether this was used or not (where 1 would mean everyone used it, and 0 would mean no-one used it). The inner red line (connecting the squares) shows our estimate of how successful this strategy was.

Fig. 5 makes it clear that participants were split on using text and diagrams, they strongly preferred the documentation to be self-explanatory, rather than using the PDF overview, more tried single words rather than synonyms, and everyone skimmed, but only a few systematically read line-by-line. As for the success of these strategies, by-and-large, the success seemed to mostly correlated with participants' expectations (they used a strategy about as much as it was successful, so the two lines go in and out together), with the notable exception of the diagrams – as discussed above, many participants wanted to use these, but they did not work out for them. Another notable result is that the PDF overview was surprisingly un-helpful.

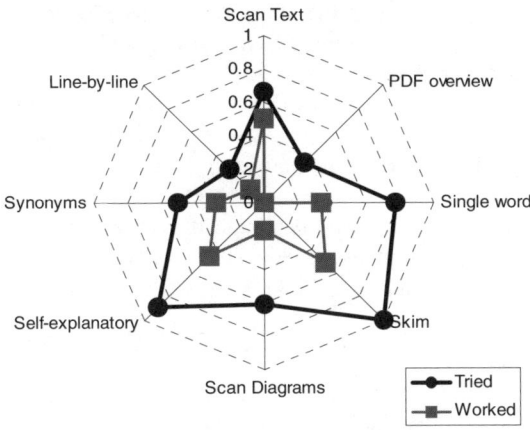

Fig. 5. Strategies the participants tried, and how well each strategy worked

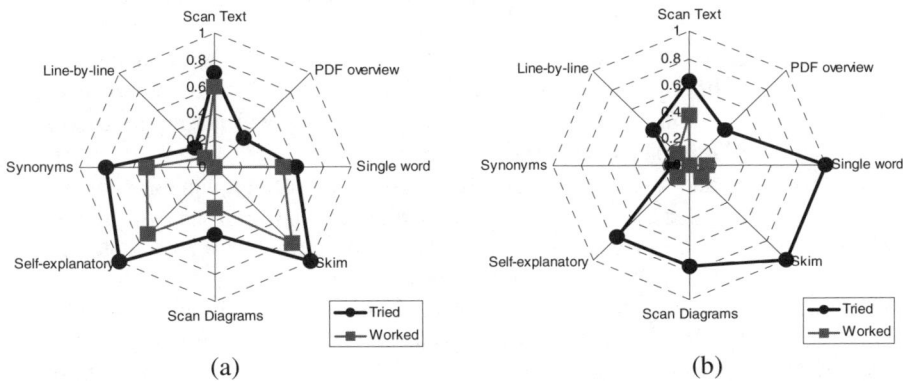

(a)   (b)

Fig. 6. Breakdown for participants with (a) and without (b) business backgrounds

Fig. 6 provides the same data broken down by whether the participants had business background or not. In terms of what they tried, it is clear that the non-business participants did not use synonyms (because they did not know the other terms that might be related), and the non-business participants were more systematic, trying to extract more meaning from the pages (whereas the business participants were more likely to be able to pick up the meaning from skimming). It is clear that few strategies worked for the participants without business backgrounds, and only scanning the text was overall successful.

5   Threats to Validity

There are many reasons why the results of this study may not generalize. First, we only used a small number of participants, and we were not able to get statistically significant results about their different behaviors. Most of the results reported here are impressions and informal analyses based on our observations of their behaviors, barriers and successes. The participants are also not necessarily representative of the target population for the documentation. eSOA APIs may be used only by people with some business background or people who have specific, relevant training. For example, SAP offers various training courses that would have explained many of the fundamental terms about which the participants were confused. Our participants were all completely unfamiliar with the documentation or the API.

The experimental set-up may have also biased the results. In real-life, users would have more than two hours to perform tasks, and they would likely go to more experienced colleagues for help when they were stuck, which was not an option in this study. Also, our task was much simpler than real-world eSOA tasks.

6 Discussion

In spite of these concerns, we feel that useful information can be learned from our study. As with other usability analyses [12], when multiple user-study participants have difficulty with something, it is highly likely that at least some of the target audience will also have trouble, so the documentation is likely to be improved by eliminating the barriers reported here.

The differences in strategies and success between the people with business experience and those without are also interesting. These can mainly be attributed to the differences in their ability to understand the many terms and acronyms used in the documentation. Participants with business backgrounds were aware of interrelated business concepts and terminology, and so understood more explanations on the web site. The navigational strategies were also very different between the two groups.

Of the four ways to navigate to the service operation, the ES index was found to be most useful to many developers, who then used the process component diagrams as a rally point. The graphical solution maps were frequently used by all participants, but tended to lead developers to the wrong services. The frequent use of the maps and process diagrams strongly suggests that a good diagram of the system is important to users. The presence of the many alternative navigation paths was itself a barrier to participants, since they had to investigate which one to use.

This study particularly focused on identifying services based on their input/output characteristics, but this turned out to be surprisingly difficult to determine from the documentation. Our previous study showed that understanding the dependencies among the parameters is also a key barrier to developers [1], since which parameters are required and which are optional depends on the values supplied for other parameters. This means that more attention is needed on documenting the parameters of services, where it is possible[2].

A consistent look and feel for the documentation was found to be important. When participants encountered the different format of the Wiki, they immediately

---

[2] Some services deal with highly customizable business processes. Customer can set up the system for their special business needs and therefore the behavior of the services can change from customer to customer. So a "create sales order" service can be used in a simple retail scenario, where you just buy 100 pencils, as well as in the aerospace industry when you order 20 Airbus A380 airplanes, which have quite different requirements.

backtracked without studying the new location. As a result, the grouped services on the wiki went unseen and unused by all of the participants.

The names of services and their types were found to be a problem. We observed one participant confused with several versions of "create sales order v1" and "v2", the differences between the same service name with "in" and "out" appended, and also with the difference between the "synchronous" and "asynchronous" versions of the same service. Another problem was the length and construction of the names themselves, which some participants found confusing (for example, SalesOrderERPCreateRequestConfirmation_In_V1).

7   Implications for Design

How can the documentation be designed to best serve developers across the whole spectrum? Improvements in the usability of the documentation are clearly necessary if users such as our participants are to succeed. We are happy to report that many of these recommendations have been implemented in the current version of the SAP documentation, and others are being investigated for future versions.

Based on our observations and user study results, we recommend the following as documentation guidelines:

- **Consistent Look-and-Feel.** Overall, the entire documentation web site should have a consistent, yet unique, format, so that developers who leave the path know it instantly, and developers who find a useful area do not backtrack. This may mean that more developer participation in a Wiki might occur if its format is not visibly different from the rest of the API documentation.
- **Provide an Overall Map.** When we were trying to understand the SAP documentation ourselves before we ran the user study, we created early versions of Fig. 1 and Table 2, which we found very helpful. Having such information at the front of the documentation web site would likely benefit users.
- **Explain Starting Points.** Make the purpose of various starting points clear. It seems that some of the paths on the eSOA documentation may be targeted at different classes of users, such as Business Experts versus developers. Alternatively, they might be used for different tasks. Users would benefit from a better explanation of *why* there are multiple paths, and how they are intended to be used.
- **Provide "bread crumbs" the documentation structure.** Users were often lost in the documentation. Providing a trail that shows where they are in the documentation structure, and what are the main nodes along the path to that page, would be helpful. However, the documentation is a graph and not a tree because some paths are in multiple paths (e.g., the same service may be used by multiple industries). This means that the trail will have to be careful to differentiate multiple possible paths to the current page, hopefully highlighting the path actually used.
- **Directly support rally points.** In addition to the bread crumbs, there should be other support for users to backtrack to well-known pages that are serving as "rally points". For example, we created a prototype which included an always-visible bookmark list into which the user could easily save pages while continuing navigation, and then these could serve as shortcuts for navigating back to a rally point. Another idea is to provide pages that *other* users or the system designers have identified as useful rally points.

- **Integrate "How-To-Use" Information.** We discovered that although a PDF guide explained how the documentation could be used, users were reluctant to leave their browsing to read a document in an external format, so the explanations should be in html format. Even better would be if the documentation was self-explanatory, with explanations integrated with the main documentation content, so there would be no need for separate documents explaining how to the API documentation. For example, pop-ups or special hyperlinks might explain "What is this?" for items that users may not be familiar with.

- **Effective Search.** The participants for whom search did not work were unhappy, so a good search facility needs to be part of all documentation. Since participants tried to search on all aspects of services, all parts of the API should be included in the search, including the parameter names and types, and the documentation of the names and types. It should be easy to navigate from data types to the fields that use those types. In order to reduce the size of the answers, the search should allow users to qualify what they are looking for (e.g., limit the answers to service operations). The grouping of the search results into categories is a good idea, but each result should be presented in a way that is easy to understand, so the user does not need to navigate into each result item to see if it is the desired one or not.

- **Provide Familiar Diagram Formats.** Our participants expected UML Class diagrams or other well-known architectural presentations to help them understand the services. Users should be surveyed on what formats they will find familiar before the decision is made to create new formats.

- **Balance of Diagrams and Text.** Some participants focused on diagrams showing the relationships among services, so these need to be clear and concise, with appropriate labels that are understandable yet not too big. At the same time, other users skipped the diagrams in favor of text, so both should be supported.

- **Curtail User Focus on Esoteric Terminology.** Specialized terminology for specialized users and use cases is absolutely necessary in API documentation. However, we observed that participants who are exploring tend to focus on unfamiliar terms, even if they are unnecessary as part of their task, and so waste time while increasing their level of confusion and frustration. However, most users will (at least eventually) be familiar with the terminology, so it is important that any definitions or other help not interfere with expert use. It is also important that users be able to quickly tell what parts of the document are important to them, so they can skip large parts (and any unfamiliar terminology in those parts).

- **Explain Crucial Terminology.** Participants could not find the correct services in our study without understanding the difference between synchronous and asynchronous services, or the meaning of "in" and "out" services. To the extent that all users must understand certain "esoteric" terminology, make sure it is clearly explained, or even better, use more generally-understood terms so less explanation is needed.

- **Make the Parameters for Services More Prominent.** Participants cited the parameters of the service signature as the main indicators of the usefulness of a service. Therefore, parameters should be given a prominent position in the description of a service operation. Our previous research showed that the distinction between optional and required parameters, and parameters used to call the service and those filled in by the service as return values was not clear to developers [1]. This needs to be particularly well explained, and certainly not left to be deduced from the WSDL files.

- **Support Comparing Services.** There are many similar services, and participants needed to compare services to find out the differences. In the current system, sometimes they needed to open up the low-level WSDL files and try to manually determine the differences. Instead, direct comparisons and explanations should be available to differentiate services. For example, side-by-side visualizations of two services might emphasize the differences in parameters or actions. If a service is an updated version of another service, the modification dates and differences should be clear with cross-links and explanations of when each might be used.

- **Clear Names for Services.** The user should be able to recognize what a service does by its name. If there are multiple versions, it should be clear why there are multiple versions, and whether they are all intended to be useful (vs. some being deprecated, for example), and which one should be selected.

- **Present Related Services.** The documentation should present related services and business objects. For example, to create a sales order required providing three different parameters that were returned by other services. Listing each of these parameters and services could help the user understand and find related services. The Bundles idea in the current documentation may help with this goal, but we were not able to evaluate how well it worked because our participants did not try the Bundles.

- **Provide Code Examples.** While web services are often advertised for their ability to be consumed in any programming language, this does not excuse the provider from showing sample code snippets. Even if it is not possible to provide example code in every target language, then it is still useful to provide some examples rather than none. It should be noted that standardization across similar services will mean that fewer examples need to be provided, because a pattern that works for one service will also work for its "sibling" services.

- **Online Service Testing.** Developers who want to see how a service works before starting to program may benefit from an interactive way to provide parameters and run the service. The current SAP documentation does have a "Test" function, where users can try out a service and see what it returns for various parameters. This kind of online service testing can have a positive effect on developers' understanding of web service consumption. It has the potential to display required and optional parameters, and allow users to verify their understanding of the service. However, without valid test data to use as parameters, the user may never be able to get a useful return value. Therefore, the testing mechanism should be combined with multiple examples, and cross-linked to other services that might return the kinds of values required for the service to operate correctly. Furthermore, once the user has configured a test call interactively, it would be useful if there was some way to generate code in the desired target language that would do the same thing.

- **New Organizations for Hierarchical Browsing.** In their think-alouds, we noticed that various participants, especially the ones without business experience, seemed to be trying to navigate based on different starting points and hierarchies. For example, some participants seemed to be trying to find particular operations (verbs) first (such as create or find), then the objects on which those operations occurred (the nouns), and finally, other parameters of the operation (adverbs such "by what" the find should get the object, or "using what" to create the object). The current documentation does allow users to start from a business object and find all of its services, or to get a global list of services, but these are always organized alphabetically. Since the services are named based with the affected business object at the front of the name (e.g., SalesOrderERPCreateRequestConfirmation_In_V1), both lists are essentially noun first. Allowing a sort by operation (sorting all the "create" service operations together) might be helpful.

8 Future Work and Conclusions

This informal study is just the beginning of a long investigation into improvements that can be made to API documentation. We are currently working on interesting new designs to see how we can make documentation even easier to search and browse, and how to make the important information more salient (e.g., [16]). For example, more commonly used items in the documentation might use a bigger font, so they stand out compared to the lesser used items.

Meanwhile, SAP is continuing to improve their APIs and the documentation for them. We plan to repeat this study with the new designs to see what problems have been solved, and if there are any new problems introduced. In the new study, it will be interesting to investigate more classes of users, from Business Expert EUDs with little programming experience to experienced programmers, and hopefully get some non-university participants from local businesses. It would also be useful to compare people who are expert users of the system and documentation to the novice users that we focused on in this study. Good documentation should also be efficient for experts, as well as helpful for novices.

In addition to providing insights into how to improve the current documentation, these kinds of studies can provide generalizable knowledge that is useful for all documentation writers for all kinds of systems, since many of the challenges will be similar. Since all programmers, from EUD to novices and to professionals, spend significant time trying to understand and use APIs, improvements to documentation can have significant impacts on the overall usability of the system as a whole.

Acknowledgements

For help with this paper, we thank many people at SAP (especially Paul Hofmann, Dan Rosenberg, Ike Nassi, Claudius Fischer, Bernhard Drittler, and Oliver Schmidt) and the participants for sharing in user study. This research was partially funded by a grant from SAP and partially by NSF under grant ITR-0325273 through the EUSES Consortium, and CCF-0811610. Opinions, findings and conclusions or recommendations expressed in this material are those of the authors and do not necessarily reflect those of the NSF or SAP.

References

1. Beaton, J., et al.: Usability Challenges for Enterprise Service-Oriented Architecture APIs. In: 2008 IEEE Symposium on Visual Languages and Human-Centric Computing, VL/HCC 2008, Herrsching am Ammersee, Germany, September 15-18, pp. 193–196 (2008)

2. Beaton, J., et al.: Usability Evaluation for Enterprise SOA APIs. In: 2nd International Workshop on Systems Development in SOA Environments, SDSOA 2008 (Co-located with ICSE 2008), May 12, pp. 29–34. Leipzig, Germany (2008)
3. Bloch, J.: Effective Java Programming Language Guide. Addison-Wesley, Boston (2001)
4. Clarke, S.: Measuring API Usability. Dr. Dobbs Journal, S6–S9 (May 2004)
5. Cwalina, K., Abrams, B.: Framework Design Guidelines. Addison-Wesley, Upper-Saddle River (2005)
6. Ellis, B., Stylos, J., Myers, B.: The Factory Pattern in API Design: A Usability Evaluation. In: International Conference on Software Engineering (ICSE 2007), May 20-26, Minneapolis, MN, pp. 302–312 (2007)
7. Forward, A., Lethbridge, T.C.: The relevance of software documentation, tools, and technology: a survey. In: DocEng, McLean. pp. 26–33 (2002)
8. Friendly, L.: The design of distributed hyperlinked programming documentation. In: International Workshop on Hypermedia Design, June 1-2, pp. 151–173. Springer, Montpellier (1995)
9. Jones, S.: SOA Anti-Patterns. Jun 19, C4Media Inc.: InfoQ.com (2006), http://www.infoq.com/articles/SOA-anti-patterns
10. Ko, A.J., Myers, B.A., Aung, H.H.: Six Learning Barriers in End-User Programming Systems. In: IEEE Symposium on Visual Languages and Human-Centric Computing, Rome, Italy, September 26-29, pp. 199–206 (2004)
11. Myers, B.: Creating More Natural Programming Languages. In: VL 2000: IEEE Symposium on Visual Languages, Seattle, Washington, September 10-14 (2000) (Invited Keynote Address), http://www.cs.orst.edu/~burnett/vl2000
12. Nielsen, J.: Usability Engineering. Academic Press, Boston (1993)
13. Purho, V.: Heuristic inspections for documentation-10 recommended documentation heuristics. STC Usability SIG Newsletter, 6(4) (April 2000), http://www.stcsig.org/usability/newsletter/0004-docsheuristics.html
14. Stylos, J., et al.: A Case Study of API Design for Improved Usability. In: 2008 IEEE Symposium on Visual Languages and Human-Centric Computing, VL/HCC 2008, Herrsching am Ammersee, Germany, September 15-18, pp. 189–192 (2008)
15. Stylos, J., Clarke, S.: Usability Implications of Requiring Parameters in Objects' Constructors. In: International Conference on Software Engineering (ICSE 2007), Minneapolis, MN, May 20-26, pp. 529–539 (2007)
16. Stylos, J., Myers, B.A., Yang, Z.: Improving API Documentation Using API Usage Information (submitted, 2009)
17. Stylos, J., Myers., B.A.: The Implications of Method Placement on API Learnability. In: Sixteenth ACM SIGSOFT Symposium on Foundations of Software Engineering (FSE 2008), Atlanta, GA, November 9-14, pp. 105–112 (2008)

End-User Development of Enterprise Widgets

Michael Spahn[1] and Volker Wulf[2]

[1] SAP AG, SAP Research, Bleichstr. 8, 64283 Darmstadt, Germany
`Michael.Spahn@sap.com`
[2] University of Siegen, Hölderlinstr. 3, 57076 Siegen, Germany
`Volker.Wulf@uni-siegen.de`

Abstract. Companies are operating in a dynamic environment, resulting in a continuous need of adapting used information systems to changing business processes and associated information needs. Viewed from a micro-perspective, business users are managing and executing business processes on a daily basis, but are not able to adapt used software to their individual needs and working practice. In this paper, we present an End-User Development (EUD) approach and prototypic environment, enabling business users to create enterprise widgets tailored to their personal information needs without the need of programming knowledge, by mashing up enterprise resources using a lightweight visual design paradigm. The approach especially considers extensibility of building blocks for widget creation even by small and medium sized enterprises (SMEs) using existing knowledge. We give evidence on the applicability of the approach in real enterprise contexts, by providing first results of an evaluation in three German SMEs.

Keywords: End-User Development, Mashup, Widget.

1 Introduction

In our today's business world, companies use enterprise software systems like Enterprise Resource Planning (ERP) systems to support and facilitate their business processes. As companies are not static and evolve like the environment of competitors, markets and customers surrounding them, a continuous need of adapting these systems to new requirements, business processes and associated information needs, exists. Due to a lack of resources and expertise, especially small and medium sized enterprises (SMEs) suffer from their inability to adapt used enterprise software to their needs [1]. They are forced to adapt themselves to the possibilities offered by the used enterprise software or to delegate adaptations to IT professionals, resulting in long and costly adaptation processes [2, 3]. As organizational and technological development are closely correlated, the inability of adapting the technical systems used, is limiting the organizational development possibilities of the companies as well [4]. As a consequence, the ability of organizations to optimize their business processes and to innovate to gain unique competitive advantages is limited.

Viewed from a micro-perspective, business users as the end-users of enterprise systems know best about changing requirements and needed adaptations, as they are managing and executing business processes on a daily basis. As end-users are domain

V. Pipek et al. (Eds.): IS-EUD 2009, LNCS 5435, pp. 106–125, 2009.

experts but not necessarily IT professionals, they are not able to adapt the used enterprise systems to their individual needs on their own. End-users are forced to indirectly influence the adaptation processes by communicating their needs to IT professionals. IT professionals are confronted with the requirements of users expressed in their domain language, which have to be interpreted and transformed into models and technical solutions matching the capabilities of the enterprise software systems. This process is not only costly and time-consuming, but also error prone due to a possible misinterpretation of requirements [5]. Furthermore many useful adaptations to the individual working practice of end-users are dropped due to limited budget, resources and expertise. One approach to improve this situation is to better enable end-users to adapt the used enterprise systems on their own. At this, the inherent challenge is to reduce the expertise tension, existing in a two-dimensional continuum of job-related domain knowledge and system related development knowledge [6].

We are approaching this challenge from an End-User Development (EUD) perspective. EUD can be defined as "a set of methods, techniques, and tools that allow users of software systems, who are acting as non-professional software developers, at some point to create or modify a software artifact" [7]. Crucial preconditions of successfully enabling EUD are on one hand systems, which are flexible enough to be adaptable in a technical sense, and on the other hand methods to leverage this flexibility at the hand of end-users [8, 9]. In the last years the dissemination of the Service Oriented Architecture (SOA) [10] paradigm led to an increased technical flexibility. SOAs, i.e. implemented using the widespread Web Services Stack, provide means to increase flexibility by recombining existing functionality of software systems using loose coupling of services, enabling the orchestration of new software solutions from existing functionality. SOAs offer rich possibilities for IT professionals, but as they are based on complex standards like SOAP, WSDL, UDDI, or BPEL, the technical flexibility is not leveraged at the hand of end-users. In this context a new type of web-based applications, known as *mashups*, has been gaining momentum. Novel lightweight design principles are currently about to emerge, allowing to mash up data from different resources into a single integrated tool and thereby creating a new and distinct service, that was not originally provided by either resource used. Popular examples for consumer mashup environments are e.g. Microsoft Popfly [11] or Yahoo! Pipes [12]. Gartner even identified mashups and composite applications as one of the top ten strategic technologies for 2008 [13].

We conducted preliminary studies in SMEs and identified several kinds of data-centric adaptation problems that end-users face in their work context [14]. We believe, that some of these adaptation problems can be adequately addressed by providing EUD tools based on a mashup design paradigm. Business users should be enabled to create data-centric tools that are tailored to their individual information needs, by mashing up enterprise resources. To further investigate that solution approach, we set up a prototypic EUD design environment for the creation of *widgets*, which can be mashed up of enterprise resources in a very lightweight way. Widgets are small, interactive applications for displaying data, packaged in a way to be executable on a users' machine [15]. By using a very lightweight mashup design paradigm and encapsulating mashups as widgets, we enable end-users to develop small, interactive applications using enterprise resources and to deploy these applications directly to their machine, without the need of any programming knowledge. Our approach especially considers extensibility of building blocks for widget creation even by SMEs using existing knowledge. Thereby the whole chain of developing building blocks and composing building blocks to widgets can be put in the hands of SMEs. To be able to evaluate the usefulness and practicability of our solution approach in real work environments, we deployed our solution to three German SMEs. We investigated if business users are able to create widgets using the lightweight design approach, and if practical problems can be addressed using such simple applications like widgets. Furthermore we classified types of end-users and analyzed how they collaborate to create solutions of practical value.

The remainder of the paper is organized as follows. In Section 2 we present the conducted preliminary empirical studies and explain our research and solution approach. In Section 3 we describe the developed EUD environment for widget creation with regard to conceptual layers, architectural components, user interface and design paradigm. First results of the evaluation phase are discussed in Section 4, before we summarize and conclude our paper in Section 5.

2   Research Approach and Preliminary Studies

An important aim of our research is to create EUD approaches and tools, which are applicable in real enterprise environments. This intent is considered by the setup of our research approach. The work presented in this paper is based on a research approach consisting of three steps, which can be characterized as follows: (i) Conducting empirical research to identify end-user adaptation problems relevant in real enterprise environments. (ii) Developing a solution approach to address identified adaptation problems. (iii) Evaluate the solution approach in real work contexts to determine its applicability for the intended purpose. In the following subsections we discuss each of the steps briefly.

2.1   Preliminary Empirical Studies

In preparation of designing EUD tools, we conducted a series of semi-structured interviews based on qualitative research methods [16] in three German midsized companies that use ERP systems to support their business processes. The addressed companies were two companies from production industry (137 and 140 employees) and one larger software vendor (500 employees). Semi-structured face-to-face interviews were conducted in an exploratory way to get a deep insight into operational tasks and work practices. The interviews focused on data-centric aspects of how end-users access information stored in the ERP system, how they flexibly process the data, and what problems they face, especially with regard to EUD related activities. With regard to EUD related activities our studies revealed, that it is common for business users to create individual information artifacts supporting them in their operative tasks. The most important information artifacts that end-users create are spreadsheets, tailored to the end-users' individual information needs. End-users commonly use predefined queries of the ERP system to import enterprise data into spreadsheets. Due to the complexity of the data model exposed by the ERP system and the complexity of the tools for query creation provided by the ERP system, most end-users are not able to create custom queries on their own to import data from the ERP system as desired.

Additionally, end-users are not able to create any kind of custom information artifact providing interaction on live data of the ERP system. Many end-users have to access a certain set of data relevant for their individual working tasks from the ERP system many times a day. In many cases, this data can not be accessed from a single location within the graphical user interface (GUI) of the ERP systems, forcing users to access multiple locations and cumbersomely collect the needed data. As they are not able to create any kind of customized GUI or interactive application, providing access to relevant data at a glance, many working tasks can only be executed in an inefficient and cumbersome manner.

Complementary to the interview studies, a participatory design workshop (PDW) was held to investigate how typical business users manage to design a software artifact using a very lightweight box and wires design paradigm. A PDW puts users in the role of designers and requires them to collaborate actively in a solution-oriented design process [17]. In the PDW business users had to design an information artifact representing a tool that should support users in an analytic task, which was taken from their work context. To create the solution, the users could add boxes to the design space that represent data or functionality. Boxes had output ports and input ports and could be connected by drawing lines to define data or control flow between the boxes. The boxes and wires model was left underspecified in a way that no concrete instructions were given to the users on how to formally specify the meaning of the used design elements. The underspecified semantics enabled to observe how users intuitively use design elements. As the participatory design workshop revealed, end-users intuitively thought of boxes as a representation of tabular data, organizing data in rows and columns. By connecting boxes, business users related data from different boxes with each other and defined the data flow of the solution. The users had no problems using the boxes and wires design paradigm itself to specify a solution, but had problems to express what data a box should represent. The users decided to specify the data by giving a short description on how they would access the data in their used ERP system. More details on the results of our preliminary empirical studies are given in [14].

2.2 Creating a Solution Approach

In our preliminary studies we identified two main problems that end-users face with regard to data-centric EUD activities. First, end-users create custom spreadsheets and rely on getting relevant business data from the ERP system by using queries, but face considerable challenges when trying to create custom queries for their individual information needs. Second, end-users need to access the same set of data within the GUI of the ERP system over and over again in a cumbersome manner, and are not able to create custom interactive applications that provide the information relevant for individual working tasks at a glance. We developed prototypic EUD environments addressing both problems identified. With regard to EUD of queries for complex enterprise information systems, we developed a prototype called "Semantic Query Designer" (SQD), which is build on an ontology-based middleware and provides sophisticated visualization, navigation, search and query building possibilities. As we are focusing on the second identified problem in this paper, we refer to [18], providing a detailed description of SQD.

With regard to EUD of custom, interactive applications providing access to data relevant for individual working tasks, we set up the prototypic EUD environment

"Widget Composition Platform" (WCP). The WCP enables business users to create custom widgets without any programming knowledge by mashing up enterprise resources in a visual design environment and deploying the created widgets to their machines. The WCP uses a very lightweight mashup design paradigm based on a simple box and wires framework. Boxes represent services that provide enterprise data that is in most cases rendered as a table. As our preliminary studies revealed, business users are able to learn simple design paradigms like boxes and wires in quite a short time and are able to use services providing data in a tabular format in an intuitive way for designing software artifacts.

For the realization of a visual mashup design environment, we could build on an early internal prototype of SAP Research that we modified and extended to suit our needs. Although we could build on a certain framework, we faced considerable challenges with regard to realizing a solution that could be deployed and used within SMEs for two main reasons. First, SMEs often use ERP systems that are not (yet) service-enabled and thus cannot provide enterprise resources as services that are accessible using standard web protocols, which is a an essential precondition for deploying developed mashups as a widget on common widget runtimes. Second, even if enterprise systems were exposing a fixed set of resources as services, this set could not be extended without programming skills and thus would limit the creatable solutions to combinations of predefined services. To address these challenges, we implemented a middleware which is able to wrap resources from not service-enabled ERP systems and provide these as services in a way accessible using standard web protocols. To enable SMEs to extend the provided services without any programming skills, new services must be creatable by SMEs using existing knowledge. As at least some advanced end-users in SMEs exist, that are able to create queries within the ERP system, we enabled the implemented middleware to wrap queries stored within the ERP system and expose these as services. Using the existing skills of query creation to enable the creation of new building blocks for widget creation, limits the entry barriers to flexibly use the new technology and can be seen as a kind of gentle slope of complexity approach [8, 19] that puts the whole chain of widget creation in the hand of SMEs. Additionally, by enabling the use of queries as services, a relation between the prototypes SQD and WCP is established, as end-users are able to use SQD for easy query creation, and WCP to mash up these queries to widgets. The conceptual layers, architectural components, and GUI of the WCP are described in detail in section 3.

2.3 Evaluating the Solution Approach

To be able to evaluate the practicability and usefulness of our solution approach in real work environments, we deployed the WCP environment to three German SMEs. In this evaluation phase we observed the usage, created widgets and services as well as the collaboration of different types of end-users. Additionally we conducted a questionnaire-based survey among the employees to refine the results of our preliminary studies and to get feedback on our WCP-based solution approach from a broad end-user base. In section 4 we provide first promising results of the evaluation phase by describing practical use cases of WCP-created widgets within SMEs, classify end-users by observed behavior related to widget creation, and discuss selected analysis results of the questionnaire-based study.

3   Widget Composition Platform

The WCP is a web-based EUD environment that enables business users to mashup enterprise resources in a visual design environment in a very lightweight way and to deploy the created mashups in the form of widgets to their local machines. In the following subsections we describe the WCP environment in detail. We describe the conceptual layers that are implemented by the WCP environment. We explain of which architectural components the WCP environment consists and how these components work together. Finally we describe the provided GUI and explain how end-users are able to create widgets by mashing up enterprise services.

3.1   Conceptual Layers

On a conceptual level, the WCP and created widgets are based on a layered architecture. Significant components of this conceptual architecture are classified and structured in the *widget stack* depicted in Fig. 1. The widget stack consists of five basic layers: resource layer, application programming interface (API) layer, wrapper layer, service layer, and mashup / widget layer. With regard to Fig. 1, we will describe the layers bottom-up, as each layer requires the functionality provided by its subjacent layer.

Resource Layer. The resource layer consists of all resources that can be integrated in mashups. Resources can be data, like customer master data stored in an ERP system, or functionality, like locating an address and returning an according image of a map provided by a map application. Resources are managed and provided by systems that can be internal or external to an organization. Internal systems might be various enterprise systems, like ERP or Customer Relationship Management (CRM) systems, custom applications tailored to the needs of the enterprise, or general purpose relational database management systems (RDBMS). External resources might be provided by systems accessible to a closed user group, like e.g. systems of suppliers, customers or B2B market places, or by systems publicly accessible over the internet, like e.g. map services or stock quotes.

API Layer. The API layer consists of the well-defined interfaces provided by the systems managing the resources. Depending on the systems, different formats and protocols may be needed to call the APIs and access the resources. APIs of modern service-enabled systems may be exposed as web services that can be called using standard web protocols, while legacy systems may expose APIs only as libraries that can be linked into source code and communicate with the system using proprietary protocols. Required formats of input parameters and formats of returned results vary accordingly and range from XML structures to proprietary binary formats.

Wrapper Layer. To abstract from the heterogeneity of APIs and respective protocols and formats, the wrapper layer provides a unified service model, consumable by the service layer. The abstraction is provided by wrapper components that transform requests to the abstract service model to concrete requests using the respective API, protocol and parameter format of the addressed resource. Raw results received from the API are transformed to a format that can be processed within the unified service

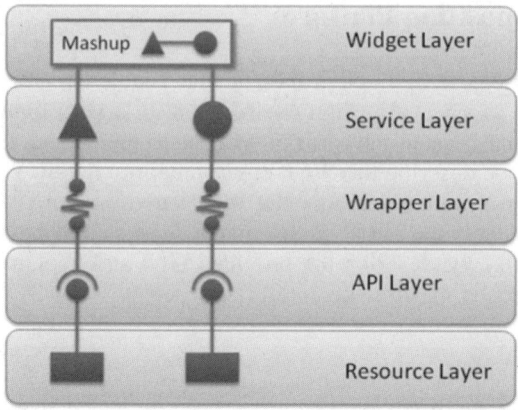

Fig. 1. Conceptual layers of widget stack in the WCP environment

model, e.g. data structures storing tables, lists or even images. Not each resource requires its own wrapper component. Generic wrappers are able to wrap certain types of resources, like SAP ERP queries or RSS feeds, in a generic way. These generic wrappers are exposed as service types in the service layer.

Service Layer. The service layer provides a repository of services that can be mashed up in the mashup environment. All services are parameterized instances of service types, relating services to a certain wrapper component in the wrapper layer. For example, a service "Customer data" providing data from a SAP ERP query is an instance of the service type "SAP ERP Query" that relates the service to an according wrapper component. The service instance uses parameters to specify which concrete query should be accessed inside the SAP ERP system via the wrapper component. Services provide further configuration possibilities that vary depending on the type of service. For example, the desired type of data visualization (e.g. rendering data as a table or a list), or the set of usable data filters that are exposed in the mashup environment, can be configured. Services can be further described by adding information like name and description text.

Mashup / Widget Layer. The mashup and widget layer is adding mashup functionality to the unified service model of the service layer and provides the functionality to deploy mashups as widgets. Mashups are defined by specifying a wiring of design elements, interconnecting design elements and defining the desired data flow. Design elements can be services or additional UI elements (like e.g. text boxes). The wiring defines how data from one design element is used to parameterize calls to other (dependent) design elements. Dependent design elements react on data updates of connected design elements and update their data accordingly. Mashups can be encapsulated as widgets and deployed as self-contained applications to individual runtimes, like e.g. the Yahoo! Widget engine [20]. The mashup creation and widget deployment functionality is provided by the mashup and widget layer to end-users by an integrated EUD environment.

To enable business users to create custom widgets supporting their individual working tasks, relevant business data needs to be available as services in the service layer. Therefore wrapper components and service types need to be implemented to be able to wrap resources from relevant enterprise systems. Any implementation of the widget stack should consider that at least some users within the organization are able to extend the services using existing knowledge. Therefore, employees should be able to create at least some types of resources and wrap these resources as services, without the help of IT professionals. If an implementation does not consider this aspect, its practical applicability will be limited by design. As an example, the usefulness of enabling the wrapping of a fixed set of web services would only be limited, as employees usually are not able to create customized web services due to a lack of programming skills. In contrast to this, the wrapping of queries enables at least some employees to create desired queries for data retrieval and flexibly include data into widgets.

3.2 Architectural Components of the Widget Composition Platform

We set up a prototypic system, instantiating the conceptual widget stack laid out in the previous subsection. Fig. 3 provides an overview of the system components, which are discussed in the following.

The central component of the system is the WCP, a web application which is implemented using Java technology and is run inside a web application server. The WCP provides an integrated graphical end-user development environment for widget creation. Its GUI can be accessed by calling a certain URL using a web browser. All services that can be mashed up within a widget are managed by a service repository. A widget deployment component within the WCP is responsible for creating source code, encoding the currently created widget for multiple runtime environments. During the process of widget composition within the WCP GUI, this component generates code for the WCP browser runtime libraries, so that the widget is fully functional within the GUI that is rendered inside a browser. If the user decides to deploy the developed widget to a widget runtime engine, the component generates code specific to that runtime environment and packages the widget to a file of according structure and format. To persist data, like the service repository, the personal repository of end-users' created widgets, or login and access right information, the WCP is using a RDBMS.

On the client side, end-users access the GUI of the WCP by using a web browser to call a certain URL. The installation of client-side software or browser plugins is not required to use the WCP. This simplifies the provisioning of the WCP to end-users and makes it very easy for end-users to start with the development of individual widgets. Within the browser, widgets are run based on a WCP runtime library implemented in JavaScript using common web standards. This enables a rendering of the widget and providing full widget functionality inside the browser during the development process without the need of any additional runtime environments installed to the client. Only if the end-user wants to use the developed widget within a certain widget runtime on the client side, this runtime environment needs to be installed on the client and the widget deployed to the runtime environment. For deployment, the WCP is delivering a single file that contains the widget packaged in the specific format required by the runtime environment.

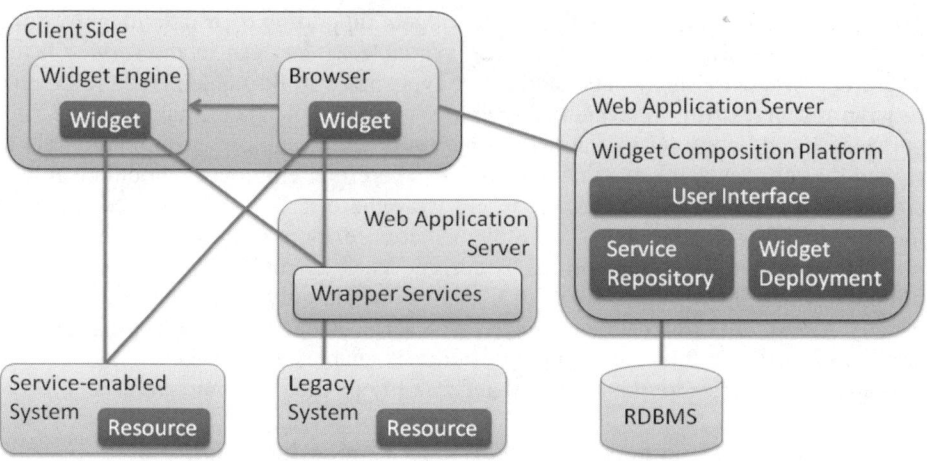

Fig. 2. Architectural components of the Widget Composition Platform

According to the widget stack described in the previous subsection, widgets access the resources that are mashed up within the widget via wrapper components. As wrapper components are encoded directly into the generated widget code, they are subject to the same technical restrictions as the technology used to implement widgets. As widgets need to run within a browser during the development process, wrapper components are limited to calls that can be realized using web standards from within a browser. If resources are managed by service-enabled systems, wrapper components are able to address the resources directly using standard web protocols. If resources are managed by legacy systems, that do not provide an API addressable using standard web protocols, wrapper components are assisted by wrapper services. Wrapper services are deployed to a dedicated web application server and provide access to legacy systems by encapsulating relevant parts of their API with a Representational State Transfer (REST) [21] based API that can be consumed by wrapper components. In our concrete setup we implemented wrapper services to access queries within not service-enabled versions of SAP ERP systems by encapsulating SAP Remote Function Calls (SAP RFC) using SAP Java Connector (SAP JCO), and execution of queries expressed in Structured Query Language (SQL) to RDBMS or Excel files using Java Database Connectivity (JDBC). By this, wrapper components are able to access resources within such systems using simple web protocols, keeping the needed technology on the client side as simple and lightweight as possible.

3.3 GUI of Widget Composition Platform

The WCP provides a browser-based GUI representing an integrated development environment (IDE) enabling the visual development of widgets without any programming knowledge. The GUI does not depend on any browser plugins and can simply be consumed by accessing an URL. A screenshot of the GUI is depicted in Fig. 3.

The GUI is separated into several panes. On the left side, a list of all services contained in the service repository is provided. The list groups services according to their service types. Users are able to add services to a mashup, simply by dragging and

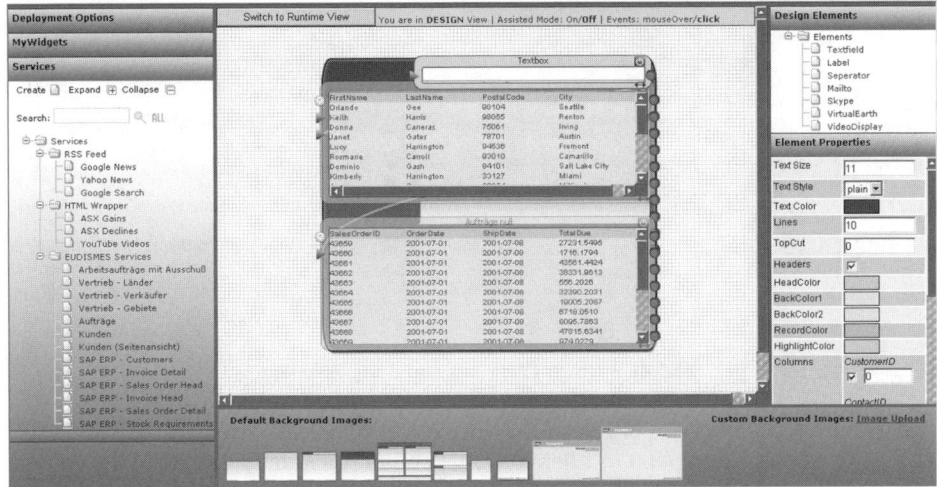

Fig. 3. GUI of the Widget Composition Platform

dropping the service to the design pane, located in the middle of the GUI. Besides services, additional design elements, like text boxes, can be dragged from the upper right of the GUI into the design pane. If an element in the design pane is selected, its properties are visible and modifiable in a properties pane on the right. Properties that can be modified include visual properties (such as color or font faces), but – more importantly – structural properties of services. For example, if service data is rendered as a table, then columns can be disabled or enabled to show exactly the desired data, or the number of displayed rows can be limited. From the background pane at the bottom of the GUI, the user is able to select a background image, enhancing the visual appearance of the created widget. Custom background images, e.g. tailored to the corporate identity of an organization, can easily be added by uploading an image in a common format like JPG. After adding services or design elements to the design pane, they are immediately populated with live data and provide runtime interaction possibilities. All design decisions create immediate effects, thus blurring design time and runtime and enabling development close to a WYSIWYG manner, increasing the confidence of the user in creating the desired results.

To mashup services, a wiring has to be defined using a simple box and wires design paradigm. As depicted in Fig. 4, services and other design elements offer input ports and output ports that can be connected to define the wiring. Input ports are visualized as orange triangles on the left side of elements and output ports are visualized as blue circles on the right side of elements. Elements are connected by drawing a line, originating from an output port of a source element to an input port of a target element. Whenever data in the source element changes, the new data is pushed as input to the target element, which updates itself accordingly. The update of data in target elements might again push new data to dependent elements, which in turn might trigger updates. Services update their data by executing a service call, which is parameterized according to the current input values. In the given example, a service providing customer master data is connected to a service providing sales order data. When selecting a customer in the customer table, the connected sales order service is automatically

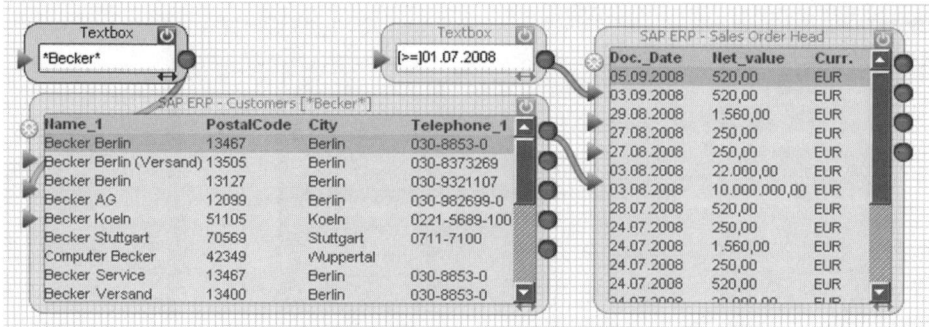

Fig. 4. Wiring of services and design elements

updated to only show sales orders of the selected customer. In case of the depicted services, input ports correspond to filters on table columns and output ports to the column values of the currently selected row. In the given example, two text boxes are used to enable the user to interactively define values that are pushed to services as input. The text box connected to the customer data service restricts the shown customers according to the given name pattern. The text box connected to the sales order service restricts shown sales orders to such sales orders that have been received at or after a given date. In addition to text boxes, other design elements exist, that provide additional functionality, if served with according data. Examples are design elements that use e-mail addresses or Skype names as input and provide the ability to send an e-mail or establish a Skype call just by clicking on an envelope or telephone symbol.

If realizing during the creation process, that a resource needed for the current mashup is missing in the service repository, an according service can be defined using the "Create" option of the service pane. To define a service, the service type needs to be selected (e.g. SAP ERP query) and then the resource that should be encapsulated by the service specified (e.g. by providing the SAP ERP system storing the query, and the name of the query). After saving the service to the repository, it can instantly be used in the mashup process.

At any point of time, the user is able to switch from the design time mode to a runtime mode. Although the widget is fully functional even in design time mode, the runtime mode hides all visual elements that are only needed at design time, like input ports, output ports, or connections, and prevents modifications to the widget. This way, the widget is presented as it would appear if deployed to an external widget engine. Widgets can be saved to and loaded from a personal widget repository managed by the WCP. This functionality is accessible through the "MyWidgets" pane on the left of the GUI. Using the "Deployments Option" pane, the widget can be deployed to multiple widget runtime environments, like Yahoo! Widget Engine [20] or Microsoft Windows Vista Sidebar [22]. When selecting deployment, the WCP is returning a single file, which can either be directly opened and thereby gets deployed to the client-side widget engine or saved as a file, that can easily be sent via e-mail or moved to a file share, to share the widget with colleagues. Widgets that are deployed to a client-side widget engine, run independently of the WCP and are small, self-contained, interactive applications.

4   Evaluation

The aim of the WCP approach is to enable business users to create custom widgets tailored to their individual information needs, without the need of any programming skills. To achieve this aim, a very lightweight composition approach was chosen, to mash up enterprise resources. This enables the creation of simple solutions by simple means. Additionally, advanced end-users are able to create new enterprise services to be mashed up within the WCP by creating and wrapping according resources within enterprise systems. With regard to validity of this approach, several questions arise. Are business users of SMEs able to create widgets using the WCP? Are widgets able to address practical problems in real work contexts, although they are very simple software artifacts composed in a very simple way? Are advanced end-users able to create and wrap enterprise resources as new services to extend the available building blocks for widget creation? What types of end-users exist with regard to widget usage and development, and how do they collaborate? To be able to evaluate our solution approach in real work environments, we deployed the WCP environment to three German SMEs. Additionally, we conducted a questionnaire-based survey among the employees to refine the results of our preliminary studies and to get feedback on our WCP-based solution approach from a broad end-user base. In the following, we describe the setup of the practical evaluation of the WCP, discuss first results of the practical use within SMEs, describe a first classification of end-users based on observed EUD behavior, and discuss first results of the questionnaire analysis. As the evaluation phase is still ongoing at the time of writing, all results have to be considered as preliminary results.

4.1   Setup of Evaluating WCP in Practice

The WCP environment has been deployed to three German midsized companies, which use an SAP ERP system to support their business processes. The companies are two midsized companies from production industry (137 and 140 employees) and one larger software vendor (500 employees). In the respective companies 57, 80 and 350 employees use a PC. Among those, 50, 70 and 116 employees have access to the SAP ERP system. 18, 60 and 70 employees use the SAP ERP system on a regular base. In two of the three companies the initial WCP installation was realized in cooperation with the IT department, and in one company with the person responsible for IT concerns, as no dedicated IT department existed. After installation, the WCP could be accessed by every employee having access to the internal network of the company.

In each company one advanced end-user was nominated as a contact person, responsible for all concerns with regard to the WCP. This person should act as an evangelist to promote the usage of the new technology, as well as provide support to end-users, if questions arise. In a first phase, the contact person was given an introduction into the WCP and should experiment freely with it to get more familiar with its concepts and usage. We defined five distinct services encapsulating SAP ERP data as a starting point for experiments. The services provided common data, like data related to customers, sales orders and invoices. To increase the motivation to go for experiments, we included some appealing external services that could be used, like a service for visualizing addresses on a map, a YouTube video service, Google news, and a stock quote service. In a second phase, we discussed any problems that might have arisen in the first phase and provided help to solve these problems. After that, we discussed potential use cases of widgets within the company with the contact person. In a third phase, we encouraged the contact person to act as an evangelist and promote the usage of the WCP by approaching employees related to the discussed use cases, giving an introduction to the WCP, and motivating its usage. If the contact person was not motivated enough or had problems acting as an evangelist, we gave additional support or acted as evangelists on our own to push the dissemination of WCP technology. During the third and ongoing phase we conduct accompanying interviews with the employees, which are using the WCP for the creation of individual widgets. We investigate what use cases exist, how end-users are able to use the WCP and widgets to address practical problems, and how different end-users collaborate to create solutions.

4.2   Adoption of WCP and Widgets in Practical Use Cases

As the evaluation phase is still in progress at the time of writing, a final analysis of the results cannot be given yet. Nevertheless we are able to discuss some of our first preliminary results, which are very promising. In the following we exemplarily discuss two use cases which describe how business users adopt widgets that have been created.

Use Case 1: Sales Support Widget. A user in the sales department is in charge of answering questions of customers related to sales orders. Customers contact the user by phone to get information related to the content and status of sales orders. Inquiries comprise e.g. questions about whether or not certain goods have been ordered in a certain sales order, or what the current state of sales order processing is. To be able to answer such questions, the user has to access multiple locations inside the GUI of the SAP ERP system. In a first step, the user needs to access customer master data to uniquely identify the customer. In a second step, the user accesses sales order header data to filter sales orders of the respective customer and the sales order of question. In a third step, the individual items of the sales order are accessed to view ordered goods, the ordered quantity and their status. If multiple sales orders are of interest, the user needs to switch back and forth between the sales order list and its details. The process of incrementally gathering required information from the GUI by accessing multiple locations and the need to switch back and forth between them is rated to be cumbersome by the user, especially as the user has to access the information many times a day.

The user was approached by the local evangelist and was shown the WCP. The user started to experiment with the WCP. Using the services we defined as standard demo services during installation, the user was able to create a suitable widget for his needs. The widget shows customer master data, sales order header data and sales order details as three distinct tables. Using text boxes the user added filters for customers by name or customer number, and filters on the order date of sales orders. The user deployed the widget to his desktop to make it easily accessible and uses it to quickly access sales order related data if customers ask for them. By using the filters on customer master data, a customer can be uniquely identified in a fast and comfortable way. By clicking on this customer in the table, all sales orders of the customer are shown in another table, directly beneath the customer table. The user then restricts the shown sales orders to the ones ordered at or after a certain order date. By clicking on a sales order, all relevant details are shown in a third table. The user configured the tables to only show data relevant for him, resulting in a compact overview providing required data at a glance. To view details of other sales orders in question, the user simply clicks on the sales order in the sales order table.

The created widget is used by the user about 40 times a day to answer standard questions of customers related to sales orders. As the user does not need to access multiple locations within the complex GUI of the SAP ERP system, but gets all relevant data at a glace, he is able to answer standard customer inquiries in approximately the half of the time compared to using the GUI of the SAP ERP system. Because of this practical value, the user sent the widget to a colleague, who needs to access such data occasionally. The user has absolutely no programming skills and was able to create a custom widget for supporting his individual working task within three hours after having seen the WCP for the first time. The user told us that experimenting with the WCP was fun for him. He perceived the WCP to have an appealing user interface and the composition of widgets to be simple, comprehensible and easy to learn.

Use Case 2: Material Lookup Widget. A user in charge of procurement needs to access certain information related to material many times a day. For instance, identifying a material by its material number and getting the quantity currently in stock and the quantity already scheduled for production. To get a first overview of the material status, the user determines a constant set of information, which she considers to be standard for her work context. Similar to the previous use case, relevant information are widely spread within the GUI of the SAP ERP system and have to be gathered in a cumbersomely manner.

As the user was approached by the local evangelist and was shown the WCP, she immediately thought of building a widget to access her standard set of material related information. As no predefined services existed that could deliver relevant data, the evangelist discussed with the user which data was actually needed and searched for possible data sources like tables and queries within the ERP system. Using a larger query as a template, the evangelist managed to create a SAP query joining five distinct tables and providing most of the requested data. The query was wrapped as a service for the WCP and was used by the user to create a suitable widget.

The widget is rather simply structured and just consists of a text box and the created service. The text box defines a filter on the material number to the service. As the service just returns a single record, the results are not rendered as a table with a single row, but as a list, showing all attributes of the record with according values as rows. The user configured the service to show only the most relevant data and arranged all design elements neatly to create an appealing widget. The widget was also deployed on the PC of an employee working in the raw material warehouse, who did not have a direct access to live data from the SAP ERP system before. By using the widget, he is able to access the most important data related to material in a very easy way, without the need of having to learn and understand a complex enterprise system.

4.3 Types of End-Users

Based on first insights obtained by accompanying interviews and observations, we distinguish different types of end-users with regard to widget usage and development. An according segmentation of end-users is given by the following classification: widget consumers, widget creators, and service creators.

Widget Consumers. Widget consumers are end-users which are only consuming widgets, but do not create widgets. Some users only use computers occasionally and are not very familiar with complex information systems. They receive widgets from more experienced colleagues and use them to access data in an easy and comfortable way without the need of learning and understanding one or more complex information systems. By this, the value of information stored in enterprise systems is leveraged, as it enables more end-users to access them and make better informed decisions. Additionally this removes the need of asking colleagues for data and thus makes data access more efficient. Another class of widget consumers consists of end-users that could create widgets for their own, but are not motivated enough to engage in widget creation. On the other hand, they willingly use widgets that are created by other end-users that turn out to be useful to support own working tasks.

Widget Creators. Widget creators are end-users that create widgets for themselves or others to support individual working tasks. They are motivated by multiple reasons to create widgets. One main reason is to simplify data access for own working tasks and thereby making these working tasks more efficient and less cumbersome. Another motivation is to provide others with especially tailored widgets, to improve data supply to others engaged into the same business processes. By this, the amount of inquiries for data is reduced and business process may be executed more efficiently. Providing better tools to support individual working tasks of processes is especially relevant for end-users being responsible for certain processes and thus motivates them to act as widget creator to optimize these processes and improve process performance. End-users successfully using widgets motivate others to engage in widget creation as they are motivated by the success of others and want to use such optimization possibilities for their own working tasks and processes. Other end-users are technology-savvy and start widget creation for the reason of having fun experimenting with new technology. They discover the usefulness for own tasks or tasks of others while experimenting.

Service Creators. Service creators are advanced end-users that are able to create new resources that can be wrapped and added to the service repository, from where they can be used for widget creation. By extending the service repository with new services, they enable widget creators to address more use cases and create more widgets that are more precisely tailored to the individual needs of end-users. Without service creators, widget creators would be limited to a certain set of predefined services which limits the amount of creatable solutions. With regard to the WCP environment service creators are end-users having the skills of creating, modifying or at least locating suitable queries inside the SAP ERP system that match existing information needs of widget creators.

4.4 Questionnaire-Based Evaluation of WCP

To refine the results of the preliminary studies and to acquire feedback on the WCP-based approach on a broad end-user base, we conducted a questionnaire-based survey among the employees of the companies participating in the evaluation of the WCP environment. Besides the WCP related aspects, the questionnaire addressed many more aspects like IT-related skills of employees, satisfaction with provided enterprise software, experience with EUD related activities, as well as working practices and problems with regard to individual information processing and access. For the sake of brevity, we focus on WCP related aspects only in the following. As not all employees participating in the survey knew the WCP environment, we provided the questionnaire online and embedded a small video presenting the WCP. The video was shown to the participants after having explained a small use case and showed the employees how to create a suitable enterprise widget and deploy it to the desktop in less than three minutes. As common office PCs mostly do not provide sound, short explanations were given by fading text in the video. Based on the video, the questionnaire asked several questions directly related to the WCP approach. Video presentation can be seen as a viable medium for demonstrating systems in a user acceptance testing context as it enables subjects "to form accurate attitudes, usefulness perceptions, quality perceptions and behavioral expectations (self-predictions of use)" [23], which are important factors for technology acceptance according to the Technology Acceptance Model [24].

Each of the three participating companies was asked to send the URL to access the questionnaire to 33 randomly chosen users of the SAP ERP system. Finally we received 73 filled and analyzable questionnaires. With regard to a total of 236

Table 1. Questions related to the WCP environment and widgets with according results

Question	Results
How do you rate the difficulty level of the shown method of widget creation?	0% too difficult, 13.8% difficult but manageable, 39.7% passable, 22.4% easy, 20.7% very easy, 3.4% declared not to answer
Do you think you could manage to create a widget using the shown method on your own?	72.5% yes, 6.9% no, 17.2% uncertain, 3.4% declared not to answer
Do you think custom-made widgets can provide benefits in real work contexts?	69.1% yes, 5.3% no, 21.3% uncertain, 4.3% declared not to answer
Do you think, you could ease or accelerate your work by using widgets tailored to your needs?	Scale from 0 (would not provide any benefits for me) to 5 (would help me a lot): 6.4% 0, 5.3% 1, 17.0% 2, 26.6% 3, 26.6% 4, 7.4% 5, 9.6% declared not to answer, 1.1% did not answer
Is there any personal, typical work situation that spontaneously comes to your mind, in which a widget would be of help for you?	47.9% yes, 27.6% no, 14.9% uncertain, 8.5% declared not to answer, 1.1% did not answer
If your last answer was "yes", would you be willing to create a widget for that purpose on your own?	58.5% yes, 8.5% no, 17.0% uncertain, 12.8% declared not to answer, 3.2% did not answer
Would you be willing to accept learning efforts to learn the creation of widgets?	5.3% no, 7.4% yes, up to half an hour, 11.7% yes, up to an hour, 19.1% yes, several hours, 21.3% yes, a day, 28.8% yes, several days, 5.3% declared not to answer, 1.1% did not answer
Can you think of using complete, predefined widgets in your everyday work, if they provide data relevant to you?	84.0% yes, 2.1% no, 8.5% uncertain, 4.3% declared not to answer, 1.1% did not answer

employees working with the SAP ERP system in these companies, we achieved a coverage of about 30.1% of the addressed test population. Table 1 lists some of the questions which have been asked in the questionnaire after the participants watched the video demonstrating the WCP environment, together with the according results.

The results are promising. The participants rate the WCP not to be too difficult. 82.8% rate the perceived difficulty level to be passable, easy or very easy. 72.5% think that they can manage to create widgets on their own using the WCP environment. 69.1% think that custom-made widgets are able to provide benefits in real work context. On a scale ranging from 0 (widgets do not provide any benefit for me) to 5 (widgets would help me a lot), 60.6% of participants rated the ability of widgets to ease or accelerate their own work with at least 3. 47.9% of the participants state, that a typical, personal work situation spontaneously comes to their mind, in which widgets would be helpful. 58.5% of these participants would be willing to create a widget on their own for that work situation. 88.3% of the participants are willing to accept learning efforts to learn the creation of widgets. 69.2% of these participants would accept learning efforts ranging from several hours to several days. 84% of the participants would use complete, predefined widgets in their every day work, if they provide data relevant to them.

The results indicate that typical business users of SMEs, which are using an ERP system in their daily work, believe that widgets are able to provide benefits in real work contexts. Many business users see application possibilities in their own, personal work context and would like to create a widget for that purpose on their own, even if they have to accept learning effort to achieve this aim. The vast majority of business users believes to be able to create widgets with the WCP environment and rates its usage to be not difficult. Overall, this can be seen as quite a positive and promising feedback with regard to the WCP environment and the practical applicability of widgets. According to the Technology Acceptance Model [24], the high degree of perceived usefulness can be seen as a strong indicator for acceptance.

5 Summary and Conclusion

In this paper, we presented an EUD approach enabling business users to create enterprise widgets tailored to their personal information needs without the need of programming knowledge. The approach is based on a prototypic, web-based EUD environment called WCP, which enables end-users to mash up enterprise resources in a visual design environment in a very lightweight way using a simple box and wires design paradigm and to deploy the created mashups in the form of widgets to their local machines. The ability of creating custom widgets enables business users to create small, interactive applications to access relevant business data in a fast and convenient way, without the need of starting heavyweight and complex enterprise systems and cumbersomely collect data from multiple locations within the GUI of such systems. This creates a new experience for end-users, as they were not able to create interactive tools providing live interaction on enterprise resources to support their individual work tasks on their own before. The approach especially considers extensibility of building blocks for widget creation by SMEs using existing knowledge, as it enables to wrap and expose enterprise resources (e.g. SAP ERP queries), which can be created by advanced end-users, as services that can be mashed up in a widget. Thus, the whole chain of widget development is put in the hand of SMEs.

We described our research approach targeted at creating EUD solutions applicable in real enterprise contexts, and motivated the need and setup of our approach with results of our preliminary empirical studies. With regard to the set up of our solution approach, we discussed the conceptual layers of the widget stack, which is instantiated by the WCP environment, and explained the architectural components of the WCP and how these work together. We presented the GUI of the WCP and explained how end-users are able to create individual mashups of enterprise resources using a simple box and wires design paradigm, and how these mashups can be deployed as widgets to the local machines of the end-users. With regard to evaluation of the approach, we presented first results of a practical evaluation of the EUD environment in three German SMEs. We provided use cases from real enterprise contexts, and gave a classification of end-user types based on our observations. Additionally, we presented results of a questionnaire-based survey conducted on a broad end-user base, which document a very promising feedback with regard to our approach.

The provided use cases from real enterprise contexts demonstrate that business users are able to create custom widgets supporting their individual work tasks using the provided EUD environment. The use cases gave evidence that widgets can be used to address practical problems in real work contexts, although they are very simple software artifacts composed in a very simple way. The results of the questionnaire-based survey support these conclusions, as they show that a broad base of typical business users believe that widgets are able to provide benefits in real work contexts, see application possibilities in their own work context, and would like to create a widget for that purpose on their own, even if they had to accept learning effort to achieve this aim. The vast majority believes to be able to create widgets with the WCP environment and rates its usage to be not difficult.

Beyond this, we observed in practical situations that advanced end-users are able to create and wrap enterprise resources as new services to extend the available building blocks for widget creation. By this, the whole development chain of widget creation can be put in the hands of SMEs and allows them to act as autonomous creators of services and widgets, without the need of external IT professionals. With regard to our aim of creating EUD approaches for enterprise environments, which can be managed even by SMEs and enable business users to better adapt software to their individual working tasks and work practice, we consider these first results as being very promising.

With our research, we contribute to the field of EUD in various ways. We give an example of how the technical flexibility of SOAs can be leveraged at the hand of end-users using approaches like mashups and widgets. We provide indications, taken from our evaluation, that a simple box and wires design paradigm, combined with a design environment blurring design time and runtime can be easily learned and used by typical business users to orchestrate simple software artifacts. We show that EUD approaches enabling business users to create simple software artifacts like widgets are able to address practical problems in real enterprise work contexts. Additionally, we provide indications from our observations, that by enabling SMEs to create enterprise resources using existing knowledge and wrapping these resources as building blocks for the EUD of software artifacts, the whole development chain of software artifacts can be put in the hands of SMEs, thus reducing the need of external IT professionals and at the same time increasing flexibility in adapting the used software infrastructure to individual and changing needs.

Acknowledgments. We would like to thank Alexander Dreiling and Kathrin Fleischmann of SAP Research for providing an early prototype of the WCP we could branch and extend. The presented research was funded by the German Federal Ministry of Education and Research (BMBF) under the project EUDISMES (number 01ISE03C).

References

1. Roth, A., Scheidl, S.: End-User Development for Enterprise Resource Planning Systems. In: Informatik 2006, pp. 596–599. GI (2006)
2. Brehm, L., Heinzl, A., Markus, M.L.: Tailoring ERP Systems: A Spectrum of Choices and their Implications. In: 34th Annual Hawaii International Conference on System Sciences (HICSS-34). IEEE, Los Alamitos (2001)
3. Markus, M.L., Tanis, C.: The Enterprise System Experience: From Adoption to Success. In: Zmud, R.W. (ed.) Framing the Domains of IT Research: Glimpsing the Future through the Past, pp. 173–207. Pinnaflex (2000)
4. Wulf, V., Rohde, M.: Towards an integrated Organization and Technology Development. In: Designing Interactive Systems 1995 (DIS 1995). ACM, New York (1995)
5. Gallivan, M.J., Keil, M.: The User–Developer Communication Process: A critical Case Study. ISJ 13, 37–68 (2003)
6. Beringer, J.: Reducing Expertise Tension. Commun. ACM 47, 39–40 (2004)
7. Lieberman, H., Paternò, F., Wulf, V.: End User Development. Springer, Heidelberg (2006)
8. Spahn, M., Dörner, C., Wulf, V.: End User Development: Approaches towards a flexible Software Design. In: 16th European Conference on Information Systems (ECIS 2008), pp. 303–314. CISC (2008)
9. Wulf, V., Pipek, V., Won, M.: Component-based Tailorability: Towards highly flexible Software Applications. IJHCS 66, 1–22 (2008)
10. Erl, T.: Service-oriented Architecture: Concepts, Technology, and Design. Prentice-Hall, Englewood Cliffs (2005)
11. Microsoft Popfly, http://www.popfly.com/
12. Yahoo! Pipes, http://pipes.yahoo.com/
13. Gartner Identifies the Top 10 Strategic Technologies for 2008 (2008), http://www.gartner.com/it/page.jsp?id=530109
14. Spahn, M., Dörner, C., Wulf, V.: End User Development of Information Artefacts: A Design Challenge for Enterprise Systems. In: 16th European Conference on Information Systems (ECIS 2008), pp. 482–493. CISC (2008)
15. Caceres, M.: Widgets 1.0 Requirements. W3C Working Draft. W3C (2008)
16. Kvale, S.: Interviews: An Introduction to Qualitative Research Interviewing. Sage Publications, Thousand Oaks (1996)
17. Muller, M.J.: Participatory Design: The third Space in HCI. In: The Human-Computer Interaction Handbook: Fundamentals, evolving Technologies and emerging Applications, pp. 1051–1068. Erlbaum (2003)

18. Spahn, M., Kleb, J., Grimm, S., Scheidl, S.: Supporting Business Intelligence by Providing Ontology-based End-User Information Self-Service. In: 1st International Workshop on Ontology-supported Business Intelligence (OBI 2008). ACM, New York (2008)
19. MacLean, A., Carter, K., Lövstrand, L., Moran, T.: User-tailorable Systems: Pressing the Issues with Buttons. In: SIGCHI Conference on Human Factors in Computing Systems (CHI 1990), pp. 175–182. ACM, New York (1990)
20. Yahoo! Widgets, http://widgets.yahoo.com/
21. Fielding, R.T.: Architectural Styles and the Design of Network-based Software Architectures. PhD thesis, University of California, Irvine, USA (2000)
22. Lal, R.: Creating Vista Gadgets. Sams (2008)
23. Davis, F.D.: A Technology Acceptance Model for empirically testing new End-User Information Systems: Theory and Results. PhD thesis, Sloan School of Management, Massachusetts Institute of Technology, Cambridge, MA, USA (1986)
24. Davis, F.D.: Perceived Usefulness, perceived Ease of Use, and User Acceptance of Information Technology. MIS Quarterly 13, 319–340 (1989)

End-User Development for E-Government Website Content Creation

Daniela Fogli

Dipartimento di Elettronica per l'Automazione
Università degli Studi di Brescia
Via Branze 38, 25123 Brescia, Italy
fogli@ing.unibs.it

Abstract. E-government websites are currently becoming more and more huge and complex. They provide citizens with several kinds of information, including services for online task payment or front office reservation. The creation and maintenance of such websites often require a distributed approach: the content publication task is transferred from software developers to personnel of the various organization departments (here called the *publishers*). To this end, a Content Management System (CMS) is usually adopted. However, CMSs do not generally satisfy all requirements and needs that emerge in this application domain. Therefore, the adoption of End-User Development (EUD) techniques, tailored to the publishers' culture, background and skills, represents a possible solution to CMSs' current limitations. In this paper, after discussing the context and the existing problems, we describe an approach to extending CMSs with EUD techniques. The approach will be discussed with reference to the creation and maintenance of the website of an existing government agency.

Keywords: e-government website, content management system, accessibility, end user, meta-design.

1 Introduction

Government agencies are complex organizations whose websites are currently becoming more and more huge and articulate. They offer to citizens several kinds of information, including sophisticated services such as online task payment or front office reservation.

For such websites, many countries all over the world have promulgated laws to establish the duty of satisfying precise accessibility standards [23][39][53], in addition to the well-known usability requirements.

The creation of websites that satisfy usability and accessibility requirements has been traditionally accomplished by software developers. Among the other activities, software developers had to perform content authoring, by gathering information from domain experts that worked in the various departments of the government agency. However, this centralized organization was doomed to fail whenever the website contents increased considerably: software developers became a bottleneck, thus determining significant delays in the publication process.

V. Pipek et al. (Eds.): IS-EUD 2009, LNCS 5435, pp. 126–145, 2009.
© Springer-Verlag Berlin Heidelberg 2009

For these reasons, a decentralized strategy is currently preferred in most government agencies: the responsibility of publishing contents on the website is assigned to the employees of the different agency departments. Distributed content authoring has a significant impact on the work organization and personnel roles, and investments are necessary to acquire proper software applications that allow storing, controlling, versioning, and publishing various kinds of web material. Web Content Management Systems (CMSs) are the software applications that meet this demand.

A CMS is usually installed and managed by software developers – personnel internal or external to the government agency who are expert in computer technology. In such a situation, their responsibility in web page creation is reduced with respect to the centralized approach. In particular, they have to develop page templates, by ensuring their accessibility and usability. They also have to design the navigation architecture, by assigning privileges to personnel committed to content publication, the so-called *publishers*. Publishers – personnel working in some agency department who possess the knowledge about the content to be published on the website – are the very end users of the CMS. As such, these personnel are expected to evolve from passive interviewees during requirements analysis to active content producers. They generally have limited competencies in computer technology, but may be acquainted with web browsers, word processors, spreadsheets and other similar office applications. Therefore, they are capable of using content authoring tools available in the CMS to add their contents to the website.

However, from our collaboration experience with a large Italian municipality, it emerged that CMS' end users are often required to acquire some programming skills, in order to cope with the limitations of the CMS. In particular, we have observed that existing CMSs often lack functionalities for generating HTML code that satisfies accessibility requirements as established by national laws (this is particularly true when the adopted CMS is out-to-date, but migration to another product is not manageable). In such a situation, publishers must access the HTML code generated by the CMS authoring tools, and modify it manually. Consequently, this requires to provide publishers with training courses and/or manuals that support them in doing this job. In spite of these precautions, people not expert in computer technologies keep on considering this task as difficult, error-prone and time consuming, and thus they arrive even at refusing to perform it.

Furthermore, software developers still remain a bottleneck in creating online services. In fact, after the elicitation of requirements from personnel of the different agency departments, they are in charge of implementing the services through the programming language available in (or compliant with) the CMS. Moreover, the communication gap [9][20][31] that often exists between developers and domain experts (the departments' employees) creates problems in correctly designing and developing these services. Therefore, tools are needed to support CMS' end users in creating not only static content, but also online services, since these people are the owners of the necessary domain knowledge.

We argue here that both HTML editing and online service creation must be regarded as two different kinds of software development activities publishers should carry out. We propose to achieve this goal by extending CMSs with proper End-User Development (EUD) facilities.

EUD [29][50] has been defined by EUD-Net, the network of Excellence on End-User Development funded by the European Commission during 2002-2003, as "the set of methods, techniques, and tools that allow users of software systems, who are acting as non-professional software developers, at some point to create or modify a software artifact" [16]. EUD activities can range from just setting parameters to the use of macro languages to extend system functionalities [8][9][28][35].

The contribution of this paper is to promote the application of results of EUD research in the field of CMSs, with a particular focus on the use of CMSs for creating e-government website content. With reference to the real case of an Italian municipality, we propose to integrate a CMS with tools that support publishers in creating contents and services, transparently with respect to their underlying representation. In this way, publishers can behave as "unwitting programmers" [11][41] by creating or modifying software components without being conscious of this. To this end, EUD tools must be designed by relying on publishers' competencies and skills, thus avoiding them to acquire new competencies in computer technologies.

In particular, we carried out a case study research [57][58] concerning an EUD-based technique that has been implemented to relieve publishers from HTML editing. This research is extensively described in [19] and briefly summarized here. A second technique has been investigated and discussed with software developers that work at the Italian municipality. It is still at the early stages of development, but it is presented here as very promising in the case of online service creation.

The paper is organized as follows: Section 2 analyses the problems concerning the development of e-government websites. Section 3 describes content management systems, the tools generally employed for creating, managing and updating an e-government website. Section 4 presents the theme of end-user development, the experiences of EUD in various application domains, and the characteristics of end users required to perform EUD activities. Section 5 describes our case study. Section 6 provides a further analysis related with the case study, which appears promising for future implementations of EUD-based techniques in the field of e-government websites. Section 7 briefly discusses the novel ideas proposed in the paper and Section 8 concludes the paper.

2 Characteristics of E-Government Websites

In many countries all over the world, several laws establish precise accessibility goals an e-government website must satisfy [39]. For instance, since 2005, websites of Italian government agencies must satisfy the requirements established in the "Disposizioni per favorire l'accesso dei soggetti disabili agli strumenti informatici" ("Provisions to support the access to information technologies for the disabled", Law no. 4 January 2004) [40].

Most of these laws on accessibility (including the Italian one) are based on the Web Content Accessibility (WCAG) release 1.0 recommendation of World Wide Web Consortium (W3C) [54]. WCAG 1.0 includes fourteen guidelines that must be followed by web developers to make their sites accessible to people with disabilities. Such people are (i) those who need to browse web pages by using assistive technologies because of physical disabilities (i.e. people having vision, hearing or mobility impairments); (ii) elder people, who experience changes in vision, hearing, dexterity, and memory as they age; (iii) people who navigate the web through obsolete or limited hardware/software technologies, including old browser versions, low bandwidth connections to the Internet, mobile phones, personal digital assistants [53]. Most of the accessibility guidelines can be followed by writing proper HTML code, while others impose constraints to the interaction experience (for example by suggesting to avoid scripting code and to limit the presence of moving objects) or suggest the creation of simpler pages in terms of layout, graphics and language.

Furthermore, nowadays, e-government websites are becoming crucial also for the services they provide to citizens. Online services can be very different one another and dedicated to different kinds of users. For examples, some citizens may find easier to pay local taxes on the web, or may find useful reserving front office services or asking for personal documents by filling in forms on the website. Online services represent a particular kind of content that, like the other information to be published on the website, needs some domain knowledge generally possessed by personnel of the various agency departments.

The necessity to publish a huge and diverse amount of content usually requires a decentralized activity. To support distributed content authoring and easy website management, content management systems are generally adopted. Their main characteristics are discussed in the following section, along with their limitations in satisfying accessibility requirements and supporting end users in the creation of complex content.

3 Content Management Systems and Their Role in E-Government Website Creation and Maintenance

Like other kinds of web authoring tools, content management systems are becoming popular in relieving web site developers from low-level details of page design and implementation. In particular, content management systems implement the so-called *content-driven* paradigm: they support a separation between page presentation and page content, and allow users to ignore those aspects related with markup and scripting languages necessary to build the pages. As far as page presentation, pre-formatted templates are usually available in a CMS, as well as WYSIWIG functionalities to support users in creating new templates. But, more importantly for website content evolution, CMSs usually include tools that allow people not expert in information technologies to create web contents. Interacting with these tools is usually similar to interacting with office applications users are accustomed to use in their daily work. For example, a typical interaction could consist in choosing a page template and filling in it by editing objects or importing them from other sources.

These characteristics permit to create websites that satisfy usability requirements (such as consistency among pages, user-error management, system feedback), and which should be compliant with existing standards, particularly those related with page accessibility. Satisfying accessibility requirements established by national and international organizations is however a difficult task. Today several CMSs claim to directly support the development of websites compliant with WCAG guidelines. They are both open source tools, such as Plone [42], Moodle [34], Joomla! [24], Drupal

[15], TYPO3 [52], and commercial tools, such as Blackboard Content System [3], QnECMS [44], Sitekit CMS [49], Microsoft Content Management Server [32] or the more up-to-date Microsoft Office SharePoint [33] (an exhaustive survey of CMS products and technology is beyond the scope of the paper). In spite of these claims, for most of these tools, evaluating which WCAG guidelines are taken into account and how is not so easy. For example, exploring Joomla! documentation, one discovers that several accessibility fixes are due in the future version of the tool. The same is true for Moodle. However, Joomla! developers have already declared that some WCAG requirements are outside of Joomla! development team, as they have to be addressed by template designers or content managers [25]. A similar claim is made by Plone's development team, who is aware that a number of WCAG checkpoints are subjective, and thus their interpretation may vary [43]. In TYPO3, an *extension* (plugin) is available for managing content accessibility, but related user manuals are unavailable at the date of writing this paper, and thus it is not possible, also in this case, to evaluate a priori the suitability of TYPO3 for creating e-government websites. A thorough evaluation is even more difficult for commercial CMSs. Generally, their vendors declare that they are WAI compliant without giving further details.

Another topic concerning CMSs is the availability of server-side or client-side languages that can be used to personalize the website created through a CMS. However, such languages almost always require advanced skills, not only in computer programming, but also in information architectures of web applications. Therefore, they are used generally by professional software developers to implement the functionalities required for the domain at hand. In e-government websites, these functionalities include online services for tax payment, document request, front-office reservation, registration to public services (e.g. schools). In order to implement these functionalities and make them available on the web, software developers must always perform requirements gathering and analysis by interviewing the personnel of the interested department. This centralized approach and the misunderstandings arising among computer scientists and people with different competencies are often the reasons for delays in service development and publication. Authoring tools suitable to this task could adequately support the personnel at various departments in creating online services. Actually, some CMSs are specialized for particular domains, such as media sharing or personal spaces. These CMSs offer tailoring techniques or component-based methodologies to create web pages with functionalities for photo or movie sharing, guestbook management, meteorological forecasting. In a similar way, domain-dependent functionalities such as those offered by e-government websites could be designed directly by publishers.

4 End-User Development: From Desktop to Web Applications

The main goal of End-User Development is to study and develop techniques and applications for "empowering users to develop and adapt systems themselves" [28]. The level of complexity of these techniques should be appropriate to the users' individual skills and situations, and possibly allowing them to easily move up from less complex to more complex EUD activities. To this end, a classification of EUD activities has been proposed in [8][9] and further elaborated in [28]. The authors called *parameterization* or *customization* all activities that allow users to choose among alternative behaviors already available in the application, resulting for example in associating specific computation parameters with specific parts of the data or in applying different functionalities to the data. Then, they classify as *program creation* or *modification* the EUD activities carried out through programming by example, incremental programming, model-based development, extended annotation.

4.1 EUD Solutions in Different Application Domains

EUD techniques have been used for many years in commercial software, such as macro recording in word processors, formula composition in spreadsheets or filter definition in e-mail clients [28]. However, on the one hand, they are far to be used extensively by a large community of end users, and, on the other hand, there exists the potential for employing EUD techniques in many other application domains and with different levels of complexity.

Research projects have been funded to design EUD techniques that support householders in programming their home appliances (e.g. digital radios, televisions, telephones) [4][5], in order to possibly obtain intelligent environments [14]. In the AutoHAN project [5], the idea is to use physical infrared remote controls that can become the syntactic elements in a program and that can be composed by the user to represent sophisticated functions. Component-based approaches for EUD are proposed in the field of computer-supported collaborative work [36], by providing visual tailoring environments that allow users to easily create search tools, chat tools and shared-to-do lists [55]. Repenning and Ioannidou propose agent-based programming as a paradigm for EUD [45]. They demonstrate the feasibility of this approach by applying it to many different domains, from game applications, to simulation environments, to software for education. Myers et al. are developing natural programming languages and environments to permit people to program by expressing their ideas in the same way they think about them [37]. They performed feasibility studies in the domain of video games, after having examined how children use and structure language to solve problems, and in the domain of business programming, after having analyzed how adults describe database access scenarios. Different techniques for EUD have been implemented in the software shaping workshops, end-user environments supporting domain experts in medical diagnosis [9], mechanical engineering [10] and geological forecasting [7]; such techniques are based on annotation mechanisms and visual programming through direct manipulation.

The area of EUD also involves the creation, modification and adaptation of web applications. This activity may turn out to be even more difficult than the development of traditional desktop applications, since it requires to know different markup languages, programming languages (both client and server side), interaction techniques with databases. In [48], the typical hurdles in web development have been identified, such as the stateless nature of the HTTP protocol and the necessity of session management, handling cross-platform compatibility, establishing and managing database connections, input validation. To overcome these problems, a software system, called Click [46], has been developed, which allows users to generate HTML code by simply instantiating and positioning components for a page under construction. In [30], Macías and Paternò propose an approach to the customization of web-based applications, which exploits intelligent mechanisms to infer customization rules from user changes. In this case, end-user web developers who need to deal with structure and presentation of web pages are facilitated by an automatic system that builds an end-user profile containing customization preferences and then uses it to regenerate web pages according to such preferences. The use of wikis for EUD is instead advocated by Anslow and Rielhe [1]: wikis are regarded as a platform to support end users not only in contributing content, but also in performing computational tasks. They applied this technique for the development of business queries in web information systems. The work of Ginige and colleagues [13][22][27] is in the field of web information systems too. However, they propose a different solution: the definition of a meta-model of web applications and a set of form-based tools that can be used by end users to customize and evolve their applications, thus making the software architecture completely transparent to them. The ideas of meta-modelling and form-based EUD techniques seem very promising also in the application domain considered in this paper. However, while the tools described in [27] require users to follow precise syntaxes to create executable code, we propose here an evolution of the technique towards a more natural and direct manipulation interaction.

4.2 End Users' Characteristics

One of the most important activities when an interactive system is designed and evaluated is the characterization of its end users, especially if such end users are required to perform EUD activities.

Cypher defines end users as people who use a computer application as part of their daily life or daily work, but not interested in computers per se [12]. They can be technicians, clerks, analysts and managers who are often required, due to new organizational, business and commercial technologies, to perform end-user computing, i.e. "to develop software applications in support of organizational tasks" [6].

Some researchers focus the attention on end users with a high professionalism, such as interior designers [18], medical doctors [9], mechanical engineers [10], geologists [7], biologists [26], urban planners [2]. This has motivated the definition of a particular class of end users, the so-called *domain experts* [8][28], that is experts in a specific domain, not necessarily experts in computer science, who use computer environments to perform their daily tasks by acting as designers and being creative [21]. According to the spectrum presented in [56], they are *software developers using domain-specific languages* to write programs in order to solve specific problems that they own.

Web applications are often developed by "sophisticated end users" [48]: they are causal webmasters who, though possessing limited competencies in web technologies, are characterized by a strong sensibility and a deep motivation in creating their own artifacts [47]. They are sophisticated in that they are experienced in web design even though they find difficulties in managing the typical complexities in web development [48]. End users of wikis (e.g. Wikipedia), media sharing systems (e.g. Flickr) and other Web 2.0 systems [38] are classified as *web contents developers* in [56]; they share with casual webmasters the high motivation. In particular, they are very motivated in contributing their contents and collaborating through the web, and they are willing to spend time for preparing web material and publishing it.

As far as the development of e-government websites is concerned, the end users of content management systems represent another kind of web contents developers. However, they are not so motivated to create web material, but often perceive such activity as an overhead with respect to their daily work. The characteristics of these users, which we consider crucial to design adequate EUD techniques, are discussed more in detail in the next section.

5   EUD in E-Government Website Content Creation: A Case Study

During our collaboration with a large Italian municipality we had the opportunity to know and analyze the needs for EUD in e-government website content creation.

This municipality adopted in 2003 a commercial CMS to support content creation by the employees of various departments. A significant personalization work was performed to adapt the CMS to the specific context and customer's requirements. Clearly, the adoption of a more recent CMS product would ensure an improvement in website management, content creation and accessibility satisfaction. However, the huge amount of content to be migrated and the necessity of performing further personalization work and personnel training have discouraged until now managers and developers to make this choice.

During first informal conversations with some publishers, we discovered that they found many difficulties in creating web contents, mainly for two reasons: 1) their own characteristics; 2) the lack of some important functionalities in the CMS. As to the first point, from conversations it emerged that publishers belong to an heterogeneous population, which includes experts in different domains, thus having different competencies, skills, and cultural background. Most of them do not hold a higher education degree and their ages range in a wide spectrum. Publishers seem often to be insufficiently motivated in doing content authoring, by perceiving such activity as alien to their daily work. Moreover, they complained that, while interacting with the CMS adopted in their agency, they were often charged with housekeeping activities. For example, the creation of some type of content required publishers to edit directly the generated HTML code, in order to satisfy accessibility requirements defined in WCAG 1.0. These activities are natural for the computer expert and manageable by casual webmasters, but they are perceived as intricate by publishers, who not rarely arrive at refusing to perform the assigned content authoring tasks. Furthermore, most publishers do not perform these tasks frequently, depending them on deadlines for tax payments or other bureaucratic issues; therefore, such users tend to forget many details of the procedure to be followed, especially when it requires some editing of HTML code.

These difficulties suggested us that an approach to CMS development aimed at integrating EUD techniques in the CMS itself could overcome different kinds of problems in e-government website creation, management and updating.

Therefore, we implemented a simple EUD technique to solve a specific problem encountered by publishers; then, a case study research [57][58] was carried out to examine in-depth the interaction with the original CMS and to evaluate how the EUD-based approach improved the situation. In the following, we describe the problem considered and a possible EUD solution. Then, the main results of the case study research are briefly presented (see [19] for more details).

5.1 EUD for Accessible Content Creation

To demonstrate the usefulness of EUD in the considered field, we faced the problem of creating tabular content to be published on an e-government website. Tabular content must satisfy guideline 5 "Create tables that transform gracefully" of WCAG 1.0 [54]. The six checkpoints of the guideline must be followed to support disabled people (users with blindness or low vision), who access tabular information through assistive technologies, such as a screen reader or a Braille display. The ability to produce accessible tabular content is of course a basic feature one would expect from a CMS (though this is not always the case). However, the EUD approach here proposed has a broader scope since it is suitable to support publishers in other and more sophisticated tasks.

To create accessible tables with the original CMS, publishers must modify the HTML code generated by the CMS. In particular, the interaction occurs as follows. The authoring tool available in the CMS provides a button in a toolbar to activate table creation. When the user selects this button, the system presents the user with a dialog window that asks for inserting the number of rows and columns of the new table. After interacting with this dialog window, a "prototype" table is created showing cells whose content is "Col 1 Row 1", "Col 2 Row 1", and so on for the first row, "Col 2 Row 1", "Col 2 Row 2", and so on for the second row, for all the rows requested by the user. Figure 1 shows the table created when the user asks for a two rows-two columns table.

When the user clicks on a table cell, its content is selected and the user can substitute it with the desired content. For example, let us suppose that the publisher inserts person names (Maria, Paola) and surnames (Rossi, Bianchi) in the first column and

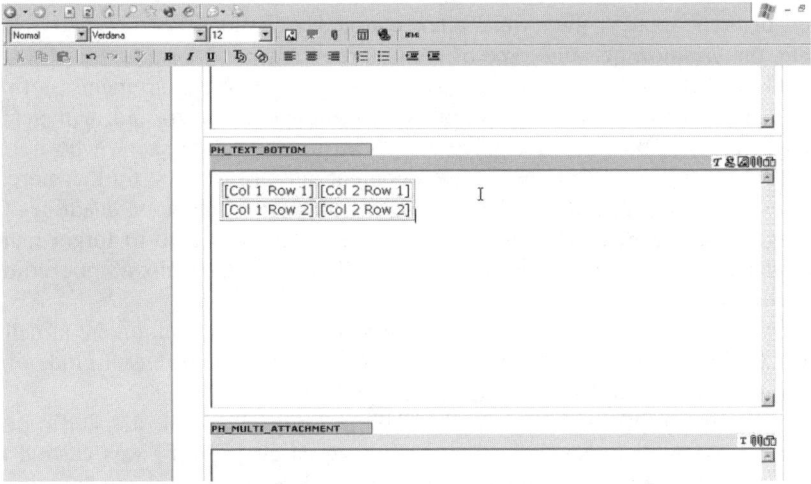

Fig. 1. The table created as a consequence of user request

second column respectively. The resulting HTML code underlying the table would be the following:

```
<TABLE>
     <TR>
             <TD> Maria </TD>
             <TD> Rossi </TD>
     </TR>
     <TR>
             <TD> Paola </TD>
             <TD> Bianchi </TD>
     </TR>
</TABLE>
```

To make this code compliant with guideline 5 of WCAG 1.0, the publisher must access this code through the proper button in the CMS toolbar and modify it as follows (users' modifications to the code generated by the CMS are highlighted):

```
<TABLE SUMMARY="This table contains name and surname of the
employees that work at the Public Relations Department of the
Brescia municipality">
            <CAPTION>Employees working at the Public Relations
       Department
         </CAPTION>
             <TR>
                 <TH ID="name">Name</TH>
                 <TH ID="surname">Surname</TH>
             </TR>
             <TR>
                 <TD headers="name">Maria</TD>
                 <TD headers="surname">Rossi</TD>
             </TR>
             <TR>
                 <TD headers="name">Paola</TD>
                 <TD headers="surname">Bianchi</TD>
             </TR>
</TABLE>
```

Actually this code aims at satisfying three of the six checkpoints of guideline 5 of WCAG and in particular:

- A tag <TH> has been added for each column by specifying the column header as a value of attribute ID of <TH>. This is to satisfy checkpoint 1 of WCAG guideline 5;
- Each cell identified by an element <TD> has been associated with the corresponding column by using attribute headers, whose value must correspond to the column header. This is to satisfy checkpoint 2 of WCAG guideline 5;
- Attribute summary has been added in tag <TABLE> and element <CAPTION> has been inserted as first child of element <TABLE>, in order to satisfy checkpoint 5 of WCAG guideline 5.

According to the municipality managers, these checkpoints are the minimum requirements to be satisfied by tables published in their website. In fact, checkpoint 6 gives additional indications for managing table linearization, but it has priority 3, while it was decided that, at the moment, the goal was to obtain Conformance Level AA for the website [53]. Checkpoints 3 and 4 refer to the use of tables for page layout; they are satisfied a priori, since page layout is managed through style sheets.

To support publishers in this work practice, they were provided with a paper-based manual, which presented a detailed example to be adapted to the case at hand. Notwithstanding this, this activity represented a problem for publishers.

In order to solve the problem by implementing a simple EUD technique based on parameterization, the source code of the CMS was properly modified. The interaction with the system for inserting a table now occurs as follows. When the user selects the tool to insert a table, after the dialog window asking for the number of rows and columns, a new dialog window is presented to the user. Such window, shown in Figure 2, asks the user for inserting a text for the caption, a text for the summary, and as much headers as the number of columns previously declared. The window autonomously adapts its size according to the number of column headers that need to be requested. It also helps the user to insert caption and summary by remembering her/him the meaning of such information directly in the text fields. The user is obliged to fill in all the text fields: in fact, when s/he selects the OK button, information are checked and, if one is missing, a warning message is presented to the user, by constraining her/him to return to the dialog window and complete data insertion. This relieves the publisher from checking the correctness of the table, making it easy to assess her/his EUD activity [28].

The new procedure is clearer and easier for people not expert in computer technologies. This was confirmed by the results of our case study research.

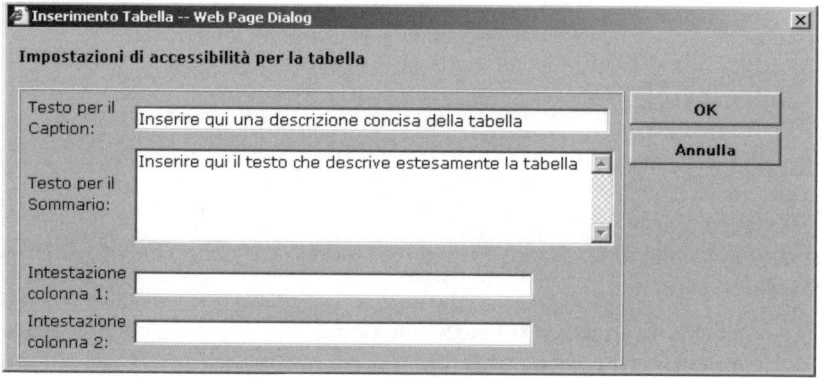

Fig. 2. The dialog window asking for accessibility parameters

5.2 Case Study Research: Methodology and Results

The goal of the case study research was to investigate the difficulties encountered by publishers in creating accessible content and to evaluate the benefits of enhancing the adopted CMS with EUD features. Therefore, our research questions aimed at understanding what happened during content creation and how the publishers faced the problems of the CMS about content accessibility. Then, our goal was also investigating if the extension of the CMS with the EUD feature would have provided significant improvements in terms of both performance and publishers' willingness to carry out activities concerned with accessible table creation.

We involved eight users chosen from different departments of the municipality. The sample, even if little, can be considered enough representative of the publisher population, because it included people expert in different domains and having different competencies, skills, and cultural background. Participants were asked for performing a task concerning the creation of an accessible table. A within groups technique was adopted, meaning that all users in the sample performed the same task using the original CMS and the extended CMS. To avoid polarization due to learning effects, different execution orders were defined.

Data gathering was carried out in the usual work place of users. The techniques adopted were *structured interviews* (after the execution of the assigned task in the two sub-cases), *observation* during task execution and *performance measures* (completion time and number of errors). The first two techniques were meant to provide us with a qualitative evaluation, while the last were meant to provide us with quantitative data possibly corroborating qualitative ones. An evaluation form was prepared to gather both qualitative and quantitative data: it included few simple questions (e.g. "Which are the main difficulties you encountered using the original CMS?", "Which are the main improvements you noticed in the new solution?") and some fields to be filled in by the observer with the observations taken during task execution and with the quantitative data.

During the execution of the task with the original CMS, we observed that most of publishers applied mechanically what was suggested by the example table in the manual and made several mistakes during the adaptation of that table. They often forgot to change some parts of the table, by leaving the information already present in the example table. Moreover, by listening to users' spontaneous comments, we discovered that difficulties and misunderstandings arose because users did not understand the meaning of tags correctly. For example, they confounded the terms `caption`, `headers` and `summary` (maybe this was also due to the translation between English and Italian). The interviews confirmed that publishers perceived the task as too difficult and requiring an exaggerate effort. In general, publishers considered the HTML code manipulation as a work alien to their competencies and tasks, useless, and time consuming. Most of them explicitly declared that they were not willing to spend energies and time in doing that job.

The new approach apparently solves all the above problems. Participants commented that the system now requires them exactly what is needed, it does not ask them anymore for thinking about the accessibility parameters, but it just drives them through table creation, and thus it also avoids them to consult the manual. These positive results, gathered through direct observation and interviews, are corroborated by quantitative data: the comparison of completion times and error numbers demonstrate that, using the procedure offered by the extended CMS, there is a significant improvement in both robustness and efficiency [19].

6 Toward Online Service Creation through EUD

We carried on the collaboration with the municipality with the aim of finding a solution also to the problem of online service development. This task is still at the hands of personnel of the Computer Science department of the municipality, since the CMS does not provide proper facilities for transferring it to publishers. This should remain valid also if a more up-to-date CMS would be adopted, since, as already mentioned, existing products provide scripting languages and macro languages that only computer experts or power users are able to manage.

This section describes a possible EUD approach to developing online services. The approach stems from the analysis of how personnel of the Computer Science department operate to create such services and from the characterization of publishers carried out during the case study research. We used unstructured interviews with a representative software developer to elicit knowledge about the kinds of services to be made available on a municipality website and about their design and development.

From the analysis of online services currently offered to citizens on the website it is possible to obtain the following classification: 1) front office reservation; 2) tax payment; 3) document request; 4) document submission; 5) registration to courses or schools. All these services are accessed by the end users of the website through form-based pages, since fill-in form interaction style has a low cognitive burden for most of people and it is easy to implement. More precisely, end users are presented with the forms composing a service through a *step-by-step instruction design pattern* [51]. This permits to drive users through the task, in order to acquire all necessary information in each step, and to perform validity checks on input data. Also inspired by the work of Ginige et al. [13][22], we think that an interaction style based on fill-in forms and a step-by-step instruction design pattern could be also at the basis of the EUD technique allowing publishers to create online services.

We illustrate this technique by an example. Currently, front office reservation services are implemented in the municipality website as a 5-step wizard, where the steps are: 1) counter choice; 2) date choice; 3) time choice; 4) input of personal data; 5) summary of data. The first three steps are implemented through radio buttons permitting exclusive choices; the fourth step presents text fields and combo boxes to input data; the fifth just presents all inserted data and asks for a confirmation. In each step, but the first, it is possible to go back one step to modify previous inserted data. An area on the right side of the page shows the steps performed, the step currently under compilation, and the steps remaining. Figure 3 shows the website page during the reservation of general registry office services: step 3 (time choice) is under compilation (see the main area of the page); on the right side, the white box and the symbol ⊙ highlight the step under compilation, whilst previous steps (counter selection and date selection) are marked as done (⊘) and next steps (input of personal data and summary of data) are marked as to be done (◎).

We argue that the implementation of such kind of wizards could be performed easily by publishers if the CMS supports them through a step-by-step form-based interaction. For creating a new online service, the publisher will first choose the class of the service, for example the "front office reservation" class. Then, the system will drive him/her through the steps for creating the service by means of fill-in forms. The

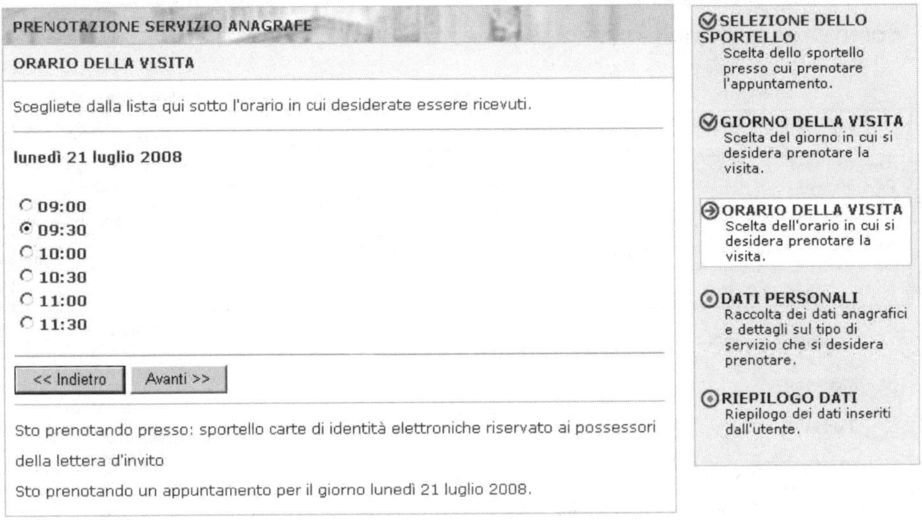

Fig. 3. Step 3 of front office reservation

first step will consist in generating the list of counter choices that pertain to the publisher's department. To this aim, a list of all counters could be available and the publisher might move items from this list to a list of selected counters, which will be presented on the website as a set of radio buttons. Figure 4 shows a mock-up of this EUD solution. (For the sake of paper readability, all mock-ups are in English).

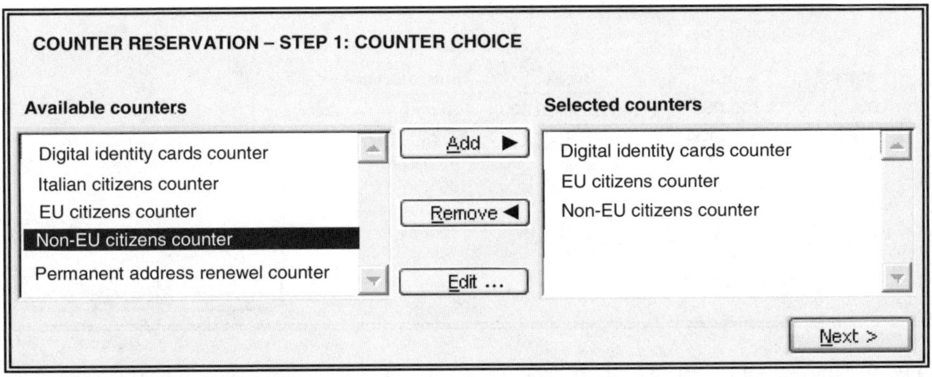

Fig. 4. Mock-up of the EUD tool for generating a list of radio buttons related with counter choice

The next step should be a calendar component customized to publishers' needs: it should support the choice of start and end dates, the indication of holidays, and the choice of week days in which the counter is open. Figure 5 shows a mock-up of this EUD solution: three calendars are used to choose start, end, and holidays; six check boxes permit to choose working days. The system must generate a set of radio buttons for date choice that satisfy all constraints defined by the publisher.

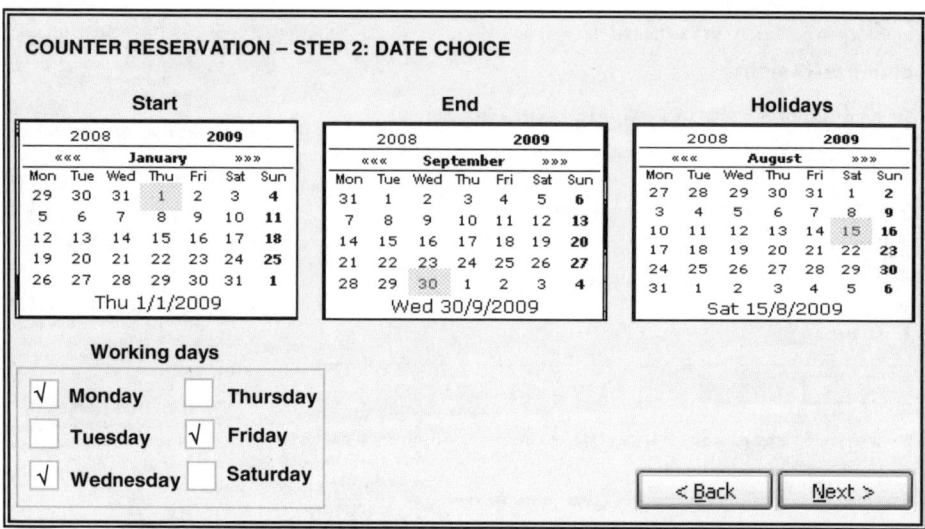

Fig. 5. Mock-up of the EUD tool for generating a list of radio buttons related with date choice

The third step should be the creation of time choices: the publisher could choose start, end, break and time intervals, and the system should generate the list of all possible times as a set of radio buttons satisfying the established constraints. Figure 6 shows a mock-up of this EUD solution: combo boxes permit time choices.

COUNTER RESERVATION – STEP 3: TIME CHOICE

Start	End	Break	Time interval
8.00	18.00	12.30-13.00	30 min
8.00	18.00	12.30-	30 min
8.30	18.30	12.45-	45 min
9.00	19.00	13.00-	60 min
9.30	19.30	13.15-	75 min
10.00	20.00	13.30-	100 min

`< Back`   `Next >`

Fig. 6. Mock-up of the EUD tool for generating a list of radio buttons related with time choice

Then the publisher should create the form for input data; also in this case, the solution foreseen for counter choice, i.e. the double-list control, can be useful: a list of all possible personal data could be available, giving the publisher the possibility to select only those s/he considers necessary to be requested in the case at hand. Finally, the step summarizing the inserted data could be generated automatically by the system on the basis of the previous steps created by the publisher.

7 Discussion

The design of EUD techniques proposed in the previous sections derives from a basic observation: end users who has to carry out some software development in the domain of e-government websites are different from casual webmasters or power users. Therefore, they must not be aware of performing software development. They should accomplish tasks that consist in just editing content (including providing information that become HTML attribute values) or selecting some content from available choices. The underlying system will be in charge of generating the correct code by exploiting the content provided by the user.

Both techniques presented in Sections 5 and 6 are based on fill-in form interaction style, which has been judged suitable for the considered end users, namely personnel used to carry out administration tasks often consisting in the compilation of paper-based forms. Therefore, this interaction style should be natural and simple for these end users, by allowing them to operate according to their mental models of the activities to be performed [11]. On the other hand, this EUD style has been applied also in other contexts with successful results [27], even though, differently from [27], we aim to drive users through all their choices, without asking them to remember some particular syntax for providing the information requested by the system.

In the case of online service creation, the fill-in form interaction style is combined with a step-by-step instruction design pattern that reflects the structure of the service to be created. The publisher should not have so much freedom (and consequent responsibility) to modify the layout of the service pages or the structure of the service. Moreover, s/he should not access the generated code.

The idea of an EUD technique based on a step-by-step instruction design pattern actually arises from the analysis of the output to be generated (i.e. the service to be made available to website's users). This analysis produces a model of the service, which helps to determine the most natural way for publishers to take care of its development.

Service analysis and model-based design of EUD techniques should remain at the hands of the software developers belonging to the organization managing the website: they should identify the classes of services that could be developed, the steps constituting each class, and the elements composing each step. Then, their work will be the development of the fill-in forms that allow publishers to create online services. These activities can be characterized as *meta-design* activities [17], in that they are carried out to "design the design process" [21], i.e. to design the EUD activities that publishers should perform. In [17], this is regarded as the first level of meta-design, which refers to the possibility offered to end users to transform and modify components and contents at use time, according to emerging needs and tasks, as it may happen in the case of online service creation. Methodologically, software developers operate at a meta-level by "establishing the conditions that will allow users, in turn, to become designers" [17].

Obviously, software developers may become again a bottleneck in those contexts that are very dynamic, where classes of services evolve over time and new classes must be designed and developed frequently. However, the approach here presented seems – at least at the moment – suitable to the dynamicity of the considered application domain. Its scalability should be studied if one would like to extend its application to other domains, such as e-commerce or e-learning websites. Further research on meta-design approaches could help to find solutions to this problem.

8 Conclusions

This paper focused on a particular application domain, namely the creation and maintenance of e-government websites. In this domain, distributed content authoring is often a necessity to avoid delays in publishing important information for citizens and to overcome communication gaps between software developers and domain experts.

However, despite the use of CMSs, this distributed activity is far to be performed in an easy, efficient and effective way. By analyzing the case of an Italian municipality we discovered that publishers find several difficulties in creating accessible contents. Therefore, a CMS extension with a simple EUD technique has been developed to eliminate such difficulties. The approach has been evaluated with publishers, by giving positive results [19].

We also observed that the creation of more sophisticated contents, e.g. online services, are still at the hands of software developers, since this task appears as too difficult to be carried out by publishers. In this paper, we tried to demonstrate the contrary: it is possible to implement proper EUD techniques devoted to these end users, whose motivation and interest in software development is low. From our analysis, it emerged that the fill-in form interaction style and the step-by-step instruction design pattern could be adopted to design EUD techniques for the domain at hand. They have been proved successful in the case of HTML editing for accessibility satisfaction, and they seem to be promising in the case of online service development.

As future work we plan to implement and test the mock-up ideas presented in this paper, as well as to identify and define meta-design guidelines for the design of EUD techniques by personnel of the Computer Science municipality department.

Acknowledgments. The author wishes to thank Sergio Colosio of Comune di Brescia, Italy, and Loredana Parasiliti Provenza of Università di Milano, Italy, for the fruitful discussions about the content of this paper. She is also indebted to Matteo Sacco for the development of the CMS extensions and to the publishers of the Comune di Brescia for their availability in participating in interviews and tests of the implemented EUD technique.

References

1. Anslow, C., Rielhe, D.: Towards End-User Programming with Wikis. In: Proc. WEUSE IV 2008, Leipzig, Germany, pp. 61–65 (2008)
2. Arias, E., Eden, H., Fischer, G., Gorman, A., Scharff, E.: Transcending the Individual Human Mind - Creating Shared Understanding through Collaborative Design. ACM Transactions on Computer-Human Interaction 7(1), 84–113 (2000)
3. Blackboard Content System,
   http://www.blackboard.com/products/Academic_Suite/
   Content_System/index

4. Blackwell, A.F.: End-User Developers at Home. Communications of the ACM 47(9), 65–66 (2004)
5. Blackweell, A.F., Hague, R.: AutoHAN: An architecture for programming at home. In: Proc. IEEE Symposium on Human-Centric Computing Languages and Environments, pp. 150–157 (2001)
6. Brancheau, J.C., Brown, C.V.: The Management of End-User Computing: Status and Directions. ACM Computing Surveys 25(4), 437–482 (1993)
7. Carrara, P., Fogli, D., Fresta, G., Mussio, P.: Toward overcoming culture, skill and situation hurdles in human-computer interaction. Int. J. Universal Access in the Information Society 1(4), 288–304 (2002)
8. Costabile, M.F., Fogli, D., Letondal, C., Mussio, P., Piccinno, A.: Domain-Expert Users and their Needs of Software Development. In: Proc. UAHCI Conference, Crete, pp. 232–236 (2003)
9. Costabile, M.F., Fogli, D., Mussio, P., Piccinno, A.: End-User Development: the Software Shaping Workshop Approach. In: Lieberman, H., Paternò, F., Wulf, V. (eds.) End-User Development, pp. 183–205. Kluwer Academic Publisher, Dordrecht (2006)
10. Costabile, M.F., Fogli, D., Mussio, P., Piccinno, A.: Visual Interactive Systems for End-User Development: a Model-based Design Methodology. IEEE Transactions on Systems Man and Cybernetics, part A- Systems and Humans 37(6), 1029–1046 (2007)
11. Costabile, M.F., Mussio, P., Parasiliti Provenza, L., Piccinno, A.: End Users as Unwitting Software Developers. In: Proc. WEUSE IV 2008, Leipzig, Germany, pp. 6–10 (2008)
12. Cypher, A.: Watch What I Do: Programming by Demonstration. MIT Press, Cambridge (1993)
13. Da Silva, B., Ginige, A.: Modeling Web Information Systems for Co-Evolution. In: Proc. ICSOFT 2007, Barcelona, Spain (2007)
14. De Ruyter, B., Van de Sluis, R.: Challenges for End-User Development in Intelligent Environments. In: Lieberman, H., Paternò, F., Wulf, V. (eds.) End-User Development, pp. 243–250. Kluwer Academic Publishers, Dordrecht (2006)
15. Drupal, http://drupal.org/
16. EUD-Net Thematic Network, http://giove.cnuce.cnr.it/eud-net.htm
17. Fischer, G., Giaccardi, E.: Meta-Design: A Framework for the Future of End User Development. In: Lieberman, H., Paternò, F., Wulf, V. (eds.) End User Development, pp. 427–457. Kluwer Academic Publisher, Dordrecht (2006)
18. Fischer, G.: Seeding, Evolutionary Growth and Reseeding: Constructing, Capturing and Evolving Knowledge in Domain-Oriented Design Environments. Int. J. Automated Software Engineering 5(4), 447–464 (1998)
19. Fogli, D., Colosio, S., Sacco, M.: Managing Accessibility in Local E-government Websites through End-User Development: A Case Study. Int. J. Universal Access in the Information Society (to appear)
20. Folmer, E., van Welie, M., Bosch, J.: Bridging patterns: An approach to bridge gaps between SE and HCI. J. of Information and Software Technology 48(2), 69–89 (2005)
21. Giaccardi, E., Fischer, G.: Creativity and Evolution: A Metadesign Perspective. Digital Creativity 19(1), 19–32 (2008)
22. Ginige, A., De Silva, B.: CBEADS©: A Framework to Support Meta-design Paradigm. In: Stephanidis, C. (ed.) HCI 2007. LNCS, vol. 4554, pp. 107–116. Springer, Heidelberg (2007)
23. Goette, T., Collier, C., Daniels White, J.: An exploratory study of the accessibility of state government Web sites. Int. J. Universal Access in the Information Society 5, 41–50 (2006)
24. Joomla!™, http://www.joomla.org/

25. Joomla! Help Site – WCAG Checklist, `http://help.joomla.org/`
26. Letondal, C.: Participatory Programming: Developing Programmable Bioinformatics Tools for End-Users. In: Lieberman, H., Paternò, F., Wulf, V. (eds.) End-User Development, pp. 207–242. Kluwer Academic Publishers, Dordrecht (2006)
27. Liang, X., Ginige, A.: Enabling an End-User Drive Approach for Managing Evolving User Interfaces in Business Web Applications. In: ICSOFT 2007, Barcelona, Spain (2007)
28. Lieberman, H., Paternò, F., Klann, M., Wulf, V.: End-User Development: An Emerging Paradigm. In: Lieberman, H., Paternò, F., Wulf, V. (eds.) End-User Development, pp. 1–8. Kluwer Academic Publishers, Dordrecht (2006)
29. Lieberman, H., Paternò, F., Wulf, V. (eds.): End-User Development. Kluwer Academic Publishers, Dordrecht (2006)
30. Macías, J.A., Paternò, F.: Customization of Web applications through an intelligent environment exploiting logical interface descriptions. Interacting with Computers 20, 29–47 (2008)
31. Majhew, D.J.: Principles and Guideline in Software User Interface Design. Prentice-Hall, Englewood Cliffs (1992)
32. Microsoft Content Management Server, `http://www.microsoft.com/cmserver/default.mspx`
33. Microsoft Office SharePoint Designer 2007 (2007), `http://office.microsoft.com/it-it/sharepointdesigner/FX100487631040.aspx`
34. Moodle, `http://moodle.org/`
35. Mørch, A.: Three Levels of End-User Tailoring: Customization, Integration, and Extension. In: Kyng, M., Mathiassen, L. (eds.) Computers and Design in Context, pp. 51–76. MIT Press, Cambridge (1997)
36. Mørch, A., Stevens, G., Won, M., Klann, M., Dittrich, Y., Wulf, G.: Component-Based Technologies for End-User Development. Communications of the ACM 47(9), 59–62 (2004)
37. Myers, B.A., Pane, J.F., Ko, A.: Natural Programming Languages and Environments. Communications of the ACM 47(9), 47–52 (2004)
38. O'Really: What Is Web 2.0 - Design Patterns and Business Models for the Next Generation of Software, `http://www.oreillynet.com/pub/a/oreilly/tim/news/2005/09/30/what-is-web-20.html`
39. Paris, M.: Website accessibility: a survey of local e-government websites and legislation in Northern Ireland. Int. J. Universal Access in the Information Society 4, 292–299 (2006)
40. Parlamento Italiano, Disposizioni per favorire l'accesso dei soggetti disabili agli strumenti informatici, Legge 9 gennaio, n. 4, G.U. n. 13 del 17 gennaio (in Italian) (2004) (in English), `http://www.pubbliaccesso.it/normative/law_20040109_n4.htm`
41. Petre, M., Blackwell, A.F.: Children as Unwitting End-User Programmers. In: Proc. VL/HCC 2007, Coeur d'Alène, USA, pp. 239–242 (2007)
42. Plone™, `http://plone.org/`
43. Plone™– Accessibility Statement, `http://plone.org/accessibility-info`
44. QnECMS – Quick & Easy Accessible CMS, `http://www.qnecms.co.uk/`
45. Repenning, A., Ioannidu, A.: Agent-Based End-User Development. Communications of the ACM 47(9), 43–46 (2004)
46. Rode, J., Bhardwaj, Y., Pérez-Quinones, M.A., Rosson, M.B., Howarth, J.: As Easy as "Click": End-User Web Engineering. In: Lowe, D.G., Gaedke, M. (eds.) ICWE 2005. LNCS, vol. 3579, pp. 478–488. Springer, Heidelberg (2005)

47. Rode, J., Rosson, M.B., Pérez Quinõnes, M.A.: End User Development of Web Applications. In: Lieberman, H., Paternò, F., Wulf, V. (eds.) End-User Development, pp. 161–182. Kluwer Academic Publishers, Dordrecht (2006)

48. Rosson, M.B., Ballin, J., Nash, H.: Everyday Programming: Challenges and Opportunities for Informal Web Development. In: Proc. VL/HCC 2004, Rome, Italy, pp. 123–130 (2004)

49. Sitekit CMS, http://www.sitekit.net/

50. Sutcliffe, A., Mehandjiev, N. (Guest eds.): End-User Development. Communications of the ACM 47(9), 31–32 (2004)

51. Tidwell, J.: Common Grounds: A Pattern Language for Human-Computer Interface Design, http://www.mit.edu/~jtidwell/common_ground.html

52. Typo3, http://typo3.com/

53. Web Accessibility Initiative, http://www.w3.org/WAI/

54. Web Content Accessibility Guidelines 1.0, W3C Recommendation (May 5, 1999), http://www.w3.org/TR/1999/WAI-WEBCONTENT-19990505

55. Won, M., Stiemerling, O., Wulf, V.: Component-Based Approaches to Tailorable Systems. In: Lieberman, H., Paternò, F., Wulf, V. (eds.) End-User Development, pp. 115–141. Kluwer Academic Publishers, Dordrecht (2006)

56. Ye, Y., Fischer, G.: Designing for Participation in Socio-Technical Software Systems. In: Stephanidis, C. (ed.) HCI 2007. LNCS, vol. 4554, pp. 312–321. Springer, Heidelberg (2007)

57. Yin, R.K.: Case study research: Design and methods. Sage, Newbury Park (1984)

58. Yin, R.K.: Case study methods. In: Green, J.L., Camilli, G., Elmore, P.B. (eds.) Handbook of complementary methods in education research, pp. 111–122. Lawrence Erlbaum Associates, Hillsdale (2006)

LWOAD: A Specification Language to Enable the End-User Develoment of Coordinative Functionalities

Federico Cabitza and Carla Simone

Università degli Studi di Milano-Bicocca,
viale Sarca 336, 20126 Milano (Italy)
{cabitza,simone}@disco.unimib.it

Abstract. In this paper, we present an observational case study at a major teaching hospital, which both inspired and gave us valuable feedback on the design and development of LWOAD. LWOAD is a denotational language we propose to support users of an electronic document system in declaratively expressing, specifying and implementing computational mechanisms that fulfill coordinative requirements. Our focus addresses (a) the user-friendly and formal expression of local coordinative practices; (b) the agile mocking-up of corresponding functionalities; (c) the full deployment of coordination-oriented and context-aware behaviors into legacy electronic document systems. We give examples of LWOAD mechanisms taken from the case study and discuss their impact for the EUD of coordinative functionalities.

1 Requirements for EUD in Document-Mediated Cooperative Work

The fact that documents are ubiquitous means to support work activities is well known. Their initially undifferentiated role has been more recently investigated and articulated to understand why documents, which are so natural and widespread, still raise problems when they are transformed in digitized counterparts, not only when electronic documents are used as stand-alone artifacts but, above all, when they are parts and components of an *electronic document system* [1,2]. The solution of this paradox calls for a stronger user involvement in the definition and maintenance of functionalities that support actors in accomplishing their duties and coordinating their action; these functionalities relate closely to how users read and write their paper-based artifacts and to the often only implicit and ad-hoc practices and conventions that regard documents' use and interpretation. A very inspiring domain where to motivate this claim and highlight requirements for an EUD-based solution is the healthcare domain. This is, on the one hand, so complex and various that almost all considerations emerged from other cooperative domains apply naturally (e.g., [3,4]); on the other hand, this domain has been widely studied and specialist literature has provided interesting findings to leverage. For instance, in his comprehensive account on the role of documents in professional work, Hertzum [5] points out the

V. Pipek et al. (Eds.): IS-EUD 2009, LNCS 5435, pp. 146–165, 2009.

paradigmatic case of the *patient record*, in regard to both its *many-sidedness* in supporting cooperative work and its ability to speak different "voices", i.e., to convey different meanings according to the actor using it (e.g., doctor, nurse). According to Garfinkel [6], the patient record contains at least two clear intertwined voices: a voice reporting what clinician did what to inpatients; and another voice attesting that clinicians have honored claims for adequate medical care. Following in the same footsteps, Berg distinguishes between the coordinative and accumulative function [7] of patient records, respectively. Patient records exhibit the accumulative function whenever they play the role of official, inscribed artifacts that practitioners write to preserve memory or knowledge of facts or events occurred at the hospital ward. Patient records exhibit the coordinative function whenever they are used to support articulation and coordination of the work activities which are tightly coupled with data production and consumption. A very important point is that the accumulative function can refer to either a long-term role of records – typically when patient's data are *archived* for research or statistical purposes – or to a short-term role– typically when these data are memorized to *keep trace* of the care trajectory during the patient's hospital stay. This latter role is necessarily entangled with coordinative functions in not always trivial ways [8,9]. Accordingly, the specialist literature distinguishes between *primary* and *secondary* purposes, respectively. Primary purposes regard the demands for autonomy and support of practitioners involved in the direct and daily care of inpatients; while secondary purposes are the main focus of hospital management, which pursues them for the sake of rationalizing care provision and enabling clinical research. The investment policies in ICT are usually focused on secondary purposes (i.e., on cost savings and new pharmacological patents) and this leads to the design of Electronic Patient Records (EPR) where document structures and functionalities are aimed at supporting information inscription and use according to data quality and usability criteria [10], which tend to neglect (or heavily overlook) the primary purposes [11]. The additional effort of articulation work on the clinical record is then usually left to practitioners; as well as, often, the burden to reconfigure their coordinative practices once their habitual paper-based artifacts have been digitized [9].

In this scenario, document templates and masks are usually imposed from above to practitioners, irrespectively of their coordinative needs. Even in the best case where documents are cooperatively and participatorily defined, they tend to be given to actors once and for all so as to neglect the frequent tuning activities and adjustments that coordinative mechanisms require for their negotiated and participated nature [12,13]. Our observational studies in two wards of a large provincial hospital in Northern Italy confirmed other accounts from the CSCW literature (e.g., [14,7,8] on how practitioners try to reconcile primary and secondary purposes on the artifacts of daily use to make them useful both to store and retrieve information but also to support mutual learning, knowledge sharing and coordination of caring activities. To this aim, actors define, renegotiate and evolve ad-hoc practices, peculiar conventions, and agreed interpretations that are local and unique to their work settings; usually, these conventions thrive either in the grey area of underspecification or through the mesh of the constraining specifications of organizational rules that the hospital management has imposed for law or quality standard compliance.

Our point is that the development of any technological support of the full usage of official records cannot do without considering these *local habits* and *conventions* as a primary source of information for the definition of functionalities that support cooperation and, to limit ourselves to our reference domain, effective care giving. Moreover, since these habits and conventions are *local and unique*, the technological support should provide *flexible* functionalities that preserve, or even foster the fluid, conventional and evolutionary nature of coordinative practices. Last but not least, these functionalities should be under the full control of actors themselves. Our research question is then how to facilitate this local management in a sustainable way. The paper aims to give a contribution in this direction by presenting a computational framework that was deeply influenced and partially tested by our field study in the above mentioned hospital [15]. The next section describes the field study context and provides the main motivations for the framework; Section 3 describes the framework and its denotational language, LWOAD, in more details; Section 4 illustrates the complex and real-life conventions we tested the framework on; Section 5 discusses the main findings of the case study; Section 6 illustrates the mockup we used as a proof-of-concept of the findings related to mechanism specification and Section 7 sums things up and sheds light on current and future directions of our research in the EUD field.

2   Bridging Conventions and EPR Applications

Our empirical research involved doctors and nurses of a major Neonatal Intensive Care Unit (NICU). We conducted this study through unobtrusive observations in the ward, informal talks, individual interviews with key doctors and nurses, and open group discussions with ward practitioners. These interactions were initially used to deal with the "descriptive" part of the research, and to reach a reasonable and common language. Yet, quite soon, the need emerged to find a more effective way to deal with what we called "local habits and conventions" in the previous section. In parallel with our investigation in the ward, practitioners had to interact with a team of software developers of a third-party IT firm, the Alpha ltd. The NICU head physician had been involved for months with this firm to produce an innovative EPR for the care of his premature newborns: a job order he was totally in charge of, with no time pressures and the concrete willingness to create a solution on the practitioners' side. Since Alpha designers had already developed a full-fledged prototype of a hospital-wide EPR, the NICU head physician soon adopted that prototype as a sort of "sandbox" where the programmer analysts of Alpha and some physicians of the NICU could experiment their innovative and peculiar ideas with no claim of officiality or exactitude. While Alpha's analysts were more oriented to the archival functionalities, we concentrated on the coordinative ones: together with the practitioners, we took the design of a new EPR as the occasion to try to preserve as many as possible efficient, though idiosyncratic, coordinative practices and "graft" them onto the archival-oriented EPR by conceiving coordinative functionalities on-top-of it.

To this aim, we felt the need to develop specific ways (a) to express coordination-oriented requirements in a user-friendly manner for ICT laymen (as clinicians were); and (b) to formalize the corresponding functionalities in a way that they could become easily computable. Our goal was to support the effort of practitioners in making explicit, symbolic and also computable the relationship occurring between recurrent patterns of context and the conventional, local ways practitioners relied on to cope with this context. During the requirement collection and preliminary analysis, we observed that the simplest, and yet powerful, concept that practitioners grasped with fewer equivocations was that of *reactive behavior* and its computable counterpart, the *rule*, i.e., a well-defined and autonomous *if-then* statement (see Figure 1).

This finding heavily influenced how we were conceiving the WOAD framework [15] (an acronym for 'Web of Documental Artifacts'). WOAD is a design framework we were articulating during the NICU case study in order to bridge the gap between informal description of coordinative conventions – expressed in terms of agreed ways to cope with the current context – and the design of document-mediated functionalities supportive of these conventions. Our point was that practitioners themselves could bridge this gap, if the the computer-based support could provide them unobtrusive and additional information to promote collaboration awareness [16,17]. In the WOAD framework, we defined (a) a conceptual model of articulation by which to characterize the main entities and relationships involved in document-mediated cooperative work in terms of minimal sets of attributes; (b) a denotational language – LWOAD – which incorporates those concepts and relationships to represent the context of cooperative document domains and conceive specific computational mechanisms that convey Awareness Promoting Information (API) depending on the current context [17]; and (c) a high-level architecture for information sharing in context-aware and distributed computing settings where LWOAD is used and implemented. Since LWOAD plays a basic role in making the specification of rules expressing the above mentioned relationships computable, we briefly introduce it and discuss how we used it in our interaction with the NICU practitioners.

3   A Language to Express Coordinative Functionalities

Within the WOAD framework, LWOAD provides a set of high-level concepts – like those of *actor, documental artifact, fact, fact space,* and *fact-interpreter* – that we propose to guide the design of a rule-based reference architecture for context-aware and coordination-oriented electronic document systems. We conceive LWOAD as an astract programming interface by which to program functionalities that (a) process the content of a document according to local conventions of coordination; and (b) convey suitable API to support actors in articulating their document-centered activities.

LWOAD encompasses a set of both static and dynamic constructs by which designers can express either contextual, organizational or procedural knowledge about a work arrangement. Static data structures and dynamic behaviors of an application are expressed by two specific constructs: *facts* and *mechanisms*, respectively. In LWOAD, designers can model a cooperative arrangement in terms of its main relevant entities and the relationships between them by declaring *facts*. Whatever is given the suffix *-fact* (e.g., *activity-fact*, *relation-fact* and *API-fact*) is a *key-value* data structures, which programmers can use to characterize the relevant entities of a documental domain just assigning a value to their specific attributes. A *relation-fact*, for instance, is characterized by five attributes: i) a name, ii) a description, iii) a property telling whether the relation-fact indicates a relationship between classes (e.g., physicians and patients) or between instances (e.g., Dr Smith and Mr Jones), iv) an attribute that specifies the fact's name of the entity that is the source (i.e., the subject) of the relationship and v) an attribute specifying the target (i.e., object) entity of the relationship. LWOAD provides designers with templates (i.e., *entity-facts*) for the most generic categories of articulation work (cf. [13]), like those of actor, activity and artifact; yet, by means of the *extends* primitive, designers can also define domain-specific entities (such as patient, doctor and clinical activity) that specialize and inherit from those general categories.

Mechanisms can be seen as simple conditional statements, like *if-then* rules. They produce some output in virtue of the actions expressed in their *consequent* (the *then* part) whenever specific contextual conditions, which are expressed in their *antecedent* (the *if* part), are true. Antecedents are considered true whenever the conditions they express on the entities they refer to are met by the current WOAD-compliant representation of the context, i.e., by the content of the facts represented within the so called *fact space*. Any single mechanism is hence a symbolic way to make a relation explicit between some contextual conditions and some functionality that the system should exhibit whenever a specific case occurs.

Although symbolic and based on rules, LWOAD is far from being usable directly by practitioners, since it must comply with the typical syntactic constraints of a language interpretable by a computational engine. For this

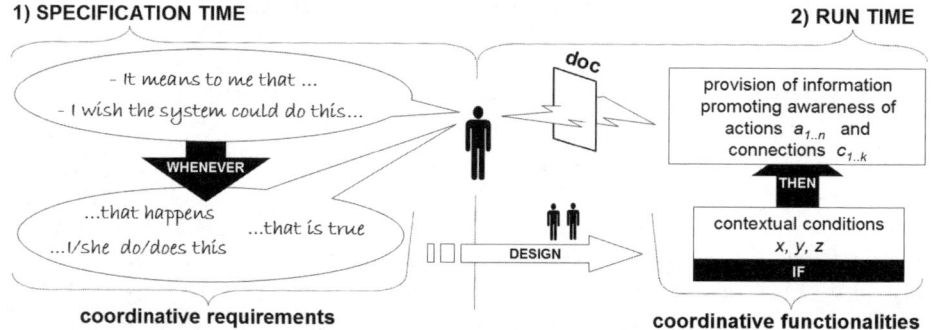

Fig. 1. The design-implementation loop inspired by the case study

reason, we adopted a two-step approach: first, for each identified coordinative mechanism, we invited the practitioners to indicate both the relevant set of attributes of the domain entities, events and documental data that the computational system should be sensitive to, and what conditions the system should evaluate on these relevant aspects of the work setting in order to activate the desired functionalities. The practitioners expressed the mechanisms in natural, tough structured and restricted, language and we translated them "on the fly' in LWOAD statements. In doing so, we could rapidly convey the "flavor" of the coordinative mechanisms envisioned by the NICU practitioners and we could support them in deciding whether the mechanisms had to be fully implemented in the hypothetical final release of the EPR. Once they had become familiar with this way of describing the desired mechanisms and had identified the basic patterns of conditions, we mocked-up an interface based on a wizard that could support practitioners in the construction of mechanisms (more details in Section 6). Our goal was to check whether the practitioners had become proficient in defining the desired mechanisms *autonomously*. Then, the needed mechanisms were translated in LWOAD to check its correctness with respect to both the application conditions and the desired outputs. Generally, practitioners did not find problems in expressing LWOAD mechanisms, probably for their intrinsic simplicity: antecedents are constituted by fact patterns and boolean tests and practitioners found natural express them as conjunction of facts that must be true in a given situation. On the other hand, consequents are sequences of WOAD primitives and practitioners mastered them in a relatively short time since our design choice was to limit LWOAD to the expression of functionalities that promote collaboration awareness and do not manipulate the data managed in the archival dimension of the EPR. Therefore, the effects of the consequents were only graphical cues added on top of documents' data. In a parallel work [17], we classified up to 13 different types of API – e.g., criticality, revision and schedule awareness – and identified together with the practitioners graphical ways to convey those various kinds of information. Although this latter identification is not completely experimented, it constituted a basis where to get an initial impression of how well the interface could be usable by practitioners on their own. In the next section, we provide the reader with two examples of mechanism specification in response to the specific coordinative requirements that we identified with the NICU practitioners during the first phase of our study.

4   Coordinative Requirements for EPRs

The patient record is the main documental artifact used in hospital care as it is the composite repository for the whole information concerning a single patient stay. During a patient stay, the whole patient record is split up into several sheets and documents; these are distributed in the ward and are very specific for a certain aspect of care so as to be usually used by different actors at the same time. During the study at NICU, practitioners recognized the need to conceive functionalities supportive of the conventional ways by which artifacts were used both to document their work and to mutually articulate their activities with each other. In the what follows, we present some cases that call for the requirements of a *flexible definition* and *flexible combination* of coordinative functionalities.

Specification Flexibility for Structure-Related Conventions. Due to the fact that clinical data are usually scattered across multiple artifacts in different places, doctors at NICU found useful to rely on a summary of clinical data that are gathered into one single sheet that they call *Summary Sheet* (SS); they update the SS quite frequently by taking and synchronizing its content from the official patient record. The summary sheet is not part of the official patient record but, nevertheless, it is a very useful working document since it is often used to jot down offhand annotations and informal communications regarding clinical conditions of the patient at hand. Moreover, due to its informality, doctors are used to bringing the SS with them either as first page of sets of papers under their arm, or even folded in their pocket. Therefore, since the SS is usually the first document doctors have got in their hand during their hectic activities, they also use it to jot clinical data and prescriptions on-the-go, which they will have to replicate into the official record later as a rule of law. Hence, the summary sheet is not only a "passive view" of previously reported data, i.e., a *view* on data fetched by querying multiple tables of a clinical database on the illness course of a single patient. It is also an active *entry form*, into which practitioners insert data at the point of care and from which they copy data into the official records for the sake of accountability and liability. Doctors were well aware of this twofold functionality during the design of the digital counterpart of the SS into the "innovative" EPR; therefore, they were willing to express constraints and define conceptual connections between sections and fields of the summary sheet and corresponding sections and fields of the artifacts compounding the patient record. These connections were seen as symmetrical, i.e., equivalent and irrespective of where the *original* data were actually inserted first. They can be traced back to the class of connections that in [18] we denoted as enabling *"redundancy by duplicated data"*, in that they make the association explicit between identical data that are reported in two or more documents of the patient record. In regard to the requirements for supportive functionalities, these kind of connections regard conventions of production and use of clinical documents: more specifically, they regard how data are organized within templates, what data type are allowed in what field (i.e., syntactic integrity) and also where people fill in data during their situated documental activities. Moreover, these connections are local and conventional both in their definition and, above all, in their use. In fact, it is only on a conventional and context-dependent basis that doctors want summary sheets be completely compiled *after* the patient record and, conversely, values reported in the SS first be fed *into* the patient record at proper time.

Two examples can better illustrate this point. Some members of the NICU staff team expressed the requirement that values on the weight of newborns would be reported into the summary sheet *only* whenever a newborn was in life-threatening conditions. In fact only in that case, these practitioners deemed

```
ANTECEDENT:

  CONSIDER THE LATEST WEIGHT PARAMETER ON THE SIGN SHEET OF A NEWBORN

  CONSIDER HER CURRENT BLOOD PRESSURE AS REPORTED IN THE VITAL SIGN SHEET

  TEST WHETHER BLOOD PRESSURE IS LOWER THAN 70mmHg,
                             I.E., WE HAVE A "CRITICAL CONDITION"
CONSEQUENT:

  HAVE THE RIGHT WEIGHT VALUE COPIED INTO THE SIGN SHEET

  MAKE ME AWARE OF THE FACT THE NEWBORN IS IN CRITICAL CONDITIONS
```

```
(antecedent
   (document-fact (record-id ?pr) (name SS) (latest-weight ?lw))
   (document-fact (record-id ?pr) (name VS) (current-weight ?cw) (current-blood-pressure ?bp))
   (patient-fact (name ?name) (patient-record ?pr) )
   (test (< ?bp 70mmHg)))
(consequent
   <write ?lw = ?cw >
   <convey (API-fact (type criticality)) on (document-fact (record id ?pr) (name SS))
                                     for (patient-fact (name ?name)) >)
```

Fig. 2. A coordinative mechanism on conventional patterns of data redundancy. Above, as expressed by practitioners in their own terms. Below, how this is translated in terms of LWOAD facts and primitives.

necessary to rely on weight data at the point-of-care, so as to calculate drug dosage precisely. In the other cases, to have these data available on the SS would only result in an unnecessary information overload and, even more annoying, would undermine the role of unobtrusive reminder on critical conditions that the presence or absence of weight data in the summary sheet could play at the point of care. Likewise, at NICU, clinical data that are reported into the SS first are often deemed as still provisional and are reported there to have colleagues consider those data but also take them as not yet definitive, or even as an invitation for further check and inquiry. The need for doctors to be aware of what is still provisional and hence different from what constitutes an unmodifiable and legal account of accomplished deeds is essential to cooperatively structure the formation of decisions and judgments, as also reported in [19].

Figure 2 depicts how the above mentioned conventions on data replication have been expressed in a dedicated and concise LWOAD mechanism. This mechanism has in its antecedent all and only the relevant aspects of context that are concerned with the coordinative functionality expressed in the consequent. While practitioners expressed this subset of contextual information in their own terms, we translated the consequent into four conditional elements, i.e., namely three patterns and an inequality test. The reason why even what seems a quite objective and scientific threshold of blood pressure is consider "conventional" (and hence ward- if not doctor-specific) is worthy a reflection. Quite surprisingly, doctors told us that also the notion of "critical condition" changes according to a number of contextual aspects that are mostly neglected by monitoring devices: their alarms are most of times consciously and rightly ignored by expert nurses, as reported in [20]. For this reason, doctors believe that these conditions are utterly difficult to hardwire into procedural application logic in all but the most obvious cases. In fact, criticality – seen along the coordinative dimension as the condition of a patient that calls for a direct and immediate intervention of some practitioner – depends on several anamnestic and physiological elements, on the illness history of the patient, and also on even more situated aspects, like the attitude of attending practitioners and their current workload. This is an important point to challenge LWOAD against the requirement of flexible definition of mechanisms. Obviously, not all the above often-tacit contextual conditions can be immediately and comprehensively externalized into a mechanism and neither should they be: however, as long as recognizing a specific situation has a relevant coordinative value, practitioners can be motivated in characterizing it formally, by relying on some shared and broader conventional interpretation of data combinations or on the mutual acquaintance of the involved actors. In all these cases, the highly incremental structure and computational autonomy of mechanisms (in terms of their inner components and role in the control flow of the application, respectively) can facilitate stakeholders in expressing and updating mechanisms that are quite specific to complex and ever new situations. For instance, if the NICU practitioners had expressed the need not to be alerted for low pressure problems of their inpatients unless in more specific cases than that represented in Figure 2, the antecedent of that mechanism would have been enriched with a new combination of conditional elements: e.g., a test to evaluate whether the basal and physiologic blood pressure of the newborn is usually low, or whether she has been already treated for low pressure after the onset of the criticality, or even whether the latest drug that had been administered to her brings low pressure normally. The progressive tuning of coordinative requirements would not require a major rewriting of the application logic behind the corresponding functionality, but just call for the addition (or deletion) of specific conditional elements within the mechanism that triggers the provision of criticality API on those critical conditions.

Combination Flexibility For Run-time Connections.   As said above, NICU practitioners expressed the need that executable mechanisms could be easy to define and modify. In addition to that, they also expressed the need the application (i.e., execution) of these constructs be dependent on the current context. In regards to this requirement, which is in the line of the major tenets of context-aware computing [21], they needed to conceive ways to manage connections that had been explicitly instantiated between data during their daily activities, and not just at schema level and at compile time as in the previous case. Thinking in terms of rules assured them that the whole set of mechanisms, once specified as a whole, is "rescaled" each time into smaller active subsets, i.e., those mechanisms whose antecedent is satisfied according to what actors do (as to any other contextual event). In fact, even multi-condition mechanisms – i.e., mechanisms that are very specific to a given situation – are considered for execution just when all their conditions are true; this releases practitioners from conceiving an arbitrarily long sequential flow of control in which this kind of mechanisms are discarded in all cases but that very specific situation. This

flexibility was deemed useful especially in the case of connections that were created at run-time across artifacts of the patient record, such as the *problem list*
and the *doctors' diary*.

The *Problem List* (PL) is the artifact of the patient record where clinicians
enumerate the patient's problems. This list is intended to document all those
conditions and events that can be related to clinical hypotheses and procedures.
The term "problem" is purposely left vague enough to comprise a number of
factors like symptoms, any alterations to vital signs, and all the concomitant
pathologies that could affect a patient's hospitalization. The PL is likely to
change during the caring process since practitioners are supposed to update its
content with respect to the actual improvements or aggravations exhibited by the
patient but also with respect to the extent they can consolidate their diagnostic
hypothesis. Therefore, the PL is more than a mere list of either concomitant
or sequential problems affecting the patient: it is the artifact where doctors
represent the main deviations and swerves of illness trajectories, and the results
of the epicrises (i.e., summings up) doctors periodically accomplish in evolving
and improving their diagnosis on a specific case. The epicrises can result in the
need to "cross out" previously unrelated symptoms and substitute them with
new comprehensive diagnostic items. On the other hand, changes that regard
the acuteness of single problems previously stated are not represented into the
PL explicitly. These are rather represented in the *Doctors's Diary* (DD). The
DD is the central repository for the notes that physicians need to write down in
order to account for the decisions and interventions they are responsible for, as
well as to make impressions, opinions, or just lines of reasoning explicit, either
for themselves as memorandum or as written notes to other colleagues.

The physicians called our attention on how useful would be for them to be
capable of making explicit on the record itself the relationships between past
problems and new problems as well as between problems of the PL and the
daily entries reported into the DD. The former capability was seen as a way
to reconstruct or, better yet, make the line of thought explicit by which symptoms have been rationalized into problems and unrelated problems into precise
diagnosis. The latter was seen as a way to facilitate the *a posteriori* reconstruction of a problem progress from its outset, in order to give indications on how
to head the course of clinical interventions towards its conclusion. These requirements point to a relevant coordinative need, besides that of keeping trace
of relevant phases during the decisional/medical process: in fact doctors were
also, sometimes implicitly, expressing the need to be informed on what problems
they should address first and on the way their colleagues had coped with these
problems that far.

We then asked practitioners which kinds of relationship they would more
naturally employ to join two or more data that are not explicitly correlated by the
patient record structure. The result was that practitioners found more natural to
consider relationships as occurring between data entries, either already recorded
or still to record on the patient record. In the former case, they pointed out the
usefulness to relate data over distributed and different artifacts; in the latter case,

they referred to the capability to draw relationships between data *values* and *fields* yet to fill in, that is between documental activities and articulated work activities still to perform. While almost any doctor expressed her preference for a number of possible relationships that had small overlap (if any) with those pointed out by the others, we noticed that when these relationships were actually applied in the field of work, they all blur into three main categories: *causal*, *temporal* and *intentional* connections [18]. The generic semantics that pertain to the nature of the relationships between a source information and a target information could then be respectively rendered as: (a) "the source *because* of the target"; doctors would use this connection in order to hint a strict causal relationship between items of the patient record: e.g., the diagnosis 'pneumonia' – reported in the PL – can be indicated as cause of the symptom 'cough' – reported in the DD – as a way to explain the symptom itself. (b) "the source *after* the target"; doctors would use this connection not only in strict temporal sense, but also to hint a very weak or just supposed causal relationship: e.g., reporting that a skin rash – a symptom from the DD – occurred after having administered a drug – an order reported somewhere else in the PR – would indicate a hypothesized correlation between these two clinical facts. And (c) "the source *for* the target", that doctors would use in order to highlight evidence supporting a particular decision or to make an intention explicit (e.g., that the bacterial culture – an order – has been prescribed to verify the diagnostic hypothesis of pneumonia – an item in the PL).

Figure 3 depicts how the need to be aware of impromptu connections (i.e., relationships) that were previously drawn by colleagues was computationally rendered in WOAD-compliant statements by practitioners with our support. The mechanism is sensitive to whether a connection exists between a specific entry and another entry anywhere else in the PR. Only whenever this situation occurs, the WOAD interpreter executes an instruction by which an API is conveyed to the actor through the form she is currently using (see last statement in Figure 3). This general mechanism can be made more specific in its antecedent by adding to the pattern for the relation-fact the explicit indication of the type of relationship

```
(antecedent
   (document-fact (name ?f1) (content (entry (id ?e1))))
            Consider any form in the EPR, e.g. the PL
   (document-fact (name ?f2) (content (entry (id ?e2))))
         and consider any OTHER form in the EPR, e.g. the DD
   (relation-fact (level instance) (source-entity ?e1) (target-entity ?e2))
      and see if someone has drawn a connection btw their data
)
(consequent
   <convey (API-fact (type inquiry)) on (document-fact (name ?f2)) for ?e2>
         then make the reader aware of that connection
)
```

Fig. 3. A list-like representation of the mechanism of run-time creation of data connections (e.g., causal) to be sensitive to. Likewise, designers can specify in the consequent what API to convey in relation to the kind of correlation.

5   LWOAD and the Flexible Specification of Coordinative Functionalities

LWOAD was presented to the clinicians as a sort of *specification language* by which to implement their coordinative requirements. These were intended to characterize an EPR that would not hinder, but rather foster, patterns of cooperative behaviors on the basis of how actors use official records and documents in their daily practice. The fact that users could be facilitated in "rapidly having a taste of a functionality" (as suggestively said by an interviewee) called for the twofold requirement that coordinative requirements must be *flexibly specified* – so as not to hinder their incremental re-definition – and the corresponding functionalities be *flexibly combined* – so as to fit an ever-changing and necessarily underspecified context.

This stress on flexibility has, on the one hand, motivated us in defining LWOAD as a language by which to render coordinative requirements in a computable but yet platform-independent and abstract manner; on the other hand, we were motivated in using it to express an upper layer of application logic that would be conceptually "on top of" a full-fledged electronic document system and that would endow that system with cooperation-oriented functionalities (see this general schema in Figure 4).

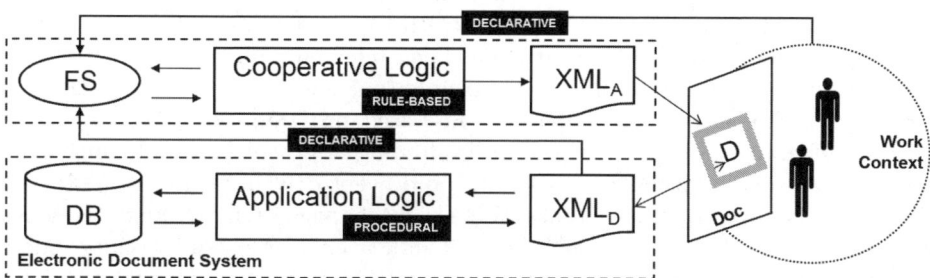

Fig. 4. The two-tier architecture designed to enhance electronic documents with collaboration awareness. FS stands for Fact Space, the memory where declarative representations of documental and working context are stored.

The adopted *declarative* and *rule-based* approach guaranteed that *coordinative functionalities* can be expressed in terms of *reactive and declarative mechanisms* [22]; these are symbolic statements intended to translate the typical question of users " ...and could I have the system do this, whenever that occurs?" into computable instructions. The declarativeness of these statements allows for the expression and formal specification of *what a system should do* rather than worrying about *how it really accomplishes it* at specification time. Declarativeness also allows mechanisms to be written without imposing a strict *control flow*, which is hardly recognizable in actual work situations. On the other hand, reactivity allows mechanisms to be written by using circumscribed units of code (i.e., rules). This "convenience of definition" relates to flexibility in terms of a greater easiness of maintenance due to better modularity and incrementality; moreover, defining mechanisms in a higher-level way than by means of traditional procedural specification is also intended towards a better participation of users in the process of modelling and defining formal expressions, so that these could reflect how users really see their domain-specific knowledge and functionalities.

The rule-based layer of cooperation logic on top of the procedural application logic of a traditional electronic document system is sensitive to both the content of documents (in Figure 4 denoted with XML_D, i.e., data rendered in XML format) and the symbolic representation of context. The output of this context-aware layer is the conveyance of *additional* information, namely API, that does not change documental data but rather how the interface of a document system displays and "affords" them (in Figure 4 denoted with XML_A, i.e., API rendered in terms of XML metadata). In doing so, data conveyed in documents (denoted with a capital D in Figure 4) would be gathered from official repositories (e.g., a hospital DB) according to procedural organizational logic; conversely, the API attached to these data (denoted as an highlighted border all around the capital D in Figure 4) would be provided according to more flexible mechanisms on the basis of coordinative conventions.

Furthermore, the rule-based approach addresses the flexibility requirement from the combination point of view. In rule-based programming, a rule is executed automatically on the basis of any significant event and data change only after that: i) its "applicability criteria" have been matched by the rule engine against current data, i.e. what constitutes the symbolic description of a situation at run-time; and ii) after that it has been selected among all other rules as the most suitable to that situation, according to some strategy (e.g., specificity, recentness). We agree with [22] that rule-based programming have some important advantages over procedural programming in grasping and aligning with cooperative work, especially for its data- and event-driven nature. In addition, the particular kind of action that LWOAD mechanisms trigger, i.e., augmenting the interface with graphical cues and indications promoting collaboration awareness, brings down the problem of mutual consistency of the rule set. This problem often makes the adoption of this form of declarative specification difficult to be understood and managed by layman users. Our case is different from production systems and expert system where possibly long chains of rules are consecutively executed to infer a line of action on the basis of progressively true conditions. Conversely, we adopt a rule-based approach in order to separate functional concerns into single mechanisms (not into chains of their executions); and, for the mechanism design, we advocate the principle that the consequent of each mechanism should be expressed as simply as possible, i.e., that each mechanism should only address a single and punctual functionality that the system must exhibit against possibly over-detailed and specific contextual conditions (which are specified in the mechanism's antecedent). Moreover, the fact that LWOAD

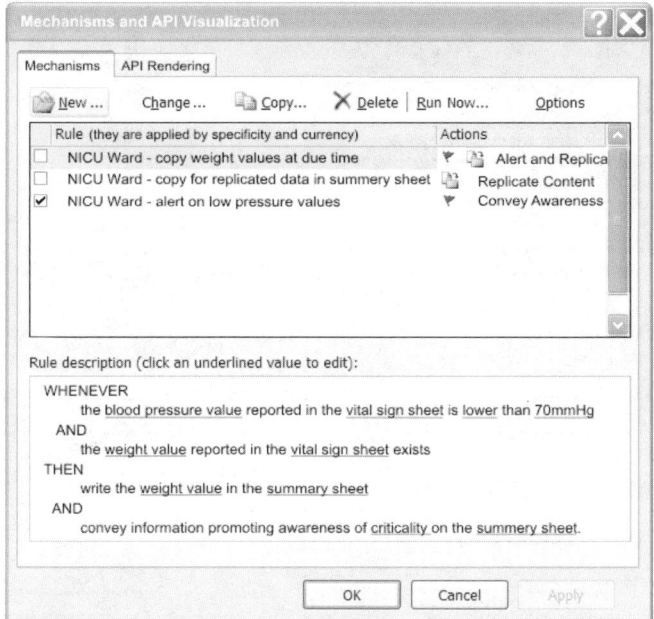

Fig. 5. Screenshot of the mockup for the mechanism editor, first windows

consequents do not change data (and hence the state of the world) but rather convey APIs, and that APIs are conceived as orthogonal guarantees that data inconsistency can not occur for their execution. Moreover, possible conflicts in alerts (e.g., when two mechanisms trigger the same API but with different values) can be "caught" before execution by the mechanism interpreter itself (i.e., by monitoring the execution agenda). In this latter case, the system can propose the conflict to users as particular situations that call for their interpretation and resolution on the basis of their experience and knowledge.

6 Simulation and Mockup Tests of LWOAD Specification

In what follows, we illustrate the mockup that we designed after the requirement analysis. This was meant as a proof-of-concept for the prospective application that users would use to develop coordinative mechanisms by themselves. Since mechanisms are but rules, the main idea was to assimilate mechanisms development to rule configuration: we then conceived the LWOAD mechanism editor similar to an interactive help utility, much alike those provided by email clients to guide users through the configuration of personal filters and mechanisms of message filing. The mockup was realized in MS PowerPoint and intended as a sequence of dialog boxes where users could select options and fill in details; each slide was endowed with active areas corresponding to the buttons and links of the prospective interface in order to simulate the typical interaction involved in mechanism creation.

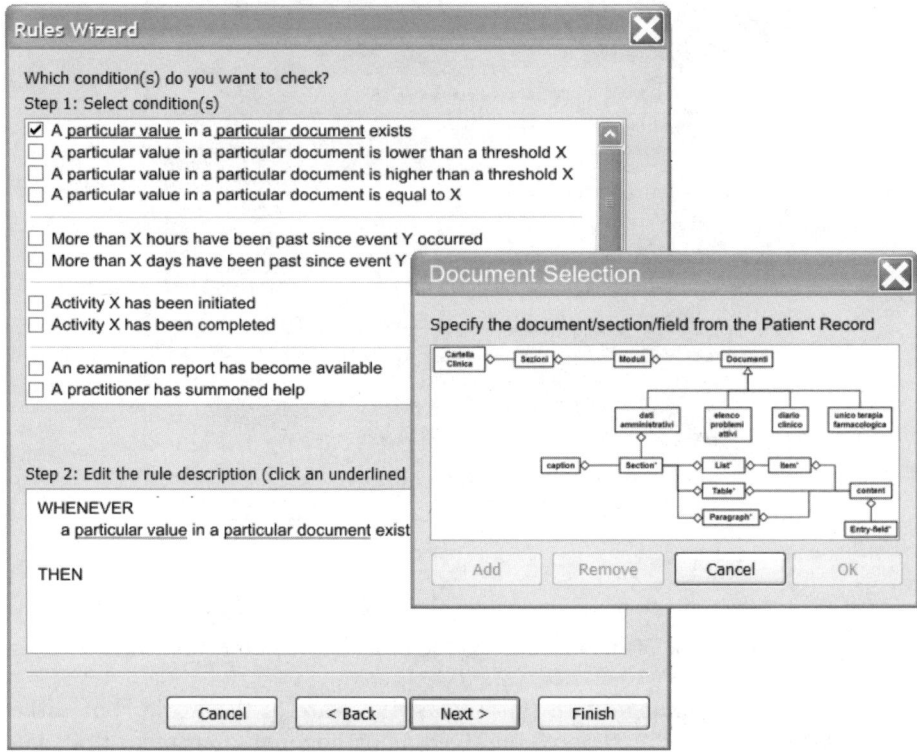

Fig. 6. Screenshot of the mockup for the definition of the mechanism's antecedent

In the first window, users have access to the macro-functionalities of the editor (see Figure 5) as regards either mechanism composition or API visualization. In this paper, we do not address the functionalities of API rendering, i.e., the association between API types and rendering functionalities (like, e.g., colors, icons, highlighting) provided by the documental platform. In regards to mechanism composition, a list of existing mechanisms is displayed in the top frame of the window. Users can read the textual description of each mechanism by selecting the corresponding row: the description is then displayed in the bottom frame (in Figure 5 we report the same mechanism illustrated in Figure 2). From the textual description of a mechanism, users can directly modify its parameters by clicking on the underlined elements (i.e., variables of the mechanism's pattern). Users can also change the structure of the mechanism (clicking on 'change...'); delete it, "activate" it (by checking the corresponding checkbox); and run the mechanism to check its functioning (clicking on 'Run Now...'). If the user clicks on 'New', the mechanism wizard starts a three-step process; in the first window, the system proposes two options: to create a mechanism from a template, or to compose it from scratch, i.e., from a blank template. We will consider this second case. In this case, the system opens a new window in place of the former, like that depicted in Figure 6 (left side, background). From the top frame of this window, the user can select any number of conditions the mechanism should be sensitive to (in its antecedent). In-depth analysis and participatory design sessions have allowed to list together all the relevant conditions that practitioners wanted to be catched with respect to the records' content, time and the clinical context. By selecting a condition from the list, the associated conditional statement is added in the bottom frame. As in the case of the first screen (Figure 5), the user can specify the value of the parameters the mechanism should monitor by clicking on the underlined parts of the statement. In doing so, corresponding input boxes are displayed to allow users insert the value (e.g., 70 mmHg, a blood pressure value as in the case reported in Figure 2). If the user wants to specify the document where to check the condition, the system opens a box like that depicted in Figure 6 (right side, foreground). Here, the user can consult a tree-like schema of the official documentation and select the document/s (or their inner sections) whose data must be matched with the pattern's values. Once the antecedent of the mechanism has been defined, the wizard proposes a third window (in place of the previous one – see Figure 7) where the user can specify what the system is supposed to do when the conditions are true, i.e., the elements of the consequent part. Also in this case, the user can select a number of different actions from the top frame; and then specify a value for each key presented in the textual description in the bottom frame. The list depicted in

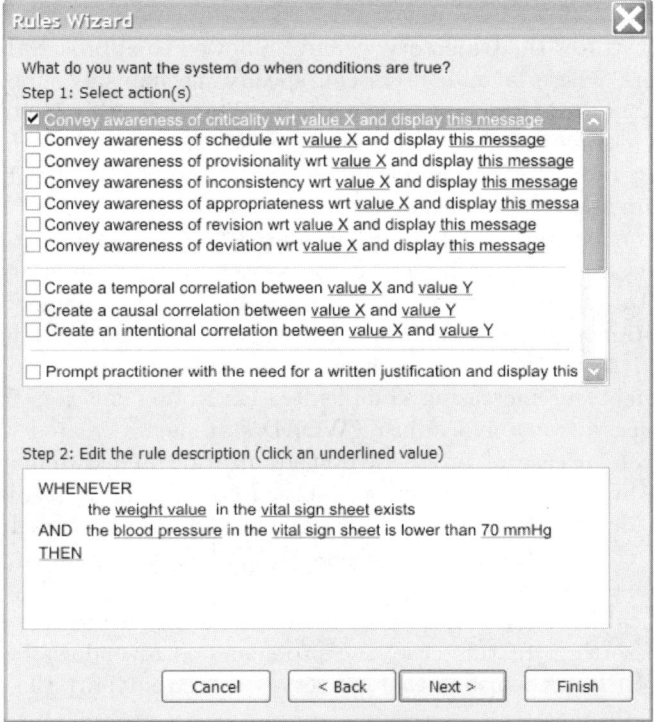

Fig. 7. Screenshot of the mockup for the mechanism's consequent definition

Figure 7 presents the main options selected by practitioners on a relevance basis during the interviews. The system groups these options together by similar category: e.g., API provision, connection definition, data replication and insertion and the like. In the case the action regards API provision, the user can also insert a textual explanation. This would be displayed on the clinical record only if requested in case a user can not interpret the API clue conveyed. By clicking the button 'Finish', the system creates the mechanism that is executable by the LWOAD interpreter. This is currently a compiler that renders LWOAD constructs into corresponding structures of Jess [1], which are then executed by the fast and reliable rule engine provided within this scripting environment. Jess was chosen after our positive experience during the development of a distributed version of Jess for the construction of applications in the Collaborative Ubiquitous Computing and Ambient Intelligence domains [23,24]. The strong decoupling we pursued in the design of the WOAD architecture between cooperative logic and the operational platform allows for the development of other compilers by which to translate LWOAD statements into other rule-based scripting languages. Currently, the implementation of a WOAD compiler compliant with the JBoss Rules[2] engine is under consideration to overcome the limits of Jess in dealing with data structures more complex than lists.

7   Conclusions and Future Work

The paper illustrates the trajectory we have followed to approach the definition of a framework where layman users can specify mechanisms supporting their cooperation mediated by documental artifacts. This trajectory is not completed but currently covers the most important part of the research path: namely, i) understanding the kind of functionalities users need; ii) identifying a way to express the functionalities and iii) defining an architecture where the functionalities can then be implemented and validated. Also in regards to how users should interact with this architecture and system, our research agenda covers the incremental involvement and increasing skills of users: namely, we started having practitioners express conditional mechanisms in natural language; then we stimulated them to use an application to compose and detail condition-action statements of increasing complexity; lastly, we envision the opportunity to have users tweak and adjust LWOAD statements created with the former application in case of progressive customization and compliance to local needs. In this study, the choice of a rule-based representation seemed the most suitable one for the different types of flexibility it allows: namely, flexibility in specifying computational mechanisms and in combining them together at execution time.

The empirical findings we gathered so far refer to the healthcare domain and to a hospital setting. In this case, the problem was to endow the implementation of an EPR with means that preserve or even support the conventions

---

[1] Java Expert System Shell:http://www.jessrules.com/

[2] See http://www.jboss.com/products/rules

that practitioners adopt to make their cooperation smooth and seamless. A first natural question regards how much our empirical findings can be generalized to other settings, even within the same domain: we acknowledge to have found a group of doctors and nurses that were extraordinarily helpful to try and co-develop innovative solutions with computer researchers and professionals; they were extremely motivated in molding any tool that could help them in providing a better care and re-delivering more healthy newborns to their parents. For this reason, scalability and generalization of our proposal is part of our research agenda. Our next activities will also include the full implementation of the interface, informally validated through the mockup illustrated in Section 6: our pilot sessions confirm its feasibility as a tool that makes users autonomous in specifying condition-action mechanisms, once the set of patterns has been identified for their antecedents and a rich palette of graphical cues has been proposed as output of their consequents. This approach however opens a new area of problems: a tool like that depicted in Section 6 interprets EUD more as a flexible kind of customization than as a real development environment [25]. In fact, the predefined set of patterns cannot fulfill the needs of increasingly skilled users wanting to extend the "localization" of the desired support. To fulfill this requirement, users must have access to the implementation environment also: here it is where the WOAD framework, and specifically its specification language – LWOAD – can play a relevant role for its declarative, abstract and modular approach that divides complex situations into a bunch of supportive functionalities that are called reactively with respect to the current context. The first phase of the study showed how (relatively) easily layman users can transform informal rules of their particular setting into executable statements, due to the "isomorphic" nature of the involved representations.

The next step is to allow users define more general rules by selecting the needed pieces of information to build the antecedent of the rules out of the documental artifacts in a natural way. Practitioners proposed a solution that could mimic how users of a spreadsheet copy data from cell to cell just by clicking on them and pasting them where needed. Likewise, users should be able to express contextual conditions from a predefined palette of templates (concerning, e.g., time, frequency, iterations, etc.) and specialize them by expressing simple key-value pairs and selecting data structures and data values directly from their documentation. Of course, this additional flexibility would ask for a strong interoperability between the coordinative layer and the archival layer, i.e., the EPR, or at least the capability to export and represent suitable views of clinical data, irrespectively of how they are organized and memorized. In our opinion, and on the basis of our interaction with practitioners, this kind of interoperability could bring data presentation strategies to EPR that are more natural and closer to the way practitioners use the current paper-based clinical record fruitfully. This positive mutual influence is the final goal we aim to pursue in our planned interactions with users in the healthcare domain.

Acknowledgements

The work presented in this paper has been partially supported by the F.A.R. 2008. The authors would like to thank the management and the Neonatal Intensive Care Unit personnel of the Alessandro Manzoni Hospital of Lecco for their kind collaboration. In particular, we would like to acknowledge the invaluable help and courtesy of Dr Bellù and Mrs Colombo.

References

1. Braa, K., Sandahl, T.: Introducing digital documents in work practices - challenges and perspectives. Group Decision and Negotiation 9(3), 189–203 (2000)
2. Sellen, A.J., Harper, R.H.R.: The Myth of the Paperless Office. MIT Press, Cambridge (2003)
3. Terzis, S., Nixon, P., Wade, V., Dobson, S., Fuller, J.: The future of enterprise groupware applications. Enterprise Information Systems, 99–106 (2000)
4. Xiao, Y.: Artifacts and collaborative work in healthcare: methodological, theoretical, and technological implications of the tangible. J. of Biomedical Informatics 38(1), 26–33 (2005)
5. Hertzum, M.: Six roles of documents in professionals' work. In: ECSCW 1999: Proceedings of the Sixth European conference on Computer supported cooperative work, pp. 41–60. Kluwer Academic Publishers, Norwell (1999)
6. Garfinkel, H.: "Good" organizational reasons for "bad" clinic records. In: Studies in Ethnomethodology, pp. 186–207. Prentice-Hall, New Jersey (1967)
7. Berg, M.: Accumulating and Coordinating: Occasions for Information Technologies in Medical Work. Computer Supported Cooperative Work, The Journal of Collaborative Computing 8(4), 373–401 (1999)
8. Fitzpatrick, G.: Integrated care and the working record. Health Informatics Journal 10(4), 291–302 (2004)
9. Winthereik, B.R., Vikkelso, S.: Ict and integrated care: Some dilemmas of standardising inter-organisational communication. Computer Supported Cooperative Work, The Journal of Collaborative Computing 14(1), 43–67 (2005)
10. Cabitza, F., Simone, C.: "You Taste Its Quality": Making sense of quality standards on situated artifacts. In: MCIS 2006: Proceedings of the First Mediterranean Conference on Information Systems, Venice, Italy, AIS (2006)
11. Berg, M., Goorman, E.: The contextual nature of medical information. International Journal of Medical Informatics 56, 51–60 (1999)
12. Schmidt, K., Simone, C.: Coordination mechanisms: Towards a conceptual foundation of CSCW systems design. Computer Supported Cooperative Work 5(2/3), 155–200 (1996)
13. Divitini, M., Simone, C.: Supporting different dimensions of adaptability in workflow modeling. Computer Supported Cooperative Work 9(3), 365–397 (2000)
14. Heath, C., Luff, P.: Documents and Professional Practice: 'bad' organisational reasons for 'good' clinical records. In: CSCW 1996: Proceedings of the international conference on computer-supported cooperative work, pp. 354–363. ACM Press, Cambridge (1996)
15. Cabitza, F., Simone, C.: "... and do it the usual way": fostering awareness of work conventions in document-mediated collaboration. In: ECSCW 2007: Proceedings of the Tenth European Conference on Computer Supported Cooperative Work (ECSCW), Limerick, Ireland, September 24–28, pp. 119–138. Springer, Heidelberg (2007)

16. Dourish, P., Bellotti, V.: Awareness and coordination in shared workspaces. In: CSCW 1992: Proceedings of the 1992 ACM conference on Computer-supported cooperative work, pp. 107–114. ACM Press, New York (1992)
17. Cabitza, F., Sarini, M., Simone, C.: Providing awareness through situated process maps: the hospital care case. In: GROUP 2007: Proceedings of the 2007 International ACM SIGGROUP Conference on Supporting Group Work, pp. 41–50. ACM Press, New York (2007)
18. Cabitza, F., Simone, C.: Supporting practices of positive redundancy for seamless care. In: CBMS 2008: Proceedings of the 21st IEEE International Symposium on Computer-Based Medical Systems, Jyväskylä, Finland, June 17-19, 2008, pp. 470–476. IEEE Computer Society, Los Alamitos (2008)
19. Hardstone, G., Hartswood, M., Procter, R., Slack, R., Voss, A., Rees, G.: Supporting informality: team working and integrated care records. In: CSCW 2004: Proceedings of the 2004 ACM conference on Computer supported cooperative work, pp. 142–151. ACM Press, New York (2004)
20. Randell, R.: Accountability in an alarming environment. In: CSCW 2004: Proceedings of the 2004 ACM conference on Computer supported cooperative work, pp. 125–131. ACM Press, New York (2004)
21. Dourish, P.: Seeking a Foundation for Context-Aware Computing. Special Issue on Context-Aware Computing HCI Journal 16 (2001)
22. Wulf, V., Stiemerling, O., Pfeifer, A.: Tailoring groupware for different scopes of validity. Behaviour and Information Technology 18(3), 199–212 (1999)
23. Cabitza, F., Seno, B.D., Sarini, M.: DJess – a context-sharing middleware to deploy distributed inference systems in pervasive computing domains. In: ICPS 2005: Proceedings of the IEEE International Conference on Pervasive Services, Santorini, Greece, pp. 229–238 (2005)
24. Cabitza, F., Locatelli, M., Sarini, M., Simone, C.: CASMAS: Supporting collaboration in pervasive environments. In: PerCom 2006: Proceedings of the Fourth Annual IEEE International Conference on Pervasive Computing and Communications, Pisa, Italy, pp. 286–295. IEEE, Los Alamitos (2006)
25. Liebermann, H., Wulf, V., Paternò, F. (eds.): End-User Development. Kluwer Academic Publishers, Dordrecht (2006)

Shaping Collaborative Work with Proto-patterns

Till Schümmer and Jörg M. Haake

FernUniversität in Hagen
Universitätsstraße 1, 58084 Hagen, Germany
Till.Schuemmer@fernuni-hagen.de

Abstract. A shared set of processes and norms as well as a shared understanding of the collaboration infrastructure is a vital aspect for collaboration. This paper investigates how practitioners of virtual organizations can be supported in creating, sharing, and applying best practices that form the basis for a shared understanding of collaboration processes. Extending the interpretation of end-user development to a the development of processes and technology, best practice descriptions document proven social processes as well as guidelines for end-user appropriation and utilization of groupware tools. We propose a practice creation process, show how proto-patterns can be used for documenting best practice, and explain how they help to gain a socio-technical perspective on the shared practices. The approach has been used to create a best practice collection for efficient meetings.

1 Introduction

Virtual organizations and virtual enterprises are becoming more and more ubiquitous in these days. According to Byrne et al. [2], virtual organizations form "… a temporary network of independent companies linked by the free flow of information. There is no hierarchy, no central office and no vertical integration: just the skills and resources needed to do the job… the key is the use of ICT [information and communication technology] which will be used to forge the alliances" (cited from [7]). Supporting collaboration in such organizations is a major challenge since all partners typically contribute their individual ways of per-forming work. They lack a shared set of processes and norms that guide the collaboration processes.

Each partner in a virtual organization contributes a different infrastructure. Thus, it is likely that different partners use different groupware systems. Johnson-Lenz and Johnson-Lenz defined groupware as "intentional group processes plus software to support them" [11]. The variety of systems used by the partners further complicated the development of shared social practices.

EUD is one approach for addressing this problem. It allows the practitioners in the individual organizations to modify their groupware systems so that the resulting infra-structures become compatible. End-users become developers in the sense of End-User Development as it was defined by Liebermann et al. who termed it as "a set of methods, techniques, and tools that allow users of software systems, who are acting as non-professional software developers, at some point to create, modify or extend a software artifact." [12].

V. Pipek et al. (Eds.): IS-EUD 2009, LNCS 5435, pp. 166–185, 2009.
© Springer-Verlag Berlin Heidelberg 2009

In the EU Project MAPPER [10], we were able to experience and observe multiple instantiations of virtual enterprises: a large automotive supplier interacting with many different car manufacturers for supplying car components, an individual car manufacturer interacting with various suppliers in order to co-construct a new car, and two small electronics design companies co-constructing a new USB chip. The above mentioned partners, a software company and several research partners formed a virtual organization with the goal of creating tools and methods for efficient distributed engineering.

All examples shared common problems typical for virtual organizations. We could confirm issues raised by Hales [7]: It was essential that the partners had a profound understanding of their core functions and that differing approaches and processes to completing tasks were embraced. All partners contributed their experience as well as their groupware systems for structuring interaction. They had different best practices for structuring the interaction among the partners. To work together effectively, the members of the virtual organization had to identify, connect, and improve their best practices and agree on a common set of shared best practices. They also had to establish a technical infrastructure that allowed them to interact. How to reach such a common set of practices with adequate technology support and thereby align the different members of the virtual organization is the topic of this paper.

We argue that EUD currently is not sufficient to bridge the socio-technical gap between the partner organizations, since EUD is primarily addressing technical systems. In this paper, we propose a method for simultaneously addressing both, the social processes and their supportive technologies.

We will show how the members of a virtual organization can be supported in the process of making their individual best practice explicit, sharing it with other partners in the virtual organization and transforming it from an individual and subjective level to an organizational level. These practices combine technical aspects with social aspects. Users shape their collaborative work by modifying both, social interaction and the technology that supports the interaction. Traditional EUD techniques (i.e., end-user programming, participatory design) are employed for shaping technology. We will also show how these shared best practices can be improved in an agile manner during application time. As a result, the virtual organization will collaboratively develop a set of shared best practices that enables efficient collaboration.

The remaining part of this paper is structured as follows: We will first discuss the problem space for sharing and improving best practice in virtual organizations both from a social and a technical perspective and identify requirements for better supporting this process. We will then discuss to what extent current approaches support the evolution of best practice knowledge and the supportive technology. Afterwards, we will present our approach that consists of a standardized best practice representation focusing both on improving social interaction and better supporting this interaction through groupware applications and a computer-supported best practice sharing process. In the final sections of this paper we will report our experiences with the approach developing meeting practices in a virtual organization.

2 Requirements for Best Practice Detection and Sharing in Virtual Organizations

In 1983, Schön published his influencing work on the reflective practitioner in which he outlines a framework of reflection in action [22]. He understands professional practice as a problem solving process. Practitioners make use of their mental model of the problem solving process. They use building blocks of knowledge and prefabricated solutions that they have in their minds in order to solve problems in their work environment. But these models only work when the anticipated context of the work situation matches the actual context. In changing work contexts practitioners have to look for new solutions for the problem at hand. Reflection-in-action means that the practitioner (1) detects that the current situation does no longer match the mental model of the anticipated context, (2) constructs a new mental model, and (3) tests the new mental model by means of ad-hoc experimentation. As a result, the practitioner will create a new model of the problem space and come up with new ways of solving the problem [22].

The improvement of the mental model can influence the concrete interaction in two ways: It can result in new strategies for interacting with the world and thus change the way how the practitioner acts. It can also result in a reconfiguration of the practitioner's context. Examples for the latter are changed layouts of offices or – in the context of computer-mediated interaction – a modified groupware infrastructure. While the practitioner is often able to build the new mental model, it is a much harder task to communicate these new social practices to others. This requires that the practitioner is able to convert his tacit knowledge into external knowledge that can be shared in a learning organization [20]. Accordingly, changed technical infrastructures can result in a better fit between the individual's mental model and the infrastructure but at the same time may create a mismatch with other practitioners' models. As a result, knowledge about changes of the infrastructure has to be shared among all involved practitioners. Again, one of the challenges is how to support the practitioner who modified the infrastructure in making his reasons for changing the infrastructure explicit and explaining how to use the improved system.

Nonaka and Takeuchi [21] have investigated this relation between tacit and explicit knowledge. They observed that "organizational knowledge creation is a continuous and dynamic interaction between tacit and explicit knowledge." [19, p. 70]. They distinguish four modes of knowledge creation: (1) socialization, (2) externalization, (3) combination, and (4) internalization. In the socialization mode, practitioners interact in the field and knowledge about practices is transferred by experiencing the practice. They work together and the apprentice observes and imitates the actions of the more experienced practitioner. When practitioners externalize their knowledge, they make it accessible for other members of the organization. Knowledge is captured in writing and can be shared in the virtual organization. The externalized knowledge of different members is then combined to reach a shared knowledge. Finally, other practitioners integrate the new externalized knowledge with their tacit knowledge. This process of internalization is required to apply the knowledge.

The different modes form a spiral of knowledge creation [21] that scales up while the knowledge is shared by a growing number of people. In the first iterations, individuals reflect on their knowledge and relate it to external representations of their knowledge. Later on, the externalized knowledge is used within the work group and even later, it may be shared in the whole organization or across organizational units of virtual organizations.

Socialization is often the most effective way of knowledge transfer. Art teaching, e.g., is normally taught by mentoring or direct observation. However, in the context of distributed virtual organizations, knowledge transfer through socialization is rarely possible since it would require co-located collaboration between the practitioners. Instead, we focus our analysis on the 'longer' path of knowledge transfer that involves externalization, combination, and internalization. From this discussion, we can draw the following requirement:

(R1) Practice knowledge must be made explicit before it can be shared in the virtual organization over distance: Here, Practitioners need to be (a) motivated to make their tacit knowledge of best practice explicit, and (b) guided in a reflection process to identify individual best practice.

Externalization is, however, a cognitive challenge for the practitioner. Traditionally, the externalization takes place by telling communication partners a story [13]. Giving the story a good plot is not always easy. According to [13], these stories should follow a narrative genre beginning with a context description that sets the stage, followed by a dramatic conflict that is resolved. This not only helps authors to write understandable descriptions, it also allows the reader faster access to the story.

(R2) Standardized practice representation: Practice descriptions should follow a common (standard) structure to ease the creation of the description as well as its application across organizational boundaries.

When writing their practice description, practitioners need to reflect on the current situation and investigate its context. Knowledge without context becomes "downgraded to information" [13]. It loses aspects that are required to interpret the knowledge and situate it in a new application context. For that reason, the context of the best practice is essential for its application. The context of a best practice can be abstracted from the concrete context to allow a wider view on the problem or it can be made more concrete to support the reader in better understanding the preconditions for the described practice. We argue that both directions need to be taken into account when describing a practice.

(R3) Abstract solution: (a) Practice descriptions need to abstract from organization infrastructures and services in order to be applicable in other contexts. (b) If practice descriptions are based on certain specifics of the organization this must be made explicit, so that the application of the practice in other contexts is informed.

By now, we have discussed the second mode of the spiral of knowledge creation: externalization. A comprehensive approach to knowledge creation in virtual organizations should also address the subsequent modes: combination and internalization including the following three requirements.

(R4) Access to practice descriptions: Individual practices or practices of one organization need to be accessible by other organizations. Hence, practitioners need to be able to store and retrieve practice descriptions. They also need support for exploring and finding best practice in the organization's existing best practice collection.

(R5) Communication: There needs to be a discussion of practice descriptions. Practitioners must have a means to comment best practice descriptions and provide feedback on their experiences with the practice.

(R6) Combination: Practitioners need to be supported in relating and aligning new best practice to the organization's existing best practice collection.

In order to become a shared practice of the virtual organization, practice descriptions need to be distributed to all members of the virtual organization. This is a prerequisite for knowledge application at an inter-organizational level.

(R7) Practice dissemination: Information about available practices must be disseminated in the virtual organization, and awareness about best practices must be raised to increase the chance of adoption.

Virtual organizations make use of information and communication technology (ICT) to mediate the interaction between partners. Best practices that involve more than one partner will thus always involve the use of ICT as well as social solutions to solve socio-technical problems. This combination may complicate the application of the practice, especially when the technical aspect of the solution requires substantial modifications to the virtual organization's ICT. Since the partners very likely enter the virtual organization with an existing local ICT, it may even be impossible to reach a full level of integration. The implementation strategy should thus describe a spectrum of implementation options ranging from social process design to using integrated technical support.

(R8) Implementation strategy: (a) The implementation of best practice must be easy-to-begin-with, i.e. by piloting a social process only. (b) However, the potential of supportive technologies to increase effectiveness must be addressed in the practice description.

The implementation strategy makes it easier for the practitioner to translate the practice to his concrete context. It eases the internalization of knowledge by providing different levels of social or technical concreteness. Linking the practice to existing tacit knowledge becomes easier since the variety of potential connection points (e.g., solely on the social level or at a level of standard ICT components) is increased. Nevertheless, we assume that a practice will still undergo a mapping process where the acting practitioner adapts the practice to his current tacit knowledge and the concrete organizational context.

(R9) Adaptation: Individual practice of members in the virtual organization should be able to change the practice of other members. Therefore, adaptation of practice to the needs of its users must be supported.

Adapted practices may then be the seeding point for the next iteration in the knowledge creation spiral. This means that changes to a practice first become an individual practice again but afterwards may emerge to a new practice that is externalized, communicated and combined again.

A solution addressing the abovementioned requirements supports the transitions between all modes of the knowledge spiral. We will now discuss supportive approaches contributing to individual requirements.

3 Current Approaches

We can group current approaches for addressing the requirements in two clusters: (1) Approaches for representing and sharing best practices and (2) processes for improving collaboration and the supportive groupware technology. In the following sections, we will provide examples of approaches in each cluster.

3.1 Representing and Sharing Best Practices

In cooperative knowledge management, numerous approaches have been developed for representing good practice. For the purpose of our analysis we take a closer look at two strategies: expert finder systems and repository approaches.

Expert finder systems support finding peers who have experienced comparable challenges. By using the current context, the system finds other users who are probably able to help the requesting user (see the EXPERT FINDER pattern in [24] for more information and example systems). This enables socialization of knowledge even in distributed settings. Practitioners talk about the context and the problems and collaboratively work on a solution given the experience of the expert found. The main problem with such an approach is that it relies on specific members of the organization. If the organization changes partners, the knowledge may get lost. Compared to our requirements, the interaction with an expert may provide implicit access to practice descriptions (R4) and foster communication on the practice (R5).

Repository approaches rely on an explicit knowledge representation. During the last years, design patterns have been discussed as a means for capturing best practices and supporting knowledge management [17]. A design pattern is a three part rule that provides a solution for a problem in a specific context. Initially developed by the architect Alexander [1] who wanted to empower lay people to shape their homes, patterns have been applied to various disciplines, especially to software development [5]. In the context of CSCW, they have been used with the following purposes:

- Describing interaction, e.g., in the context of ethnographic fieldwork where patterns were used to describe typical scenarios observed by the field worker [16].
- Improving social interaction, e.g., in the context of organizational change [15], or to support changes in the networked society [26].
- Designing socio-technical systems, e.g., for knowledge management [9] or community-based learning [3]. The most recent and largest collection of socio-technical patterns is the pattern language for computer-mediated interaction [24]. It includes 71 patterns addressing, among others, issues of community design, small group interaction, and the design of infrastructures for collaborative systems.

While descriptive approaches help to better understand interaction, they do not necessarily provide guidance for improving a concrete situation. Patterns for improving social interaction can be used to describe the social part of the best practice. But as soon as technology is required for distributed interaction, they lack appropriate guidance for mapping the social processes to technology. Socio-technical patterns combine social and technical aspects and thereby support the co-evolution of group processes and supportive technology. However, the different implementation strategies are not addressed by current approaches (R8).

Pattern approaches capture solutions in a standardized way (R2, R4) together with an intended application context (R3). But they do not address the evolutionary change of the patterns (R5, R6, and R9). Neither do they address the process of pattern creation needed to generate a pattern language for a virtual organization (R1).

3.2 Processes

In the context of groupware development, appropriation, and application, several process models have been proposed that help the users to improve their work place and share their improved practice with others. The Integrated Organizational and Technical Development (OTD) [27] model is an evolutionary process that assumes that users constantly analyze the actual state of the organization. They should detect problems and create alternatives. As a result, the users apply interventions looking simultaneously at three levels, namely the technology used in the organization, the organizational structures, and the qualification. In summary, OTD satisfies the requirements for applying new practices (R8&R9) but does not provide explicit support for the creation of best practices (R1-R7).

The Seeding, Evolutionary Growth, and Reseeding (SER) approach [4] puts a special focus on knowledge transfer in knowledge intensive work. In the seeding phase, users contribute their subjectively relevant knowledge and design objectives. The collected knowledge influences the future collaboration. During work, users contribute to the initial seed. In a reseeding phase, the user-generated knowledge is restructured so that it is compatible with the initial seed. SER supports shared access to common knowledge (R4), fosters communication (R5) and combination (R6) in the reseeding phase, and embraces adaptations (R9) that are fed back into the development process (R7). However, it neither propagates a standardized knowledge structure (R2) nor supports practitioners in making their knowledge explicit (R1).

In the Oregon Software Development Process (OSDP) [23] practitioners make use of design patterns to modify their groupware environment. While working with a groupware system, practitioners constantly reflect on their interaction. As soon as they encounter a collaboration breakdown, they look for design patterns that help to resolve the conflict that caused the breakdown. The application of the patterns may either result in tailoring activities where the practitioners change the groupware system or in development activities where practitioners ask developers to change the groupware system. A pattern scout observes the practitioners' behavior and seeks for interesting tailorings that may lead to new patterns.

By using patterns, OSDP employs a standardized practice representation (R2) that encourages adaptation (R9). The distinction between tailoring and development activities fulfils parts of the implementation strategy requirement (R6). However, it does only provide little guidance on how the patterns should emerge and states that this should be the task of the pattern scout. It thus lacks concepts for making tacit knowledge explicit (R1), and discussing (R5), relating (R6), and disseminating (R7) it within the organization.

With a focus on tailoring activities, Pipek and Kahler discussed different levels of collaboration involved in tailoring [19]. Based on empirical findings on tailoring behavior and sharing of tailoring, the authors identified several aspects that need to be addressed when supporting shared tailoring including a mechanism for sharing tailoring (in line with R4) and the need for communicating about tailoring (R5). The authors also argue that tailoring as a collaborative design process (in the sense of Oberquelle [18]) should foster reflection on breakdown situations and ease the process of articulation during the design process. We share this requirement and extend it to the discussion of both social practices and technology (including adaptations to the technology).

Lyons [13] as well as May and Taylor [17] argued that practitioners should create patterns of their best practice as a result of the reflection process. They should use these patterns for knowledge transfer in virtual teams. This is the closest approach to our requirements. However, Lyons did not provide guidelines on how to create and improve patterns as well. May and Taylor proposed to use shepherding and writer's workshop techniques known from pattern conferences to improve the pattern quality. However, they still make a distinction between pattern authors and practitioners since the act of writing a pattern is considered as an extremely difficult task. Supporting end-users in end-user pattern writing is thus still an open issue (R1). In addition, their patterns address social aspects only which means that a more detailed pattern structure is required in order to support the co-evolution of social practices and groupware support (R8 & R9).

In summary, while the processes provide important advice for best practice sharing, none of them provides sufficient support for making implicit practice knowledge explicit. To our knowledge, there is no process or knowledge representation that fulfils all requirements for a best practice sharing approach needed in our virtual organization setting.

4   A Proto-pattern Oriented Approach to Best Practice Sharing in Virtual Organizations

In order to fulfill all requirements, we propose the knowledge creation process shown in Figure 1. The process makes use of the pattern format as a means for documenting best practice. Unlike traditional pattern approaches, we guide the practitioners through the process of pattern creation, improvement, dissemination, and application. Our process consists of three major phases:

1. In the pattern creation phase, users make their tacit knowledge explicit. This phase maps to the externalization mode of Nonaka and Takeuchi.
2. The pattern sharing phase focuses on reviewing and relating patterns. Members of the virtual organization interact with the author and provide hints for improvement. This phase maps to the combination mode of the knowledge creation spiral.
3. During the pattern application phase, the pattern is applied by other members of the virtual organization. Findings from the application are fed back to the sharing phase or directly to the creation phase. The application phase maps to the internalization mode of Nonaka and Takeuchi.

We will now briefly describe our pattern format. Afterwards, we present each phase of our process in detail.

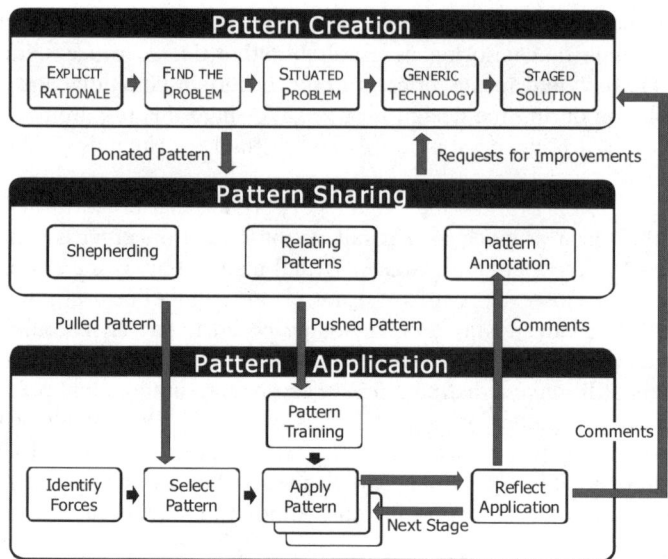

Fig. 1. Pattern-oriented best practice creation

4.1 The Proto-pattern Structure

We modified the pattern structure of [24] in order to make it suitable for capturing best practice of individual practitioners (R2). The main difference is that we refine the structure of the solution statements so that social solutions, solutions that require tailored off-the-shelf technology and custom-built groupware solutions are presented separately. In addition, we encourage practitioners to describe their personal best practices even though they may not have a long track record of successful applications across different teams. This is the reason why we also talk of proto-patterns (we will use the terms pattern and proto-pattern interchangeably in the remaining part of this paper). Proto-patterns contain at least the following sections:

Pattern Name (and alternative names): Patterns should carry metaphoric names where possible. They are the shortest description of the pattern's solution.

Context: A pattern provides a best practice for a problem in a specific context. The context section summarizes the original context that was in the author's focus.

Problem: One of the two most important parts of the pattern is the problem description. It answers why the solution is really needed and serves as a hint for the user of the pattern to understand what the pattern really solves.

Symptoms: The symptoms section lists potential observations that indicate the presence of the problem and the applicability of the pattern.

Social Solution: The social solution explains changes of the social practice needed to solve the problem. As mentioned above, we clearly distinguish between social and technical solutions. This allows the practitioner to implement the pattern with different implementation strategies (R7). When no common infrastructure is in place and no budget for creating or installing additional applications is available, the practitioners can implement the pattern by adapting their interaction process.

Although such an implementation strategy reduces the costs for technology change, it can still be difficult and expensive to implement since changes in social processes rely on the respective participation of all involved team members. Adapting social practice is done by employing participatory design techniques for creating, improving, and applying patterns in the organization.

Instant Technology Solution: The easiest way to get technical support for interaction in a virtual organization into the workplace is to make use of technology that is already there. The Instant Technology Solution section explains how the social solution proposed by the pattern can be implemented using standard collaboration technology. We assume that the partners have access to a common set of core applications. Even though our selection of core technologies is short, it is important to note that most complex technologies can be emulated by a less complex technology. From an abstract point of view, the members of the virtual organization need access to shared data and be able to send data from one participant to one or more other participants. The most common technology supporting this basic service is IMAP. It allows users to access content stored on a mail server and send content to other users on the same or a different server. We assume that the virtual organization has either agreed on the following set of basic services or that the members have found ways to emulate these technologies:

- Audio- or text-chat tools for synchronous communication. E-mail may be used to emulate chat interaction (by polling the mail server for new messages).
- A wiki [14] or a SHARED FILE REPOSITORY [24] allowing participants to store, modify, and access shared documents. An IMAP mail system that allows group access to mail folders can emulate a SHARED FILE REPOSITORY. To upload a new file, users send it as an attachment to the target mailbox that can be accessed by all group members.
- A shared view area can be used to project the content of the screen to any other user (following the APPLICATION SHARING [24] pattern). The shared view area can be emulated with a SHARED FILE REPOSITORY. However, the participants in this case will need a good communication channel so that instructions for updating local views can be given.

Modifying their ICT infrastructure thus becomes selecting common technologies, typically involving EUD techniques for tailoring the selected technologies. Some technologies also allow customization by means of macro programming or template design. In these cases, the practitioner starts to program structural and/or process-oriented support for the virtual organization.

Groupware Solution: Participants may need to use highly sophisticated tools for performing specialized tasks during collaboration. Integrating the collaboration infrastructure with these applications can help to better support the collaboration. The groupware solution section describes how the social solution can be supported using collaboration techniques that emerged from CSCW research (e.g., patterns for computer-mediated interaction [24]).

In this case, EUD techniques for participatory design empower the practitioners to play an active role in the design process of the common future groupware solution.

Drawbacks: Each change in a socio-technical system can cause new problems, arising from complex social dependencies. For the users of the patterns, it is therefore important to get guidance on issues that they should carefully observe after they have put a specific pattern in place.

Related Patterns: The related patterns section lists patterns that are closely related to the current pattern in the sense that they solve comparable problems or that they are often applied together with the current pattern.

The proto-pattern format provides the basis for addressing the other requirements. Since it is not trivial to create proto-patterns of high quality, the proposed knowledge creation process guides the practitioner through the writing and application of the patterns. We will now present the individual phases of this process. Note that we will use a shortened form of the pattern format to describe best practice for pattern writing as well.

4.2 Pattern Creation

The pattern creation phase is triggered by practitioners or pattern scouts [23]. Either practitioners reflect their current practice and identify successful episodes or pattern scouts observe practitioners and interact with the practitioners to externalize their tacit knowledge. In both cases, the practitioner reflects on his current practice and the way how he solves a specific problem. He starts by describing the social process of his practice. Afterwards, he explains, why the process has this form. The following patterns support the practitioner in this process:

Explicit Design Rationale

Problem: People cannot understand why elements of a practice are present and what their purpose is.

Solution: Annotate each part of the practice description with an explanation why the specific part is needed. Formulate the need in terms of a force, i.e., as a sentence that explains the underlying requirement for implementing this solution part.

Find The Problem

Problem: Practitioners make implicit decisions based on their understanding of the world. Less experienced practitioners can often not understand the purpose of specific actions performed by the experienced practitioner.

Solution: Create a punchy problem statement that contrasts the most important conflicting forces that will be resolved in the solution. To implement this, you should basically perform the following 5 steps:

1. Maintain relations to all requirements that are addressed or affected by the solution (we will call these requirements forces).
2. Create a network of forces that contains relations between all forces whenever one force positively or negatively influences another force.
3. Identify conflicting forces that are balanced when the solution is in place.
4. List all other forces that are influenced by the solution as indications for applying the pattern.
5. Create a contrast phrase that explains the conflict between the most important conflicting forces and use this as a problem statement.

The process of detecting forces and creating the problem statement is the most important analytical step in the pattern creation phase. After this is in place, the pattern contains the most important aspects of a successful story: The forces unfold a dramatic conflict that is resolved by a social solution. Such proto-patterns can already be shared with other practitioners sharing the same context. For wider applicability, the tacit context must be externalized, too.

Situated Problem
Problem: Depending on the state of the environment, practitioners make different decisions to solve a specific problem. While guidelines mostly focus on the mechanics of the solution, they often neglect the prerequisites for applying the solution. But when practitioners apply the solution, these prerequisites are of special importance since they have to be compatible to the practitioner's current context.
Solution: Capture the context when documenting the solution for a problem. Keep records of your context such as a diary or video recordings in order to ease the reconstruction of the context when reflecting on the solution.

In summary, the above mentioned patterns in combination with the role of the pattern scout who accompanies the practitioner in the process of making his tacit knowledge explicit address the requirements of explicit practice knowledge (R1) and the solution abstraction (R3). The two remaining steps in the pattern creation phase aim at supporting the applicability of the pattern in a virtual organization that relies on ICT for collaboration (R7).

Generic Technology
Problem: Describing a concrete technical implementation in the solution statement of a proto-pattern makes it difficult to apply the proto-pattern in a similar but not identical context. Especially, technology constraints in the target context may prohibit the direct use of the pattern.
Solution: Separate solution ideas from technology specific parts of the solution. For example, speak of version management services instead of naming a specific version management system (CVS).

Staged Solution Description
Problem: Changes in socio-technical systems affect both the social process and the technology that supports the process. But users willing to apply the change may not have the technical expertise to change the technology that is currently in use. Restricting the solution description to actions that can be performed by every practitioner on the other hand forces the creator of the proto-pattern not to go beyond the technical state of the art and thereby restricts his ability to describe advanced technology solutions.
Solution: Split the solution statement of the pattern into three parts: the social solution describing changes in the interaction process, the instant technology solution describing how off-the-shelf software systems can be used to support the social solution, and the integrated groupware solution describing how the process can be supported by an integrated and domain-specific collaborative system.

With the integrated groupware solution, the practitioner is able to contribute his understanding of how the process should be integrated with the domain-specific tasks. This takes into account that practitioners often have a clear vision on how to improve their work environment. As an example for the level of integration, one may consider design meetings in the automotive industry. In these meetings, participants need to be able to access CAD and Simulation systems. They need to relate their discussion to elements of the CAD model of the constructed car. An integrated groupware solution for sharing annotations would thus become a part of the CAD system so that users could share their annotations directly in their domain-specific CAD application.

4.3 Pattern Sharing

Once the pattern contains the most important sections, the context, the problem, and the solution, it can be donated to a common pattern repository. Our proposed process makes use of a structured wiki [6] to store the individual patterns. Each pattern is stored as a wiki page that has fields for the required sections of the pattern. In addition, each pattern has an associated BLOG that allows pattern-centric discussions and annotations.

From a process perspective, donated patterns will be taken up by a shepherd [8], i.e., an experienced pattern author who helps the author to further improve his practice description. The assumption is that the practitioner remains the expert for his practice but that the shepherd can help to better structure the proto-pattern and detect forces that were up to then not seen by the practitioner. The shepherd sends requests for improvement to the pattern author who in return updates the pattern description accordingly.

Pattern authors as well as other practitioners also work on relating patterns to the pattern language of the virtual organization. Here, all members can become active and forge links by editing the wiki page of the pattern.

Shepherding as well as the process of relating patterns contribute to the communication (R4) and the combination (R5) requirements.

4.4 Pattern Application

We distinguish two different motivational factors for applying proto-patterns: the breakdown and the group policy. When the pattern application is triggered by a breakdown, the practitioner observes obstacles in his current activities. He starts to analyze the different forces that cause the breakdown and compares these forces with the forces of the available patterns. Assuming that a matching pattern exists, the practitioner can directly apply the pattern. Since the user is actively seeking for a matching pattern, we speak of a pull mode here (cf. Figure 1).

In contrast, the group policy trigger assumes that patterns are pushed to relevant practitioners (cf. Figure 1). In this case, the management board of the virtual organization has agreed on a specific set of patterns that are then presented to the practitioners of the individual organizational units in forms of tutorials, reports, or newsfeeds. The practitioners are expected to study the patterns independently of a concrete current breakdown and apply these patterns when appropriate situations come up in the future.

The application of the pattern may go through different stages. Typically, practitioners start applying the pattern on a social level implementing the changes in the social interaction processes. As soon as the new process shows that the practice was improved and better usability or effectiveness is needed, practitioners may think about supportive technology. This is done by tailoring existing infrastructures according to the solution outlined in the instant technology solution of the pattern. Finally, if tighter integration with existing groupware infrastructures is requested, the practitioner may initiate new development activities performed by groupware designers and assisted by practitioners in the sense of a participatory design setting.

Whenever practitioners have applied a pattern, the process encourages them to reflect on the application to identify aspects that improved or to spot new problems. They can share their observations by annotating the patterns in the shared pattern repository or by directly asking the pattern author to improve the pattern.

Note that the application process is closely related to the tailoring iteration in the Oregon Software Development Process [23]. The main differences are that our approach differentiates the triggers for starting the pattern application and that it distinguishes the different application stages.

5   Experiences

We evaluated our approach through several case studies taking place in the context of a 30 months European project. During this time, we observed the behavior of (1) the members of a virtual organization running a research project with 9 partner organizations distributed all over Europe, (2) a virtual organization in the automotive suppliers sector, (3) a virtual organization formed by a major European automotive company and its suppliers, and (4) a virtual organization of two electronics design companies.

The first case was our main observation target for understanding the whole best-practice creation process. We intentionally focused our attention on this virtual organization since it was highly distributed (6 countries throughout Europe) and had a high variety with respect to the partners' organizational cultures ranging from research cultures brought in by research partners to industrial interaction cultures brought in by participating manufacturing companies. The latter three industrial cases provided additional experiences with respect to the application of the patterns.

During the first phases of the project, meetings showed to be a relevant activity for all cases. Each partner contributed his or her own view on how a meeting should be prepared and performed. It was thus required that the group as a whole grew a meeting culture.

In the following sections, we will first show how a concrete pattern was created. We will then report on anecdotal experiences of the pattern sharing process and finally show how the patterns were applied in the different cases.

5.1   Pattern Creation

The members of the virtual organization first performed meetings as they were used to in their home organizations. This means that meetings were differently structured dependent on the origin of the specific meeting facilitator. After several weeks of experience, one practitioner started to reflect his practice of organizing meetings and compared it to the other user's practices. He found out, that his way of organizing meetings was different with respect to the agenda creation. While other facilitators simply fixed an agenda, he felt that the participants of the meeting should contribute to the agenda.

He started to use a wiki for collaboratively organizing the agenda and noticed that this worked reasonable well for his meetings. This was the starting point to create a pattern for collaborative agenda creation. He wrote down the advice for agenda creation that contained detailed descriptions of how to set up an initial agenda in the wiki, how to invite participants by mail and ask them to add their agenda items, and on how to finalize the agenda.

He then identified 10 forces and analyzed whether or not the forces were in conflict. Two examples for conflicting forces were:

– *F3: Owner sets topic. The meeting owner wants to set the topic of the meeting.*
– *F5: Participants show interest. Participants will not contribute to the meeting if the agenda is not interesting for them.*

From this list, the practitioner was able to deduct a problem statement. He then described the context and checked the situations in which he used the solution. Finally, he situated the pattern in the context of meeting preparation.

The initial description of the solution referred to a concrete technical infrastructure. While refining the pattern, the practitioner abstracted from the concrete wiki and exchanged references to concrete mail addresses that were present in an early draft of the pattern with explanations of the receiver's role.

Finally, he split up the solution by distinguishing between technical aspects of the solution and social aspects. In the instant technology solution, the practitioner created templates for agenda pages that could be re-used in the whole virtual organization. By creating the template, he extended the existing infrastructure (he performed end-user programming activities). He also envisioned how an integrated solution would look like and became a driving force in convincing the developers of the virtual organization's infrastructure to implement an integrated meeting support mechanism (the practitioner became the driving force ion a participatory design process).

The pattern creation process resulted in the following pattern (some parts have been abbreviated for space reasons).

It's My Agenda – It's My Meeting
Context: You are calling for a meeting and create an agenda for it. There are stakeholders who have different backgrounds and interests.
Problem: The owner of the meeting normally creates an agenda. All other invited participants have only limited possibilities to participate in the agenda creation. This can lead to incomplete or wrong agendas.
Symptoms:
– Agreeing on the agenda takes a lot of time at the start of the meeting.
– Many new topics pop up during the meeting, which have not been foreseen.
– Important topics do not make it to the agenda early enough for allowing good preparation of the topics.

Social Solution: **Define a shared place where all invited meeting participants can collaboratively prepare the meeting agenda up to a specified deadline.**

Instant Technology Solution: Create a wiki page as a shared artifact of the agenda. Invite participants to change the wiki page by sending them a link to the page. Tell them that and how they should update other participants on agenda changes (i.e. by replying to the invitation mail). Create a section on the wiki page where the participants can express their approval after the agenda was finalized (one week before the meeting).

Groupware Solution: Implement the agenda preparation workflow as part of your collaboration environment. Make use of a SHARED FILE REPOSITORY [24] or a ROOM [SL07] as a shared place where agenda items for the meeting are stored. Initially the shared space is only accessible to the meeting organizers. After the meeting organizers have created an initial agenda, they can invite additional participants. Invited participants will receive a message in which they can confirm their attendance. From then on, participants can modify agenda items. After saving an updated agenda item, the system sends a notification to all other participants. The final acceptance of the agenda can be supported by a VOTE [24] that is automatically triggered at a defined time before the meeting.

Drawbacks: If the agenda is created by the group, the meeting owner may need to be the MODERATOR [24] so that the meeting stays in line with the general meeting goals.

Related Patterns:
–   WHY SHOULD I BE THERE: The discussion of the agenda can help the participants to better understand why they should attend the meeting.

5.2 Pattern Sharing

We provided practitioners with a structured wiki to store their patterns. Practitioners contributed their patterns to the wiki so that they could be discussed afterwards. However, we observed that users hesitated to comment on the patterns. One reason for this may have been that the users did not consider themselves as experts for the specific topic and thus did not want to question the pattern author's expertise. Another reason that was reported by one user was the lack of time.

However, when we discussed the patterns in face-to-face meetings, the members of the virtual organization contributed valuable feedback ranging from confirmations over suggestions for improving the social process up to new ideas for an integrated groupware solution.

When more meeting patterns were created, the practitioners started to connect the patterns. Connections were established using wiki links. Currently, the meeting pattern language contains 21 patterns each connected to 2-11 other patterns.

All meeting patterns have undergone a shepherding process. After an internal shepherding of peer practitioners, the meeting pattern language was passed on to an external shepherd who spent six weeks giving comments to the patterns and checking updated versions. The final version of the patterns was in addition shared with the European patterns community and received high attention [25].

5.3 Pattern Application

Initially, the meeting patterns were applied as a group policy in the research consortium. During a project meeting, one pattern author gave an overview of the pattern language and explained how the patterns can be used together. Notably, this had an immediate effect on the meeting. While the first day of the meeting started without a detailed agenda, the second day was prepared by the facilitator much more precisely. In addition, the facilitator changed the way how he collected input for the agenda. Agendas were no longer created only by the facilitator. Instead, all meeting participants started to contribute to the agenda creation process and thereby helped to create an agenda that suits the group's needs.

In subsequent distributed project meetings, the practice of agenda creation was further improved according to the pattern. One group moved from the social implementation level to the instant technology level. They created a wiki template for meetings as it is shown in Figure 2 (using the CURE wiki engine [6]). Participants could from then on directly edit the agenda of the meeting.

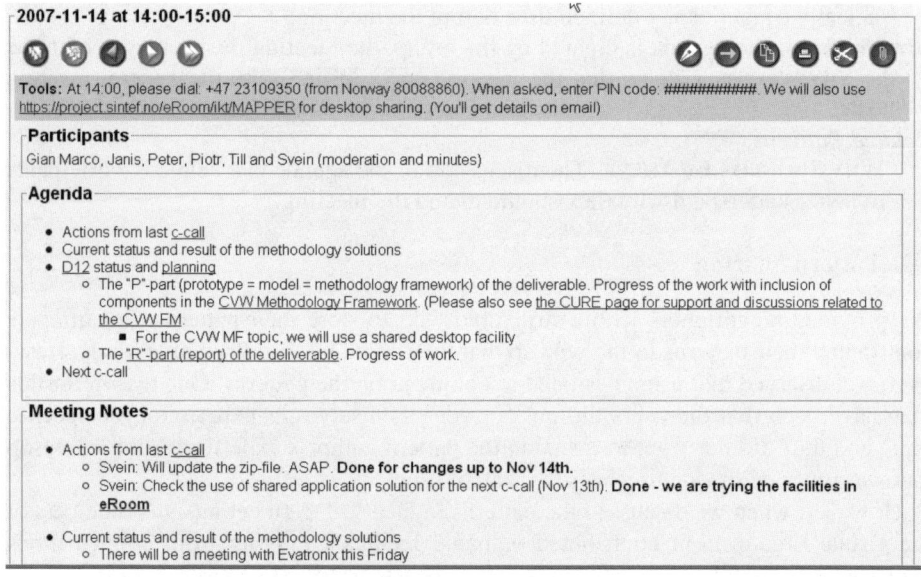

Fig. 2. A meeting page in CURE

Since the agenda creation gained more and more importance during the project, the technology providers in the project finally decided to implement the envisioned solution so that the meeting planning process was integrated in the CURE system. The development activities were accompanied by users of the system who contributed their visions for system design. The CURE developers provided new wiki page types that aggregate other pages and that could be used as overview pages for meetings (i.e. the agenda was a composite of agenda items). The invitation of participants was done by giving the intended participants access rights to the meeting place and change notifications for changes of the agenda were automatically sent to all participants of

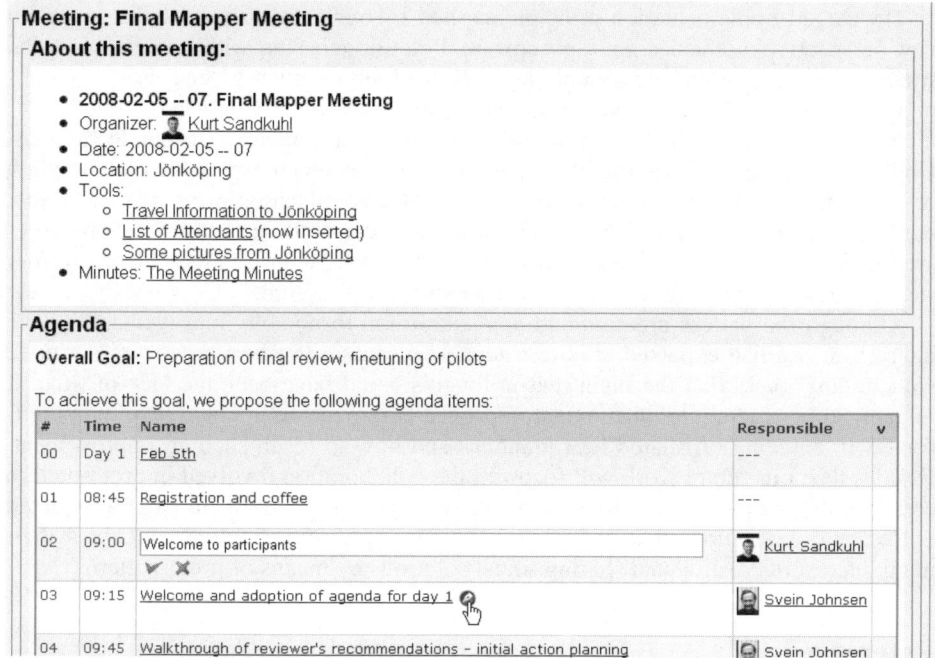

Fig. 3. Integrated Groupware Solution for the It's my Agenda – It's My Meeting pattern

the meeting. Figure 3 shows how the resulting meeting page looked after the pattern was implemented in CURE.

One industrial consortium decided to directly adapt the solution that was developed and used in the research project by adapting the existing meeting templates. Another industrial consortium decided to implement the patterns on the social level. The third consortium made use of the advice given in the instant technology solution and tailored their MS SharePoint installation so that meeting preparation was better supported. All industrial partners reported on perceived efficiency improvements as a result of applying the patterns. In summary, this shows that all three implementation levels were used by the partners and that it depends on the concrete application context how much technology support is required.

6 Conclusion

In this paper, we presented a process model and a knowledge representation for best practice sharing in virtual organizations. This process uses EUD techniques for adjusting supportive technologies to changing social practice. It makes use of proto-patterns for capturing and communicating social practice. We showed how practitioners can use proto-patterns to make their tacit knowledge explicit so that it can be shared and discussed with other practitioners. This allows other practitioners to internalize the shared practice and create a common conception of collaborative work.

The staged implementation principle applied by our proto-patterns helps to gain a new perspective on the design of groupware. Practitioners start with implementing the social process, continue with applying EUD techniques such as end-user programming or tailoring of off the shelf components and occasionally decide to create a domain-specific integrated groupware solution using participatory design techniques. Unlike in other approaches that have a focus either on social aspects of collaboration or on the technical implementation of the groupware application, we experienced that our approach helps practitioners to gain a good understanding on how the processes are mapped to technology. This means that the presented approach may be one further step towards bridging the socio-technical gap in CSCW design.

Although the pattern creation and application led to notable improvements of the interaction, we had expected a more extensive discussion of best practices. For now, we can only guess that the main reason for this could have been the lack of time. It remains to be studied, to what extent improved communication could help the practitioners in agreeing on shared best practices and how to reach such an improvement. Besides this, our future work will focus on the collaboration involved in proto-pattern creation. We are currently working towards transferring the results to large distributed voluntary organizations that make few use of groupware technology and show their main interest in creating and sharing social solutions by means of proto-patterns.

References

1. Alexander, C., Ishikawa, S., Silverstein, M., Jacobson, M., Fiksdahl-King, I., Angel, S.: A pattern language. Oxford University Press, New York (1977)
2. Byrne, J., Brandt, R., Port, O.: The virtual corporation. Business Week 8, 98–102 (1993)
3. Carroll, J.M., Farooq, U.: Community-based Learning: Design Patterns and Frameworks. In: Proceedings of ECSCW 2005, Paris, France, pp. 307–324 (2005)
4. Fischer, G., Grudin, J., McCall, R., Ostwald, J., Redmiles, D., Reeves, B., Shipman, F.: Seeding, Evolutionary Growth and Reseeding: The Incremental Development of Collaborative Design Environments. In: Olson, G., Malone, T., Smith, J. (eds.) Coordination Theory and Collaboration Technology, pp. 447–472. Lawrence Erlbaum Associates, Mahwah (2001)
5. Gabriel, R.P.: Patterns of Software. Oxford University Press, New York (1996)
6. Haake, A., Lukosch, S., Schümmer, T.: Wiki-templates: adding structure support to wikis on demand. In: Proc. of WikiSym 2005, pp. 41–51. ACM Press, New York (2005)
7. Hales, K.: Value Creation in a Virtual World, PhD thesis, Bond Univ., Qld, Australia (2005)
8. Harrison, N.B.: The Language of Shepherding. In: Proceedings of PLoP 1999 (1999), http://hillside.net/patterns/EuroPLoP2001/shepherding.doc
9. Herrmann, T., Hoffmann, M., Jahnke, I., Kienle, A., Kunau, G., Loser, K.-U., Menold, N.: Concepts for usable patterns of groupware applications. In: Proc. Of GROUP 2003, pp. 349–358. ACM Press, Sanibel Island (2003)
10. Johnsen, S., Schümmer, T., Haake, J., Pawlak, A., Jørgensen, H., Sandkuhl, K., Stirna, J., Tellioglu, H., Jaccuci, G.: Model-based Adaptive Product and Process Egineering. In: Rabe, M., Mihók, P. (eds.) New Technologies for the intelligent Design and Operation of Manufacturing Networks, pp. 7–27. Fraunhofer IRb Verlag, Stuttgart (2007)

11. Johnson-Lenz, P., Johnson-Lenz, T.: Consider the Groupware: Design and Group Process Impacts on Communication in the Electronic Medium. In: Hiltz, S., Kerr, E. (eds.) Studies of Computer-Mediated Communications Systems: A Synthesis of the Findings, Computerized Conferencing and Communications Center, New Jersey Institute of Technology, Newark, New Jersey (1981)
12. Lieberman, H., Paternó, F., Klann, M., Wulf, V.: End-User Development: an Emerging Paradigm. In: Lieberman, H., Paterno, F., Wulf, V. (eds.) End-User Development, pp. 9–16. Springer, Berlin (2006)
13. Lyons, K.: Using Patterns to Capture Tacit Knowledge and Enhance Knowledge Transfer in Virtual Teams. In: Malhotra, Y. (ed.) Knowledge Management and Virtual Organizations. Idea Group Publishing (2000)
14. Leuf, B., Cunningham, W.: The Wiki Way. Addison-Wesley, Reading (2001)
15. Manns, M.L., Rising, L.: Fearless Change: Patterns for Introducing New Ideas. Addison-Wesley, Reading (2005)
16. Martin, D., Rodden, T., Rouncefield, M., Sommerville, I., Viller, S.: Finding Patterns in the Fieldwork. In: Proc. of ECSCW 2001, pp. 39–58. Kluwer, Germany (2001)
17. May, D., Taylor, P.: Knowledge management with patterns. Commun. ACM 46(7), 94–99 (2003)
18. Oberquelle, H.: Situationsbedingte und benutzerorientierte Anpaßbarkeit von Groupware. In: Hartmann, A., Herrmann, T., Rohde, M., Wulf, V. (eds.) Menschengerechte Groupware - Software-ergonomische Gestaltung und partizipative Umsetzung, Teubner, Stuttgart, pp. 31–50 (1994)
19. Pipek, V., Kahler, H.: Supporting Collaborative Tailoring. In: Lieberman, H., Paterno, F., Wulf, V. (eds.) End-User Development, pp. 315–345. Springer, Berlin (2006)
20. Prange, C.: Organizational Learning – Desperately Seeking Theory? In: Easterby-Smith, M., Burgoyne, J., Araujo, L. (eds.) Organizational Learning and the Learning Organization, pp. 23–43. SAGE Publications, Thousand Oaks (1999)
21. Nonaka, I., Takeuchi, H.: The knowledge creation company. Oxfort University Press, New York (1995)
22. Schön, D.: The Reflective Practitioner: How Professionals Think in Action. Basic Books, New York (1983)
23. Schümmer, T.: A Pattern Approach for End-User Centered Groupware Development. Josef Eul Verlag, Lohmar – Köln, Gemany (2005)
24. Schümmer, T., Lukosch, S.: Patterns for Computer-Mediated Interaction. John Wiley & Sons, Chichester (2007)
25. Schümmer, T., Tandler, P.: Patterns for Technology Enhanced Meetings. In: Proceedings of EuroPLoP 2007, Konstanz, Germany, pp. 97–120 (2008)
26. Schuler, Douglas: Liberating Voices: A Pattern Language for Communication Revolution. MIT Press (2008)
27. Wulf, V., Krings, M., Stiemerling, O., Iacucci, G., Fuchs-Fronhofen, P., Hinrichs, J., Maidhof, M., Nett, B., Peters, R.: Improving Inter-Organizational Processes with Integrated Organization and Technology Development. Journal of Universal Computer Science 5(6), 339–365 (1999)

Web Design Patterns: Investigating User Goals and Browsing Strategies

Paloma Díaz[1], Mary Beth Rosson[2], Ignacio Aedo[1], and John. M. Carroll[2]

[1] DEI Lab. Universidad Carlos III de Madrid Spain
[2] Information Science and Technology College, Pennsylvania State University USA
paloma.diaz@uc3m.es, ignacio.aedo@uc3m.es,

Abstract. Design patterns document in a systematic way design solutions to re-current problems and they are expressed using non-technical terms, so that a wider audience can understand them. Thus they could be useful tools to im-prove communication in interdisciplinary teams and to integrate end-users in participatory design processes. However, the difficulties of using patterns go beyond the lexicon used in the patterns description. The individuals who might use the patterns may be following different strategies when browsing a collec-tion of patterns, strategies that are determined by their goal at a specific point during the development process. Moreover, the strategy they follow can have some influence in the quality of the proposed solution. In this paper we describe an empirical study that has been performed to answer some of these questions. In the study we gathered information on browsing strategies and user goals when using a patterns catalogue to design a web system. We also analyzed the relation among the goal and the strategy as well as their impact in the quality of the use of the patterns. This investigation is part of a larger project intended to design patterns catalogues that take into account the goals and expectations of their end-users, who are not necessarily experts either on web design or on design patterns.

Keywords: web design patterns, design, end-user development.

1 Introduction

The design of large-scale web information systems is a complex and multifaceted task that must consider issues such as information structure, navigation options, the design of the user interface and interaction mechanisms, personalization, and security assur-ance [1, 2]. One consequence is that inter-disciplinary web development teams, made up of members with complementary abilities and knowledge, are often preferred to generalist software engineers, because they provide greater depth and breadth of knowledge [3]. In the web domain, such teams typically integrate specialists in web design and programming, information architecture, HCI and security. Further, to en-sure that the final system is both usable and useful, end users or other problem domain stakeholders are often asked to contribute to design decisions through a user-centered or a participatory design process when they are integrated as first-class designers who can take active part in the design decisions and not just as evaluators of prototypes.

V. Pipek et al. (Eds.): IS-EUD 2009, LNCS 5435, pp. 186–204, 2009.
© Springer-Verlag Berlin Heidelberg 2009

Unfortunately, inter-disciplinary teams are not always as efficient as one would hope. Communication difficulties that can affect the quality of the final product [4], may worsen in the case of web development, where there are often particularly onerous time pressures on the schedule. Researchers such as Jan Borchers have suggested that design patterns might be used to improve communication in inter-disciplinary teams; such patterns document established solutions to recurrent problems using a language characterized by its cross-discipline readability [5]. The work reported here is part of a larger effort investigating the usefulness of web design patterns in the context of inter-disciplinary development teams that include end-users as first-class designers.

In addition to improving communication among team members with differing expertise, design patterns may be of particular benefit to end-users and other nonprogrammers who wish to contribute to the development of a web system, because they may help to address the technical challenges of the web development process [6]. We are exploring this possibility within a pattern-driven framework for web development, where users select and compose design patterns to specify a system, rather than learning and using complex programming techniques [7, see also 8]. We propose that a pattern language integrates patterns from different design disciplines (including web design patterns [10, 11, 12, 13] and interaction design patterns [14]), may be useful to inter-disciplinary designers and end-users — but only if these individuals can navigate the patterns to find solutions to their problems and fulfill their requirements. For example, problems of different types that are correlated in the real world (for example, a dynamic navigation interface that violates security guidelines) should also be correlated in the pattern language. In this way we will help designers to consider different but inter-related knowledge when dealing with a problem; failure to do so is one of the most common errors in inter-disciplinary development [4].

Even if we succeed in creating a cross-disciplinary pattern language of this sort, we must also consider how users with varying background will explore and apply these patterns. To ensure that our pattern-based framework will be useful for teams that include diverse users, we must first understand how such individuals approach design problems, so that we can provide them with the representation(s) that helps them to efficiently locate and apply the patterns they need.

In this paper, we report a preliminary empirical study of pattern-based web design that we conducted to explore the browsing strategies that non-experts use when trying to apply patterns to web information system design. Our goal was to understand the implications that such browsing strategies have for a design tool that supports pattern exploration. We describe the results of the study in terms of how browsing strategies were related to users' goals in design problem-solving. We also consider how the different browsing strategies impacted users' effectiveness in using the patterns.

The remaining of the paper is organized as follows. Section 2 reviews related work. Section 3 describes the patterns collection used in the study, and Section 4 reports the study. Conclusions and further work are summarized in Section 5.

2 Related Work

Design patterns document in a systematic way the successful solutions to recurrent problems. They achieve this purpose through an organization that includes sections with information about the pattern's utility, its limitations and how to apply it. For example, the Alexandrian or canonical format includes the sections such as the *Name*; the *Problem*; the *Context*; the *Forces*; the *Solution* and *Example*; the *Resulting Context*; a *Rationale*; the *Know Uses* and the *Related Patterns*.

A comprehensive information resource like a pattern can be used for very different purposes. For instance, in the conclusions of the CHI '97 Workshop on Pattern Languages, Bayle et al [15] summarized five different uses for design patterns that had been suggested by workshop participants: *Capture and Description*, when patterns are used as a mechanism to record features of a design entity, whether static or dynamic, in a specific context; *Generalization*, when patterns are used to generalize properties across places and situations; *Prescription*, when patterns are used as a way to determine the right solution to a specific problem; *Rhetoric*, when they are used as a kind of *lingua franca* to talk about design in an easy and understandable way and *Prediction*, when patterns are used to analyze the impact of a specific design decision.

These different possible uses of patterns suggest they may contribute to different points in the software development lifecycle, and not only for design generation as is commonly believed. For example, during the analysis process, design patterns may be used to identify features or requirements of the system as they *capture* and *describe* problems and solutions and *generalize* aspects. During design, solutions *described* by patterns can be applied and even they can be used as a communication tool between designers given their *rhetorical* value. Moreover, if we have competing designs, the predictability can be used to select the most appropriate one [14]. Finally, patterns can also be used to evaluate a system's quality according to their *prescriptive* value. Focusing just on the design process, the empirical study reported in [16] enumerates four different activities that may be supported by patterns during design: *discovery*, when designers browse the collection to identify those patterns that could be useful; *ideas generation*, when designers look for patterns fulfilling a specific high-level goal; *issue clarification*, when they look for a specific solution to a fully specified problem; and *re-reference*, when they look back to the collection just to reference something they saw before.

A central problem in practical use of patterns is the identification of a candidate pattern. Problems arise because of the typical ways in which patterns are organized and presented in current tools [17], especially once we consider that users may be operating within different use contexts or pursuing different purposes when using the patterns. Design patterns are normally found in text-based or web-based catalogues that emphasize browsing or searching the collection with pre-defined criteria, usually a design concern. For example, the ACM-SIGWEB Hypermedia Design Patterns web repository [18] offers two exploration options: an alphabetically ordered list of patterns, including the name and creation date for each item; and three broad categories of patterns (Interface/Layout; Structure/Navigation or Content oriented).

Patterns may also be integrated within a cohesive pattern language that makes explicit the relationships amongst patterns (typically composition and association). In this case, exploration tools can include links enabling users to move from one pattern to other related patterns. For example, HyperPatterns [19], a language of web design patterns, supports navigation via web design concerns (navigation, structure, presentation, interaction, personalization and security) as well as browsing via hyperlinks embedded in the pattern description. However both of these navigation options may create difficulties for non-experts because they require knowledge of either design patterns (to identify a pattern by name) or web design (to identify the design issue that might be related to a potentially useful pattern). Moreover, once selected a pattern is presented in a comprehensive and sequential fashion – including all its sections – that may make the content difficult to read and understand.

A richer approach to pattern exploration is described in [20]; here each pattern is rewritten as a *forces hierarchy* that shows the benefits and trade-offs for each pattern individually, so designers can understand the consequences of applying a specific pattern. However, in this approach the relation between patterns, which makes up the core of the pattern language, is lost. As another alternative, we have described a visual tool that would enable pattern browsing by design goals extracted from the *problem* section of patterns [7]. We have re-written the HyperPatterns language using soft-goal graphs [21]. Users are first presented a number of web design goals (like "Guide the user through the information space" or "Ensure system security"); these are organized in a hierarchy of soft-goal graphs that consider the relationships in the pattern language. Both positive relationships (goals that contribute to reach another goal) and negative relationships (goals that can make it difficult or prevent for meeting another goal) are highlighted in the graph. Users can interactively browse this goal space and see the patterns that support each goal.

Even though a visual goal-based approach such as this might be more efficient for non-experts than textual-based descriptions, it does not consider the requirement that pattern browsing and application is likely to occur with different purposes by different individuals, and at different points of development. If the patterns have different uses, their users - whether experts, casual designers or end-users – are likely to be pursuing different goals when identifying and applying the patterns. These variations in purposes may in turn imply the need for supporting different browsing strategies.

The work reported in this paper elaborates this general idea. We seek to analyze the browsing strategy used by the designer as a function of her goal, and to analyze the relation between strategy and goal, and between strategy and the effectiveness of pattern use of. In contrast to other work, we are not interested in measuring the quality of the designs produced through application of a patterns catalogue or language. Our goal instead is to study the goals and strategies of users and how well they understand the pattern when they apply a specific strategy or try to meet a goal, so that we can identify flaws that might guide design of patterns exploration tools that can make users more efficient in their use of patterns. Such exploration tools could be integrated into development frameworks, like the one described in [22], which make it possible to generate conceptual designs and prototypes from a list of selected patterns. In this way, end user development would be completely supported using the patterns as the main interface.

3   HyperPatterns: A Language of Web Design Patterns

In order to study the strategies users apply to their search for patterns and the goals that drive these explorations, we need a collection of patterns that can be explored by users. Because one of our goals is to provide tools dealing with different web design perspectives, including information structure, navigation tools, presentation and interaction mechanisms, security and personalization, we selected an existing patterns language called HyperPatterns [19]. This language is a compilation of patterns belonging to several existing pattern languages. Moreover, all the patterns include some kind of design rationale, so designers will have additional resources for deciding whether or not to apply each pattern. However, HyperPatterns has some usability and readability problems. First, the patterns description is often too long. Taking into account the time pressure on most web site development projects, it is not realistic to expect designers to devote significant time reading and understanding the patterns, especially if we consider that patterns do not provide a *cut-and-paste* solution but rather solution guidelines that are only more or less precise, depending on the pattern's level of abstraction. Secondly, the solution proposed by the patterns is often rather abstract and verbose, with no additional examples or illustrations, so that users might find it difficult to understand quickly as required in a domain like web development.

As a result of these issues, we have created a new version of HyperPatterns, available in [23] where the essence of the pattern language was maintained. Here, each pattern description includes nine sections (see figure 1): the *identifier*, *name* as well as the *reference* to the original pattern (see first line in the figure); the *context*, that describes the situation leading to the application of the pattern (see second line in the figure); the *intent*, that describes in a very short sentence the problem addressed by the pattern (see the centered bold line in the figure); the *solution* that consists of an image and a description of the proposed solution (see description and figure below the solution); the *discussion* that analyzes the implications of applying the pattern; *related patterns* that links to some related patterns; and *references* that links to the original source of the pattern as well as other sources used to improve the original pattern. Most patterns are slightly modified to shorten the description of the problem in order to make them more readable; some also include new sections like images of application examples, in order to improve their comprehensibility. Moreover, the different sections of the pattern have been reordered and formatted to improve readability. For example, each problem has been described using the shortest and clearest sentence possible, with a placement that is centered and bold at the beginning of the pattern to give it a strong emphasis, so that users can quickly determine if the pattern is potentially useful for them depending on whether it deals or not with a problem they are concerned with. We also considered important to put the reference to the original source as soon as possible to use authority as a criteria to promote the confidence in the pattern quality.

Recall that we selected HyperPatterns as a focus for investigation because it contains patterns that consider six different design views. This gives us the flexibility to consider different kinds of web design problems. Moreover, patterns deal with problems at different levels of abstraction so we have patterns that could be useful for different kinds of users. For example, the pattern [HI1] Interaction describes at a very high level how to deal with interaction design as a global task, acting as a kind of integrator for the rest of the patterns dealing with this design perspective; the pattern [MI1] Information on Demand is a medium level pattern that provides several guidelines to let the user control the amount of information she wants to receive. [LI1] Action Buttons is a low-level pattern that describes the user interface technique of links that may be used to evoke actions.

[MN2] Guided Tour Navigation based on [Garzotto et al, 1999]

The information has been organized using a [BE1]Hierarchical Organization or [BE2]Task-based Organization patterns and you want to guide the user to explore a set of nodes.

How can an overview of the system be provided to new users?

- You have to select those nodes or pages of your system that can provide users an accurate feeling of the utility of the system
- You have to identify an order among the set of selected nodes and to create sequential links among them. Links can be uni- or bi-directional.
- A variant is a circular guided tour, where the last node links to the first one. You can also have an upper node in the structure to get out from the cycle.
- You have to put an access anchor to the first node of the collection.

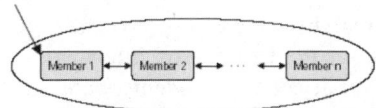

Provide an itinerary to the users to access for first time to the application ([Garzotto et al, 1999])

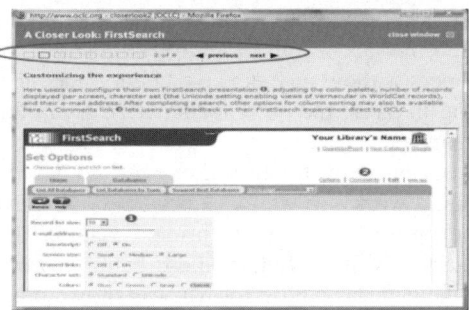

Discussion

Some users, who have very few knowledge of the application domain or who are accessing the system for the first time, need sometimes to get familiar with the system content and tasks before using it. Other users could just want to get a quick overview of the system to decide whether to use it or not.

Related to

- To use the [BE1]Collection Center to define the enter point. This pattern can be combined with the [MN1]Index Navigation pattern to go out from the initial itinerary to the final of the tour or in any time.
- To adapt this navigation mechanism to different contexts, you can use the [MN3]Navigational Context pattern.

Sources

[Garzotto et al, 1999]
[12]

Fig. 1. One of the design patterns in the new version of HyperPatterns used in the study

4   Analysing User Goals and Browsing Strategies

To study users' design goals as well as their browsing strategies we conducted a preliminary empirical investigation of casual developers as they attempted to find and
apply patterns to a web design problem. This was an exploratory study, in that our
focus was on participant observation as they worked on problems, so that we could
answer questions like which and how many strategies they appied, and what goals
they were pursuing as they progressed through the activity. There were no predefined
categories for goals or strategies — the goal of this initial study was precisely to discover what such categories might be. In this section we first describe the study set-up

and procedures. We follow this with an analysis of results, and finish with implications for design tools that support user-centered exploration of design patterns.

4.1 Methods

Goal. The goal of the empirical study was to study the strategies users follow when browsing a design patterns collection to design a web site. We were interested in finding out how the users access and read patterns and with what purposes, in order to devise useful browsing tools.

Participants. We recruited volunteers from two classes of students currently taking an HCI course offered within the College of Information Sciences and Technology College at Penn State University. These students were not experts in either web programming techniques or design patterns. 21 students volunteered for the study; 3 were women. They were organized into 10 pairs plus one single student. Five pairs had never worked together, two occasionally (once or twice), and three of them very often (several times or quite often according to them). In general, we can describe participants as casual developers without an extensive history in cooperating together.

Procedure. Working in pairs, the participants were given the task to design a personal information organizer. The task description is included in Annex I. They received a high-level description of this task (i.e., with no details as to what should be included or how it should work), as well as a printed book containing a set of Hyper-Patterns patterns. The book contained the printed version of the patterns listed in Table 1. The book started with an Index where patterns were organized by design concern, followed by the patterns whose format was shown previously in Figure 1.

Table 1. Index of the design patterns used in the study

Design view	Pattern (ID + Name)
Interaction	[MI1] Information on Demand based on [10]
	[MI2] Process Feed-back based on [10]
	[LI1]Action Buttons based on [14]
Navigation	[MN1] Index Navigation based on [11]
	[MN2] Guided Tour Navigation based on [11]
	[MN3] Navigational Context based on [10]
	[LN1] Location Bread Crumbs based on [14]
	[LN2] Site Map based on [13]
	[LN3] Search Action Module based on [14]
	[LN4] One Jump Home based on [24]
Presentation	[MP1] Information-Interaction Decoupling based on [12]
	[MP2] Information-Interaction Coupling based on [12]
	[MP3] Behavioral Grouping based on [10]
	[MP4] Define and Run Presentation based on [25]
	[MP5] Synchronize Channels based on [25]
	[LP1] Navigation Bar based on [14]
	[LP2] Footer Bar based on [13]
Structure	[ME1] Hierarchical Organization based on [14]
	[ME2] Task-based Organization based on [14]
	[LE1] Collection Center based on [11]
	[LE2] Node as a Single Unit based on [10]
	[LE3] Home Page based on [14]

Participants were given 45 minutes to generate a high-level design. Their deliverables were a paper and pencil sketch of the interface and a narrative description of how it worked. They were asked to browse the patterns catalogue as they developed their design and to annotate their sketch to show which pattern(s) they had applied. Once the design was completed the participants completed individual surveys that posed questions about the way they had used the catalogue. Finally, the participants responded to semi-structured interview questions, so that we could clarify and validate both the design and their answers to the survey questions. During the interview we also probed more deeply how they thought of patterns as a communication tool between designers, to analyze the rhetorical use of patterns as a *lingua franca*, as well as their expectations about the role of patterns in designing a more complex and unfamiliar web site. This final question was aimed at understanding what aspects of our findings might be tied to the particular design problem assigned, as well as to gather information about how the results could be applied in a different setting.

Recording mechanisms and data gathered. As mentioned earlier, we had three main sources of data: the designs; the questionnaires and the interviews. Designs were pen and pencil drawings of the interface, and included marks showing where and which patterns has been used (see an example in figure 2).

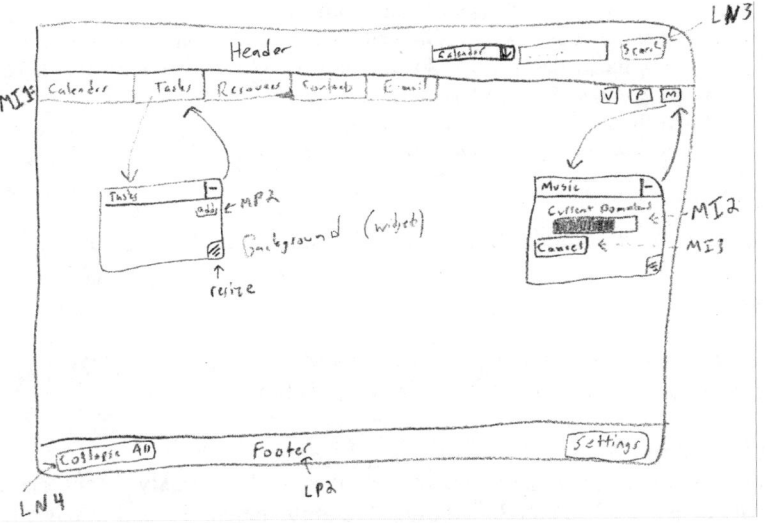

Fig. 2. A design with patterns marked where used

The questionnaire (see the questions in the figure 3) included five open-ended questions about the use of the patterns, and a few more specific questions about the participants' background. The semi-structured interview began by asking evaluators to describe their design. Then we followed an informal script to ask about four main issues: the criteria they used to decide whether the pattern was useful or not; the sections of the pattern they found more useful; the use of the pattern as a communication tool between them; and their intention to use these patterns to design a completely new and unfamiliar web site. We introduced this last question after the first three sessions and interviews, when we realized that most participants said that the web site assigned as a design problem for the study was so familiar to them as web users that they would have used probably the same patterns even without realizing they were doing it. Overall, we collected 11 designs and interviews and 21 completed surveys.

Data were gathered from the sources summarized in Table 2. We had no pre-established categories for user goals or strategies because this project was an exploratory study where we were observing users to understand their behaviour; in such settings a predefined set of categories would have biased the results. Concerning the "Quality in the design of the patterns, for each of the patterns in the catalogue we assigned a value according to its suitability to the design problem being faced. We used 4 values: 0 if pattern should not be applied; 0.25 if its use is slightly recommended (it is not necessary but it could be used if the system is complex enough); 0.5 if it is strongly recommended and 1 if it is considered mandatory.

Table 2. Data gathered in the empirical study

Goal	Data source
User goals	Questionnaire: questions 1, 2 and 3
	Additional information from interviews
Browsing strategy	Questionnaire: questions 1 and 2
	Additional information from interviews
Most/less useful	Questionnaire: questions 2, 4 and 5
parts of the pattern	Additional information from interviews
Quality in the use of	Designs
the patterns	
Patterns as a com-	Interviews
munication tool	
Using patterns in	Interviews
unfamiliar contexts	

4.2   Results

In this section we summarize the main results of our empirical study, organized according to the data we gathered for the issues in Table 2.

4.2.1   User Goals

To identify the different user goals our evaluators had, we analyzed the answers collected from questions 1, 2 and 3 (see Fig. 3), complemented by additional information provided in the interviews. We have identified three categories of goals:

1. Adhering to design goals: some evaluators established in the first place a number of goals, usually through brainstorming, or they worked having in mind the general goal of improving usability and easiness of use and design.
2. Recreating similar systems: some evaluators have had previous experience with this kind of web systems and they just tried to include the same services and structures they are used to.
3. Looking for ideas: some evaluators just went through the catalogue to identify design solutions that could be useful, with no preconceived idea or goal.

POST-TASK SURVEY

Now that you have completed the web design task, we would like to ask you a few
questions about how you approached it, and how the design patterns were used.

1. How did you browse the material in the design patterns catalogue? If you did this in
    multiple ways, please compare your strategies in terms of effectiveness.

2. Once you found a pattern of interest, how did you assess its potential for the design
    problem you were addressing?

3. Describe how you used the patterns in your design, giving examples if possible.

    As you worked on your design and explored the patterns, what if any relationships
    among the patterns did you notice? How did this affect your design process?

4. Choose one pattern you remember using, what was it? _____

5. Looking back at this pattern, what part(s) of it did you find most useful? Why? What
    parts did you find least useful? Why?

    Finally, we'd like to gather a bit of information about your background, so that we can
    make better interpretations of your experiences and reactions.

1. What is your current semester standing in IST?

2. Rate check your level of expertise in web user interface design:

Novice	Modest	Average	Good	Expert

3. Rate check your level of expertise in web programming:

Novice	Modest	Average	Good	Expert

4. Rate your history of working together with this partner in other contexts:

Never	Once	Twice	Several times	Quite often

Fig. 3. Questions included in the post-task individual questionnaire

According to the data collected, the most common goal was "Adhering to design
goals" (16 participants), followed by "Recreating similar systems" (12 participants)
and, finally, "Looking for ideas" (4 participants). As can be seen by these tallies,
some users described two different strategies, a non-surprising result considering that
the phrasing of question 1 raised this as a possibility. In particular, 8 participants said
they were pursuing both goals 1 and 2 at different moments. According to one team
during their interview:

> *"We used the categories at the beginning, in the index of the book, to
> go through the patterns. We used the category to decide if the pattern
> could be relevant for our goals. We also used our personal experience
> in this kind of systems. We were trying to combine ideas from social
> networks and organizers."*

4.2.2 Browsing Strategies by User Goals

From participants' answers to questions 1, 2 and 3 and the interviews we extracted the
strategies that users applied for browsing the patterns. In this case we have identified
4 different strategies:

1. *Skim information*: some participants were looking for information to decide whether to apply a pattern or not (e.g., the title, the problem, the solution, the example).
2. *Flip through pages looking for images*: some participants used visual information (examples of use and image of the solution).
3. *Read one-by-one*: some participants went through all the patterns as a first strategy to identify candidates and look for ideas
4. *Use of category index*: some participants went to the index as a first strategy to identify potential patterns matching their concerns

In Figures 4, 5 and 6 we have graphed participants' reported strategies according to the three types of goals they had reported (see previous subsection).

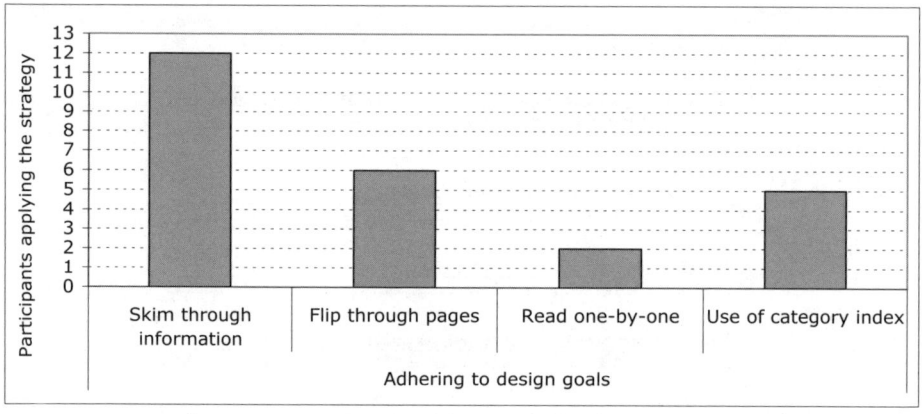

Fig. 4. Browsing strategies for the "Adhering to design goals" user goal

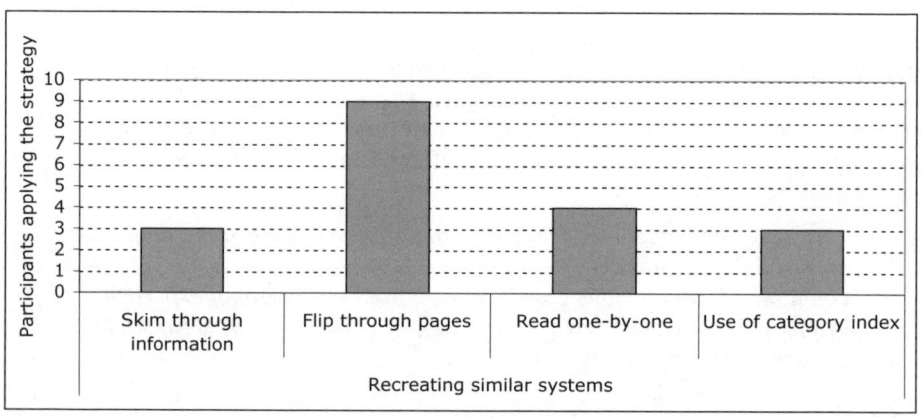

Fig. 5. Browsing strategies for the "Recreating similar systems" user goal

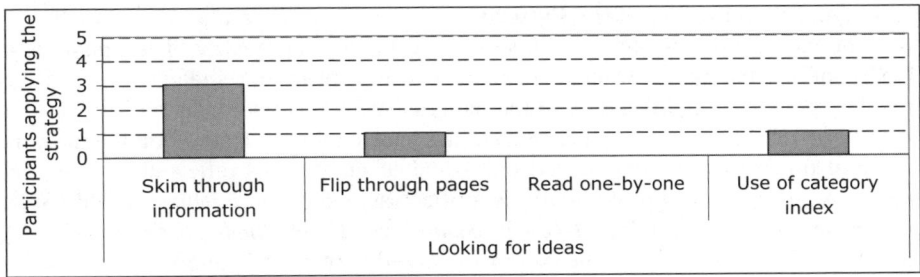

Fig. 6. Browsing strategies for the "Looking for ideas" user goal

As these graphs convey, "Skim through information" (i.e., browsing descriptive sections like the problem or solution section of a pattern) is most common as a strategy when the participants were trying to work with specific design principles, as well as when they were looking for ideas. In contrast, when they had a clear idea about what they wanted, mainly because they were frequent users of this kind of web systems, the preferred strategy was "Flip through pages"; that is, they have an image of the interface they wanted to create based on previous experience with similar systems, and are presumably looking for some example image that could match what they have in mind. "Read one-by-one" is rarely used and only when participants were attempting to recreate some other system. "Use of category index" was used less frequently across all types of goals.

4.2.3 Most- and Least-Used Sections of Patterns

In order to generate ideas about how to organize or highlight the information contained in each pattern, we included a specific question about the sections of each pattern that were considered most relevant. In general, participants reported that the name of the pattern, the problem description and the images were most useful. The following are some specific comments concerning this issue:

> - *When paging we were looking for the bold titles* (problem section)
> *and pictures* (Example and Solution sections) *to make sure we have
> included such things. Quickly find patterns to apply.*
> - *Pictures help to draw your attention*
> - *Examples and figures were really useful.*

Notably, the "Related Patterns" section was not reported as useful by any of the evaluators. Even though such information is usually considered to be fundamental to the pattern language, because it makes it possible to navigate through related patterns, it seems that the enumeration of related patterns, even when the relationship is explained, was not very useful in this task context. It seems that other ways to deal with issues involving related patterns are needed. Perhaps techniques that are more visually engaging like graphs [7], or more proactive like pop-up windows that draw the attention of the user, will be effective in promoting discovery of related patterns.

As a caveat, the results we report about these users' attention to different aspects of the pattern information might have been influenced by the limited amount of time they had to create their designs. However even if so, we expect that real-world web development projects often take place under similar time pressures.

4.2.4 Quality in the Use of the Patterns

As mentioned earlier, we had no interest in evaluating the quality of the patterns in HyperPatterns, but rather wanted to know if users' browsing strategy might affect how they perceived and understood the patterns. With this goal in mind we analyzed the sketched designs and the patterns that had been explicitly marked on them. In the course of doing this, we discovered that some of the designs reflected patterns that had not been recognized or explicitly identified (as one of our evaluators said *"Since they* (patterns) *are so familiar I can presume I would use them even without being aware of"*). However because the pairs were asked to mark the patterns they used, we only considered the marks like those in Figure 2 to analyze their use of the patterns.

The results are summarized in figure 7. Generally the most commonly used patterns were those that are relatively intuitive and concrete, a result that has also been obtained in similar studies [17, 28]. A counterexample is the most used pattern [MI2, Process Feedback], a medium level pattern that was used by all the teams. In this case, the example image accompanying the pattern was particularly clear, perhaps making it was very easy to understand. Looking across the patterns, we see that interaction patterns were most effectively used; it may be that interaction schemes are quite easy to understand while the other categories deal with more abstract concepts like navigational context or information decoupling. For example, two patterns that were relevant but were not mentioned in any design were MN1 and LE2. MN1 ("Index Navigation") concerns organizing a collection of items. Because it is about organization and the example in the printed catalogue is a complex hierarchy with several levels, participants might have thought it was not needed and would complicate unnecessarily the interface. Concerning LE2 ("Node as a single unit"), this is an example of rather abstract concept that everybody uses but few are aware of as an explicit guideline.

With respect to design goals, it is worth noting that the only incorrect application of a pattern (misuse of the pattern MN2 "Guided tour") occurred in two groups that were using the "Flip through the pages" strategy. In these cases they did not read the

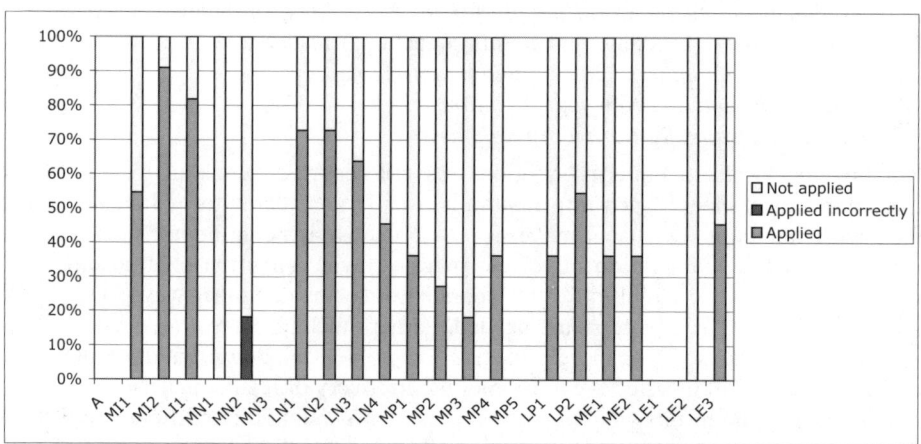

Fig. 7. Data about the quality of the use of the patterns; for pattern names see in Table 1

pattern, but rather just looked at images and examples and got the wrong idea about the solution proposed. For this pattern (intended to demonstrate how web navigation can be designed as a guided tour), one of the groups said:

> *"We began with an idea we had and combined the idea with the layout on page 18"... The combination of tabs and buttons was most useful, however we altered the buttons to links...."*

This comment reveals that when they were analyzing their design they adapted the interface layout of the example provided, but without realizing that the solution being exemplified (see Figure 1) was not the layout but rather the buttons that enable navigation between the items in the guided tour.

4.2.5 Patterns as a Communication Tool

We included a question in the interview to assess whether patterns could be used with a rhetorical purpose by end users or casual developers. Even though our results may be biased by the fact that the participants had been exposed to the patterns only during a 45 minutes work session, it is common among patterns developers to claim that patterns use an intuitive vocabulary that can be understood by casual designers and end users without problems.

Our results show that users found the idea behind the pattern more intuitive than the name of the pattern itself; only three participants mentioned the name. Some of the comments we recorded in the interview suggest some possible causes of this rather modest acceptance of pattern names:

> Answering to the question, Did you use the names of the patterns as a communication tool between both of you?
>
> *- Yes, not using the entire name in some cases cause names are too long but the idea of the pattern*
>
> *- Yes both the code and the idea behind the pattern. We moved from familiar concepts (like collapsable) to the patterns code (MI1) when documenting the system*

Also we realized that participants who had a predefined concept for their web design based on experience with similar web systems, said they used the pattern as a way to acquire some "vocabulary". One way to understand this comment is that learning a pattern's name became a goal for them as it made them feel more technically sound.

4.2.6 Using Patterns in Unfamiliar Contexts

Considering that the design problem used for the study was familiar enough that may participants chose to adapt the design of similar systems, we included a question in the interview to get their opinion about using this patterns catalogue in a much less familiar context - a military intranet. In this case, all of the groups agreed they would want to use the patterns. Because this was an open-ended question we include some of the most revealing comments we gathered:

> *- Even if it is something really new you always can pick up some ideas from patterns*
>
> *- If you come from the web design area, probably you would need to read carefully the requirements and try to address them before applying patterns*

- It would have been definitely harder (to use them to design an unfamiliar site) *but it would have been easier to come up with something completely new since you need to decide what the system has to do first*

- They help because once you have the requirements list they could help you to figure out solutions, they can be applied to meet the requirements, to pick up ideas and how they can be applied. Examples and figures were really useful.

4.3 Preliminary Conclusions of the Study

Even though we are aware that further empirical work is required to draw strong conclusions about strategies and to envision the right tool for each strategy, we did collect a number of interesting findings in this first exploratory study. We summarize them below, illustrating each with comments of individual participants.

Since they (patterns) *are so familiar I can presume I would use them even without being aware of it.*
This is perhaps the main weakness of patterns. The patterns that are most used are those that reflect practices that are so evident and broadly spread that would have been used without even thinking about them in an explicit fashion. Good designers are good designers, with or without patterns. Patterns are supposed to be oriented towards those who have little or no experience in design, or to communicate complex ideas to expert designers. However, our study is consistent with other studies [17, 28] in demonstrating that designers prefer only very concrete and visual patterns, especially those with clear images illustrating the solution. In fact one participant reported that "*Originally tried reading text but it was confusing and time-consuming*". Note that participants had 45 minutes to produce the design applying patterns they had not been exposed to in advance.

So, what is the use of abstract patterns and their narrative sections if designers do not look at them except perhaps on occasion? In some sense their use is obvious; they provide design rationale for reuse of design knowledge. Looking only at images can lead designers to misconceptions, as happened with two of our groups that relied on the images and thought they had used a pattern but had not. Informative sections like the problem, the consequences or the context might help users to understand the pattern and how and why to apply it. Our primary challenge might be in the way we are deploying patterns - i.e., as extensive narratives that must be read by designers who have no time for reading. Maybe we should consider more efficient ways to organize and present information. We should go further in analyzing which are the needs of designers in terms of information and representation. We should explore alternative visualization tools that go beyond the plain representation of the full text pattern, including graphs like in [7, 20] that make possible to visualize the problem space with contributions and trade-offs or applying adaptation techniques for presentation and navigation purposes, reusing knowledge from the hypermedia community [27].

In the beginning I quickly scanned the entire catalogue and took some mental notes of things I saw. I then used the index on the first two pages to quickly locate what I was looking for.

It was clear that participants used different browsing strategies to look for the patterns they needed depending on the stage of the design they were and on their goal. Some started by selecting patterns by its name and then reading them thoroughly to check if they were suitable. Some did just the opposite, scanned the catalogue picking up ideas using mainly the bold title and the images. Others just were flipping pages to see images that reinforced the idea they had about the interface or that suggested new ideas to incorporate.

These findings suggest not only that we should support different access strategies to the patterns but that strategies are likely to vary for the same designer over time. In any case further empirical research is required to provide valid guidelines about the design of exploration tools.

If you come from the web design area, probably you would need to read carefully the requirements and try to address them before applying patterns

This is an idea repeated by several participants in the study; it points to the close tie between patterns and requirements, already studied by different researchers. Because patterns address recurrent problems in a specific domain, the space defined by the Problem section of patterns can be directly linked with the system requirements, whether to trace requirements [28], to identify requirements [14] or to generate designs from requirements, whether automatically [22] or not [29].

As another participant mentioned, *"Once you have the requirements list they* (patterns) *could help you to figure out solutions, they can be applied to meet the requirements, to pick up ideas and how they can be applied"*.

5   Conclusions and Further Work

In this paper we have described a study of non-expert users attempting to apply design patterns to a simple web design task. Our results suggest that users apply different strategies to browse pattern depending on their goal and previous experience as user of the kind of system being developed. Exploration tools could be improved to support such strategies and assist users in applying all the patterns their design needs, not only those that are so evident that are applied unintentionally but those who are more complex and abstract. Moreover, patterns must be presented in a way that is useful and usable by end users and casual designers, not only to expert designers who are much less likely to need them for assistance. Consequently, further work on the design of the exploration tools is required to map the content and representation of design patterns to their less expert users, who do not have experience either with design tasks or design patterns. In this sense, the investigation we have reported is a first step in this challenge. We need to carry out more studies of with different kinds of users and with different exploration tools, to define a set of useful guidelines to improve the reuse of the design knowledge underlying the patterns by supporting efficient browsing strategies.

Acknowledgments

This work is funded by the Spanish Ministry of Science and Innovation through the grant MEC PRY2007-0267 and the MODUWEB project (TIN2006-09678).

References

1. Lowe, D., Hall, W.: Hypermedia and the Web: an engineering approach. John Wiley and Sons, Chichester (1999)
2. Díaz, P., Montero, S., Aedo, I.: Modelling hypermedia and web applications: the Ariadne development method. Information Systems 30(8), 649–673 (2005)
3. Rideout, T.B., Uyeda, K.M., Williams, E.L.: Evolving the software usability engineering process at Hewlett-Packard. In: IEEE International Conference on Systems, Man and Cybernetics, vol. 1, pp. 229–234 (1989)
4. Safoutin, M.J., Thurston, D.J.: A communications-based technique for interdisciplinary design team management. IEEE Transactions on Engineering Management 40(4), 360–372 (1993)
5. Borchers, J.: Interdisciplinary Design Patterns. In: INTERACT 1999 7th International Conference on Human-Computer Interaction, Edinburgh, UK, August 1999. Position Paper, Workshop on Usability Pattern Language (1999)
6. Rode, J., Rosson, M.B., Perez, M.: End user development of web applications. In: Lieberman, H., Paterno, F., Wulf, V. (eds.) End-User Development. Springer, Heidelberg (2006)
7. Díaz, P., Aedo, I., Rosson, M.B.: Visual representation of web design patterns for end-users. In: AVI 2008, pp. 408–411 (2008)
8. Radeke, F., Forbrig, P., Seffah, A., Sinning, D.: PIM Tool: Support for Pattern-Driven and Model-Based UI Development. In: Coninx, K., Luyten, K., Schneider, K.A. (eds.) TAMODIA 2006. LNCS, vol. 4385, pp. 82–96. Springer, Heidelberg (2007)
9. Gamma, E., Helm, R., Johnson, R., Vlissides, J.M.: Design Patterns: Elements of Reusable Object-Oriented Software. Addison-Wesley Professional, Reading (1995)
10. Garrido, A., Rossi, G., Schwabe, D.: Patterns systems for hypermedia. In: Proceedings of The 3rd Pattern Language of Programming Conference (1997)
11. Garzotto, F., Paolini, P., Bolchini, D., Valenti, S.: Modeling-by- Patterns of web applications. In: Advances in Conceptual Modeling: ER 1999 Workshops on Evolution and Change in Data Management, Reverse Engineering in Information Systems, and the World Wide Web and Conceptual Modeling, pp. 293–306 (1999)
12. Rossi, G., Schwabe, D., Lyardet, F.: User interface patterns for hypermedia application. In: Proceedings of Advanced Visual Interfaces 2000, pp. 136–142 (2000)
13. van Melie, M.: Web design patterns (last accessed September 2, 2008), http://www.welie.com/patterns/
14. van Duyne, D.K., Landay, J.A., Hong, J.I.: The Design of Sites: Patterns, Principles, and Processes for Crafting a Customer-Centered Web Experience. Addison-Wesley, Reading (2002)
15. Bayle, E., Bellamy, R., Casaday, G., Erickson, T., Fincher, S., Grinter, B., Gross, B., Lehder, D., Marmolin, H., Potts, C., Skousen, G., Thomas, J.: Putting It All Together: Towards a Pattern Language for Interaction Design (last accessed on September 2, 2008), http://www.visi.com/~snowfall/Patterns.WrkShpRep.html
16. Saponas, T.S., Prabaker, M.K., Abowd, G.D., Landay, J.A.: The impact of pre-patterns on the design of digital home applications. In: Proceedings of the 6th Conference on Designing interactive Systems, DIS 2006, University Park, PA, USA, June 26 - 28, pp. 189–198. ACM, New York (2006)
17. Kampffmeyer, H., Zschaler, S.: Finding the Pattern You Need: The Design Pattern Intent Ontology. In: Engels, G., Opdyke, B., Schmidt, D.C., Weil, F. (eds.) MODELS 2007. LNCS, vol. 4735, pp. 211–225. Springer, Heidelberg (2007)

18. Bolchini, D.: Hypermedia Design Patterns Repository (last accessed September 2, 2008), http://www.designpattern.lu.unisi.ch
19. Montero, S.: Hypermedia Patterns: Semantic Repository (last accessed September 2, 2008), http://hypatterns.no-ip.info:8080
20. Araujo, I., Weiss, M.: Linking Non-Functional Requirements and Patterns. In: Proceedings of the Ninth Conference on Pattern Language of Programs (PLoP 2002), September 8–12 (2002)
21. Chung, L., Nixon, B.A., Yu, A., Mylopoulos, J.: Non-Functional Requirements in Software Engineering. Kluwer Academic Publishers, Dordrecht (2000)
22. Montero, S., Díaz, P., Aedo, I.: From requirements to conceptual modeling of web applications through design patterns. In: Workshop on HCI Patterns: Mapping User Needs Into Interaction Design Solutions, in conjunction with INTERACT 2005, Rome, Italy, September 13 (2005)
23. http://dino2.dei.inf.uc3m.es/hyperpatterns (last accessed September 2, 2008)
24. Irons, M.L.: Patterns for personal web sites (last accessed September 2, 2008), http://www.rdrop.com/~half/Creations/Writings/Web.patterns/index.html
25. Cybulski, J.L., Linden, T.: Composing Multimedia Artefacts for Reuse. In: Pattern Languages of Program Design, vol. 4, pp. 461–488. Addison-Wesley Longman, Amsterdam (1999)
26. Chung, E.S., Hong, J.I., Lin, J., Prabaker, M.K., Landay, J.A., Liu, A.L.: Development and evaluation of emerging design patterns for ubiquitous computing. In: DIS 2004: Proceedings of the 2004 conference on Designing interactive systems, pp. 233–242. ACM Press, New York (2004)
27. Brusilovsky, P.: Adaptive hypermedia. Kobsa, A. (ed.) User Modeling and User Adapted Interaction, Ten Year Anniversary Issue 11(1/2), 87–110 (2001)
28. Cleland-Huang, J., Schmelzer, D.: Dynamically Tracing Non-Functional Requirements through Design Pattern Invariants. In: Workshop on Traceability in Emerging Forms of Software Engineering, in conjunction with IEEE International Conference on Automated Software Engineering (October 2003)
29. Weiss, M.: Pattern-Driven Design of Agent Systems: Approach and Case Study. In: Eder, J., Missikoff, M. (eds.) CAiSE 2003. LNCS, vol. 2681. Springer, Heidelberg (2003)

ANNEX I. DESCRIPTION OF THE DESIGN TASK

Designing a Web Personal Organizer using design patterns

The goal of this experiment is to determine whether and how the patterns in the catalogue are useful to you, as well as to gather ideas for how to make them more useful.

INSTRUCTIONS

- Read the task description and create with your pair a design for the proposed web site applying some of the web design patterns included in the catalogue. A design is a sketch of the interface, done with paper and pencil, plus a narrative description of how it works.

- Browse the patterns catalogue to produce your solution. The design has to include at least the home page and some second-level pages where patterns are used.

- Mark in the sketch the pattern(s) you have applied (use the alphanumeric IDs to refer to the pattern in the sketch). You have to use at least one pattern of each category (Interaction, Presentation, Navigation and Structure).

- Fill the survey about the web design patterns usage.

DELIVERABLE
- Design (sketch + narrative)

- Survey

TASK DESCRIPTION
The task consists of designing your own web personal organizer (WPO). In your organizer you can manage your public personal page, agenda, list of contacts, tasks and assignments, multimedia files (videos, music...), urls to resources (courses, chats...), alarms or whatever you consider necessary to make your organization more efficient. Think about useful and innovative ways of organizing and displaying information according to your needs and don't imitate existing interfaces if you don't consider they have the appropriate interface. To manage the WPO means that you browse, add, modify, structure and remove items from the web system.

Males' and Females' Script Debugging Strategies

Valentina Grigoreanu[1,2], James Brundage[2], Eric Bahna[2], Margaret Burnett[1],
Paul ElRif[2], and Jeffrey Snover[2]

[1] Oregon State University, School of Electrical Engineering and Computer Science,
Corvallis, Oregon, USA 97331
{grigorev,burnett}@eecs.oregonstate.edu
[2] Microsoft, One Microsoft Way,
Redmond, Washington, USA
{t-valeng,jamesbru,ebahna,pelrif,jsnover}@microsoft.com

Abstract. Little research has addressed IT professionals' script debugging strategies, or considered whether there may be gender differences in these strategies. What strategies do male and female scripters use and what kinds of mechanisms do they employ to successfully fix bugs? Also, are scripters' debugging strategies similar to or different from those of spreadsheet debuggers? Without the answers to these questions, tool designers do not have a target to aim at for supporting how male and female scripters want to go about debugging. We conducted a think-aloud study to bridge this gap. Our results include (1) a generalized understanding of debugging strategies used by spreadsheet users and scripters, (2) identification of the multiple mechanisms scripters employed to carry out the strategies, and (3) detailed examples of how these debugging strategies were employed by males and females to successfully fix bugs.

Keywords: Gender, Debugging, Scripting, Debugging Strategies.

1 Introduction

At the border between the population of professional developers and the population of end-user programmers, lies a subpopulation of IT professionals who maintain computers, and they accomplish much of their job through scripting. As Kandogan et al. argue, this population has much in common with end-user programmers [14]: as in Nardi's definition of end-user programmers, they program as a means to accomplish some other task, not as an end in itself [22]. Scripting is also becoming much more common by end-user programmers themselves through the advent of end-user oriented scripting languages for the desktop and the web. However, despite the complexity of some scripting tasks, little attention has been given to scripters' specific debugging needs, and even less to the impact that gender differences might have on script debugging strategies and the mechanics used to support them.

We therefore conducted a qualitative study to address this gap by identifying the debugging strategies and mechanisms scripters used. *Strategy* refers to a reasoned plan or method for achieving a specific goal. *Mechanisms* are the low-level tactics

V. Pipek et al. (Eds.): IS-EUD 2009, LNCS 5435, pp. 205–224, 2009.

used to support those strategies: through environment and feature usage. Our work was guided by the debugging strategies reported in an earlier end-user debugging study with spreadsheet users [32].

There are several reasons to ask whether strategies used by scripters working with a scripting environment might be different from strategies used by end-user programmers with a spreadsheet system. First, the populations are different; for example, one might expect scripters to have more experience in debugging per se than spreadsheet users. Second, the language paradigms are different: scripting languages are control-flow oriented, in which programmers focus primarily on specifying sequence and state changes, whereas spreadsheet languages are dataflow oriented, in which programmers focus primarily on specifying calculations (formulas) that use existing values in cells to produce new values. The language paradigm differences lead naturally to a third difference: the environments' debugging affordances themselves are different, with scripting environments tending toward peering into sequence and state, whereas spreadsheets' affordances tend more toward monitoring values and how they flow through calculations. Therefore, the research questions we investigated were:

RQ1: What debugging strategies do scripters try to use?
RQ2: What mechanisms do scripters employ to carry out each strategy?
RQ3: How do our findings on scripters' strategies relate to earlier results on strategies tied with male and female spreadsheet users' success?

Thus, the contributions of this paper are in (1) identifying the strategies scripters try to use in this programming paradigm, (2) identifying the mechanisms scripters use to carry out their different strategies, and (3) exploring details of successful uses of the strategies by males and females.

2 Background and Related Work

Although there has been work in how to effectively support system administrators in *creating* their scripts [14], we have been unable to find work addressing scripters' debugging *strategies*. Instead, most of the work on script debugging has been on tools to automatically find and fix errors (e.g., [35, 37]).

However, there has been considerable work on professional programmers' debugging strategies, and some work on end-user debugging strategies. One study on professional programmers' debugging strategies classified debugging strategies as forward reasoning, going from the code forward to the output, and backward reasoning, going from the output backward through the code [15]. See Romero et al. for a survey of professional programmers' debugging strategies [29].

End-user programmers have elements in common with novice programmers, so the literature on how novice programmers differ from experts is relevant here. For both novices and experts, getting an understanding of the high-level program structure before jumping in to make changes relates to success [19, 21]. However, experts have been found to read programs differently from novices: reading them in control flow order (following the program's execution), rather than spatial order (top to bottom).

In end-user programming, gender differences have been found in attitudes toward and usage of end-user programming and end-user programming environment features [3, 4, 5, 10, 13, 16, 27, 28, 30, 38]. Especially pertinent is a series of end-user debugging studies reporting gender differences in debugging strategies for spreadsheets [9, 32]. The first of these studies pointed to behavior differences that suggested strategy differences, and the second reported a set of eight strategies end users employed in their debugging efforts. In both of these studies, the strategies and behaviors leading to male success were different from those leading to female success. For example, in [32], dataflow strategies played an important role in males' success, but not females'. Prabhakararao et al.'s spreadsheet debugging study with end users also reported a strong tie between using a dataflow strategy and success [25], but participant gender was not collected in that study.

In fact, gender differences that relate to processing information and solving problems have been reported in several fields. One of the most pertinent works is the research on the Selectivity Hypothesis [20, 23]. It proposes that females process information in a comprehensive way (e.g., attending to details and looking for multiple cues) in both simple and complex tasks. Males, on the other hand, process information through simple heuristics (e.g., following the first cue encountered), only switching to comprehensive reasoning for complex tasks.

Self-efficacy theory may also affect the strategies employed by male and female debuggers [1]. Self-efficacy is a person's confidence about succeeding at a specific task. It has shown to influence everything from the use of cognitive strategies, to the amount of effort put forth, the level of persistence, the coping strategies adopted in the face of obstacles, and the final performance outcome. Regarding software usage, there is specific evidence that low self-efficacy impacts attitudes toward software [3, 11], that females have lower self-efficacy than males at their ability to succeed at tasks such as file manipulation and software management tasks [33], and that these differences can affect females' success [3].

Gender differences in strategies also exist in other problem-solving domains, such as psychology, spatial navigation, education, and economics (e.g., [8]). One goal of this paper is to add to the literature on gender differences in problem solving relating to software development, by considering in detail the usage of different strategies by male and female scripters.

3 Study

3.1 Participants

Eleven IT professionals (eight males and three females) volunteered to participate in the study by responding to invitations on an IT-related internet forum and on a PowerShell email discussion list. Participants received software as gratuity. Although we had hoped for equal participation by females and males, female IT professionals are in short supply, and only three signed up. Almost all participants had a technical college degree (in computer science, engineering, or information systems), with the exception of two males whose education ended after high school. Despite their technical degrees, six of the eleven participants rejected the label of "software developer." Those who did classify themselves as software developers were the three females and two of the eight males; the remaining six males described themselves as IT professionals or scripters. All participants reported that, in their everyday jobs, they accomplished their IT professional tasks using PowerShell. As examples of these regular tasks, participants mentioned moving packages, moving machines out of a domain, modifying the registry, initializing software, automating IT tasks, automating tests, and creating test users on servers.

All participants had written two or more scripts within the past year, using Windows PowerShell. The females had written fewer scripts in the past year than the males (number of scripts written by females: 2, 3, and 5; number of scripts written by males: 6, 6, 7, 20+, 30, 30+, 50, 100+).

3.2 Scripting Language and Environment

PowerShell is a new implementation of the traditional Command Line Interface and scripting language developed by Microsoft, which aims to support both IT professionals' and developers' automation needs. We used an as-yet unreleased version of this language and environment in our study. PowerShell supports imperative, pipeline, object-oriented, and functional constructs. Its pipelining, unlike traditional UNIX commands that pipeline *text* to one another, pipelines *objects* to one another. PowerShell has both a command line shell and a graphical scripting environment, and participants used both. Both the command line and graphical scripting environment provide common debugging features such as breakpoints, the ability to step into, error messages, and viewing the call stack. Fig. 1 shows a version of the graphical scripting environment that is similar to the one our participants used.

3.3 Tasks, Procedure, and Data Collection

We instructed the participants to debug two versions of a PowerShell script, which included a "main" section and eight called functions, each of which was in a separate file within the same directory. We used the same script (two versions) for both tasks in order to minimize the amount of time participants spent getting an understanding of the scripts so as to maximize the amount of time they spent actually debugging.

The script was a real-world script that one of us (Brundage) had previously written to collect and display meta-data from other PowerShell scripts. We introduced a total of seven bugs, which we harvested from bugs made by the script's author when he originally wrote the script. Each version of the main script contained one different bug. The eight functions called by both versions contained five other bugs. The seven total bugs fell into two categories: three errors *in data*: using an incorrect property, allowing the wrong kind of file as input, and omitting a filter; and four *errors in structure*: an assignment rather than a comparison, an off-by-one error, an infinite loop, and omitting the code that should have handled the last file.

After participants completed a profiling survey, we gave them a description of what the script was supposed to do. Participants then debugged one version of the script using a command line debugger and a second version using a graphical debugger. The order of the script versions and environments was randomized to control for learning effects.

Participants were instructed to talk aloud as they performed their debugging tasks. Data collected included screen captures, video, voice, and measures of satisfaction.

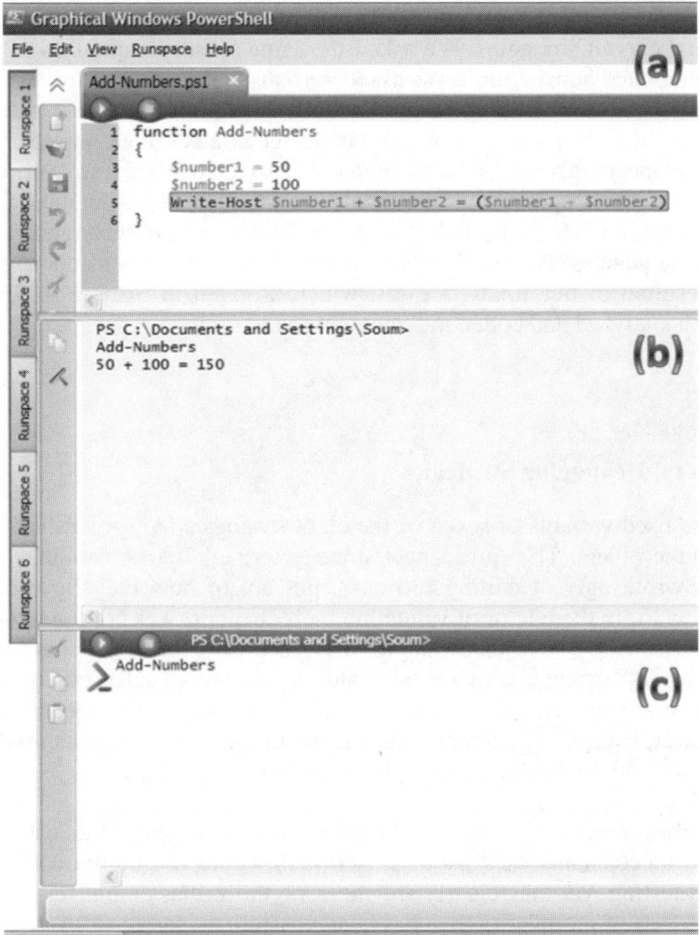

Fig. 1. This is the graphical version of the Windows PowerShell environment. (a) Scripts are written in the top pane, and the example shows a function that adds two numbers. (b) The output pane displays the result of running the script or command. (c) The command line pane is used exactly like PowerShell's command line interface. In this case, it is running the function to add two numbers. This figure is an adaptation of a figure in [36].

After completion of each task, participants were given a post-session questionnaire that included an interview question about the debugging strategies they used.

3.4 Analysis Methodology

We analyzed the data using qualitative content analysis methods. We analyzed two data sources: participant responses to the questionnaire, and the videos. Because we wanted to measure the extent to which males' and females' debugging strategies identified in previous work [32] would generalize to our domain and population, we began by mapping that code set to the Powershell domain of the current study.

One researcher applied these codes to participants' post-session open-ended interview responses about strategies. We asked the same strategies question as in the earlier work mentioned above, but it was asked verbally, rather than on paper. This led to generalizations of a few of the codes and the introduction of a few new codes.

Two researchers then used this revised code set as a starting code set for the videos. They independently coded 27% of the videos (six tasks from various participants), achieving 88% agreement. The dually coded set included the three participants described in 4.2, for which the two researchers also collaboratively analyzed the circumstances, sequences, and mechanisms, resolving any disagreements as they arose. This also resulted in our final code set, which is given in Section 4. The first researcher then analyzed and coded the remaining videos alone.

4 Results

4.1 Scripters' Debugging Strategies

Our scripters used variants of seven of the eight strategies the spreadsheet users used [32], plus three others. The spreadsheet strategy termed "fixing formulas" (in which participants wrote only of editing formulas, but not of how they figured out what, where, or how to fix the bug or of validating their changes) was not found in our data.

As Table 1 shows, five of the strategies they used were direct matches to the earlier spreadsheet users' strategies, two were matches to generalized forms of the spreadsheet users' strategies, and three arose that had not been viable for the spreadsheet users. However, even for the direct matches, the mechanisms scripters used to pursue these strategies had differences from those of the spreadsheet users.

Direct Matches. *Testing* is trying out different values to evaluate the resulting values. Some of the mechanisms used by these scripters would not traditionally have been identified as testing, yet they clearly are checking the values output for correctness— but at finer levels of granularity than has been possible in classic software engineering treatments of the notion of testing.

Specifically, we noticed three types of testing mechanisms used by participants: testing different situations from a whole-program perspective, incrementally checking variable values, and incrementally testing in other ways. The first type is classic testing methodology to cover the specifications or to cover different parts of the code (testing both the antecedent and the consequent parts of an if-then statement, for example). The latter two are informal testing methods to see whether, after having executed part of the code, the variables displayed reasonable values. For example, from a whole-program perspective:

Female P0721081130 ran the code and examined both the error messages and the output text in order, rather than focusing on either one or the other.
Female P0718081400 tried different contexts by cd-ing back to the root directory in the command line before running the file again using the menu.
Male P0717080900 changed the format of the output so that he could understand it more easily when he ran the program.

Table 1. Participants' responses when asked post-session to describe their strategies in finding and fixing the bugs (listed in the order discussed in the text)

Strategy	Definition
	Direct Matches
Testing	Trying out different values to evaluate the resulting values.
Code Inspection	Examining code to determine its correctness.
Specification Checking	Comparing descriptions of what the script should do with the script's code.
Dataflow	Following data dependencies.
Spatial	Following the spatial layout of the code.
	Generalized Matches
Feedback Following	Using system-generated feedback to guide their efforts.
To-Do Listing	Indicating explicitly the suspiciousness of code (or lack of suspiciousness).
	New Strategies
Control Flow	Following the flow of control (the sequence in which instructions are executed).
Help	Getting help from people or resources.
Proceed as in Prior Experience	Recognizing a situation (correctly or not) as one experienced before, and using that prior experience as a blueprint of next steps to take.

However, incrementally checking variable values was much more common, and participants did it in many different ways:

Male P0718081030 hovered over variables to check their values.

Male P0117081130 also hovered over, but in conjunction with breakpoints to stop at a particular line to facilitate the hover.

Female P0718081400 ran the code by accessing it through the command line interface. Others preferred reaching it through the menu.

Female P0718081400 typed the variable name in the command line.

Male P0717080900 added temporary print statements to output variable values at that point in time.

Male P0721081330 added temporary print statements to check whether a particular part of the code was reached/covered by the input.

Female P0718081400 would have liked to use a watch window to examine variable values.

Male P0718081030 examined an entire data structure using tabs (auto-complete) to determine the correctness of its property values.

Other forms of incremental testing focused on running part of the code to check its output. For example:

Female P0718081400 did not understand why she was getting an "access denied" message and therefore tried performing the action manually with Windows Explorer and navigating to that directory (to see if she would get the same message in that different context).

Female P0718081400 first ran a variable to see its output, and then started adding the surrounding words to get more information about that variable and how it is being used.

Female P0717081630 used "stepping over" to see the script's output appear incrementally as she passed the line in the code that produced it.

Male P0721080900 wanted to break into the debugger once a variable had a particular value.

Primarily only the first category of testing is supported by tools aiming to support systematic testing for professional programmers or end-user programmers (e.g., WYSIWYT [6]). However, our scripters were very prone to incremental testing, and although the scripting environment gives them good access to checking these values, there is no support in that environment or most others for using this incremental testing to *systematically* track which portions of the code are tested successfully, which have failed, and which have not participated in any tests at all.

Code inspection is examining the code to determine its correctness. Code inspection is a counterpart to testing with complementary strengths [2]. It is heavily relied upon in the open source community [26]. Not surprisingly, as in the spreadsheet study, testing and code inspection were the most common strategies. Participants' mechanisms for code inspection revealed a surprisingly large set of opportunities for supporting code inspection better in scripting environments, spreadsheets, and other end-user programming environments.

Besides simply reading through the code, some of the basic mechanisms the participants used were:

Female P0718081400 opened up all of the files in the same directory as the script (to view functions the main script was calling), and quickly scanned through all of them one after the other.

Male P0718081030 resized the script pane to show more of the script.

Male P0717080900 used the "Find" function to jump to the part of interest.

Male P0718081030 used the command line to find out all the contextual information he could about a variable he was inspecting (its type, for example).

Male P0717080900 used the integrated scripting environment as a code editor for the command line task because he disliked inspecting the code without syntax highlighting.

The above five mechanisms may seem obvious, but many end-user programming environments do not support these functionalities. For example, they are not well supported in spreadsheets; in that environment performing these actions is awkward and modal. Given the heavy reliance on code inspection by the participants in both this study and the previous spreadsheet study, a design implication for end-user programming and scripting environments is to provide support for the flexible and easy ability to inspect large amounts of the code when desired.

Finally, there were many instances of integration between testing and code inspection, such as this participant's fine-grained mixing of the two:

Female P0718081400 hovered over variables in the code view for simultaneously seeing both the code and output values.

Most participants in the earlier spreadsheet study also used testing and code inspection together. The preponderance of mixing these strategies suggests that programming environment designers should strive to support this mixture, allowing "drill down" into related testing information during code inspection, as in the example above, and conversely allowing drill down into related code information during testing. Getting directly to the code that produced certain values is well supported in spreadsheets and in some end-user languages and environments such as Kid-Sim/Cocoa/Stagecast [12] and Whyline [17], but is rarely present in scripting environments.

Specification Checking is somewhat related to code inspection, but involves comparisons: namely, comparing descriptions of what the script should do with the script's code. This strategy is not well supported in any scripting or end-user programming environment—code comments are the primary device to which users in these environments have access for the purpose of specification checking.

Both the spreadsheet study and this one provided (informal) specifications in the form of written descriptions of the intended functionality, and these were widely used by both the previous study's spreadsheet users and the current study's scripters. In addition, they relied on comments and output strings embedded in the code for this purpose, as in the examples below.

Male P0717080900 read the informal description handout related to the script.
Male P0717080900 read the comments in the code related to what that part of the code was supposed to do.
Male P0117081130 looked in the code for the places producing constant string outputs, with the view that those string outputs helped describe what nearby code what supposed to do.
Female P0718081400 read the comments one-by-one, as she was reaching the parts that they referred to in control flow order.

Thus, specification checking is an under-supported strategy for both spreadsheet users and scripters.

Dataflow means following data dependencies through the program. Following dataflow is a natural fit to the dataflow-oriented execution model of spreadsheets, and some spreadsheet tools provide explicit support for it such as dataflow arrows and slicing-based fault localization tools [6]. Even in imperative programs, dataflow mixed with control flow (i.e., "slicing") is commonly used [34], and ever since Weiser's classic study identified slicing as an important strategy for debugging [34], numerous tools have been based on slicing. Our scripters followed dataflow a little, but it was not particularly common, perhaps because the scripting environment did not provide much explicit support for it:

> Female P0717081630 said, "Wish I could go to where this variable is declared."
> Female P0717081630 tried to "find all references" to a variable, in any file.
> Male P0718081030 wanted to know how a particular variable got to be a certain value, and therefore followed the flow of data to see what other variables influenced this variable, and how it got to be the value it was.

Spatial is simply following the code in a particular spatial order. For example, scripts can be read from top to bottom. (This is different from following execution order; execution order deviates from top to bottom at procedure calls, loops, etc.) Most participants demonstrated a little of this strategy, but nobody relied on it for very long. It was fairly uncommon in the spreadsheet study as well, in which fewer than 10% of the participants mentioned that strategy.

Generalized Matches. The two strategies that matched generalizations of strategies observed in the spreadsheet study were Feedback Following and To-Do Listing.

Feedback Following is using system-generated feedback to guide debugging efforts. This is a generalization of the strategy "Color Following" in the spreadsheet study. To draw users' attention to them, the spreadsheet system colored cells' interiors to show their likelihood of containing errors (based on the judgments made by users about the correctness of each cell's value). The users who followed this type of feedback directly were considered to be color following. The scripting environment used certain messages (not colors alone) to draw users' attention to code with possible bugs, a generalization upon following colors toward possible bugs.

Our script participants paid particular attention to the feedback messages, including reading them, navigating backward and forward in them, looking at more or fewer of them, and drilling down to get more information about them. For example:

> Male P0117081130 looked at the last error message.
> Male P0718080800 changed the display settings so as to show only the first error message.
> Male P0717080900 cleared the command line screen so he could easily scroll up and stop at the first error message.
> Female P0718081400 resized the output window to see more of the messages at once.
> Female P0718081400 opened up Windows Explorer to better understand what path the error message is talking about.

To-Do Listing is indicating explicitly the suspiciousness of code (or lack of suspiciousness) as a way to keep track of which code needs further follow-up. Some spreadsheet users did this by checking cells off or X-ing them out. (These features were designed for another purpose, but some participants repurposed them to keep track of things still to check.) Like the spreadsheet users, our scripters found mechanisms to accomplish to-do listing, such as:

Male P0117081130 put a breakpoint on a line to mark that line as incorrect, and to stop on it whenever he ran the code.
Female P0721081130 closed files that she thought to be error-free, leaving possibly buggy ones open.
Male P0718081030 used pen and paper to keep track of stumbling points.
The same male, P0718081030, also mentioned sometimes using bookmarks to keep track of stumbling points.

Keeping track of things to do and things done is a functionality so dear to computer users' hearts, they have been reported to repurpose all sorts of mechanisms to accomplish it, such as appropriating email inboxes [7] and code commenting [31] for this purpose. Yet, other than bug trackers (which do not work at the granularity of snippets of code), few programming environments support to-do listing. A clear opportunity for designers of end-user programming environments and scripting environments is providing an easy, lightweight way to support to-do listing.

New Strategies. Finally, there were three strategies that had not been present in the spreadsheet study: control flow, getting help, and proceeding as in prior experiences.

Control Flow means following the flow of control (sequence in which instructions are executed). Pennington found that expert programmers initially represent a program in terms of its control flow [24]. Since spreadsheets do not provide a view of execution flow, it is not surprising that following control flow did not arise in the spreadsheet study. The scripting environment, however, provided multiple affordances for viewing control flow, and participants used them. For example:

Male P0717080900 used the call stack to see what subroutines were called and in what order.
Female P0718081400 placed a breakpoint on the first line to run the script in control flow from there in order to understand it.
Male P0117081130 stepped over and into to examine and execute the code in the order it was run.

Providing support for following control flow is relatively widespread in programming environments for professional programmers, but less so for end-user programming environments. A notable exception is the approach for allowing control flow following in the rule-based language KidSim/Cocoa/Stagecast [12], which features the ability step through the program to see which rules fire in which order.

Help means getting help from other people or resources, a common practice in real-world software development. For example, Ko et al. reported that developers often sought information in hard-to-search sources, such as coworkers' heads, scanned-in diagrams, and hand-written notes [18]. In our study, examples of following help included searching for help on a bug using Google Search, consulting the internal help documentation in order to set a breakpoint, or asking the researchers what a particular function does. This strategy was not available in the spreadsheet study but our script participants used it extensively.

Female P0717081630 sought help from the observers.
Male P0718081030 sought online help.
Male P0117081130 used the interface's help menu item.
Female P0718081400 used the command line's "-?" and "/?" commands.
Male P0718081030 used the function key to bring up the internal help. Later, he also brought help up on a particular word by first highlighting it and then hitting the function key.

Finally, one participant attempted to integrate external help with code inspection:

Male P0718081030 restored down the help window, to be able to look at the code and still have the help in an open window next the code.

Proceeding as in Prior Experience was recognizing a situation (correctly or not) as one experienced before, and using that prior experience as a blueprint of next steps to take. Sometimes the recognition was about a feature in the environment that had helped them in the past and sometimes it was about a particular type of bug. Once recognition struck, participants often proceeded in a trial-and-error manner, without first evaluating whether it was the right path. For example:

Male P0717080900: "Ah – I've seen this before. This is what must be wrong."
Female P0718081400: "It obviously needs to go up one directory."
Male P0721080900 said: "Just for kicks and giggles, let's try this."
Male P0718081030 felt something strange was going on and, from an earlier experience, decided that it was PowerShell's fault. He therefore closed the environment and opened it up again.

We suspect that proceeding as in prior experience is quite widespread, but it has not been reported in the literature on debugging. Given humans' reliance on recognition in everyday life, this strategy could be having a powerful influence on how people debug. It is an open question whether and how designers of debugging tools might leverage the fortunate aspects of this and take steps to help guard against the unfortunate aspects.

4.2 Sequential Usage of Strategies: Three Participants

To investigate how the participants used these strategies when succeeding, we analyzed three participants in detail. The first two were the most successful male (who fixed four bugs in one task) and the most successful female (who fixed one bug in one task). We then analyzed a male with the same scripting experience as the female (who also fixed one bug in one task). Each of these participants thus provided at least one successful event to analyze, in addition to several failed attempts. Fig. 2 shows the sequence of strategies used in one of the two tasks by these participants.

As an aside, the overall low success rate on the number of bugs fixed was expected, because we deliberately designed the tasks to be difficult, so that strategizing would occur even with expert scripters. For example, one of our participants (the most successful male) was extremely experienced, having written more than 100 PowerShell scripts in the past year. He fixed all seven bugs in the two tasks. (Reminder: the figure shows only one of those two tasks.)

The most successful female described herself as a software developer. She was about 30 years old, and had nine years of scripting experience (in JavaScript, Power-Shell, Perl, and Bash/UNIX Shell Scripting). Within the past year, she had written about five PowerShell scripts and was a frequent PowerShell user, normally using it about two to three times per week.

As Fig. 2 shows, after reading the task description, this female began by running the script: "First thing I'm going to do is to try to run it to see what the errors are." Using the error message which stated there was an error at a line which contained "Type = 'NewLine'" because "Type" is a read-only property, she navigated directly to that line of the script. She right away noticed that the equal sign was doing an assignment instead of a comparison, thereby finding the first bug (the dashed bar at the beginning of her session in Fig. 2). But, although she knew what the error was, she fixed it incorrectly based on her prior experience with other languages (the solid line with a dot followed by 45 seconds of testing). Fortunately, testing her change made her realize that her fix was incorrect: "Ok, perhaps it was wrong..." Despite her experience with scripting and using PowerShell, she said she felt silly about not remembering what the correct syntax was, but that it is due to her not writing scripts from scratch in PowerShell often, but rather reusing and extending existing scripts.

Knowing what she wanted the program to do but not the syntax to accomplish it, she started to use code inspection to find a suitable fix by looking for examples in related code: "That's why I usually start looking at other files, to see if there's an 'equal' type thing." She went on to skim two other PowerShell files, rejecting two Boolean operators she did not believe would fix her problem. However, the second one, even though it was not exactly what she needed, was close enough to enable her to fix the bug by patterning her change after that code: "Aha! '–like' isn't it because that would be like a 'starts with' type thing. So, maybe I need to do '-eq'?" This use of code inspection is what enabled her to actually fix the bug, and is a good example of *how* increased use of this strategy might have led to greater female success in [32].

The female's use of code inspection to actually *fix* the bug above, rather than just to *find* it, is interesting. It suggests a possible new debugging functionality, code mini-pattern recognition and retrieval, to support searching and browsing for related code patterns to use as templates. The female's beneficial use of code inspection in this study is consistent with the results from [32] that code inspection was statistically tied to female spreadsheet users' success. These combined results suggest the following hypotheses to more fully investigate the importance of code inspection to female debuggers:

Hypothesis 1F: Code inspection is tied to females' success in *finding* bugs.

Hypothesis 2F: After a bug has been found, code inspection is tied to females' success in correctly *fixing* the bug.

Hypothesis 3F: Environments that offer explicit support for code inspection strategies in fixing bugs will promote greater debugging success by females than environments that do not explicitly support code inspection strategies.

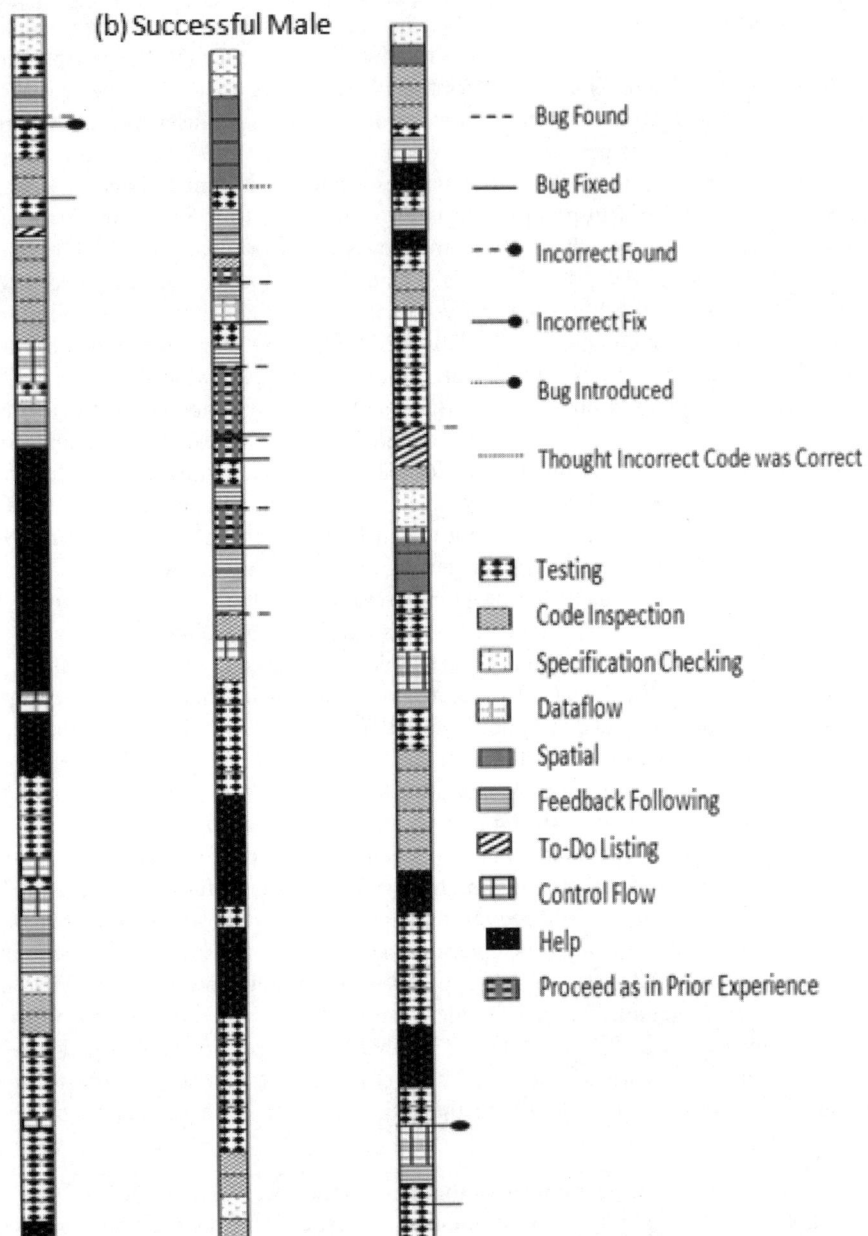

Fig. 2. The strategies used by three participants during one of the two tasks, as well as when bugs were found and fixed. Each patterned square is a 30-second use of the strategy shown in the legend, and the lines display a bug found / fixed also shown in the legend. The start of the session is at the top and the end at the bottom.

In contrast to the female, for males, code inspection did not appear to be tied to success, either in the earlier spreadsheet study or in this one. As the figure shows, the successful male used very little of it, and used none in the periods after finding, when working on actually fixing the bugs. Although the low-experience male did use code inspection, it did not seem to help him very much. Thus, we predict that a set of hypotheses (which we will refer to as 1M, 2M, and 3M) about males like the female-oriented Hypotheses 1F, 2F, and 3F will produce different results in follow-up research, because instead of emphasizing code inspection, the periods near the low-experience male's successful finding of a bug and near his successful fixing of the bug contained a marked emphasis on testing. (We will return to this point shortly.)

The successful male, whose sequence of strategies is also shown in Fig. 2, was a very experienced scripter. He described himself as a scripter (not as an IT professional or developer) and had 20 years of experience writing scripts in languages such as Korn Shell, BIN, PowerShell, Perl, and Tcl. He had used PowerShell since its inception and had written over 100 PowerShell scripts within the past year alone.

After reading the task instructions, the successful male did not begin as the female did by running the script, but instead first began by reading the main script code from top to bottom for a couple of minutes, "The first thing I'll do is to read the script to find out what I believe it does." Once he got to the bottom of the script, he stated that "this code didn't seem to have anything wrong with it," denoted by the dotted line in Fig. 2. He was incorrect about this.

After the dotted line, this successful male switched to running the script to see its outputs (testing) and to consider the resulting error messages (feedback following). The first error message this male pursued was the second error message that the successful female had also tried addressing: "cannot find path because it does not exist." Without even navigating to the function to which that the error referred, the successful male was able to draw from his prior experience, immediately hypothesizing (correctly) that the error was caused by a function call in the main script that used the "name" property as a parameter, rather than the "full name" property of a file. He stated, "I know that the file type has a 'full name' property, so that's what we need to do." After changing the code, to check his change before really declaring it a fix, he opened the function that the error message referred to, checking to see how the file name that was being passed as a parameter was being used (dataflow). At this point, he declared the first bug fixed, and reran the script to see what problem to tackle next. He used a similar sequence of testing, feedback following, and prior experience for the next three bugs he found and fixed.

But when the successful male found the fifth bug (see the fifth dashed line in Fig. 2), he did not have prior experiences relevant to fixing it. As the right half of the figure shows, he spent the rest of the session trying to fix it, mainly relying on a combination of fine-grained testing (checking variable output values) and help (documentation internal to the product on debugging PowerShell scripts), with bits of code inspection, control flow, and specification checking also sprinkled throughout.

Thus, the successful male provided interesting evidence regarding code inspection, testing, prior experience, and dataflow. We have already derived hypotheses about code inspection, and we defer hypotheses about testing until after discussing the second male. Regarding prior experience, both the successful male and the successful female drew on prior experience in conjunction with feedback following, but the female's prior experience had negative impacts when she tried to fix a bug by re-membering the syntax from a different language. The interplay between feedback following and proceeding as in prior experience is thought-provoking, but there is not as yet enough evidence about this interaction and gender differences for us to propose hypotheses for follow-up.

Dataflow, however, was also a successful strategy for the males in [32], and this successful male's experience with it suggests exactly *where* it might be contributing to males' success:

> Hypothesis 4M: Dataflow is tied to males' success in *finding* bugs.
> Hypothesis 5M: After the bug has been fixed, dataflow is tied to males' success at *checking their fix.*
> Hypothesis 6M: Environments that offer explicit support for dataflow will promote greater debugging success by males than environments that do not explicitly support dataflow.

We do not expect the corresponding female Hypotheses 4F, 5F, and 6F to show significant effects, since we have seen no evidence of it in either study.

The successful female was much less experienced than the successful male, so we also compared her strategies to those of a less experienced male to obtain insights into strategy differences due solely to experience. This male had nearly identical experi-ence to the female: 10 years of scripting experience (in CMD, VBScript, PowerShell, T-SQL, and SSIS). In the past year, he had written about six PowerShell scripts, and used PowerShell about three times per week.

Like the successful male, this less experienced male also started out with inspect-ing the code from top to bottom. The less experienced male examined most of the script very carefully, highlighting the lines he read as he went along. He used several strategies (including testing, feedback following, control flow, and help) to better understand a construct he had never run into before. After about four minutes of try-ing, he noted not completely understanding that part of the code and assumed that it was correct (which was true), stating that the part he had been studying seemed like a "red herring" and "a no-op". He therefore went on to examine the next line.

Directly following about three minutes of incremental testing (running only frag-ments of the code at a time to see what they output), the lower-experience male found a bug (dashed line in Fig. 2). At that point, he stated "I'm making a note of a bug that's here; that we're not making a path here... And we're going to fail, because the system is simply not going to find those files." After having made the note, he went on trying to use several strategies (mainly testing and code inspection) to understand the rest of the code.

In the earlier study, we saw some evidence pointing in the direction of to-do listing being a strategy used more by females [32], and two of the three females used it in this study too. This male employed a pen-and-paper version of to-do listing, but to-do listing was so scarcely used overall in this study (perhaps since it was not supported by the environment) that we could not derive hypotheses based on these data alone.

By inspecting the code in control flow order, the less experienced male realized that an incorrect property used for one of the variables was the cause of the faulty output. Returning to the first bug he had written down on paper, he succeeded at fix-ing the bug through the use of testing. Specifically, he copied that variable and its property into the command line and ran the command. He stated that the output was incorrect, since it was the name of the file instead of its full path. Using tab-completion in the command line, he deleted the property, and tabbed through the list of all properties. He then also used a command to output a list of all properties and skimmed through them, wondering, "Is there a FullPath property?" There, he found a "FullName" property. He tried it out by typing the variable name and property in the command line again. The output was exactly what he wanted, so he put that small code fragment into the script's code, thereby fixing the bug. This suggests a possibility that a programming environment that supports *systematic debugging-oriented testing* mechanisms, such as tracking incremental testing and testing of small fragments of code, may be helpful to testing-oriented debuggers.

The testing evidence from both males above, combined with that of the previous study, suggests the following hypotheses for follow-up investigation.

Hypothesis 7M: Testing is tied to males' success in *finding* bugs.

Hypothesis 8M: After a bug has been found, testing is tied to males' success at correctly *fixing* the bug.

Hypothesis 9M: After the bug has been fixed, testing is tied to males' success at *evaluating their fix.*

Hypothesis 10M: Environments offering explicit support for incremental testing and testing of small code fragments will promote greater debugging success by males than environments that do not explicitly support incremental testing strategies.

We are also proposing identical hypotheses for testing with females (7F, 8F, 9F, and 10F). Our prior study provided no ties between testing and success by females, so we do not predict significant effects for 8F-10F. However, the successful female in this study used testing in conjunction with feedback following to successfully find a bug; 7F might therefore also hold true for females.

As we have been bringing out in our hypotheses, the above evidence from all three participants suggests that the debugging stage at which a strategy is used (finding a bug, fixing a bug, or evaluating a fix) might have an influence on females' and males' success with the strategy, and we consider this to be an interesting new open research question. For example, although everyone successfully found at least one bug by incorporating testing, only the lower experience male *fixed* a bug using that strategy. One concrete instance of this open question is, therefore, whether there is a difference in *how* males and females use testing. For example, might males incorporate testing into both finding and fixing, whereas females use it for only in the finding stage? We express this open question as a general hypothesis:

Hypothesis 11MF: Males' and females' success with a strategy differs with different debugging stages (finding a bug, fixing a bug, or evaluating a fix).

---

5 Conclusion

This paper presents the results from a think-aloud study we conducted to see how well end-user programmers' spreadsheet debugging strategies generalize to a different population and a different paradigm: IT professionals debugging Windows Power-Shell scripts. Our results show that:

- All but one of the strategies found with the spreadsheet users also applied to IT professionals debugging scripts, along with three more that emerged. The seven strategies we observed in both studies were: *testing, code inspection, specification checking, dataflow, spatial, feedback following* (a generalization of the strategy previously termed *color following*), and *to-do listing*. In addition, we observed the following three strategies that had not been present in the spreadsheet study: *control flow, help,* and *proceeding as in prior experience*.
- The mechanisms scripters used revealed several opportunities for new features in scripting environments, such as support for *systematic* incremental testing, for easy inspection of large amounts of code and of code mini-patterns, for "drill down" into related testing information during code inspection and into related code information during testing, for informal specification checking, and for to-do listing.
- The evidence of the earlier statistical study on spreadsheets combined with the qualitative analysis of this study's participants produced several detailed hypotheses on gender differences in successful strategy usage.

Perhaps the most important contribution of this study is that it raised a significant new open question: whether males' and females' uses of debugging strategies differ not only in *which* strategies they use successfully, but also in *when* and *how* they use those strategies.

Acknowledgements. We thank the participants of our study and are grateful to Jennifer East, Curtis Posadas, and Siddhika Nevrekar for recruiting them. Finally, we thank the anonymous reviewers, whose feedback helped us significantly in improving the paper.

References

1. Bandura, A.: Social Foundations of Thought and Action. Prentice Hall, Englewood Cliffs (1986)
2. Basili, V., Selby, R.: Comparing the Effectiveness of Software Testing Strategies. IEEE Trans. Soft. 13(12), 1278–1296 (1987)
3. Beckwith, L., Burnett, M., Wiedenbeck, S., Cook, C., Sorte, S., Hastings, M.: Effectiveness of End-User Debugging Software Features: Are There Gender Issues? In: Proc. ACM CHI 2005, pp. 869–878 (2005)
4. Beckwith, L., Kissinger, C., Burnett, M., Wiedenbeck, S., Lawrance, J., Blackwell, A., Cook, C.: Tinkering and Gender in End-User Programmers Debugging. In: Proc. ACM CHI 2006, pp. 231–240 (2006)
5. Beckwith, L., Inman, D., Rector, K., Burnett, M.: On to the Real World: Gender and Self-Efficacy in Excel. In: Proc. IEEE VLHCC (2007)
6. Burnett, M., Cook, C., Rothermel, G.: End-User Software Engineering. Comm. ACM 47(9), 53–58 (2004)

7. Danis, C., Kellogg, W., Lau, T., Stylos, J., Dredze, M., Kushmerick, N.: Managers' Email: Beyond Tasks and To-Dos. In: ACM CHI Extended Abstracts, pp. 1324–1327 (2005)
8. Gallagher, A., De Lisi, R., Holst, P., McGillicuddy-De Lisi, A., Morely, M., Cahalan, C.: Gender Differences in Advanced Mathematical Problem Solving. J. Experimental Child Psychology 75(3), 165–190 (2000)
9. Grigoreanu, V., Beckwith, L., Fern, X., Yang, S., Komireddy, C., Narayanan, V., Cook, C., Burnett, M.: Gender Differences in End-User Debugging Revisited: What the Miners Found. In: IEEE Symposium on Visual Languages and Human-Centric Computing, pp. 19–26 (2006)
10. Grigoreanu, V., Cao, J., Kulesza, T., Bogart, C., Rector, R., Burnett, M., Wiedenbeck, S.: Can Feature Design Reduce the Gender Gap in End-User Software Development Environments? In: IEEE Symposium on Visual Languages and Human-Centric Computing, pp. 149–156 (2008)
11. Hartzel, K.: How Self-Efficacy and Gender Issues Affect Software Adoption and Use. Communications of the ACM 46(9), 167–171 (2003)
12. Heger, N., Cypher, A., Smith, D.: Cocoa at the Visual Programming Challenge 1997. Journal of Visual Languages and Computing 9(2), 151–169 (1998)
13. Ioannidou, A., Repenning, A., Webb, D.: Using Scalable Game Design to Promote 3D Fluency: Assessing the AgentCubes Incremental 3D End-User Development Framework. In: Ioannidou, A., Repenning, A., Webb, D. (eds.) IEEE Symposium on Visual Languages and Human-Centric Computing, pp. 47–54 (2008)
14. Kandogan, E., Haber, E., Barrett, R., Cypher, A., Maglio, P., Zhao, H.: A1: End-User Programming for Web-based System Administration. In: ACM UIST 2005, pp. 211–220 (2005)
15. Katz, I., Anderson, J.: Debugging: An Analysis of Bug-Location Strategies. In: Human-Computer Interaction, vol. 3, pp. 351–399 (1988)
16. Kelleher, C., Pausch, R., Kiesler, S.: Storytelling Alice Motivates Middle School Girls to Learn Computer Programming. In: Proc. ACM CHI 2007, pp. 1455–1464 (2007)
17. Ko, A.J., Myers, B.A.: Designing the Whyline: A Debugging Interface for Asking Questions about Program Failures. In: Proc. ACM CHI 2004, pp. 151–158 (2004)
18. Ko, A., DeLine, R., Venolia, G.: Information Needs in Collocated Software Development Teams. In: International Conference on Software Engineering, pp. 344–353 (2007)
19. Littman, D.C., Pinto, J., Letovsky, S., Soloway, E.: Mental Models and Software Maintenance. In: Soloway, E., Iyengar, S. (eds.) Proc. ESP. Ablex, Norwood, NJ, pp. 80–98 (1986)
20. Meyers-Levy, J.: Gender Differences in Information Processing: A Selectivity Interpretation. In: Cafferata, P., Tybout, A. (eds.) Cognitive and Affective Responses to Advertising, Lexington, Ma, Lexington Books (1989)
21. Nanja, N., Cook, C.: An Analysis of the On-Line Debugging Process. In: Olson, G.M., Sheppard, S., Soloway, E. (eds.) Proc. ESP, Ablex, Norwood (1987)
22. Nardi, B.: A Small Matter of Programming: Perspectives on End-User Computing. MIT Press, Cambridge (1993)
23. O'Donnell, E., Johnson, E.: The Effects of Auditor Gender and Task Complexity on Information Processing Efficiency. Int. J. Auditing 5, 91–105 (2001)
24. Pennington, N.: Stimulus Structures and Mental Representations in Expert Comprehension of Computer Programs. Cognitive Psychology 19(3), 295–341 (1987)
25. Prabhakararao, S., Cook, C., Ruthruff, J., Creswick, E., Main, M., Durham, M., Burnett, M.: Strategies and Behaviors of End-User Programmers with Interactive Fault Localization. In: IEEE Symposia on Human-Centric Computing Languages and Environments, pp. 15–22 (2003)

26. Rigby, P., German, D., Storey, M.: Open Source Software Peer Review Practices: A Case Study of the Apache Server. In: International Conference on Software Engineering, pp. 541–550 (2008)
27. Rode, J.A.: An Ethnographic Examination of the Relationship of Gender & End-User Programming, Ph.D. Thesis, University of California Irvine (2008)
28. Rode, J.A., Toye, E.F., Blackwell, A.F.: The Fuzzy Felt Ethnography - Understanding the Programming Patterns of Domestic Appliances. Personal and Ubiquitous Computing 8, 161–176 (2004)
29. Romero, P., du Boulay, B., Cox, R., Lutz, R., Bryant, S.: Debugging Strategies and Tactics in a Multi-Representation Software Environment. International Journal on Human-Computer Studies 61, 992–1009 (2007)
30. Rosson, M., Sinha, H., Bhattacharya, M., Zhao, D.: Design Planning in End-User Web Development. In: Proc. VLHCC. IEEE, Los Alamitos (2007)
31. Storey, M., Ryall, J., Bull, R.I., Myers, D., Singer, J.: TODO or to bug: Exploring How Task Annotations Play a Role in the Work Practices of Software Developers. In: International Conference on Software Engineering, pp. 251–260 (2008)
32. Subrahmaniyan, N., Beckwith, L., Grigoreanu, V., Narayanan, V., Bucht, K., Drummond, R., Fern, X., Wiedenbeck, S., Burnett, M.: Testing vs. Code Inspection vs. ...What Else? Male and Female End Users' Debugging Strategies. In: Proc. ACM CHI (2008)
33. Torkzadeh, G., Koufteros, X.: Factorial Validity of a Computer Self-Efficacy Scale and the Impact of Computer Training. Educational and Psychological Measurement 54(3), 813–821 (1994)
34. Weiser, M.: Programmers Use Slices When Debugging, Comm. ACM 25(7), 446–452 (1982)
35. Whitaker, A., Cox, R., Gribble, S.: Configuration Debugging as Search: Finding the Needle in the Haystack. In: 6th Symposium on Operating System Design and Implementation (2004)
36. Windows PowerShell Wikipedia entry (accessed on August 20, 2008), http://en.wikipedia.org/wiki/Powershell
37. Yuan, C., Lao, N., Wen, J., Li, J., Zhang, Z., Wang, Y., Ma, W.: Automated known problem diagnosis with event traces. In: Proc. ACM Sigops/Eurosys European Conference on Computer Systems (2006)
38. Zang, N., Rosson, M.B.: What's in a Mashup? And Why? Studying the Perceptions of Web-Active End Users. In: IEEE Symposium on Visual Languages and Human-Centric Computing, pp. 31–38 (2008)

Hypertextual Programming for Domain-Specific End-User Development

Sebastian Ortiz-Chamorro[1,4], Gustavo Rossi[1,2], and Daniel Schwabe[3]

[1] LIFIA, Universidad Nacional de La Plata, Argentina
[2] CONICET, Argentina
[3] Departamento de Informática, PUC-Rio, Brazil
[4] Departamento de Electrónica e Informática, Universidad Católica de Asunción, Paraguay
{sortiz,gustavo}@lifia.info.unlp.edu.ar, dschwabe@inf.puc-rio.br

Abstract. Domain-specific languages (DSLs) have successfully been used for end-user development. However, dealing with language syntax poses significant learning challenges. In this paper, we introduce hypertextual programming, a technique that represents language syntax as hypertext. With this technique, instead of dealing with textual languages, users can inspect and construct their programs mainly by using navigation. Beyond merely representing the syntax, hypertext can be used to provide various views of a single program code. Nevertheless, to reap the benefits of this technique, adequate hypertextual editors must be built. This paper argues that many of the lessons learned in the web engineering area can be used to deal with this problem. Millions of users navigate the World Wide Web. Hypertextual programming leverages this widely available end-user skill to facilitate the construction of computer programs.

Keywords: hypertextual programming, end-user development, interfaces for end-user development, domain-specific languages, web engineering.

1 Introduction

Domain-specific languages (DSLs, a.k.a. scripting languages) have successfully been used for end-user development [1,2,3]. These languages help domain experts construct, inspect and test computer programs that operate within defined realms. Part of their success may be attributed to the fact that they present a set of familiar concepts to the end-user. However, DSLs force the user to "learn the arcane syntax and vocabulary conventions of the language" [2]. This initial step constitutes a difficult and undesirable challenge for the end-user.

Even in the case of DSLs, language syntax may be very complex. Consider the case of writing business rules in Jess [4], a popular rule-engine. The following is an example of a valid sequence of Jess commands:

```
(defglobal ?*threshold* = 20)

(bind ?age = 15)

(if (> ?age ?*threshold*) then
```

V. Pipek et al. (Eds.): IS-EUD 2009, LNCS 5435, pp. 225–241, 2009.
© Springer-Verlag Berlin Heidelberg 2009

```
        (printout t "adult" crlf)

    else

        (printout t "minor" crlf))
```

The syntax of these commands is correct, but one missing or extra parenthesis would render the whole program syntactically invalid. We also have to take into account that dealing with language syntax in order to write a program goes way beyond avoiding syntactic errors. Executing the above set of commands in Jess 7.0 would actually generate a runtime error: *Not a number: "="*

This is because of a subtlety: even though syntactically correct, the second line actually assigns the string *"="*, not the number 15, to the *age* variable. If the user's intention was to assign the numeric value 15 to this variable, the following would be the correct Jess instruction:

```
(bind ?age 15)
```

Other language conventions may involve constantly memorizing and recalling (or at least searching through) an ever changing set of available elements to use. For example, in Jess, the set of available functions at a given program point contains all the predefined language functions and also any functions that the user has already defined. This is representative of many other languages where users are required to declare, define or import variable declarations, functions and other language elements before using them.

A different dimension of dealing with the language syntax in programming involves understanding the program code. Programming is an iterative process where, typically, the programmer has to read and understand existing code, identify the part or parts of the program that will be modified in a particular iteration and then perform the changes. Going back to the Jess example, a beginner will need significant effort to understand the complex language syntax. This adds a heavy burden to the authoring process.

Visual programming techniques have been developed to mitigate this problem by giving users graphic representations that may be more easily recognizable in some cases. These techniques have been used for end-user development [3]. However, visual programming has problems of its own. Among other things, some authors argue that visual programming may have scalability problems [5].

Graphic or not, the length and complexity of the end-user's programs, together with the limitations stated above and the need to focus on the specific parts that are undergoing modification call for a representation of the program code as a set of manageable pieces that the user can browse for inspection.

If a program is divided into units to be presented to the user, this user will need an intuitive and consistent way to select the specific parts to be viewed and modified.

This paper presents a technique based on the use of hypertext development environments that embody the syntax and conventions of the underlying language and use navigation as the main tool to inspect and modify programs. Hypertext systems [6] provide interactive environments where users can navigate through defined pieces of information (nodes). Beyond code browsing, in this paper we argue that by adequately using widely available tools like the World Wide Web, users can be provided with explicit controls that present them with a carefully chosen set of modification options for each specific node given the underlying language syntax. This has the potential to greatly reduce the programming learning effort.

This technique grew out of more than a decade of experience in the construction of web-applications that had various end-user development features. These ranged from small business process management rule definitions to the complete development environment presented in this paper as a concrete example of hypertextual programming: Benefit Catalog and Benefit Configurator. This dyad of applications constitutes a complete end-user development, versioning, testing, deployment and run-time environment for dynamic health-care insurance policy programming.

Expressing language syntax through navigation poses a significant engineering challenge. Hypertextual programming draws heavily on ideas from web engineering [7]. Several web design methodologies address the problem of expressing an underlying structure (usually a domain model) through a web-application [8,9,10,11,12]. In this case, the underlying structure is the syntax of a domain-specific language. The description of hypertextual programming that we present in this paper is a first attempt towards applying the lessons learned in web engineering to the problem of constructing hypertextual programming environments for a given DSL.

The structuring of this paper loosely follows the chronological development of hypertextual programming. In our experience, it is easier to understand this technique by starting with a concrete example and then exploring the general ideas and definitions behind it. Section 2 contains a description of Benefit Catalog and Benefit Configurator and includes some general requirements, architecture and hypertextual programming characteristics. In section 3, we present a more general description of hypertextual programming and some web engineering ideas that may help in the construction of hypertextual developing environments. Section 4 discusses related work. Finally, the conclusions of this paper and future research are presented in section 5.

2   Benefit Catalog and Benefit Configurator

Health-care insurance is a fertile ground for domain-specific end-user development. The process of administering health care insurance policies involves complex decision-making based on knowledge gained throughout decades of industry experience. Domain experts in this area may take years to learn the intricacies of just the sub-areas of the business that they work on. Merely the first step of the process from the client's point of view, which is helping to choose, customize and issue a health care policy, involves maintaining a sizable catalog of products that can be tailored to a specific client's needs. The health insurance products rendered by this process must comply with a considerable number of company guidelines and policies, and also any applicable laws.

Benefit Catalog and Benefit Configurator allow domain experts (*benefit engineers*) to: i)collaboratively develop a dynamic catalog of health-care insurance products (each dynamic product definition is called a *product template*); ii)maintain a library of parts to be used by different product templates; iii)test the product templates; iv)promote the approved versions of product templates for use in a production environment; v)run the product templates developed as an interactive sequence of questions to be asked to specialized company sales representatives; vi)based on the answers, generate and store health-care insurance policy specifications (called *answer sets*) as the output of these interactive questionnaires; and vii)provide support for the full product development life cycle, including the management of different versions of product templates and reusing previous answer sets for health care policy renewal.

An important requirement of this application is that the whole process described above has to be done without the intervention of professional programmers or company IT staff. This project required benefit engineers, that is, domain experts that do not have any professional programming background, to develop, test and manage product templates by themselves using a web environment. This requirement clearly prompted us to focus on the construction of tools that facilitate end-user development.

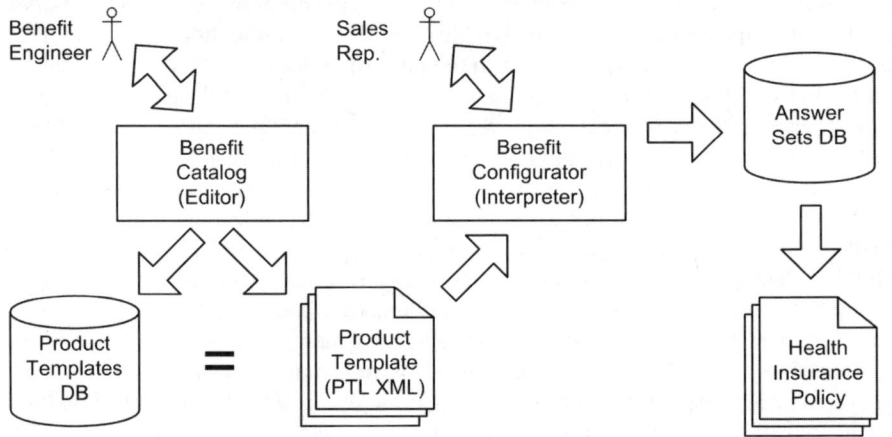

Fig. 1. Benefit Catalog and Benefit Configurator architectural diagram. Product templates are stored in the product template database, then, they are rendered as "executble" PTL XML.

An architectural diagram of the applications is shown in Fig. 1. Benefit Catalog is a fully web-based product template development environment. This tool saves product templates both in the product template database and also as programs written in the PTL[1] XML language. This allows users to query the product template database and obtain information about the various product templates that have been developed.

Additionally, benefit engineers can test and manage product templates' versions and the product part libraries that are used to build them.

Benefit Configurator is a PTL interpreter that runs these programs and generates an interactive series of questions to be answered by specialized sales representatives; then, based on the answers provided, it produces a health care insurance policy for the client (an answer set) and saves it to the answer set database.

The answer sets database is then transformed and imported into various downstream systems, including legal (text) contract generators and various claims systems among others.

---

[1] PTL stands for Product Template Language.

2.1 Product Template Language

We created an internal domain-specific language for product template specification. The Product Template Language (simply called *PTL*) is an XML [13] language that was built as an extension of the Cytera.Rules language [14]. Cytera.Rules is a Cytera Systems Inc. proprietary XML business rules language that allows the creation and evaluation of basic string, mathematical and boolean-based rules. PTL allows the representation and processing of rules involving objects and operations that are specific to the health-care insurance area.

In order to run PTL, almost all of the Cytera.Rules language interpreter had to be rewritten. To avoid this inconvenience in future projects, we developed a business rules language called AtOOmix with the aim of allowing the creation and implementation of XML domain-specific languages as extensions of existing AtOOmix languages without the need to fully rebuild the original languages and interpreters [15].

2.2 Benefit Catalog Hypertextual Programming Environment

It is important to point out that the benefit engineers never had direct contact with PTL. A fully web-based PTL editor was developed as the core of the Benefit Catalog application. This editor has several features aimed at facilitating the benefit engineers' tasks. Benefit Catalog represents the PTL code of an existing product template as a hierarchical collection of web pages that the user can navigate through.

Benefit Engineers never had to learn PTL, they only had to use the web-application that serves as user-interface. This is similar to the case of users that employ a web-application to populate a database: these users never have to deal directly with the database tables; they merely have to interact with the web-application.

Benefit engineers can also create and modify PTL code with Benefit Catalog. Fig. 2 shows how a new question is created. First, the user activates the *Attach Plan Choice Question* anchor in the *Grouping* node. This takes the user to the *Question* node. In this case, since it is a new question, users must fill-in the appropriate fields and then click on the *Attach* button. A benefit engineer can also create a new question by copying and then modifying an existing one. The *Copy* link is also shown in Fig. 2.

Right after a question has been created, and also throughout subsequent development sessions, benefit engineers can use navigation to go back to the question to inspect or modify it, e.g. change the grouping it belongs to, add a rule to turn-on the question or change the set of possible answers.

As a comparative example, the following code is a simplified PTL representation of a plan choice question:

```
<grouping name="Deductible">
  <pcq question_part="fam_ded">
    <when_turned_on_rule>
      <operation op="=">
          <var type="String">ded_yn</var>
          <const type="String">Yes</var>
```

```
    </operation>
  </when_turned_on_rule>
  <quality_type>core</quality_type>
  <funding_type>SI</funding_type>
  <seq>1</seq>
  <eff_dt>05/11/2005</eff_dt>
  <trm_dt>05/11/2007</trm_dt>
  <save>Y</save>
  <txt>Do you want a family deductible?</txt>
  <answer type="String" qi="Core" cc= "Y"
         mndt="Federal">Yes</answer>
  <answer type="String" qi="Core" cc= "Y"
         mndt="Federal">No</answer>
</pcq>
. . .
```

Writing these rules manually requires an important effort. The syntax is complex and many language conventions have to be taken into account. For example, all questions have to reference previously defined question parts and answers. This is also true of quality types, funding types, quality indicators, cost containment and mandate indicators. In all these cases, with Benefit Catalog, values are assigned by simply choosing them from select lists. The application interface enforces the language conventions instead of leaving that burden to the user.

Reading questions directly from PTL would also a problem for the end-user, especially as the number of questions becomes large (a template with more than 200 rule-activated questions is not unusual). The background web page shown in Fig. 2 is an example of high-level code visualization. Questions belonging to a specific group are displayed on a single page. At this level, only the most critical question information is displayed to provide the user with a comprehensive view of the set of questions that form the group.

Using this web interface, benefit engineers can add other constructs used in product templates like cost sharing components and define rule-driven properties for them. Users can also define benefit options, benefit service levels for the benefit options and rules to populate them with the dynamic cost sharing components previously defined. For sake of space and simplicity, we do not provide the details of all these programming primitives in this paper. The number of these additional primitives is at least five times higher than the ones related to plan choice questions and involve more health-care insurance-specific concepts that are not as easy to explain as questions and answers. The main features of hypertextual programming on this system are adequately illustrated with plan choice questions.

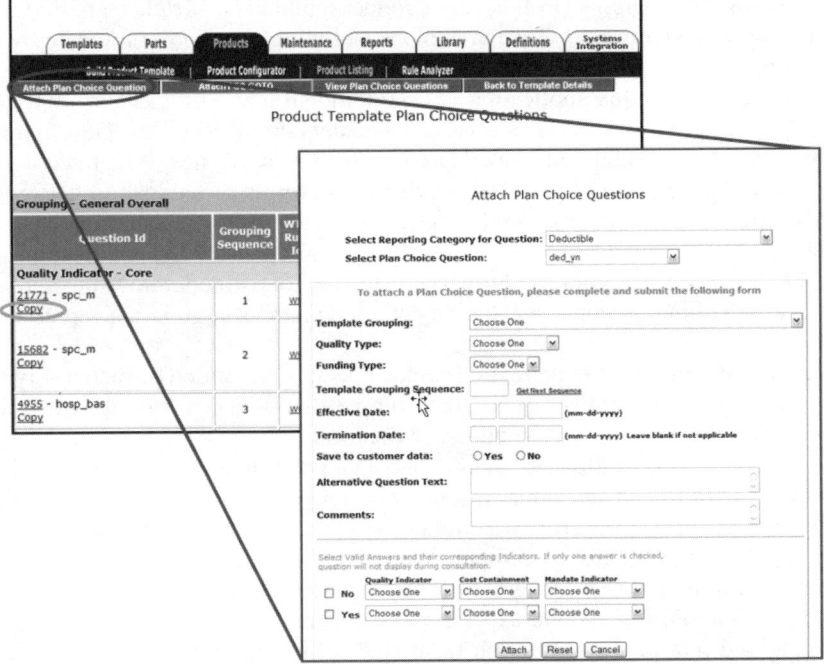

Fig. 2. Creating a new question in Benefit Catalog

To complete the program lifecycle, benefit engineers can run their product templates in a test environment, manage different versions of the same product template and activate it for it use in a production environment where it is used to interactively configure health-care plans. It is important to point out that all of this process is done by the benefit engineers themselves through Benefit Catalog and without the intervention of IT staff or professional developers.

3 Hypertextual Programming

Benefit Catalog and other applications that provide similar features cannot be adequately characterized neither as visual programming tools nor as text or structure based editors either. Rather, Benefit Catalog can be seen as an example of hypertextual programming.

We define *hypertextual programming* as a form of programming that uses navigation as the primary tool to inspect and edit the application code, and is supported by a computer system that: i) represents the entire program source code as hypertext; and ii) allows all the possible finite language instances to be generated as navigation paths through it.

In contrast to hypertextual programming, visual programming provides the user with a set of mainly graphic (as opposed to purely textual) elements that users can manipulate in order to develop a program. Benefit Catalog does not provide a graphic representation of programs (in this case product templates); it rather provides an interactive system where the users can explore and modify the program code by using navigation.

At the same time, this application is no traditional text editor either. Text editors usually present programs as collections of characters divided in files. Development is achieved mainly by adding and deleting characters in those files. Integrated development environments like Eclipse [16] provide some forms of navigation between different portions of the program code and features like auto-complete; however, we consider that they do not provide all the necessary features for hypertextual programming. First, navigation is not the primary means for source-code browsing and –most importantly– editing. Second, the source code structure at large is not represented as hypertext.

One basic definition of hypertext describes it as text structured in such a way that it has several possible reading paths. An example that satisfies this definition is the famous novel "Rayuela" by Argentinian writer Julio Cortazar. However, several authors insist on having automated navigation support for an artifact to be considered a hypertext system [6]. In the same fashion, we view hypertextual programming as an activity that is inseparable from a computer system that provides automated support for its key aspects. We call this computer system a *hypertextual editor*.

This definition requires program inspection and editing to be done primarily through navigation, but in our experience, the combination of this and other programming and interface construction techniques offer bigger potential. As an example, we found that mathematical and logical formulas may not always be well suited for hypertext representation. Breaking up such formulas in various nodes would lead to unnecessarily long navigation paths that contain very little information in each one of them. Consider the following formula:

```
1 + (2 * (Math.cos(a + b)))
```

If we represent it as eight nodes (1, +, 2, *, Math.cos, a, +, b) and provide the corresponding navigational links between them, very little information would be displayed in each node and the user would have to traverse a long navigation path just to read it.

This example is representative of other cases where better results might be obtained simply by using text to represent sub-parts of a language. In these cases, the text subparts can be used as node components.

In other cases, graphic elements may be more expressive to represent sub-parts of a language. Again, these graphic elements may also be used as node components.

When creating or altering language elements (e.g. adding a question or a group), users are creating or modifying node and link instances; they expect these changes to be reflected in the space that they are navigating (the specific instance of the navigational model at a given time). In other words, with hypertextual programming, the development of a computer program can be viewed as the construction of a navigation space, or more formally, as the iterative instantiation of a given navigational model.

Our definition requires the language syntax to be represented through hypertext. In the next section, we give a more detailed description of how a widely used language syntax definition can be represented in this way.

3.1 Expressing Language Syntax through Hypertext

Several web engineering methodologies separate conceptual design from navigational design in such a way that the nodes and links in navigational models are based on the objects, attributes and relations found in the conceptual model [8,9,10,11,12]. For example, Fig. 3 shows the conceptual and navigational models for part of a health care information website in OOHDM [8].

In OOHDM, navigational objects (nodes and links) are explicitly defined as views on conceptual objects. Nodes are composed of attributes that potentially belong to several classes in the conceptual model. In the conceptual model shown in Fig. 3, a *Medical Condition* class has as attributes the *Name* and *General Information* about it. The symptoms associated with a condition are a related but separate class. Treatment is also on a separate class.

In the navigational model, a node based on the *Medical Condition* conceptual class shows more than merely the *Name* and *General Information*. A list of *Symptoms*, *Tests* and available *Treatments* are also displayed in this node. Here, only *Test* names are displayed (other attributes are hidden at this level), and these names are anchors that trigger navigation to the *Test* node. A similar thing occurs with the Treatment node. However, not necessarily all conceptual classes become nodes. In our example, there is no node corresponding to the *Symptom* class.

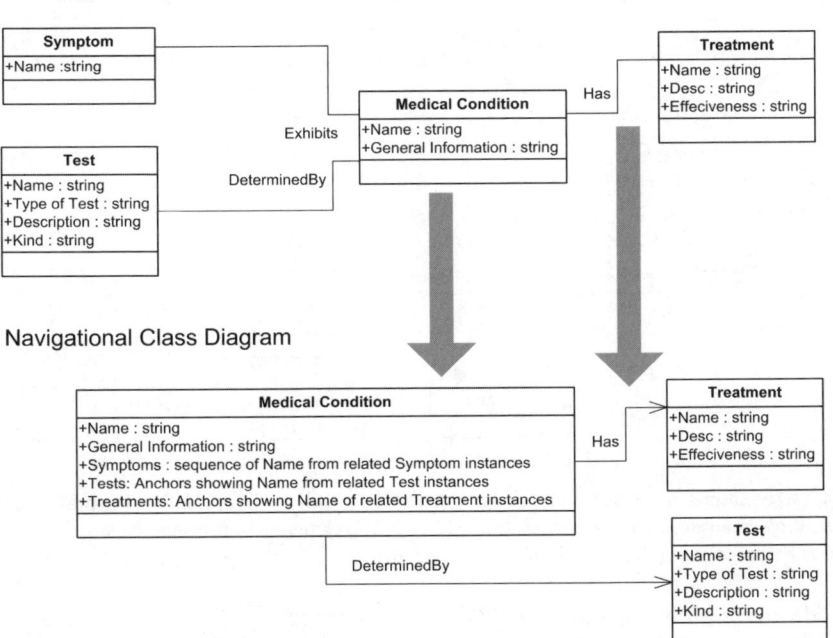

Fig. 3. Conceptual and Navigational models for a health care information website

Links are the navigational realization of relations appearing in the conceptual model. In our example, the *Has* relation between the *Medical Condition* and *Treatment* conceptual classes becomes the *Has* link between the *Medical Condition* and *Treatment* nodes.

This separation of concerns allows web developers to deal with the understanding of complex domains and the creation of a navigational scheme that expresses this underlying domain as separate issues. At the same time, these practices force the developers to elaborate a solid and coherent underlying foundation (the domain model) that will be rendered to the web site user in the form of a concrete navigation structure.

A hypertextual editor's navigational design should also express an underlying structure. The key difference is that the underlying structure being expressed through navigation is not an object model, but rather the syntax of a domain-specific programming language. In order to do this, there must be a correspondence between language syntax and navigational design. Fig. 4 is an example of the correspondence between PTL syntactic elements as defined in XML Schema [17,18] and part of Benefit Configurator's navigational classes.

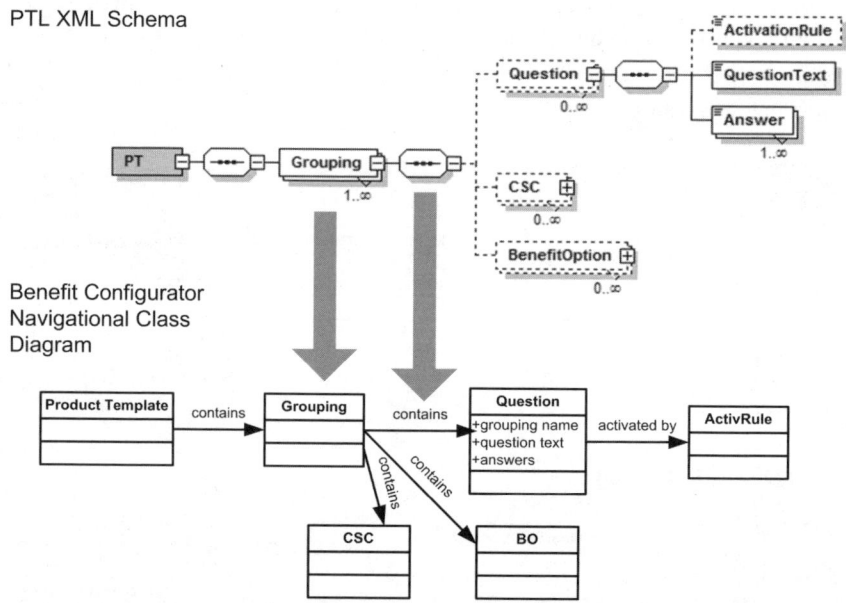

Fig. 4. An example of correspondence between PTL's XML Schema-defined syntax and Benefit Catalog's navigational class diagram. PTL's XML Schema is presented using XML Spy's visual schema notation. Tag attributes are not shown.

Nodes have a correspondence with XML language tags. The node's content may come from the data contained in the tag that it represents and also from related tags. For example, the *Question* node contains, among other things, the *grouping name*, from the parent *Grouping* tag; the *question text* attribute, from the *QuestionText* child tag; and the list of *answers* for the question, from the *Answer* tags below.

Not all tags become nodes. For example, there is no node that corresponds to the *Answer* tag. The contents of these tags are displayed in the *Question* node. Also note that not all the complete contents of a tag are shown in the node that represents it. For example, the *Grouping* node does not show all the details of the *Question* tags that it contains. The question of what tags should constitute nodes and what information to include in them are design choices that have to be decided by the software engineers in charge of the project. General Web design and usability guidelines should be taken into account [19].

Nodes are weaved by the links that connect them in such a way that links correspond to the syntactic rules that define the language structure. The links in Benefit Catalog correspond to the XML Schema definitions that specify the tag structure. For example, the *contains* link from *Grouping* to *Question* corresponds to the *xs:sequence* XML Schema definition that specifies the content of the *Grouping* tags to include a sequence of *Question* tags.

One last element that needs to be defined in order to complete the navigation design is the context diagram. The context diagram groups navigational objects into sets and defines access structures that the user can employ to reach and move through these objects. Fig. 5 shows part of the context diagram for Benefit Catalog.

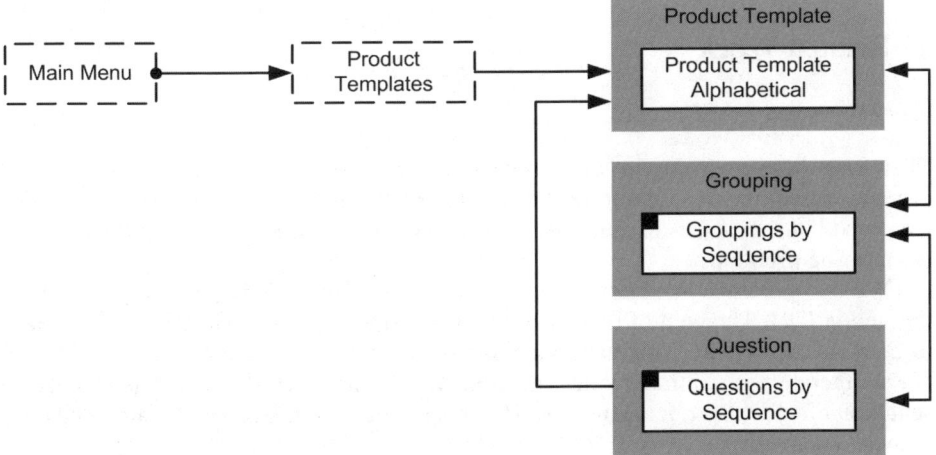

Fig. 5. Part of the Benefit Catalog context diagram

From the main menu, users have direct access to an index of product templates, listed alphabetically. When users access this index, they enter into the *Product Template Alphabetical* context, where product templates are listed by name. From that context, the user can go to the *Groupings* context where groupings are displayed by sequence order.

Although Benefit Catalog does not use this feature, in OOHDM, navigational classes may be decorated when appearing in a particular context. Decorating navigational classes may become important as more potent context diagrams are built.

3.2 Navigating beyond Syntax

Benefit Catalog has a very simple context diagram that stems directly from PTL's hierarchical XML Schema definition, e.g. groupings and questions are only displayed by sequence.

It is important to point out that many other contexts can be built around these navigational elements, providing the user with different views of the program code. For example, a possible improvement for Benefit Catalog could be displaying questions indexed by the variables that are used in its activation rules, or by its answers. This would help visualize what questions a certain variable helps turn on and off, or in what questions a certain answer is used in.

In fact, navigational design in web engineering in general is to a large extent, the definition of the various navigational contexts that the user will be traversing while performing the various tasks the applications purports to support. Therefore, the natural place to look for them is in the task descriptions (for example, in user interaction diagrams).

The potential features of hypertextual editors go beyond merely representing the underlying language syntax. The various tasks performed by end-users should be an important guide for organizing sets of navigational elements.

4   Related Work

4.1 Hypertext CASE Tools

There are different ways in which hypertext can support the software engineering process. Sometimes, these approaches are hard to compare because they may all use hypertext but they use it in completely different ways or to address different software engineering problems.

Østerbye developed a system to explore the idea of using hypertext for literate programming [22]. The goal of this work was to use the linking capabilities of hypertext to help weave together smalltalk code and documentation to facilitate inspection. In classic literate programming spirit, the aim was to construct a human-oriented representation of code and documentation. By using hypertext, the program can go beyond a linear document.

However, the advantages of this technique come at a great cost. The developer has to design all the navigation for the hypertext program representation. Even the authors point out that a drawback of this technique is "the well-known problem of hypertext, that one looses the feeling for where the information presently available at the screen belongs in the overall document".

First, it is important to point out that this system, and literate programming in general, assumes that there is an underlying programming language that will be used in the development process (Smalltalk in this case). Literate programming (with or without hypertext) uses this basic tool –the programming language(s)–, rearranging and combining source code with documentation in order to make them easy to absorb by a human reader; we can say that literate programming is at least one-level above purely textual programming languages. Hypertextual programming is proposed as an alternative to textual programming languages. Moreover, hypertextual programming could be used for literate programming.

There are some similarities between this literate programming system and the hypertextual environments described in this paper. In this literate programming system, some of the Smalltalk constructs are represented as nodes and some of the syntax rules as links. However, this relationship is not strict and the nodes contain important portions of textual code.

This Smalltalk literate programming system does not conform to our definition of hypertextual programming. Although the result of the programming process is hypertext (a program-document that developer can navigate through) and navigation may be used throughout the development process, programming is done primarily by editing text, not by using navigation. The most important criterion or our definition is not met. By using this or a similar system, the end-user would still have to learn a textual programming language. That's precisely what we are trying to avoid.

Using hypertext for end-user development also has to address the user disorientation problem. In order to do this, the web engineering techniques discussed in this paper were developed in part to deal with this problem. However, using these techniques for designing navigation is in turn a costly task usually done by professional web engineers. As opposed to this Smalltalk literate programming system, the present proposal does not leave navigational design to the developer (in our case, an end-user doing development). When designing a hypertextual editor, engineers have the responsibility of transforming language syntax into navigational design and create an application where the user is less likely to get lost.

Then, when end-users add or modify navigational elements, they may create links and nodes, but these actions do not alter the underlying navigational model (they simply instantiate it).

The Chimera open hypermedia system [23] uses hypertext to help manage and combine heterogeneous software engineering tools. Some of these engineering tools are programming language IDEs. Chimera also uses hypertext at a level above programming languages. The same can be said about Ishys [24].

Hypertextual programming editors may be one of the many systems combined by Chimera and other open hypermedia systems.

4.2 Visual and Textual Programming

Visual programming languages provide "some visual representations (in addition to or in place of words and numbers) to accomplish what would otherwise have to be written in a traditional one-dimensional programming languages" [25]. Despite its advantages, visual programming may have scalability problems [5], including scalability from a program-size standpoint and also scalability from a problem-domain standpoint.

From a program-size standpoint, the Benefit Catalog example that we presented was successfully used by end-users to develop programs (dynamic health care products) that are sizable and complex by various measures: i) the programs had several thousand rules; ii) they were collaboratively developed; iii) the development process of these programs typically takes several months; iv) these programs went through several maintenance cycles.

The various levels of abstraction and potentially different views of the source code given by a well-designed hypertextual editor, provide an adequate tool to deal with large programs.

From a problem-domain standpoint, this paper has provided guidelines to build hypertextual editors for any character-based, domain-specific language. Since domain-specific languages have been used in several areas, this suggests that hypertextual programming may also be scalable on this respect. In fact, we have used this technique in health-care insurance, small business rules definitions and programming email alerts for an academic system.

Visual programming techniques may be more appropriate to express some programming concepts. Even in these cases, hypertextual programming is well-suited for use in combination with visual and other programming and interface construction techniques.

In the case of textual programming, having to learn the syntax and conventions of character-based programming languages constitutes a considerable problem for end-users. The importance of this problem cannot be overstated. Providing a hypertextual editor that embodies the syntax and language conventions, transforming them in navigational paths to be traversed by the end-user significantly reduces this burden.

However, in the case of end-users who have already learned a textual domain-specific language, there may be no clear advantage in starting to use a hypertextual editor for the same language.

5   Conclusions and Future Research

In this paper we introduced the concept of hypertextual programming. This programming technique represents the program code as hypertext [6], allowing the end-user to inspect and modify this code mainly by using navigation.

Millions of users navigate the World Wide Web. Hypertextual programming leverages this widely available end-user skill to facilitate the construction of computer programs.

The user is provided with an environment that allows interactive source code exploration through navigation. A well-designed environment could facilitate reading and understanding by providing various views of the source code at potentially different levels of abstraction and a consistent way to move between them.

In a hypertextual editor, the user interacts with interface elements in order to modify the program code. On any given node, a carefully chosen set of relevant editing controls allows program modification without overwhelming the user. When combined with DSLs, many of these interface components may represent concepts that are familiar to the user. This technique is expected to significantly reduce the learning effort needed to begin developing domain-specific programs.

We presented and discussed a concrete example of a hypertext editor, Benefit Catalog, both as validation and to illustrate this technique. On this application, end-users have been effectively developing, testing, debugging, maintaining, deploying and running complex programs for dynamic health care policy configuration without the intervention of professional programmers or IT staff.

Beyond syntax representation, various navigational contexts may be created in order to provide the user with a rich set of navigation paths that take into account the various tasks that form the software development process.

However, reaping the benefits described above requires well-designed hypertextual editors. This entails significant engineering challenges. Among other things, editors have to express the syntax of the underlying language through a concrete navigational and interface design to begin with. In this paper, we argue that many of the techniques used in web engineering, most noticeably design methodologies [8,9,10,11,12], can be helpful on this respect, leveraging years of academic research and real-world experience.

Hypertext has been used in programming before. We reviewed three representative examples [22,23,24]. In general, all of these tools and techniques assume that there are one or more underlying programming languages and use hypertext to rearrange and/or link the potentially different program sources with other documents and products of the software engineering process. In general, they use hypertext on an above-language level. As an exception, in the Smalltalk literate programming system that we reviewed [22], some of the Smalltalk syntax is expressed in the form of links. However, nodes still contain significant portions of textual code and the rendering of the program in the form of nodes and links is guided by the literate-programming goal of human readability. In this system, although navigation may play a role in the development process, it is not the primary means to edit the program code. Text editing is still a central part of the development process. Therefore, this system does not conform to our definition of hypertextual programming. More importantly, the user has to know Smalltalk in order to use this system. The need to learn a textual language is precisely what hypertextual programming tries to avoid.

We made a comparison with these tools mainly to clarify that their use of hypertext is different and addresses other problems related to software development. The side-by-side comparison should not be with these techniques, but mainly against visual and textual programming.

Hypertextual programming is different from visual programming. The first does not rely mainly on the expressive power of graphics to facilitate the development process; it rather relies on the organization of the source code as a set of nodes and an intuitive mechanism to move around these nodes: navigation.

It has been argued that visual programming may have scalability problems [5]. Hypertextual programming can help to mitigate the problem of dealing with a great number of visual primitives at one time by providing different views of the program code and a systematic mechanism to tie them up: navigational links. At the same time, hypertextual editors can benefit from the use of visual techniques as part of their interface.

We provided general guidelines to build hypertextual editors for textual, domain-specific languages. This suggests that hypertextual programming may also be useful in different areas (domain-scalability). In fact, we have used this technique in health-care insurance, small business rules definitions and programming email alerts for an academic system.

With textual programming, the user has to learn the syntax and conventions of character-based programming languages. This constitutes a significant problem that hypertextual programming may help to solve. Providing a hypertextual editor that embodies the syntax and language conventions, transforming them in navigational paths to be traversed by the end-user may significantly reduce this burden.

We discussed some basic correspondence principles that should exist between XML Schema [17] syntax elements and a navigational model that may serve as guides in the design process. Still, more formal and detailed methodologies for designing hypertextual editors could be developed in the future.

Moreover, a careful and detailed review of the use of navigational contexts for building hypertextual editors may be beneficial.

Several design patterns for hypertext in general have been developed [20] since they were first introduced in [21]. Design patterns that are specific to hypertextual editors may be needed. In our experience, building nodes that are overly small or providing an excessive number of editing controls on a single node are not desirable. However, some of these problems may be related to more fundamental limitations of this technique. The answer may lie in the fact that some languages may be more suitable than others for use with hypertextual programming.

Our definition requires the hypertext editor to be able to generate all possible finite instances of the language and it requires navigation to be the main inspection and editing mechanism. Although a more formal demonstration should be performed, one seemingly direct consequence is that all (or at least the main) editing tasks for the given language should be achievable through navigation.

This paper discusses mainly languages defined in XML Schema. The specifics of other grammars deserve further investigation.

Since a hypertextual development environment has a correspondence with the syntactic elements of the underlying code, it may be viewed simply as a mapping between the language syntax and the possible ways of representing these elements as a web-application (the formatting and layout could be specified separately with CSSs). We are currently designing a web-based hypertextual editor generation application for XML Schema-defined languages.

The development environments discussed on this paper are mainly web-applications. Other forms of hypertext should also be considered.

References

1. Martin, J.: An Information Systems Manifesto. Prentice-Hall, Englewood Cliffs (1984)
2. Cypher, A. (ed.): Watch What I Do: Programming by Demonstration. MIT Press, Cambridge (1993)
3. Lieberman, H., Paternò, F., Klann, M., Wulf, V.: End-User Development: An Emerging Paradigm. In: Lieberman, H., Paternò, F., Wulf, V. (eds.) End User Development, pp. 1–8. Springer, Netherlands (2006)
4. Jess, the Rule Engine for the Java Platform, http://herzberg.ca.sandia.gov/
5. Burnett, M.M., Baker, M.J., Bohus, C., Carlson, P., Yang, S., van Zee, P.: Scaling up Visual Programming Languages. IEEE Computer 28(3), 45–54 (1995)
6. Conklin, J.: Hypertext: an introduction and survey. Computer 20(9), 17–41 (1987)
7. Murugesan, S., Desphande, Y.: Web Engineering. Software Engineering and Web Application Development. LNCS-Hot Topics. Springer, New York (2001)
8. Schwabe, D., Rossi, G.: An Object Oriented Approach to Web-Based Application Design. Theory and Practice of Object Systems 4(4) (1998)

9. Fons, J., Pelechano, V., Albert, M., Pastor, O.: Development of Web applications from Web enhanced conceptual schemas. In: Song, I.-Y., Liddle, S.W., Ling, T.-W., Scheuermann, P. (eds.) ER 2003. LNCS, vol. 2813, pp. 232–245. Springer, Heidelberg (2003)

10. Ceri, S., Fraternali, P., Matera, M.: Conceptual modeling of data-intensive Web applications. IEEE Internet Computing 6(4), 20–30 (2002)

11. Knapp, A., Koch, N., Zhang, G., Hassler, H.M.: Modeling business processes in Web applications with ArgoUWE. In: Baar, T., Strohmeier, A., Moreira, A., Mellor, S.J. (eds.) UML 2004. LNCS, vol. 3273, pp. 69–83. Springer, Heidelberg (2004)

12. De Troyer, O.: Audience-driven Web design. In: Rossi, M., Siau, K. (eds.) Information Modeling in the New Millennium. IDEA Group Publishing, Hershey (2001)

13. Bray, T., Paoli, J., Sperberg-McQueen, C.M., Maler, E., Yergeau, F.: Extensible Markup Language (XML) 1.0., 3rd edn. W3C Recommendation (2004)

14. Ortiz-Chamorro, S.: Cytera. Rules Language Specification. Technical Report, CyteraSystems (2001)

15. Ortiz-Chamorro, S., Aquino, N., Rubin, R., Cernuzzi, L.: AtOOmix: un Lenguaje Extensible de Reglas de Negocios. In: Proceedings of CLEI 2008 (to appear) (2008)

16. Eclipse Home, http://www.eclipse.org/

17. Thompson, H.S., et al.: XML Schema Part 1: Structures, 2nd edn. W3C Recommendation (2004)

18. Biron, P.V., Malhotra, A.: XML Schema Part 2: Datatypes, 2nd edn. W3C Recommendation (2004)

19. Nielsen, J.: Designing Web Usability: The Practice of Simplicity. New Riders Publishing, Indianapolis (1999)

20. Hypermedia Design Patterns Repository, http://www.designpattern.lu.unisi.ch/index.htm

21. Rossi, G., Schwabe, D., Garrido, A.: Design reuse in hypermedia applications development. In: Proceedings of Hypertext 1997, pp. 57–66 (1997)

22. Østerbye, K.: Literate Smalltalk Programming Using Hypertext. IEEE Transactions on Software Engineering 21(2), 138–145 (1995)

23. Anderson, K.M., Taylor, R.N., Whitehead, E.J.: Chimera: hypermedia for heterogeneous software development enviroments. ACM Transactions on Information Systems 18(3), 211–245 (2000)

24. Garg, P.K., Scacchi, W.: ISHYS: Designing an Intelligent Software Hypertext System. IEEE Expert: Intelligent Systems and Their Applications 4(3), 52–63 (1989)

25. Shu, N.: Visual Programming. Van Nostrand Reinhold, New York (1988)

Fast, Accurate Creation of Data Validation Formats by End-User Developers

Chris Scaffidi, Brad Myers, and Mary Shaw

Carnegie Mellon University
5000 Forbes Ave
Pittsburgh, PA 15217
{cscaffid,bam,mary.shaw}@cs.cmu.edu

Abstract. Inputs to web forms often contain typos or other errors. However, existing web form design tools require end-user developers to write regular expressions ("regexps") or even scripts to validate inputs, which is slow and error-prone because of the poor match between common data types and the regexp notation. We present a new technique enabling end-user developers to describe data as a series of constrained parts, and we have incorporated our technique into a prototype tool. Using this tool, end-user developers can create validation code more quickly and accurately than with existing techniques, finding 90% of invalid inputs in a lab study. This study and our evaluation of the technique's generality have motivated several tool improvements, which we have implemented and now evaluate using the Cognitive Dimensions framework.

Keywords: Data validation, web macros, web applications.

1 Introduction

The success of Web 2.0 hinges on enabling end-user developers to create programs that collect information via the web. For example, accountants and financial analysts might create web macro scripts to automatically "screen scrape" data from web pages into spreadsheets [6][15], and marketing specialists or even administrative assistants might create web applications to receive information directly from people via web forms. This wide range of different users can then write programs to use the collected information for computation, report-generation, or generating new web pages.

Inputs often contain typos and other errors, so values should be validated when they are first received in order to prevent invalid data from jeopardizing the program's purpose. For example, if an end-user developer creates a web macro that scrapes data from a certain place on a web page, and the web page is later modified by the site owner, then the web macro may begin to read incorrect information and malfunction as a result [6][7]. Even when information is not collected automatically, inputs can still contain errors. For instance, prior studies have shown that people sometimes type the wrong kind of data into web form fields such as entering "12 Years old" into a street address field [16], which limits the usefulness of this information for generating maps, mining data, or creating reports.

V. Pipek et al. (Eds.): IS-EUD 2009, LNCS 5435, pp. 242–261, 2009.

However, existing tools for designing web macros and web forms can validate only a limited set of input types, and they present high barriers to specifying custom validation. For instance, end-user developers can create web forms with Microsoft Visual Studio.NET (which comes in an "Express Edition" for hobbyists, students, and end-user developers), and they can specify that textfield inputs should be validated against certain regular expressions (regexps), such as email addresses and zip codes. However, the list of available regexps is extremely short compared to the range of actual input fields that appear in real web applications. Examples of data types that lack pre-packaged regexps include city names and company names as well as organization-specific data types such as project numbers. Creating custom regexps or writing intricate JavaScript is beyond the abilities of many administrative assistants, accountants, and other end-user developers. Spreadsheets and other end-user development tools share these limitations.

Solving this problem is not as simple as providing an online repository of regexps that end-user developers could copy/paste into programming tools. Such repositories already exist, but they do not completely meet the users' needs, mainly because it is so difficult to obtain specialized regexps needed for particular applications. For example, the forum for the largest existing online repository[1] includes postings from people who want regexps that:

- Only accept a password if it has "at least 7 characters, at leaset [sic] 1 number, 1 lower case, 1 upper case and no spaces"
- Only accept a URL if its domain is not in a set of certain disallowed domains
- Only accept a zip code if the first three digits fall into a certain range

When people fail to find what they need in these repositories, the main problem is with the underlying regexp notation rather than with the repository per se, as it is extremely cumbersome and sometimes impossible to write regexps with the characteristics of the examples above (complex character counting, compound negative disjunctions, and numeric ranges).

To address the underlying need for a better notation, this paper presents a new interaction technique based on describing inputs as a series of constrained parts, resembling the way that end-user developers actually describe data. This reduces the time required to implement custom validation, and the automatically generated validation code displays targeted human-readable error messages to help application users fix invalid inputs. Our technique is integrated with programming-by-example and direct manipulation in a prototype editor called Toped. Given examples of the data to validate, Toped infers a format describing that data. It presents the format to the end-user developer, who can iteratively review, test and edit the format before using it to validate data in spreadsheets, web applications, web macros, and other programs.

Previous work described how to algorithmically infer formats from examples [17], how to use Toped formats to validate data in web macro editors and other programming platforms [6][18], and how to formally model collections of formats [16]. While this work briefly mentions Toped, it does not describe Toped's internal details, nor does it evaluate Toped's expressiveness and usability.

---

[1] http://regexlib.com/

In the current paper, we describe our format editor in detail as well as three studies: a formative interview-based formative study that originally led to our editor's design, an empirical evaluation of the editor's expressiveness and generality, and a user experiment evaluating its usability. Finally, we briefly summarize improvements in our most recent implementation of the editor, which we evaluate using the Cognitive Dimensions framework [5]. The contributions of this paper are:

- An interaction technique for describing formats as a sequence of constrained parts, which is adequate for representing a wide range of short, human-readable strings.
- A prototype tool that enables end-user developers to quickly create accurate formats, as well as editor innovations that will likely further enhance usability.

We review related work in Section 2 In Section 3, we describe the formative study that guided the design of the format editor, which we describe in Section 4. We evaluate the expressiveness and usability of the editor in Sections 5 and 6. These evaluations prompted improvements to our editor, which we describe and evaluate in Section 7. Finally, in Section 8, we conclude with a discussion of future work.

2 Related Work

To help end-user developers overcome some difficulties of the regexp notation, SWYN infers a regexp from example strings and presents it using a visual language for review and editing [1]. This language replaces regexps' exotic characters with shapes (for example, representing the Kleene operator * as a visual stack of letters and the disjunction operator | as a colored circle containing a set of options). SWYN adds simple negation to the regexp notation, using red shading to express substrings that are not allowed. Grammex [8] and Apple data detectors [13] describe strings as character sequences with context-free grammars (CFGs) rather than regexps. No usability studies have been done on Grammex or Apple data detectors, but we expect that the relative complexity of CFGs versus regexps make them less usable than SWYN. Unlike Toped, regexps and CFGs are ultimately expressed in terms of character sequences, which forces users to figure out how to translate high-level constraints into character sequence patterns. This can be difficult or even impossible, as in the case of examples mentioned in Section 1 (e.g.: a password if it has "at least 7 characters, at leaset [sic] 1 number, 1 lower case, 1 upper case and no spaces"). While Toped generates CFGs internally, users never see the grammars and can instead describe data as a series of constrained parts.

Lapis infers a pattern in a specialized textual language that end-user developers can edit and use to find outliers that do not match the pattern [9]. Whereas regexps, SWYN, and CFGs require end-user developers to describe a string as a character sequence, Lapis allows end-user developers to describe a string as a sequence of parts, each of which matches a regexp, literal string, or a certain primitive refined by "starts with", "contains", or "ends with" constraints. Toped eschews regexp-based constraints and instead offers a broad range of human-readable constraints that can be combined to validate parts of strings.

Toped also significantly differs from regexps, CFGs, and Lapis in that it supports soft constraints that need not always be true. This makes it possible to flag inputs that are questionable, but which should be accepted if they are double-checked.

Several tools check constraints over numeric data in particular programming platforms, rather than a format over string-like data. For example, Cues infers constraints over web service data [14], and Forms/3 infers numeric constraints over spreadsheet cells [2]. From a conceptual standpoint, Toped generalizes these number-oriented systems to include string-like data.

3   Formative Study

To learn how end-user developers describe data, we asked four administrative assistants to verbally describe two types of data (American mailing addresses and university project numbers) so a hypothetical foreign undergraduate could find those data on a hard drive. (We used this syntax-neutral phrasing to avoid biasing participants toward or away from regexps or any other particular notation.)

Participants described data as a series of named parts, such as city, state, and zip code. They did not explicitly provide descriptions of those parts without prompting, assuming that simply referring to those parts would enable the hypothetical undergraduate to find the data. When prompted to describe the parts of data, participants hierarchically described parts in terms of other named parts (such as an address line being a number, street name, and street type) until sub-parts became small enough that participants lacked names for them.

At that point, participants used constraints to define sub-parts, such as specifying that the street type usually is "Blvd" or "St". They often used adverbs of frequency such as "usually" or "sometimes", meaning that valid data occasionally violate these constraints. This use of not-always-true constraints stands in stark contrast to regexp-based validation, which classifies inputs as valid or invalid, with no shades of gray.

Finally, participants mentioned the punctuation separating named parts, such as the periods that punctuate parts of our university's project numbers. Such punctuation is common in data encountered on a daily basis by end-user developers, such as hyphens and slashes in dates, and parentheses around area codes in American phone numbers.

4   Toped Format Editor

Based on the formative study results, we have designed a new tool for end-user developers to describe the format that inputs should match (Fig. 1). After a developer creates a format, its specification is stored and later used to check inputs. The process is conceptually similar to creating a regexp and using it to check inputs, except that Toped describes data as a sequence of named parts with constraints (Table 1). Toped is forms-based, a style of user interface known to help reduce memory load and errors, though at the risk of limited expressiveness and generality [12].

Step 1: Tell what kind of data your format is for... [Mailing Address]
     Give your format a descriptive name... [NNN Street Name Type.]

Step 2: Describe the parts that make up each Mailing Address ...

[+ part]   You can start from an example: [   ] [Ok]

Each Mailing Address has a part called the [street number]   [X]

The street number [always ▼] has [1-5] of the following characters: [X]
☐ lowercase letters ☐ uppercase letters ☑ digits other characters: [   ]

[+ info]

[+ part]

Each Mailing Address has a part called the [street name] [▲]   [X]

The street name [always ▼] has [3-10] of the following characters: [X]
☑ lowercase letters ☑ uppercase letters ☑ digits other characters: [   ]

[▲]

The street name [always ▼] is preceded by [§] and followed by [   ]   [X]
(You can leave one of these two fields blank if it does not apply.)

[▲]

The street name can repeat [1-3] times, separated by [§]   [X]
The last separator in any list of repetitions is [also §   ▼]

[+ info]

[+ part]

Each Mailing Address has a part called the [street type] [▲]   [X]

The street type [always ▼] has [2-9] of the following characters: [X]
☑ lowercase letters ☑ uppercase letters ☐ digits other characters: [.]

[▲]

The street type [always ▼] is preceded by [§] and followed by [   ]   [X]
(You can leave one of these two fields blank if it does not apply.)

[+ info]

[+ part]

Step 3: Test your format...   [Test Now]

When you click the Test Now button, your format will be tested.

If you like, you can specify several Mailing Address examples in the left
column of this spreadsheet ⟶
When you click Test, these examples will be checked to see if they
match the format.

Copy All	Paste All
15211 4th St	Ok
501 Highland Ave.	Ok
433 Amazon River Trail	Ok
767 Burgh Boulevard	Ok
#12 Locomotive Terr.	Does not match format

The street number always has 1-5 digits

Step 4: Save your format...   [Save Now]

Fig. 1. Editing a format in Toped, after providing example street addresses and giving human-readable names to the inferred format and its three parts. Adding, removing, and reordering parts/constraints is accomplished with the [+] , [X] , and [▲] buttons. Each § indicates a space.

Table 1. Constraints that can be applied to parts

Constraint	Description
Pattern	Specifies the characters in a part and how many of them may appear
Literal	Specifies that the part equals one of a certain set of options
Numeric	Specifies a numeric inequality or equality
Substring	Specifies that the part starts/ends with some literal or number of certain characters
Wrapped	Specifies that the part is preceded and/or followed by a certain string
Optionality	Specifies that the part may be missing
Repeat	Specifies that the part may repeat, with possible separators between repetitions
Reference	Specifies that the part matches another format

We named the editor "Toped", after the Greek word "tope" for "place", because each format validates a kind of data that has a natural "place" in the problem domain. That is, problem domains involve email addresses and salaries, rather than strings and floats, and it is the problem domain that governs whether a string is valid.

Our editor has four sections, as shown in Fig. 1. First, the user names the data to validate, such as "phone number" or "person name", and names the format. It is important to distinguish between the name of the data and the name of the format, since many kinds of data can appear in more than one format (such as "08/16/2008" and "Aug 16, 2008" formats for US dates). Our system includes a format browser so the user can browse for formats using these names. Prompting the user to name the data also enables the editor to refer to the data by name in the next three steps.

Second, the end-user developer defines the format's parts. For example, a US phone number has three parts: area code, exchange, and local number. The end-user developer can add, remove and reorder parts, and he can specify constraints on parts. Table 1 shows the available constraints, which we initially identified based on the formative study and later expanded as we used Toped to validate a variety of data.

In the third step of the editor, the end-user developer can enter example strings to test against the format. The editor displays a targeted error message in a mouse-over tooltip for each invalid test example. These targeted messages show a list of violated constraints. The end-user developer can iteratively debug the format.

Finally, the format is saved to a file, which can be reloaded and further edited.

4.1 Specific Editor Features

To help the end-user developer get started, Toped includes a textbox that accepts an example string. The editor identifies non-alphanumeric characters in the example and treats these as separators between parts. It then initializes a part in the editor for each part of the example and looks for a few basic constraints (e.g.: noticing that a word-like part starts with an uppercase letter). To provide further help, Toped can examine multiple examples of data and infer a single format describing the majority of those examples [17]. The examples are automatically copied into the testing feature (Step 3) to help the end-user developer review, test, and customize the format.

One problem with some editing tools is that spaces are invisible and (we suspect) hard to debug. To counter this, Toped makes spaces visible by representing them with a special symbol, §. Though this slightly reduces readability, it is preferable to having spaces that the end-user developer cannot see or debug. (In error messages, spaces appear as SPACE to avoid font-related problems.) To further improve readability and directness, Toped allows numeric ranges in textboxes that accept an integer. For example, users can specify that a part starts with "1", "2-3", or "4+" uppercase letters.

The Pattern, Literal, Numeric, Wrapped, and Substring constraints can be marked as "never", "rarely", "as often as not", "more often than not", "almost always", or "always" true. We selected these adverbs of frequency because there is surprisingly little variance in the probabilities that people assign to these words, corresponding within a few percentage points to probabilities of 0%, 10%, 50%, 60%, 90%, and 100%, respectively [10]. This robust correspondence makes it feasible to integrate constraints with formal grammars (below). As users have trouble grasping mixtures of conjunction and disjunction [11], all constraints are conjoined, and disjunction is expressed as two constraints with parallel sentence structure that are each not always true. Toped has an advanced mode, not shown in Fig. 1, for specifying conditional constraints that span multiple parts, such as the intricate leap year rules for dates.

4.2 Validating Data

Formats are not used to validate data directly. Instead, they are converted automatically into a grammar, which is then used at runtime to validate strings in web forms, web macros, and other end-user development platforms.

Generating a grammar and parsing strings. To create a grammar, Toped generates a hierarchy of CFG productions to represent Reference constraints, indicating that a part should match another format. It inserts separators between parts based on Wrapped constraints, and it inserts repetition productions based on Repeat constraints. Toped generates leaf productions based on Numeric, Pattern and Literal constraints, which indicate that certain characters or literal values appear in a part.

Like other CFGs, this basic CFG can only accept or reject strings. But the soft constraints supported by the Toped user interface are more expressive, since they can identify questionable inputs that might or might not be valid. Toped reflects this additional expressiveness in the grammar by augmenting the basic CFG with additional productions and constraints on productions. Each production constraint has a "penalty", which indicates that if a substring matches the production but violates the constraint, then the substring is questionable and might be invalid. This penalty is between 0 and 1, depending on the probability corresponding to the adverb of frequency on the constraint.

The Numeric, Pattern and Literal constraints can be directly attached to productions of respective parts. If a Wrapped constraint has an adverb of frequency, indicating that separators should occur but are not mandatory, then Toped augments the basic CFG with alternate productions where the separator does not occur, and it attaches a penalty to the alternate productions. Toped also generates alternate productions from Optionality constraints, but without penalties.

At runtime, strings are parsed according to the augmented grammar. Our parser is based on GLR [19], which runs in linear time (with respect to the length of the input string) when the grammar has low ambiguity, as is generally the case with grammars generated from Toped formats. We adapt GLR by incorporating constraints. When a production is completed, producing a variable v, GLR automatically treats this variable as valid and uses it to complete other productions waiting for v. In contrast, our adapted version of GLR associates a score with each variable instance (a parse tree node), ranging from 0 through 1. When a production p for a variable v is completed, the parser evaluates any constraints on p. It downgrades the score of v by multiplying the score by each violated constraint's penalty. If a variable instance with a downgraded score is later used on the right hand side of a production, then the parser uses this score to multiplicatively downgrade the score of the variable on the production's left-hand side. Thus, the score of each node in the parse tree depends on child nodes' scores.

In short, these multiplications use penalties from violated constraints to score each node, including the root. That way, when the tree is complete, the parser can return a score between 0 and 1 for the input as a whole. In cases of ambiguity, the parser selects the parse with the highest score.

Generating error messages. To generate error messages, the parser tracks a list of violated constraints and concatenates them into a message (e.g.: the tooltip in Step 3 of Fig. 1). When a parse totally fails (making it impossible to identify specific violated constraints), the parser generates a message by concatenating constraints associated with failed productions that should have been completed. The resulting message is targeted and descriptive, a significant improvement over typical hard-coded error messages such as "Please enter a valid phone number" on web sites, or "The formula you typed contains an error" in Excel.

Toped has been integrated with several end-user development tools, including Visual Studio.NET [18], the Robofox web macro tool [6], and Microsoft Excel [18]. Formats can be reused without modification in each of these programming platforms. While error messages are generated in the same way for each platform, they are displayed in different ways.

For example, when a format is associated with a web form field using Visual Studio.NET, targeted human-readable error messages appear alongside textfields when inputs are invalid (Fig. 2). If an input matches the CFG but violates soft constraints, the code shows the message so that the end user can correct the input, but the message is displayed in a popup window so that the user can override the warning. End-user developers can also specify alternate settings, such as showing overridable messages with an "Ignore" button alongside textfields rather than in a popup, or configuring the web form to always reject any input that violates soft constraints.

Phone:	911-555-1212	The area code never ends with 11
Address:	373Maple Dr.	The street number always has 1-5 digits The street name always is preceded by SPACE
City:	New haven	The city's word always starts with 1 uppercase letter
State:	CX	The state abbrev always is one of these: AL, AK, AZ...
Zip:	8445	The zip always has 5 digits

Fig. 2. Validating web form data

A second programming platform, web macros, enables end-user developers to create scripts that scrape data from web sites, but scripts can sometimes read the wrong data from web pages if the pages are modified by site owners after the scripts are created. Toped formats help make Robofox web macro scripts more robust to web page changes. When constructing a script, an end-user developer can highlight a clipboard item, which is a variable that is initialized by a copy operation in the script. This opens Toped so the end-user developer can create a new format or select an existing format. Robofox then creates an assertion specifying that after the copy operation, the clipboard should contain a string that matches the format. At runtime, if a string violates any constraint in the format, then Robofox displays a warning popup to explain that the assertion is violated, enabling the end-user developer to modify the script or cancel execution if necessary.

To validate Excel spreadsheets, end-user developers highlight some cells, click a button, and select a format file, which can be customized if desired. Alternatively, clicking another button causes Toped to infer a new format using the highlighted cells as examples, and then the new format is presented for editing. Based on the grammar generated from the format, the plug-in validates each highlighted cell and flags each invalid cell with a red triangle and a tooltip showing a targeted error message. End-user developers can browse through comments using Excel's Reviewing feature.

Toped's format editing user interface runs on Microsoft .NET 2.0 and is implemented in C#. Toped's parser for validating data against formats is available as a .NET library and as a Java library. All code has been made available as open source so that other researchers can continue to apply formats in new and innovative ways.

5 Expressiveness Evaluation

In many cases, "forms-based systems lack generality" [12] since they provide a relatively small set of primitives. Consequently, we evaluated the expressiveness of Toped by implementing formats for a range of data types commonly encountered by end users. As this was an evaluation of expressiveness, not usability, we implemented the formats ourselves as expert users.

5.1 Data and Method

To identify test data, we ran logging software for three weeks on four administrative assistants' computers. When a user filled out a web form in Internet Explorer (these users' preferred browser), the logger recorded the fields' HTML names and some text near each field (to capture the fields' human-readable labels).

For each field, the logger recorded a regexp describing the string that the user entered. (We recorded a regexp rather than the literal string to protect users' privacy.) To generate regexps, we converted each lowercase letter to the regexp [a-z], uppercase to [A-Z], and digits to [0-9], then concatenated regexps and coalesced repeated regexps (e.g.: user0@XYZ.EDU → [a-z]{4}[0-9]@[A-Z]{3}.[A-Z]{3}).

We manually examined many of the 5897 logged regexps and wrote scripts to gather fields into semantic families such as "email" and "currency" based on HTML names and human-readable text near the fields. As shown in Table 2, 5527 (93.7%) fell into one of 19 semantic families. Using the regexps as a reference, we created formats for the 14 asterisked families. We omitted 3 families (justification, description, and posting title) because each would have simply required a sequence of any characters. That is, it is doubtful that these fields have any semantics aside from "text." We omitted usernames and passwords because we wanted to post formats online and did not want to reveal formats of our users' authentication credentials. Finally, we used our parser to test formats with sample strings, which we generated by referring to concrete regexps in the log and by using our knowledge of formats' semantics (such as what might constitute an email address).

Table 2. Semantic families gathered from user data. Asterisked groups were used for testing.

Family name	Strings	Example regexp from logs	Formats Needed	Strings Not Covered
project number *	821	[0-9]{5}	1	1
justification	820	*Very long*		
expense type *	738	[0-9]{5}	1	
award number *	707	[0-9]{7}	1	
task number *	610	[0-9][A-Z]	2	
currency *	489	[0-9]\.[0-9]{2}	2	6
date *	450	[0-9]{2}V[0-9]{2}V[0-9]{4}	2	2
sites *	194	[a-z]{3}	1	
password	155	*Several characters*		
username	121	*Several characters*		
description	96	*Very long*		
posting title	65	*Very long*		
email address *	50	[a-z]{8}@[a-z]{7}\.[a-z]{3}	2	7
person name *	48	[A-Z][a-z]{5}\s[A-Z][a-z]{8}	2	
cost center *	41	[0-9]{6}	1	
expense type *	41	[0-9]{5}	1	6
address line *	37	[0-9]{3}\s[A-Z][a-z]{5} \s[A-Z][a-z]{4}	1	
zip code *	28	[0-9]{5}	1	
city *	16	[A-Z][a-z]{8}	1	

5.2 Results

We had little trouble expressing families as formats. Some required 2 formats, but this was reasonable, as web forms generally require inputs to be in a certain format. For example, we needed a format for dates like "10/12/2004" and another for dates like "12-Oct-2004".

When testing formats, we found that we had made 4 errors. Three were cases where we failed to mark a part as optional. The fourth error was an apparent slip of the mouse, in which we indicated that a constraint was often true rather than always true. The version of the editor that we used for this evaluation did not have the testing feature (Step 3 in Fig. 1). We noted that these errors probably could have been found if we had been able to test our formats when we created them. Therefore, after our evaluation, we added the editor's testing feature.

After correcting these errors, our formats covered 99.5% of the 4250 strings used for testing. The 22 strings not covered included 17 apparent typos in the original data and 4 cases that probably were not typos by the users (that is, they were intentionally typed), but we suspect that they may have been invalid inputs, nonetheless. For example, in 2 cases, users entered a month and a year rather than a full date. The final uncovered test value was a case where a street type had a trailing period, and the editor offered no way for us to express that a street type may contain a period but only in the last position, a limitation that has recently been addressed. Formats' effectiveness at identifying invalid values suggests that they are powerful enough for validating a variety of data types.

6 Usability Evaluation

We conducted a between-subjects experiment to assess Toped's usability. As a baseline, we compared Toped to Lapis (which was described in Section 2) because Lapis patterns are more expressive than regexps or CFGs, and were previously shown to be usable by end-user developers [9].

Using emails and posters, we recruited 7 administrative assistants and 10 graduate students, who were predominantly master's students in information technology and engineering. None had prior experience with Toped or Lapis, but many had some experience with programming or grammars. We paid $10 to each.

We randomly assigned each to a Toped or Lapis group. Each condition had four stages: a background questionnaire, a tutorial for the assigned tool, three validation tasks, and a final questionnaire.

The tutorial introduced the assigned tool, coaching subjects through a practice task and showing all tool features necessary for later tasks. Subjects could ask questions and work up to 30 minutes on the tutorial.

The validation tasks instructed subjects to use the assigned tool to validate three types of data. Subjects could spend a total of up to 20 minutes on these tasks and could not ask questions. Subjects could refer to the written tutorial as well as an extra reference packet extensively describing features of the assigned tool.

6.1 Task Details

In Lapis, text appears on the screen's left side, while the pattern editor appears on the right. End-user developers highlight example strings, and Lapis infers an editable pattern. Lapis highlights each string in purple if it matches the pattern or yellow if it does not. For comparability, we embedded Toped in a text viewer with the same screen layout and highlighting. Each example string on the left was highlighted in yellow if it violated any constraints or purple otherwise.

Each task presented 25 strings drawn from one spreadsheet column in the EUSES corpus, an existing collection of spreadsheets from the web [4]. Each column also contained at least 25 additional strings that we did not show but instead reserved for testing. All 50 strings were randomly selected.

The first task used American phone numbers, the second used street addresses (just the street address, not a city or state or zip), and the third used company names. We selected these types to exercise Toped on data ranging from highly structured to relatively unstructured. The data contained a mixture of valid and invalid strings. For example, most mailing addresses were of the form "1000 EVANS AVE.", but a few were not addresses, such as "12 MILES NORTH OF INDEPENDENCE".

We told subjects that the primary goal was to "find typos" by creating formats that properly highlighted valid strings in purple and invalid strings in yellow. To avoid biasing subjects, we did not use Toped or Lapis keywords in the description of validity. To further clarify the conditions for validity, the task instructions called out six strings for each data type as valid or invalid.

Table 3. Results comparing Toped to Lapis

	Toped	Lapis	Relative Improvement	Significant? (Mann-Whitney)
Tasks completed	2.79	1.75	60%	p<0.01
Typos identified				
On 75 visible strings	16.50	5.75	187%	p<0.01
On all 150 strings	31.25	9.50	229%	p<0.01
F1 accuracy measure				
On 75 visible strings	0.74	0.51	45%	No
On all 150 strings	0.68	0.46	48%	No
User satisfaction	3.78	3.06	24%	p=0.02

6.2 Results

We asked subjects to think aloud when something particularly good or bad occurred in the tool. One Toped subject interpreted these instructions differently than the other subjects, as she spoke aloud about virtually every mouse click. We discarded her data from analysis, leaving 8 subjects assigned to each group.

As shown in Table 3, we used the conservative Mann-Whitney (Wilcoxon) statistical test, since our sample was small and we could not assume normally distributed data (though all measures' medians were very close to the respective means).

Tasks completed. In the allotted time, Toped subjects completed an average of 2.79 tasks, while Lapis subjects averaged 1.75 (Table 3), a significant difference (Mann-Whitney, p<0.01). Toped subjects were more successful at their primary goal, finding typos. Of the 18 actual invalid strings in the 75 visible strings, Toped subjects found an average of 16.5 invalid strings, compared to 5.75 for Lapis subjects, which was a significant difference (Mann-Whitney, p<0.01). In addition, of the 35 typos in the total set of 150 test strings, the completed Toped formats found an average of 31.25 invalid strings, whereas completed Lapis patterns found only 9.5, a significant difference (Mann-Whitney, p<0.01).

Accuracy. Finding invalid data is not sufficient alone. Validation should also classify valid data as valid. We evaluated accuracy using F1, a standard statistic commonly used to evaluate classifiers, with typical F1 scores in the range 0.7-1.0 [3]. F1 combines measures for "false negatives" and "false positives". Compared to simply counting classification errors, F1 more effectively "discourages classifiers that sacrifice one measure for another too drastically" [3]. The 23 completed Toped formats had an F1 of 0.74 on the 75 visible strings and 0.68 on all 150 strings, whereas the 14 completed Lapis patterns had respective scores of 0.51 and 0.46, though these inter-tool differences were not statistically significant (Mann-Whitney, p<0.05). Thus, Toped subjects completed more tasks without sacrificing accuracy.

User satisfaction. We assessed user satisfaction because end-user developers such as students and administrative assistants typically do not need to program to get their work done: they can choose a manual approach rather than a programmatic approach if they do not like their programming tool [12].

Subjects generally commented that Toped was easy to use, "interesting" and "a great idea". Most suggested other types of data to validate, such as email addresses, license plate numbers, bank record identifiers, and other application-specific data. One subject commented that it was unintuitive to represent "two options" (disjunction) as two constraints with parallel structure.

The satisfaction questionnaire asked subjects to rate on 5-point Likert scale how hard the tool was to use, how much they trusted it, how pleasant it was to use, and if they would use it if it was integrated with spreadsheets or word processors. We found that we could combine answers into a moderately robust scale (Cronbach's alpha=0.74). On this scale, subjects reported an average satisfaction of 3.78 with Toped and 3.06 with Lapis, a significant difference (Mann-Whitney, p=0.02).

No confounds with background. Subjects had different job categories and varying experience with grammars and programming. Yet for each tool, we found no statistically significant effects (Mann-Whitney, p<0.05) on task completion, format accuracy, or user satisfaction based on this prior experience or job category.

6.3 Comparisons to Other Studies

Regexp study. Though not perfectly comparable, it appears that subjects completed our tasks with Toped more quickly and accurately than subjects completed tasks with regexps in a study during SWYN's development [1]. For each of 12 data types presented in random order, that study asked 39 graduate students to identify which of 5 strings matched a provided regexp that was written in one of four notations. Average speeds on the last six tasks (after subjects grew accustomed to the notations) ranged from 14 to 21 seconds per string, and error rates ranged from 27% to 47%. (No F1 was reported.) In contrast, Toped subjects were faster and more accurate, not only checking strings, but also constructing a format at an average of 15 seconds per string (373.8 sec / task) with a simple classification error rate of only 19%.

Formative study. As in our formative study, our initial questionnaire (prior to validation tasks) asked subjects to write descriptions of US postal addresses and person names. Slightly more than half of responses (17) were sentences calling out parts by name. In some cases, they specified constraints on parts, whether implicitly in names ("street *number*" implies the presence of digits) or explicitly ("5 digit zip code"). Constraints often included an adverb of frequency. This description style is consistent with the earlier results and a close match to Toped's style of interaction.

Our questionnaire also uncovered an additional way that people describe data as a series of constrained parts. Many questionnaire responses (15) were non-sentence templates listing parts by name and visually showing spaces or punctuation separating parts. As in the sentence-like descriptions, many constraints were implicit in names, but explicit constraints were rarely specified. Our earlier study probably did not uncover this visual way of describing a series of constrained parts because the formative study required participants to *verbally* describe data, whereas this questionnaire asked participants to *write* descriptions, and the written medium is much more conducive to communicating template-like (visual) descriptions.

7 Recent Editor Improvements

During the evaluations described above, we observed the need for several editor improvements, which we have implemented and will evaluate below.

7.1 Requirements for Improvements

Sharing parts between formats. During the expressiveness evaluation, we observed that implementing validation for a semantic family often required more than one format. In most cases, these formats had the same parts but different separators and different ordering of parts. For example, person names could be written as "Otto von Bismark" or as "von Bismark, Otto". In addition to the multi-format semantic families shown in Table 2, we have observed many other kinds of multi-format strings such as credit card numbers (written as "1234 5678 9012 3456" or "1234567890123456" or "1234-5678-9012-3456") and phone numbers. The parts in these formats have identical constraints—it is merely the manner of combining the parts that differs.

In such cases, it would be ideal if the user could create a part and reuse its constraints in multiple formats. In the existing editor, this would only have been feasible by putting the first name into a format of its own, the last name into a format of its own, and then referencing these formats when creating the person name formats. This would lead to a rapid increase in the number of formats and format management complexity. Perhaps a particular user might still want to store the first and last name formats separately, in order to validate fields that should only contain a first or last name rather than a full person name, but at least the end-user developer should be able to make that choice rather than having it forced onto him.

Referencing collections of formats. Another consequence of the multi-format nature of users' data is that a format's part might match one of several formats. For example, a month can be written as "Aug", "August", "08", or "8", and when a month is referenced in a date, humans typically can understand the date regardless of which format is used for the month (with caveats about ambiguity among the day, month and year parts, which we discuss later). The implication for our format editor is that it would be ideal if a user could not only reuse one format in another format, but if they also could reference a collection of formats when specifying a part in another format.

Tailoring constraints to kinds of parts. In our expressiveness study, we noted that several kinds of parts frequently appeared, and the kind of the part strongly influenced the applicable constraints. Numeric parts always contained numeric characters, never contained alphabetic characters, always had Numeric constraints, and rarely needed Substring constraints. Word-like parts rarely contained numeric characters (with exceptions like usernames in email addresses), always contained alphabetic characters, sometimes contained punctuation, and often needed Substring constraints.

Despite the existence of these kinds of parts, Toped treated each part as a "generic" part, rather than tailoring the interface to each kind of part. Consequently, adding a new constraint to a part required selecting the desired constraint from the full list of available constraints, rather than a shortened list of constraints relevant to that kind of part. It would be ideal if the editor instead showed the most relevant constraints for each kind of part, with an option to add other kinds of rarely-relevant constraints.

Showing disjunction more clearly. Finally, during the user study, a single participant commented that it was unintuitive to represent "two options" (disjunction) as two constraints with parallel structure. Disjunction most commonly occurred when different separators could be used between parts (such as writing a North American phone numbers as "888-888-8888" or "(888) 888-8888"), or when the part could start or end with certain particular options. The disjunction of separator options is actually the same issue as having multiple formats with the same parts (discussed above). As for Substring disjunctions, it would be ideal if choices for starting or ending strings could be listed within the same constraint, so as to avoid multiple parallel constraints.

7.2 Toped+: An Improved Prototype for Editing Formats

Our latest format editor, called Toped+, refers to a collection of formats as a "data description" (Fig. 3). The data description can contain one or more variations that contain parts interspersed with separators. This presentation was inspired by the 15 cases where usability study participants used non-sentence templates listing parts by name and visually showing spaces or punctuation separating parts. Toped+ supports drag/drop and copy/paste operations for creating and manipulating parts, as well as instantiation of parts or an entire data description from examples.

Each part has constraints, which can be edited by clicking on the part. Toped+ supports three kinds of parts—Numeric, Word-like, and Hierarchical (referencing another data description—and each icon in the Toolbox corresponds to a prototype instance of a part or separator. When the user drags a new part from the Toolbox on the left, the part's editor is "pre-loaded" with a default set of constraints that are usually appropriate for that kind of part. In addition, the user can add Pattern, Literal, Substring, and Repeat constraints to any kind of part. Substring constraints can contain a disjunction of options. To test part constraints, each part icon has a user-editable example, which is validated using the part's constraints (generating a targeted message in a tooltip if the example fails to meet the constraints).

Thus, this improved interface directly meets three of the four requirements above: sharing parts between formats, tailoring constraints to kinds of parts, and showing disjunction more clearly. Support for the fourth requirement, referencing collections of formats, is more complex and has implications that require deeper explanation.

Referencing collections of formats. Toped+ allows users to create a Hierarchical part that references an existing data description, which may contain multiple variations. As a result, each variation actually corresponds to multiple formats. In this way, it is possible to quickly build up quite complex validation code.

For example, a month data description might have three one-part variations (the first of which would recognize "August", the second for "Aug", and the third for "8"),

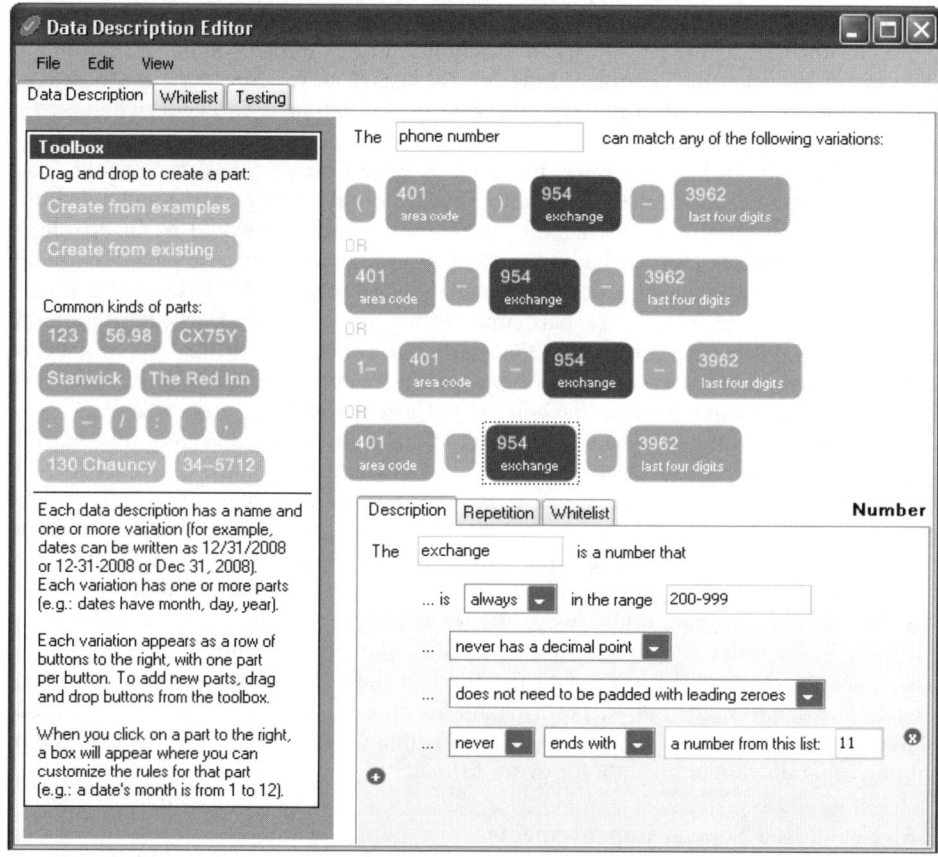

Fig. 3. Using Toped+ to edit variations of a phone number data description. Each variation appears on one row and consists of a series of parts (each of which may appear on multiple rows). Dragging and dropping a prototype's icon from the Toolbox creates a new part, and the editor also supports drag/drop re-arrangement of parts as well as copy/paste. Users can click the example in a part's icon to edit it, while clicking other parts of the icon displays widgets for editing its constraints, which are shared by every instance of the part. As in Toped, clicking ⊕ adds a constraint, while clicking ⊗ deletes the constraint. Users can toggle whether each space character is shown with a special character or as an invisible blank.

a day data description might have one variation, and a year data description might have two one-part variations (for two-digit and four-digit years). Concatenating hyphen separators with month, day and year parts (each referencing the respective data description) would yield 6 formats visually represented on-screen by a single date variation. The user could duplicate this variation by copy/paste, then change the new variation's separators to slashes, yielding another six formats in just a few user inter-face operations. Dates are perhaps the most complex kind of string data that we have encountered, in terms of the number of formats. Yet because the parts are shared be-tween variations, and because parts reference data descriptions rather than particular formats, it is possible to show many formats in relatively little space. This conciseness helps to greatly reduce the data description's visual complexity.

Ambiguity. A consequence of parsing against collections of formats, rather than particular formats, is the possibility of ambiguity. For example, should "02/06/08" be interpreted as a date in February, June, or August? Careful consideration, however, reveals that this is a false dilemma: the role of validation is to check whether this string matches *any* valid date, so it does not matter which date it refers to.

Forgetting about Toped for the moment, it would be perfectly reasonable for a skilled programmer to validate dates with a (very complex) regexp that had a disjunction of many different date formats, even though the regexp would be incapable of indicating which date format had been used. The regexp's job is to identify invalid dates, not to identify a valid date's format. On the other hand, if the programmer wanted users to enter values in a particular format, then he would instead use a more specific regexp that only recognized that particular format. Unfortunately, this would require the programmer to maintain a separate regexp for each particular format, since it would not be feasible to reuse the general-purpose format.

The same reasoning also applies to Toped+, but with improved reusability of validation code. If an end-user developer wants to validate dates against a specific format, then (unlike in the case of regexps), a general-purpose data description can still be reused. In this case, the user associates the data description with the input field and provides an *example* of the preferred format to our plug-in for Microsoft Excel or Visual Studio.NET. The plug-in calls our parser to parse the example in order to identify the desired format. (Obviously, the example must match one format, as in "12/31/99", in order to unambiguously specify the preferred format.) The plug-in associates this preferred format with the field so that at runtime, inputs are *checked against the demonstrated format* rather than the entire data description. Thus, Toped+ supports validating inputs against particular formats, but without the hassle of maintaining separate validation code for every format.

7.3 Evaluating Toped+ Improvements

Cognitive Dimensions is an established framework for qualitatively evaluating non-orthogonal aspects ("dimensions") of a notation, programming language or user interface, and for discussing trade-offs between different designs [5]. Example dimensions include Closeness of mapping, Abstraction gradient, Juxtaposability, and Visibility. Below, we consider 12 dimensions that are highly relevant to the task of creating formats, in order to identify strengths and weaknesses of Toped+ relative to Toped.

Closeness of mapping. Both Toped+ and Toped have excellent closeness of mapping to the problem domain, since like end-user developers, they describe formats as a sequence of constrained parts. We believe that this closeness of mapping was a key ingredient to Toped's success in the user study. Moreover, Toped+ constraints are associated with parts, rather than appearances of parts in particular formats, yielding better closeness of mapping to the kinds of data that appear in the real world.

Abstraction gradient and Hidden dependencies. Both Toped and Toped+ require users to comprehend and manipulate constraint, part, and format abstractions. In addition, Toped+ requires users to comprehend variations and data descriptions. Yet Toped+ is not "abstraction-hungry" in the sense of requiring users to create multiple variations if they are not needed for a particular data description.

The usual problem introduced by reusable abstractions is the possibility of hidden dependencies. This caution applies to Toped+, since if a user edits a part by clicking on its icon in one variation, then any changes will also affect the part as it appears in other variations. We have attempted to mitigate this potential for confusion by high-lighting every one of a part's icons throughout the data description when a user clicks on a part (Fig. 3). Another form of hidden dependency, which applies to both Toped and Toped+, is the fact that formats are indirectly affected when referenced formats change. Future versions of Toped+ should mitigate this potential for confusion by listing the data descriptions that reference the data description currently being edited.

Juxtaposability, Diffuseness, and Visibility. In Toped, it was impossible to view two formats side-by-side at the same time. Toped+ places formats adjacent to one another, making it straightforward to see differences in separators and part ordering.

Toped and Toped+ both suffer from a common problem of visual languages in requiring a great deal of screen space. Toped+ mitigates this diffuseness by only show-ing a part's constraints when the user clicks on the part's icon, which frees up enough screen space to show several variations at the same time. This design decision im-proves visibility but decreases the juxtaposability of parts' constraints, since it is therefore impossible to view two parts' constraints simultaneously. Fortunately, it is fairly rare that two parts need to have similar constraints, so we believe that it is more valuable to show multiple variations than multiple parts at the same time.

Error-proneness and Premature commitment. We expect the constraint editors in Toped+ will help reduce error-proneness relative to Toped, since users would need to make a special effort to create senseless combinations of constraints.

The trade-off with this decision is that users must choose a particular kind of part before configuring the part's constraints. This is a form of premature commitment, since the user must manually back out of an error to a previous state (by deleting the part) before performing a more correct operation. It would be ideal if Toped+ pro-vided a feature to change the kind of a part, but we believe that it is infeasible to pro-vide such a feature because of the richness of the supported constraints. Therefore, we have attempted to mitigate this problem by making it simple to delete a part (by click-ing on it and typing Control+Delete, or selecting Delete under the Edit menu) and to create a part (by dragging a prototype from the Toolbox).

Viscosity. Toped+ greatly reduces the effort required to make changes to programs (viscosity). One reason is that simple operations are faster because Toped+ supports drag/drop and copy/paste. Another reason is that fewer user interface operations are required because it is so easy to reuse constraints and data descriptions.

Hard mental operations, Progressive evaluation, and Secondary notation. We have tried to minimize the need for hard mental operations in both Toped and Toped+ through support for inferring formats (or even particular parts in Toped+) from examples. Progressive evaluation is supported in Toped+ by letting the user enter an example (in the part's icon) that is validated with the part's constraints. In addition, the user can enter a list of examples to test the data description as a whole—just as a format could be tested in Toped. Moreover, unlike in Toped, the example strings entered for testing in Toped+ are actually stored with the data description, so they can serve as a form of "use case" secondary notation that provides additional information about the function of the data description. In both editors, users provide human-readable names for parts and data descriptions, which is a form of secondary notation.

8   Conclusion and Future Work

The central insight described in this paper is that end-user developers tend to describe string inputs as a series of constrained parts. We have found that this way of describing data is expressive enough for validating many kinds of data, and we have used this insight to design a tool that helps end-user developers create validation formats more quickly and accurately than is possible with existing tools. Our studies identified the need for editor improvements that we have implemented. Based on an analysis using the Cognitive Dimensions framework, we believe that the enhanced editor will be even more usable than the first version. We conclude that describing strings as a series of constrained parts is an effective approach for structuring validation code.

Future work will continue to develop Toped+ by providing highly-usable support for implementing functions that transform strings among the different formats of a data description. We have already prototyped a minimalist tool for implementing basic inter-format transformations, such as fixing capitalization and tweaking separators [16]. However, we have not integrated this tool with Toped+, since we anticipate that can do even better by developing algorithms that *automatically* implement these basic transformations based on the layout of a data description's variations. We will also support custom transformations with a general-purpose language such as JavaScript.

In addition, we are designing a repository that will enable end-user developers to publish, find, and reuse data descriptions. As noted in the introduction, the main problem with existing repositories is with the underlying notation, rather than the idea of a repository per se. Since Toped+ provides a means for end-user developers to inspect and modify formats in a notation that has strong closeness of mapping to the problem domain, we anticipate that a final summative user study will show that integrating a repository with Toped+ enables end-user developers to conveniently browse, select, reuse and customize data descriptions to validate data.

Acknowledgements

This work was funded in part by the EUSES Consortium via NSF (ITR-0325273) and by NSF under Grants CCF-0438929 and CCF-0613823. Opinions, findings and conclusions or recommendations are the authors' and not necessarily those of sponsors.

References

1. Blackwell, A.: SWYN: A Visual Representation for Regular Expressions. In: Your Wish Is My Command: Programming by Example, pp. 245–270. Morgan Kaufmann, San Francisco (2001)
2. Burnett, M., et al.: End-User Software Engineering with Assertions in the Spreadsheet Paradigm. In: Proc. 25th Intl. Conf. on Software Engineering, pp. 93–103 (2003)

3. Chakrabarti, S.: Mining the Web: Discovering Knowledge from Hypertext Data. Morgan Kaufmann, San Francisco (2002)
4. Fisher II, M., Rothermel, G.: The EUSES Spreadsheet Corpus: A Shared Resource for Supporting Experimentation with Spreadsheet Dependability Mechanisms. Tech. Rpt. 04-12-03, Univ. of Nebraska (2004)
5. Green, T., Petre, M.: Usability Analysis of Visual Programming Environments: A "Cognitive Dimensions" Framework. J. Visual Lang. and Computing 7, 131–174 (1996)
6. Koesnandar, A., et al.: Using Assertions to Help End-User Programmers Create Dependable Web Macros. In: Proc. 16th ACM SIGSOFT Intl. Symp. on Foundations of Software Engineering (to appear) (2008)
7. Lerman, K., Minton, S., Knoblock, C.: Wrapper Maintenance: A Machine Learning Approach. J. Artificial Intelligence Research 18, 149–181 (2003)
8. Lieberman, H., Nardi, B., Wright, D.: Training Agents to Recognize Text by Example. J. Auton. Agents and Multi-Agent Systems 4(1), 79–92 (2001)
9. Miller, R., Myers, B.: Outlier Finding: Focusing Human Attention on Possible Errors. In: Proc. 14th Symp. on User Interface Software and Technology, pp. 81–90 (2001)
10. Mosteller, F., Youtz, C.: Quantifying Probabilistic Expressions. Statistical Science 5(1), 2–12 (1990)
11. Myers, B., Pane, J., Ko, A.: Natural Programming Languages and Environments. Comm. ACM 47(9), 47–52 (2004)
12. Nardi, B.: A Small Matter of Programming: Perspectives on End User Computing. MIT Press, Cambridge (1993)
13. Nardi, B., Miller, J., Wright, D.: Collaborative, Programmable Intelligent Agents. Comm. ACM 41(3), 96–104 (1998)
14. Raz, O., Koopman, P., Shaw, M.: Semantic Anomaly Detection in Online Data Sources. In: Proc. 24th Intl. Conf. on Software Engineering, pp. 302–312 (2002)
15. Safonov, A.: Web Macros By Example: Users Managing the WWW of Applications. In: CHI 1999 Extended Abstracts on Human Factors in Computing Sys., pp. 71–72 (1999)
16. Scaffidi, C., Myers, B., Shaw, M.: Topes: Reusable Abstractions for Validating Data. In: Proc. 30th Intl. Conf. on Software Engineering, pp. 1–10 (2008)
17. Scaffidi, C.: Unsupervised Inference of Data Formats in Human-Readable Notation. In: Proc. 9th Intl. Conf. on Enterprise Information Systems-HCI Volume, pp. 236–241 (2007)
18. Scaffidi, C., et al.: Using Topes to Validate and Reformat Data in End-User Programming Tools. In: Proc. 4th Workshop on End-User Software Engineering, pp. 11–15 (2008)
19. Tomita, M.: An Efficient Augmented-Context-Free Parsing Algorithm. J. Computational Linguistics 13(1-2), 31–46 (1987)

Part III
Refereed Notes

Cicero Designer: An Environment for End-User Development of Multi-Device Museum Guides

Giuseppe Ghiani, Fabio Paternò, and Lucio Davide Spano

ISTI-CNR, HIIS Lab, Via Moruzzi 1,
56124 Pisa, Italy
{Giuseppe.Ghiani,Fabio.Paterno,Lucio.Davide.Spano}@isti.cnr.it

Abstract. This paper describes the design and implementation of a tool to allow people without programming experience to customize the functionality and user interface of a multi-device museum guide. It consists of a direct-manipulation visual environment that supports editing of the main features of a museum guide and the creation of the associated interactive games. The tool then generates application versions for access through both mobile and large screen stationary devices. We also report on a first empirical evaluation carried out with museum curators.

Keywords: End User Development, Multi-Device User Interfaces, Mobile Museum Guides.

1 Introduction

End-User Development (EUD) [8] has focused mainly on desktop applications. However, mobile technology has penetrated many application domains and mobile devices are more and more powerful in terms of processing and interaction resources. There is an increasing number of applications that aim to exploit such technological offerings. Non-professional developers already have difficulties in developing applications for desktop systems, and targeting multi-device environments is too complex, unless they are adequately supported [4]. The prototype described in the paper is an example of a domain specific EUD environment. The identification of key semantic building blocks and target scenarios guided the creation of an intuitive metaphorical tool to configure context-sensitive museum guides, including educational games and multi-device deployment.

In particular, we consider the museum application domain, in which software applications are increasingly used to assist visitors in accessing the relevant information. In addition, museums are dynamic entities and often change the items on exhibit or their locations. Thus, it is important to allow their curators, who presumably have no programming experience, to be able to (re)configure the mobile guide, its content and interactive behaviour.

Our work aims to allow museum curators to easily create and modify guides accessible through both mobile and large screen stationary devices, providing a rich set of

V. Pipek et al. (Eds.): IS-EUD 2009, LNCS 5435, pp. 265–274, 2009.

interactions with the museum information, including some interactive games, which can be useful to improve and assess the learning experience.

2 Related Work

A visual strategy for developing context-aware applications was proposed in [7]. Such a system, called iCAP, allows end-users to design application prototypes by defining elements (objects, activities) and rules (associations between actions and situations). The rules are graphically edited through basic operations like dragging the defined elements onto rule sheets. Another framework to support people without program-ming experience is eBlocks [6]: it facilitates the creation of customized sensor-based systems and the configuration of condition tables.

Differently from iCAP and eBlocks, which are not specifically dedicated to end user development for mobile environments, our investigation is focused on solutions for facilitating the management of content and the associated interactive functionality also on mobile devices (namely, PDAs and smartphones).

Akesson et al. [1] present a user-oriented framework to ease the reconfiguration of ubiquitous domestic environments. The support, running on a tablet PC, adopts a different paradigm, based on jigsaws.

Carmien and Fisher [5] describe a framework for customizing mobile applications to help people with cognitive disabilities. A graphic editor, intended to be used by the caretakers, facilitates the management of the task-support scripts for helping the dis-abled. The evaluation of the editing environment, called MAPS-DE, revealed that the caretakers appreciate the possibility of customizing the prompting system for the needs of individuals with specific disabilities. Like MAPS-DE, our environment also allows the customization of mobile solutions, but it has educational purposes rather than disabled support and it also allows the generation of application versions for stationary systems with large screens.

The use of educational games on mobile phones for enhancing scholars' visit of ar-chaeological sites is treated in [2] which, however, does not deal with the develop-ment and modification of application content and behaviour.

Bellotti et al. [3] propose a framework for developing edutainment applications, such as mobile tourist guides. The paper also deals with the issues related to the inter-action between the user and the mobile device when rich multimedia content is pre-sented, but it does not provide solutions for end-user development.

Some ideas regarding general environments for end-user development of multi-device interactive applications are in [4] but such ambitious goal has not found a definitive solution. In this work we focus on a specific application domain (museums) and present a solution that can be applied to other domains as well, and which can be extended to support adaptation to a broader set of devices.

3 The End-User Development Environment

In order to facilitate content creation for the guide of a new museum and/or changes to an existing one and the associated interactive behaviour, we have developed a specific visual environment for the desktop PC. The guide editor tool (as well as the resulting mobile and stationary versions of the guide) has been written in the .NET C# language. This tool accesses an XML-based description of the museum, which defines rooms, their layout, and artwork positions as well as additional information. Starting with such data, which includes the photos and descriptions of the artworks, the editor allows users to:

- Create museum rooms or sections by simply drawing polygons on the overall museum map;
- Create links for navigation among rooms using icons (e.g.: arrows or stairs) or text boxes;
- Add, remove or change artwork icons and select the associated photo, information, video and text files, used by the TTS (Text-to-Speech) engine to create the vocal comments on the fly. Each artwork can be associated with a tag (RFID, in our case) for automatic user localization purposes at run time (see Figure 1). The tag ID inserted in the editor is basically a string and the editor functionality is independent of the localization technology actually used by the guide application: the matching between the detected tag(s) and the associated artwork(s) is solved at run time when a new tag event occurs. This type of event is triggered by the localization module that interfaces with the hardware;
- Create help sections;
- Insert interactive regions on the overall museum map for quick room selection (allowing the user to manually change room by clicking them);
- Create instances of educational games;
- Insert, by drag-and-drop, game instances, which are associated with specific artworks.

3.1 The Museum Maps

Figure 1 shows the interface for editing the museum virtual environment. The rooms and the associated items are listed on the left side in a tree structure (elements can be expanded for editing). The same strategy is used in the right panel for listing the available resources (e.g.: photos). The central part is dedicated to the room currently being edited. New elements can be added to the room by just selecting the corresponding icons from the toolbox and locating them in the museum map through drag-and-drop.

After saving the configuration, the tool generates a collection of XML files, which define the corresponding database and can be simply deployed on the devices (mobile and stationary). The two database versions differ mostly in the detail level of the multimedia resources. The stationary device package contains pictures and videos with higher quality than the mobile one. In this way it is possible to exploit the better resolution of the large screen (e.g.: for items preview) and to save storage space on the mobile device. On the guide application at run-time the information available is presented differently depending on the type of device (thus, for example, long descriptions are presented only on request on the mobile, while they are immediately rendered on the large screen).

Currently, the rules determining how the user interface will appear in the two different platforms are pre-defined. In future work they will be generated from logical descriptions taking into account the capabilities of the target devices.

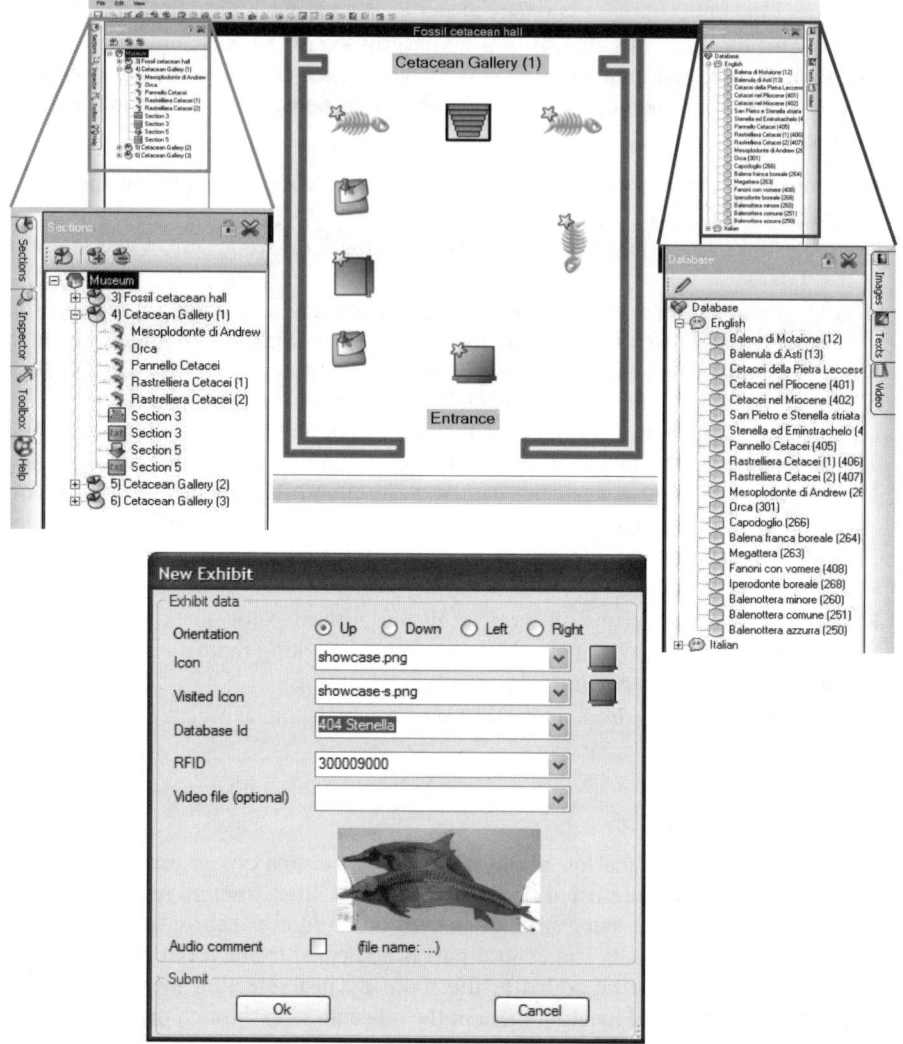

Fig. 1. The main window of the museum maps editor (top) and the form for setting the exhibit parameters (bottom)

3.2   The Games

The environment supports six types of individual games. Figure 2 shows the user interface for each:

- *Associations* requires the player to link images to information items, e.g. the picture of an artwork with its name.

- *Details* shows an enlargement of a small portion of an image. The player has to guess which of the items the detail belongs to.

- *Chronology* requires the user to order the images of the artworks shown according to their creation date.
- In the *find the word* game the user is requested to guess a "hidden word" related to an exhibit attribute: the number of characters composing the word is provided as a facility.
- In the *memory* game, the user has to observe an image for a while. After the image has disappeared s/he has to answer a question related to the image.
- The *quiz* is a single-answer multiple-choice question.

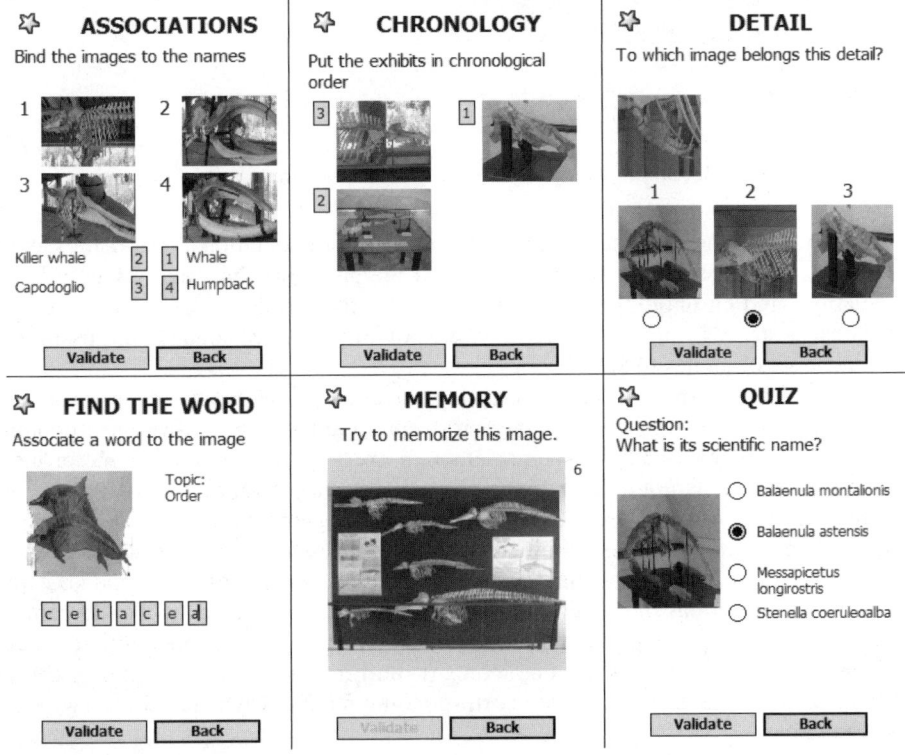

Fig. 2. The six individual games displayed on the PDA

We chose these types of games with the aim to enhance the museum visitor's experience without interfering with the visit: users need not spend time in understanding the game rules, but should exploit the museum information in order to find the solution. For this reason the games are simple, and the difficulty depends mostly on the content.

The interface for editing a game has been designed to look like a preview of the corresponding game: the user enters the questions, the images and the captions, and provides the solution for the game.

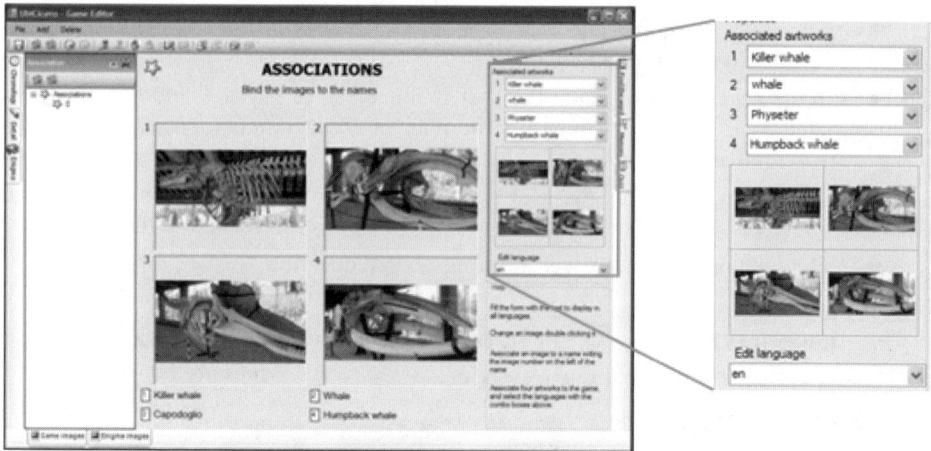

Fig. 3. The window for creating an "associations" game

To create a game, the user selects the game type (associations, chronology etc.), then associates the artwork (or the artworks if the game involves more than one, i.e. associations and chronology), and finally provides the proper content. After creating the game, a star will appear over the corresponding artwork icon. It is possible to associate a set of games to an artwork.

Figure 3 shows an example of creating an association game: the environment prompts the user (i.e., the museum curator) to provide the images, the corresponding names and the relations among them. Although every game is bound to one or more artworks, the game is not a field of the artwork data structure, that is to say it is not contained in the artwork definition. Thus, the game generation is a more dynamic process than a simple content addition. Indeed, each new game consists of a set of resources (texts, pictures) contained on, or referred by, a piece of XML code compliant to the specifications of the template. The association between artwork and game is then solved by the editor preview form, as well as by the guide application, to enable the graphic engine to draw the game icon. At run time, museum visitors may try the possible associations and receive the corresponding feedback whether the answers are correct or not.

This high configurability of the environment has made it possible to create a guide for the Natural History Museum of Calci involving one collaborator of our laboratory for about one week. The availability of an EUD tool for museums is judged important, especially after the guide application deployment, since the layout of a museum can often change. The museum curators can thus directly update the data and functionality of the guide, even without knowing the underlying implementation language.

4   The Resulting Application

The resulting application can be used through either a PDA or a desktop system, including desktops with large screens. While the two application versions have a similar logic, their user interfaces vary in order to better adapt the different screen sizes (3.5 and 42 inches). In addition, users can dynamically transfer part of the user interface from the mobile to a large screen when one is nearby in order to opportunistically exploit its better resolution or share information and comments on it with other visitors. Figure 4 shows how, after migration to the stationary device, the user can access the content that was available on the PDA through richer presentations. On the PDA, the map items are icons (A1), while on the large screen images are used (A2). The artwork/exhibit preview on the desktop (B2) has a picture with a better resolution than in the PDA (B1), and the text is shown in its entirety (while on the PDA the description is provided vocally) and the position of the visited section with respect to the museum map is presented as well.

Thus, the user interfaces differ depending on the mode in which the application is accessed: mobile only, desktop only, distributed across the two platforms.

In the case of mobile access:

- The item has a label, a low resolution photo (about 150x200 px), chronology and a summary of main information (e.g., authors for artworks or scientific names for animals). The description is automatically read by text to speech software;
- The games are represented by title and description (or question, if any), item photo, UI for answering through PDA-designed interaction (e.g., four clicks in sequence for chronology order);
- Museum visit consists of presenting section/room maps with low resolution icons of the items.

In the case of stationary access through large screens:

- Items are presented by name, high resolution photo (about 800x600 px), detailed description, context information (life of the author and historical descriptions for artworks, species information for animals etc.), related items, position in the museum and path from current position.
- Games are represented as in the PDA, with high resolution photos of the items and standard desktop interactions.
- Museum visit is supported through high resolution section or room maps with the possibility to change the display of the items using icons, previews or both, and whole museum map with current position, as well as collaborative game status

In the case of distributed user interface:

- The PDA shows game title, description (or question) and the UI for answering through a PDA-designed interaction technique;
- the desktop shows same title, description and high resolution photo of the items

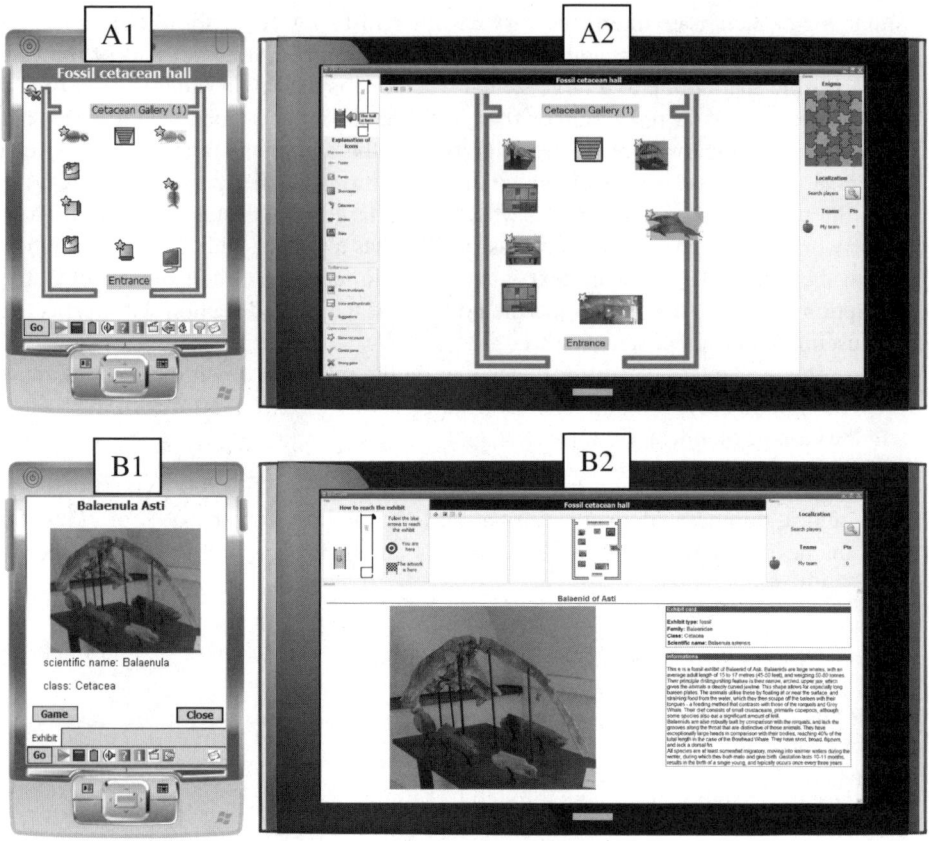

Fig. 4. Device dependent representations: virtual section on PDA (A1) and large screen (A2); artwork preview on PDA (B1) and large screen (B2)

5   User Test

We performed a first user test of our end-user development platform for museum environments. In order to get feedback from the target users, we involved the curators of the Museum of Natural History in Calci (Italy). Two of them participated in the test session. Both had several years of experience on personal computers and applications, however they had never used any environment for managing museum content or, more generally, visual builders.

Before starting the test, the participants viewed a short demonstration on the capabilities of the tool and received explanations on the main components. Then, they were provided with the list of tasks to perform:

- Set up one room (reflecting the real layout)

  o Extract the room map from the global museum map
  o Create, configure the exhibits and put them on the map
  o Insert the link items for section changes

- Add a new item to an existing room
- Generate two educational games and bind them to existing exhibits.

Both users were able to accomplish the assigned tasks. After performing the test, the users were requested to answer a questionnaire providing ratings (1 to 5) as well as subjective opinions and suggestions for improving the tested solution. Users rated the tool's features 4 and 5, and provided positive feedback. The museum curators appreciated the possibility of quickly editing the museum guide descriptions, not only for setting up new sections but also for managing the rooms whose layouts often change. This was considered a key feature for a museum guide: the curators often change the presentation of exhibits or artworks (for special exhibitions, artists celebrations etc.), and a software without this possibility would soon be considered obsolete.

One user reported that the ease of editing would enable easily creating ad-hoc games for teachers in order to evaluate their knowledge before actually accompanying students to the museum. The other user suggested enhancing the game editor interface with previewing capabilities, in order to let the user immediately see the actual presentation provided to the visitors on the PDA.

6 Conclusions and Future Work

End-User Development has mainly focused on desktop applications, but people use more and more mobile devices as well in order to access interactive applications. In this work we present an environment to support end-user development of museum applications that can be accessed through both mobile and desktop devices. This work shows a systematic design pattern: domain analysis to define target functionality and building blocks for component-based design time, use of direct manipulation design principles, templates (in this case game patterns, for example). These principles can be transferred to other domains as well.

Future work will be dedicated to the possibility of extending the approach in such a way to generate application versions accessible also through different modalities (such as voice) exploiting the use of XML-based declarative descriptions of user interfaces and a set of adaptation rules customizable by users. We also plan to conduct further empirical validation of the approach proposed.

References

1. Akesson, K.P., Crabtree, A., Hansson, P., Hemmings, T., Humble, J., Koleva, B., Rodden, T.: "Playing with the Bits" User-Configuration of Ubiquitous Domestic Environments. In: Dey, A.K., Schmidt, A., McCarthy, J.F. (eds.) UbiComp 2003. LNCS, vol. 2864, pp. 256–263. Springer, Heidelberg (2003)
2. Ardito, C., Buono, P., Costabile, M.F., Lanzilotti, R., Pederson, T.: Mobile games to foster the learning of history at archaeological sites. In: VL/HCC 2007, pp. 81–86 (2007)
3. Bellotti, F., Berta, R., De Gloria, A., Margarone, M.: MADE: Developing Edutainment Applications on Mobile Computers. Computers & Graphics 27, 617–634 (2003)
4. Berti, S., Paternò, F., Santoro, C.: Natural Development of Nomadic Interfaces Based on Conceptual Descriptions. In: End User Development, pp. 143–160. Springer, Heidelberg (2006)

5. Carmien, S.P., Fischer, G.: Design, Adoption, and Assessment of a Socio-Technical Environment Supporting Independence for Persons with Cognitive Disabilities. In: Proc. CHI 2008, pp. 597–606 (2008)
6. Cotterell, S., Vahid, F.: A Logic Block Enabling Logic Configuration by Non-Experts in Sensor Networks. In: Proc. CHI 2005, pp. 1925–1928 (2005)
7. Dey, K.A., Sohn, T., Streng, S., Kodama, J.: iCAP: Interactive Prototyping of Context-Aware Applications. In: Fishkin, K.P., Schiele, B., Nixon, P., Quigley, A. (eds.) PERVASIVE 2006. LNCS, vol. 3968, pp. 254–271. Springer, Heidelberg (2006)
8. Lieberman, H., Paternò, F., Wulf, W.: End-User Development. Springer, Heidelberg (2006)

Observing End-User Customisation of Electronic Patient Records

Cecily Morrison and Alan F. Blackwell

University of Cambridge, Computer Laboratory
JJ Thompson Avenue, Cambridge, UK, CB3 9EU
{Cecily.Morrison,Alan.Blackwell}@cl.cam.ac.uk

Abstract. The contemporary practice of medicine, which is concerned both with national standards of audit and innovation through local customisation, is a prime domain for end-user development. In this paper we describe four experiences of end-user development in this domain that offer interesting empirical examples. We look at existing practices through considering end-user customisation of paper charts (1), compare the end-user customisation facilities provided by two applications for electronic patient records (2), assess the structure of an actual end-user development using one of these (3), and propose a longitudinal study of end-user customisation building on this work (4).

Keywords: Patient records, Healthcare, End-user customization.

1 Introduction

Contemporary medical practice is fundamentally concerned with the definition and execution of standardised procedures. The creation of new standard procedures by individual hospitals or units, and the local refinement of existing procedures, is commonplace. Such local customization, even if minor, can be seen in a positive light, encouraging reflective professional practice [1], as well as innovation. Despite these potential benefits that procedural diversity carries, it causes problems for the application of information technology to clinical practice, which for economic reasons is often deployed across a large number of client institutions. This conflict is well illustrated by the significant difficulties encountered in the implementation of the British National Program for Information Technology, a very large scale deployment of standardised clinical administration software [2].

The combination of requirements, for both standardisation and customisation, means that Electronic Patient Record (EPR) systems are a natural target for end-user development or end-user customisation. (In this paper, we will refer to both as EUD.) Indeed, leading EPR products offer in addition to their standardised set of procedures and record formats, significant capabilities to support local end-user development. The already established medical practice of defining and refining procedures makes EUD application use in medical environments particularly interesting to study, as the practitioners are familiar with the process but not the technology. Such a situation provides the opportunity to assess customisation procedures without the use

V. Pipek et al. (Eds.): IS-EUD 2009, LNCS 5435, pp. 275–284, 2009.

of technology as well as a capability to home in on the problems stemming from the technology use, as we can assume that the process of negotiating customised procedures is already smoothly established.

This paper highlights a number of examples from our experiences with customisation procedures and EUD technology employed in healthcare environments. We begin by investigating the process of customisation without technology, by detailing how paper charts were developed in an intensive care unit (1). Moving on to look at customisation of technology, we present a comparison of the initial customisation procedures of two EPR systems, GE Healthcare *Centricity EMR* [3] and IMDsoft *Metavision* [4] (2). We then focus on a single system, Metavision, and explore how system structure affects end-user development (3). Finally, we change focus from the initial to the long-term practice of customisation, and propose how one might study long-term EUD usage in a medical environment (4). Despite the brevity of these examples, we aim to demonstrate in our conclusion that studies in the medical environment can offer insight into a wide variety of issues in the EUD application development process.

2   Customisation on Paper (Case 1)

As noted in the introduction, the creation and refinement of new procedures in medical contexts is both common and productive. Indeed it is considered an important skill for senior clinical practitioners and a way to provide innovative patient care. These procedures are traditionally deployed through the development of appropriate charts. Below we look at the customisation of paper charts found in an intensive care unit (ICU) of a cardiothoracic specialist, research-oriented hospital in the UK. We first detail a brief example of process and then discuss the end-result.

2.1   Customisation of the CCOC Paper Chart

A tremendous amount of data about a patient's state is collected from the many machines to which she is attached – heart rate, fluid balance, oxygen levels and blood results to name just a few. This data is organized in various charts, perhaps as many as 10, for use by different kinds of practitioners (e.g. nurses vs. doctors). In order to utilize such a wealth of information, the director of this ICU discouraged narrative observations on charts, in favour of formalised tabular formats that could be easily reviewed and compared. The most commonly used chart shared by all practitioners, the Critical Care Observation Chart (CCOC), became, as a result, formalised to an extent that it did not accommodate the more diverse aspects of patient care with which nurses are concerned.

In response, nurses developed the habit of turning the CCOC over, to write less structured observations on the back. However, as unstructured text presents problems in consistency and standard interpretation, the ICU nursing staff decided to define a standardised structure for nursing observations too. They revised the CCOC by printing another grid on the reverse side, providing another, but different, knowledge structure for use by nurses.

We might note two points from this example of the customisation process. First, the process of formalisation and categorisation is a feature of organisational data management, a point observed by Bowker and Star [5] in an analysis of case studies that included the formalisation of nursing practices. It is therefore a process that is well practised, even when customisation happens without any EUD technology, a point that will be discussed further in section three. Second, it demonstrates a reactive, incremental developmental process which suggests the importance of looking at long term usage of patterns of EUD application and not just the initial period of customisation, something that will be done in section four.

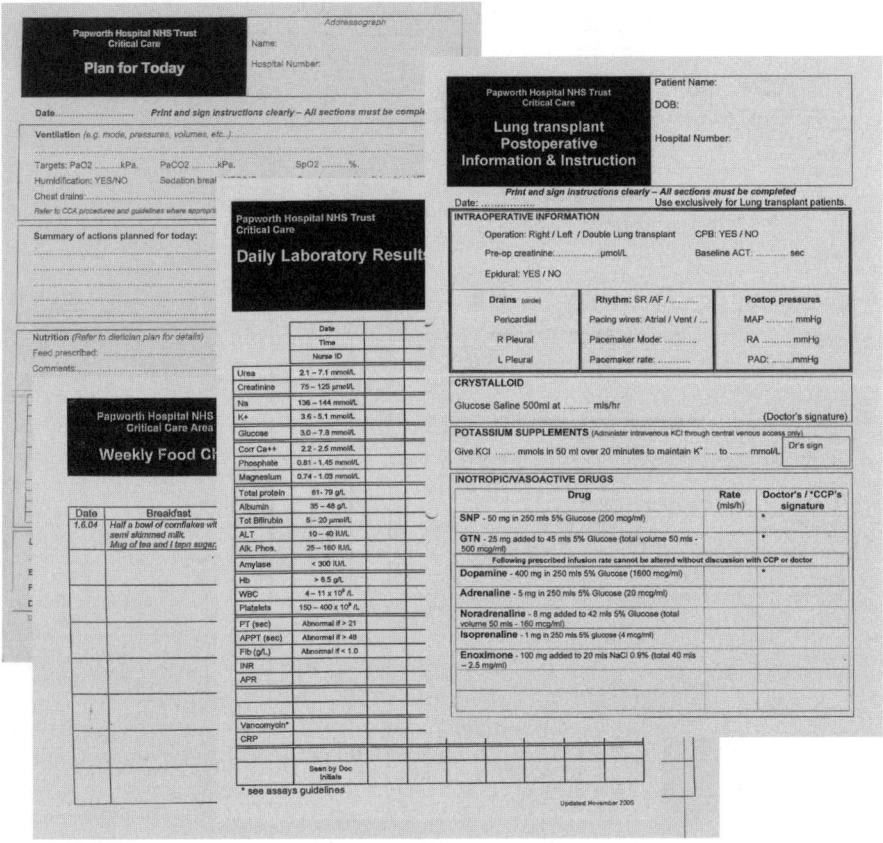

Fig. 1. A selection of more recently design paper charts in use at the ICU

2.2 Examples of Paper Chart Customisation

In Figure 1 and 2 we present a collection of charts from this ICU unit. Those in Figure 1 are newer and more standardized than those in Figure 2. In particular, we would like to draw attention to the visual coherence that begins to appear in the newer charts. This suggests that not only is customisation happening on a chart-by-chart basis as the

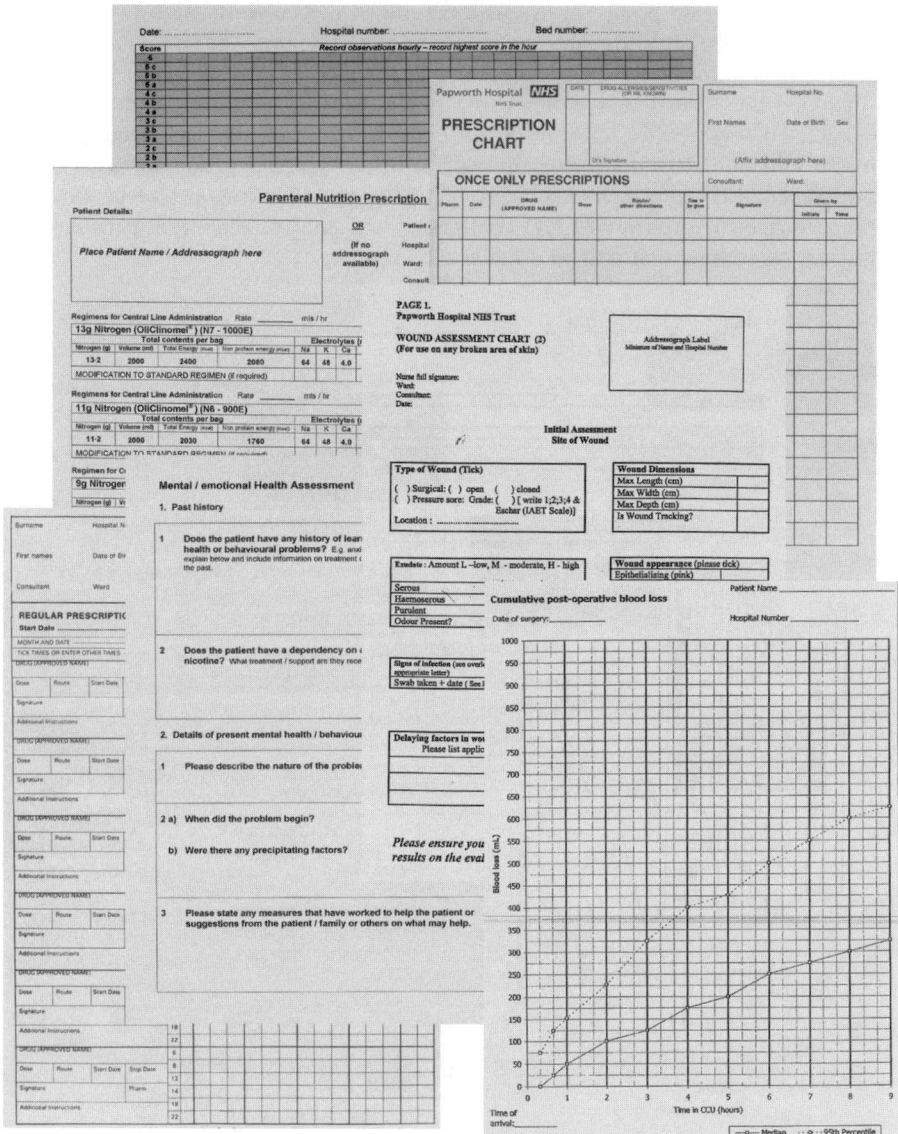

Fig. 2. A selection of older paper charts in use at the ICU

need arises (as above), but that there is concerted design of the information structure. Customising fields on a chart might be seen as end-user programming while design of an information structure may be likened to end-user software engineering. This distinction will be considered in more detail below.

3   Comparison of Two Health EUD Applications (Case 2)

3.1   GE Healthcare

The CHI 2006 workshop on End-User Software Engineering [6] included a representative of GE Healthcare, who described the customisation facilities of the Centricity Electronic Medical Record product [7]. The aspect of the system providing the focus of discussion was its facility for generating medical reports. Medical reports are standardised in structure and terminology, to an extent that suggests they might easily be generated automatically. Indeed, Centricity allowed doctors to define the content of an individual patient's report using menus and checkboxes, then automatically generate the full prose text report from the resulting data fields. However, despite the clear advantages of standardised text (consistency, quality control, efficiency), individual doctors often have strong preferences for particular expressions or writing approaches, to an extent that makes them reluctant to use standardised text.

The solution offered by the Centricity product is that doctors can customise report text generation in accordance with their own preferred style, using a "medical expression language." Unfortunately, the computational complexity of transforming a predefined set of terms into arbitrary prose constructs is such that this language includes most of the data and control features of a general purpose programming language (typed variables, conditionals, iteration and others). The instruction manual for the medical expression language resembled an introductory programming course, in both content and structure. Few doctors have the time to develop programming skills from scratch, leading on the one hand to a thriving third-party industry offering customisation services for Centricity, and on the other hand to a variety of costs and risks associated with the specification and debugging of any scripts written by relatively inexperienced doctors.

3.2   IMDsoft Metavision

The director of the above mentioned ICU considered the GE Healthcare product when implementing a new Electronic Patient Record system, but eventually selected the MetaVision product from IMDsoft. He reported to us, at the outset of our research, that customisation facilities had been a significant factor in that decision. Although MetaVision has a different set of customisable features, the encounter with a different product did provide us with an opportunity to compare end-user customisation and deployment issues associated with different products in the same market. At this ICU, report formats also provided an initial focus for customisation. However, it was not prose reports that were the main priority, but the layout and content of patient charts to monitor patient's vital signs, drug administration and fluid balance.

Implementation of Metavision at this ICU was mainly concerned with replicating the structure of these existing paper charts within the Electronic Patient Record. We observed the necessary customisation work being carried out by a small team of system "super-users" – the clinical director of the unit (a consultant anaesthetist) who had been the initiator and driver of new policy, the director of nursing, and the computer system administrator. Their approach to the project closely resembled professional practice. Having collected samples of all the paper charts used in this ICU, the team identified all data fields. They arranged these on flipcharts posted around the walls of their workspace and carried out the customisation in the centre of the room at workstation with a collection of Metavision manuals. A second workstation was used by IMDsoft staff who were present as trainers at the start of the one week initial customisation period.

The professional and systematic approach to end-user development was not accidental. Metavision training material has an explicit focus on project management, including recruiting suitable members of the development team, and establishing a systematic development process. This typically starts with the definition of "parameters" (patient data and measurements), followed by layout of a patient "flowsheet" that provides interactive access to various data entry forms as well as charts and reports. It is clear that the Metavision product takes as its starting point the importance of end-user software engineering (EUSE) concerns, somewhat in contrast to the Centricity training material, which at the time we saw it had a far more conventional focus on end-user programming (EUP) facilities.

From the perspective of a computer science researcher, the Metavision documentation was rather irritating, because basic description of language syntax and library functions are located in obscure parts of the documentation. The Centricity documentation offered far more conventional programming reference – perhaps a sign that the two audiences, end-user software engineering and end-user programmers should be clearly separated. In other EUP research in our group, we encourage the use of personas to distinguish between the two, characterising the approaches to programming that might be found among different professional groups [8].

4 EUD Application Structure

End-user development activities in Metavision are largely structured around the predefined dataflows and interaction model at the core of the product. It would not be possible for users to modify these system behaviours. Customisation of certain operations can be done using a scripting language that is invoked during particular operations, which include "triggers," relatively advanced messaging, action and automated notification functions. During the initial customization period, the team focused on creating parameters and forms rather than on triggers. However, they did use scripting facilities to write "formula" scripts that can calculate new parameters derived from directly captured data.

Formula scripts provided the main opportunity for us to observe conventional programming activity. IMDsoft training staff were able to assist with script syntax, but this threw attention onto the need for a shared domain understanding between technical and practical expertise. We observed a sustained debate over the interpretation of physical dimensions and data types, as clinical staff and trainers disagreed whether the built-in type "millimoles" represented a concentration or a quantity of potassium (ion balance in ICU patients was a key clinical concern of the ICU director).

A less contentious, although laborious, consequence of using formula scripts to implement local clinical concerns was the process of creating many formulas to calculate patient fluid balance – almost all drug administration and nutrition introduces fluids into the patient that must be taken into account alongside ion balance. As the base product did not anticipate this particular cross-cutting concern, customisation activity had to include the creation of many small scripts throughout the system to account for fluid intake.

We also observed the consequences of conflict between the built-in operational model of the software, and the operational conventions of existing paper-based data processing. One of the primary displays in the Metavision software is a chart that can be customised to plot various parameters along a continuous timeline. The navigation of the chart and control of the timeline itself are sophisticated, and of course cannot be customised by end-users. However, this seemed to cause a major obstacle for the nursing staff. The local clinical concern with continuous monitoring of fluid balance meant that nurses were accustomed to noting that a patient had passed a quantity of urine, and attributing this retrospectively to a loss of fluid over the previous hour. However, the underlying model of the Metavision timeline seemed to assume that all observations related to events in the current, rather than previous time period.

The above three examples demonstrate a number of problems. The first and the third note the issue of having a sufficiently shared understanding between technicians and end-users to achieve a task. In the latter example particularly, neither the team nor the IMDsoft staff found it easy to identify this fundamental difference in the way they described the relationship between observations and intervals. Most likely, a common level of description would have required a shift to a more abstract conception of time [8]. The second and third examples indicate the importance of appropriate design even when customisation abilities are present. Although many problems can be worked around, as in the second example of writing many scripts to calculate fluid balance, others, such as the notion of time and flow, are more problematic. Research into requirements gathering for EUD systems that distinguishes between items that can and cannot be customised would be useful.

5 Studying Long-Term EUD Usage

In the second section we highlight the need to focus not just on the initial process of end-user customisation (as in cases two and three) but also on long term usage, enabling us to understand how customization becomes embedded in the social context. Lieberman et al [9] also stress the need for empirical studies of long-term EUD usage in their vision of EUD research of the next 15 years. This vein of research aims to answer questions ranging from when software is customised as opposed to when workarounds are found, to what role does cooperation play in the customisation process. We are now commencing a retrospective study of the ICU unit described above, investigating the day-to-day process of the customisation process of the Metavision system. This section describes how we intend this to be done.

5.1 Background

The majority of work that focuses on usage of EUD systems is carried out during the design, rather than evaluation phase. Rode et al. [10] for example, look at what features non-professional web-designers use in order to build an EUD system that addresses the needs of this particular group. Stevens et al. [11] focus more on the social context of system use, describing problems with data control between two organizations and how that can be accounted for in an EUD system. In contrast, we concentrate on the long-term usage of the system. One expects a significant amount of customisation when a system is first bought and used. When, by whom, and for what purpose is the system customised after the initial burst? Noting Blackwell's attention investment theory of abstraction use [12], if users are given the opportunity to customise, when do they decide to adapt themselves rather than the system? How does the technology and the social context change the answer to this question?

5.2 Study Design

We have chosen two complementary approaches to address these questions: (1) a catalog of customised elements; (2) contextual interviews about specific changes made. The catalog will be used to explore patterns in what, when, and who does the customisation, while the contextual interviews are intended to investigate the social context in which customisation happens. The interviews will be broken into two parts, the first focusing on understanding the context for making changes and the second one concentrating on how the EUD capabilities are employed to achieve changes.

The catalog will be comprised of a database of all changes made in the past two years, documenting what change was made, when, and by whom (if possible). After categorizing the changes using grounded theory, it will be possible to look for patterns. We are particularly interested in whether there will be correlations between any of the following:

(1) the time elapsed since the initial customisation and the number of changes made
(2) time and what kind of changes are made
(3) time and who makes changes
(4) what changes are made by whom

We would also like to know if repeated changes are made to the same element. Not only will this data give us a general overview of customisation over time, but will provide fodder for the contextual interviews.

In the first part of the interview, the respondent will be asked about four changes in the catalog. Three will be randomly chosen to sample a range of possible user concerns and the fourth will be one of interest to the researchers, such as an element that has been changed several times. We have chosen to discuss concrete examples for two reasons. First, we want to understand the average case, rather than just extraordinary ones that are likely to be remembered. Second, it is usually easier for people to recall something specific (e.g. the change of the haemoglobin parameter) rather than something more general (what kinds of parameters have changed). The respondent will also be given an opportunity to discuss any significant changes that they remember in order to identify the most burdensome problems.

The questions used for both sections of the first part are listed below. They are open-ended and thus designed to elicit more information than is strictly implied in the question. Other questions will be used as necessary to develop themes that emerge.

1) Who made this change? (Does this person usually make changes?)
2) Why was this change made?

3) How was the decision made to make this change?
4) Were there any difficulties making this change?
5) Was the change tested after it was made?
6) How was the change communicated to the medical staff?
7) Was the accuracy of the change ever questioned?

The first question hopes to draw out comments about how people think of those making changes and perhaps how that affects their attitude towards or description of the changes. The second question will help us understand when changes are made and perhaps when they are not, and whether this varies over time. Questions 3 & 6 are oriented towards discovering the official and unofficial policies for making and distributing changes. Question 4 is an initial question to probe difficulties, either social or technical ones, which arise during customisation. Lastly, question 7 is an exploration of the social context of customisation.

The second part of the interview looks more specifically at interaction with the customisation interface and language. Again we employ the strategy of talking about concrete episodes, this time asking them to recall a specific incident. We also use a strategy of repetition, making the later questions refinements of the earlier. The questions are meant to address the social and technical issues raised when non-programmers use a programming language.

1) Is there any change that you would like to make but are unable? If so, can you describe how you would like to make this change?
2) In the past have there been problems that have been difficult to solve? What did you do?
3) Do you work on customisation with your colleagues?
4) How is this work similar and/or different from designing the paper charts?
5) Do you use metaphors or images or other aids when customizing?

6 Conclusion

We have presented a description of research work in progress, investigating the relationship between existing professional customisation practices, and software-based EUD practices, in a medical environment. It is clear that current commercial products already incorporate relatively sophisticated EUD facilities, and that these (unsurprisingly) are drawing attention to the importance of end-user software engineering, both in the formal interventions of software vendors, and the informal appropriation of technical capabilities within clinical teams. As such, we find that these experiences offer a valuable case study for comparison to experiences of EUD in educational or research contexts. Furthermore, they offer an opportunity for the long-term observation and analysis that is still in progress. This kind of long-term professional deployment is unusual in research contexts, and includes longitudinal study of individuals that is unusual in educational contexts (where studies of individual students usually last for a year at most). We believe that this research context will offer a valuable opportunity for further investigation of EUD in practice.

References

1. Schon, D.A.: The Reflective Practitioner: How professionals think in action. Basic Books (1983)
2. Martin, D., Rouncefield, M., O'Neill, J., Hartswood, M., Randall, D.: Timing in the Art of Integration: That's How the Bastille Got Stormed. In: Proc. of Group 2005 (2005)
3. GE Healthcare: Centricity EMR product description (August 29, 2008), http://www.gehealthcare.com
4. IMDsoft MetaVision MVICU product description (August 29, 2008), www.imd-soft.com
5. Bowker, G.C., Star, S.L.: Sorting Things Out: Classification and Its Consequences. MIT Press, Cambridge (1999)
6. Burnett, M., Myers, B., Rosson, M.B., Wiedenbeck, S.: The next step: from end-user programming to end-user software engineering. In: CHI 2006 (extended abstracts)
7. Orrick, E.: Position Paper for the CHI 2006 Workshop on End-User Software Engineering (2006), http://eusesconsortium.org/weuseii/docs/ErikaOrrick.pdf
8. Blackwell, A.F., Church, L.E., Green, T.R.G.: The abstract is an enemy. In: Proc. of PPIG (2008)
9. Lieberman, H., Paterno, F., Klann, M., Wulf, V.: End-User Development: An Emerging Paradigm. In: Lieberman, Paterno & Wulf (2006)
10. Rode, J., Rossen, M.B., Perez Quinones, M.A.: End-User Development of Web Applications. In: Lieberman, Paterno & Wulf (2006)
11. Stevens, G., Quaisser, G., Klann, M.: Breaking it up: An Industrial Case Study of Component-Based Tailorable Software Design. In: Lieberman, Paterno & Wulf (2006)
12. Blackwell, A.F.: First steps in programming: A rationale for Attention Investment models. In: Proc. of the IEEE Symposium on Human-Centric Computing Languages and Environments (2002)
13. Lieberman, H., Paterno, F., Wulf, V. (eds.): End-User Development. Springer, Heidelberg (2006)

Author Index

Aedo, Ignacio   186
Andersen, Renate   31

Bahna, Eric   205
Beaton, Jack   86
Blackwell, Alan F.   275
Brundage, James   205
Burnett, Margaret   15, 205
Busse, Daniela K.   86

Cabitza, Federico   146
Carroll, John. M.   186
Costabile, Maria Francesca   70

Díaz, Paloma   186

Efeoglu, Arkin   86
Ehret, Ralf   86
ElRif, Paul   205

Fischer, Gerhard   3
Fogli, Daniela   126

Ghiani, Giuseppe   265
Grigoreanu, Valentina   205

Haake, Jörg M.   166

Jeong, Sae Young   86

Karstens, Jan   86

Mørch, Anders I.   31
Morrison, Cecily   275
Mussio, Piero   70
Myers, Brad A.   86, 242

Ortiz-Chamorro, Sebastian   225

Parasiliti Provenza, Loredana   70
Paternò, Fabio   265
Piccinno, Antonio   70
Pipek, Volkmar   50

Rossi, Gustavo   225
Rosson, Mary Beth   186

Scaffidi, Chris   242
Schümmer, Till   166
Schwabe, Daniel   225
Shaw, Mary   242
Simone, Carla   146
Snover, Jeffrey   205
Spahn, Michael   106
Spano, Lucio Davide   265
Stevens, Gunnar   50
Stylos, Jeff   86

Wulf, Volker   50, 106

Xie, Yingyu   86

Printing: Mercedes-Druck, Berlin
Binding: Stein+Lehmann, Berlin